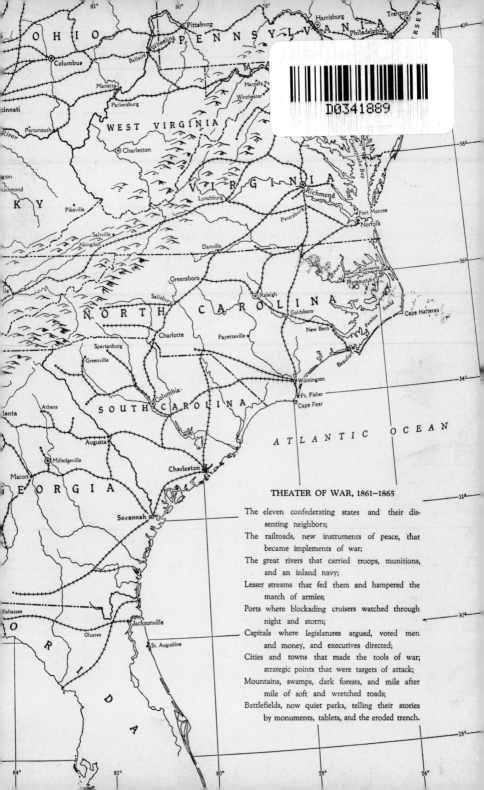

THEATER OF WAR, 1861–1865

The eleven confederating states and their dissenting neighbors;

The railroads, new instruments of peace, that became implements of war;

The great rivers that carried troops, munitions, and an inland navy;

Lesser streams that fed them and hampered the march of armies;

Ports where blockading cruisers watched through night and storm;

Capitals where legislatures argued, voted men and money, and executives directed;

Cities and towns that made the tools of war; strategic points that were targets of attack;

Mountains, swamps, dark forests, and mile after mile of soft and wretched roads;

Battlefields, now quiet parks, telling their stories by monuments, tablets, and the eroded trench.

LINCOLN FINDS A GENERAL

THE MACMILLAN COMPANY
NEW YORK · BOSTON · CHICAGO · DALLAS
ATLANTA · SAN FRANCISCO

MACMILLAN AND CO., Limited
LONDON · BOMBAY · CALCUTTA · MADRAS
MELBOURNE

**THE MACMILLAN COMPANY
OF CANADA, Limited**
TORONTO

SECRETARY OF WAR EDWIN M. STANTON

KENNETH P. WILLIAMS

LINCOLN
FINDS A GENERAL

*

A Military Study of the Civil War

WITH MAPS BY CLARK RAY

VOLUME TWO

NEW YORK

THE MACMILLAN COMPANY

1949

Gen'l.

COPYRIGHT, 1949, BY KENNETH P. WILLIAMS

FIRST PRINTING

PRINTED IN THE UNITED STATES OF AMERICA

more and Ohio Railroad by Edward Hungerford (1928), and *Ulysses S. Grant and the Period of National Preservation and Reconstruction* by W. C. Church (1926); Charles Scribner's Sons—*The Life and Letters of General George Gordon Meade* by George G. Meade (1913), *Lee's Lieutenants* by Douglas S. Freeman (1942), *R. E. Lee* by Douglas S. Freeman (1934), *Letters from Lee's Army* by Susan Leigh Blackford (1947), and *War Years with Jeb Stuart* by Lt. Colonel W. W. Blackford (1945); University of Alabama Press—*The Civil War Diary of General Josiah Gorgas* by Frank E. Vandiver (1947); The University of North Carolina Press—*George B. McClellan, The Man Who Saved the Union* by H. J. Eckenrode and Bryan Conrad, copyright, 1941, by The University of North Carolina Press, and *I Rode with Stonewall* by Henry Kyd Douglas, copyright, 1940, by The University of North Carolina Press; University of Pennsylvania Press—*South After Gettysburg* by Cornelia Hancock (1937); The University of Wisconsin Press—*Lincoln and the Radicals* by T. Harry Williams; Yale University Press—*A Volunteer's Adventures* by John W. De Forest (1946), and *The Campaign of Chancellorsville* by John Bigelow, Jr. (1910).

CONTENTS

VOLUME TWO

CONTENTS

ILLUSTRATIONS

VOLUME TWO

MAPS

LINCOLN FINDS A GENERAL

VOLUME TWO

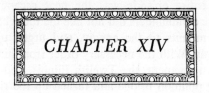

CHAPTER XIV

THE VICTORY WHICH WAS A FAILURE

Nothing of importance happened with McClellan yesterday. This morning he was up with the enemy at Sharpsburg, and was waiting for heavy fog to rise.
Lincoln to Curtin

FRANKLIN's men were pressing—but in a careful and prudent manner —upon the line which McLaws had thrown across Pleasant Valley. Word came to the Confederates that Harpers Ferry had surrendered, and the sequel is related by the Confederate officer Blackford: "A skirmisher of the enemy, as our cheers rang out in response, sprang up on a stone wall and called over to us, 'What the hell are you fellows cheering for?' We shouted back, 'Because Harpers Ferry is gone up, G—— d—— you.' 'I thought that was it,' shouted the fellow as he got down off the wall." [1] It scarcely can be claimed that Franklin had shown "the utmost activity that a general" could exercise, enjoined upon him by his chief. But Franklin, who was one of McClellan's favorites, probably had formed his idea of "activity" by observing his chief. He must have noted McClellan's careful respect for the repose of the Sixth Corps on the night of the 13th, and so it was not strange that he showed similar care on the 14th. The fall of Harpers Ferry was a catastrophe. General White had retired to the place with his regiments from Martinsburg, and had deferred command to Miles. About 14,000 men were surrendered with much equipment. The town was absolutely untenable after McLaws had dragged guns to the top of Maryland Heights; but Miles held out about twelve hours longer than Lee may have expected he would. The one really creditable feature in the entire episode was the neat escape of the cavalry regiments, whose commanders did not like the thought of surrendering their men and mounts to the enemy, and urged upon Miles their ability to get away. With the necessary order from him, Colonel Arno Voss led his own regiment, the Twelfth Illinois, and the Eighth New York across the pontoon bridge and turned up the river between the canal and the steep slopes of Maryland Heights about eight o'clock on Sunday evening. Rapidly and as quietly as possible, in column of twos, without led horses or wagons, the 1,200 troopers rode at a trot or gallop until the Confederate outposts had been passed. At nine the next morning, after a march of about sixty miles around Lee's "main body," Voss reached Greencastle, Pennsylvania, and reported to General Wool.[2] On the way he had encountered a Confederate wagon train which Longstreet had ordered back to Virginia when he had marched from Hagerstown back to Boonsboro; Voss destroyed about sixty wagons with ammunition, and took 675 prisoners. When boldness and enterprise were tried, they paid off for the Federals, quite as well as for the Confederates. Word of the fine exploit by the cavalry reached McClellan in a telegram from Governor Curtin, who had begun to pick up considerable good information;[3] but the news also came from people of the countryside.[4]

Colonel Miles, an officer well on in years, was killed during the few moments of firing that continued after the white flag had been raised at Harpers Ferry. A military commission was presently to investigate the unhappy affair.[5]

When Lee realized that South Mountain was lost, he moved at once to the town of Sharpsburg and deployed his force of some 18,000 men behind the Antietam [6]—a stream of no great dimensions, but nevertheless of considerable military value for four or five miles above the point where it flows into the Potomac. It was a location which his absent units could reach by a six hours' march from Harpers Ferry without being dangerously exposed, and from which he could retire at need across the Potomac into Virginia. Elements of McClellan's army must have reached the east bank early in the afternoon, and when the general himself arrived he was greeted with cheers and cap-throwing.[7] In his report he wrote: "After a rapid examination of the position, I found that it was too late to attack that day, and at once directed the placing of the batteries in position in the center, and indicated the bivouacs for the different corps, massing them near and on both sides of the Sharpsburg turnpike." [8] In placing batteries in position McClellan was doing what an artillery officer should have done, and in massing his corps near the roadside he was quite likely delaying deployment.

"Too late to attack that day." The words make the reader hopeful about the morrow. But then hour after hour passed away, and precious minute followed precious minute as Little Mac puttered about, while Lee's absent divisions marched to join their endangered comrades. Anxiously the man in the White House waited, knowing full well that a great opportunity must exist after the success of the 14th. With no news coming, the President wired Governor Curtin at noon: "What do you hear from General McClellan's army? We have nothing from him to-day." The Governor replied promptly that he had had no definite news, but that his telegraph operator at Hagerstown reported a battle in progress between Sharpsburg and Williamsport. Hopefully he inquired, "What success did McClellan meet with yesterday?" In the meantime a delayed message had reached Washington that brought little cheer. Nevertheless, Lincoln at 2:35 considerately passed on the meager news: "Since telegraphing you, dispatch came from General McClellan, dated 7 o'clock this morning. Nothing of importance happened with him yesterday. This morning he was up with the enemy at Sharpsburg, and was waiting for heavy fog to rise." [9] Was there irony and double meaning in the President's closing words?

So McClellan waited for the fog to rise on a day which had begun hot but was relieved by a breeze toward noon, as staff officers became bored with "tedium and inaction," and troops lay about in idleness.[10] His report gave the plan for the "impending general engagement," which he matured that day: to attack the enemy's left with the corps of Hooker and Mansfield (commanding Banks's old corps), supported by Sumner's corps, and if necessary by that of Franklin. Then, as soon as matters looked favorable in that direction, he would move "Burnside's corps against the enemy's extreme right, and, whenever either of these flank movements should be successful," advance his "center with all the forces then disposable." [11]

The plan looks well enough, but one wonders about the word "successful." Did it mean the complete rout of the enemy, or his retirement, or mere signs of his exhaustion and the imminence of breaking? Did McClellan have the ability to judge events on a battlefield, and could he tell when the moment had arrived to put in "all the forces then disposable"? And (a greater test of a general) did he have the high moral courage to do so? One is to remember, in reading the story of the battle, that McClellan himself had said that he intended to put in all disposable forces when the proper time came.

McClellan's plan certainly paid high tribute to John Pope, for the initial heavy work was allotted to the old Army of Virginia, of which Porter—who was to sit the battle out—had spoken with a sneer when he first came to it. Hooker had McDowell's old corps, Mansfield had that of Banks, and most of Burnside's troops had been under Pope. McClellan's old commanders of the Peninsula—Sumner, Franklin, and Porter—were to have supporting or reserve roles. McClellan had an excellent opportunity to remove the cloud which had hung over Porter since Second Bull Run, and it looks as if he may have intended to have that general deliver the final thrust that would win the battle.

On the afternoon of the 16th, Hooker's corps crossed the Antietam by one of the upper fords and took position for his attack the next day, McClellan accompanying it, or at least inspecting the operation. At 5:50 a message was sent to Sumner directing that Mansfield's corps cross and take a position to be designated by Hooker; his own corps was to be prepared to march an hour before daylight. Though it was specified that Mansfield should be "ready for action early in the morning," not a word was said about an attack, in what apparently was the nearest thing to a written order for the coming battle. Not until after midnight was Franklin ordered to join the army, for McClellan first considered having him continue his operation against Maryland Heights.[12]

Hooker's movement was discovered, and some brisk action took place. Thus, when night came Lee not only had been joined by a large part of his absent troops but knew exactly where McClellan would strike his main blow. The management of the left part of Lee's line was given to Stonewall Jackson.

Palfrey wrote, "The night before the battle passed quietly, except for some alarms on Hooker's front, and most of the men in both armies probably got a good sleep." One wonders just how good the sleep was. Even the veterans must have been restless, with memories that let them picture the ordeal ahead. Then there were new regiments of men who had never yet faced the ordeal of fire, who had never

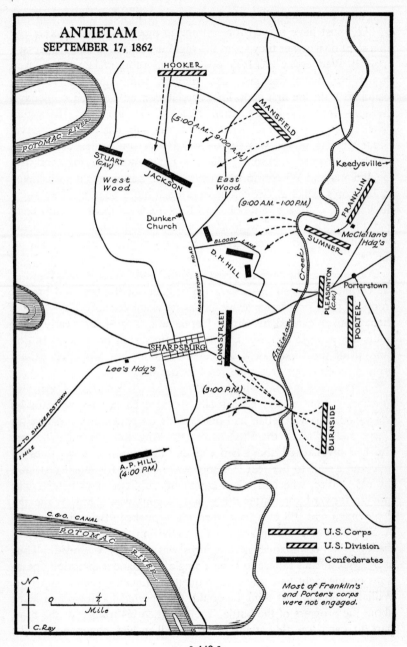

ANTIETAM
SEPTEMBER 17, 1862

HOOKER

(5:00 A.M. - 9:00 A.M.)

MANSFIELD

Keedysville

STUART
(CAV.)

JACKSON

West
Wood

East
Wood

FRANKLIN

(9:00 A.M. - 1:00 P.M.)

Dunker
Church

McClellan's
Hdq's

SUMNER

BLOODY LANE

D. H. HILL

Creek

Antietam

PLEASONTON
(CAV.)

Porterstown

PORTER

HAGERSTOWN ROAD

LONGSTREET

SHARPSBURG

Lee's Hdq's

(3:00 P.M.)

TO SHEPERDSTOWN
1 MILE

BURNSIDE

A. P. HILL
(4:00 P.M.)

C. & O. CANAL

POTOMAC RIVER

N

0   ⅟₂   1
Mile

C. Ray

⬛ U.S. Corps
⬛ U.S. Division
⬛ Confederates

*Most of Franklin's
and Porter's corps
were not engaged.*

[449]

seen their comrades fall, and who must have wondered what it would be like, must have prayed for courage to meet the test. Whether the men slept or whether they spent the night in controlled and suppressed anguish, Wednesday the 17th was not a morning of late rising, even though the dawn was gray and somber, with light mist reducing visibility. With the first good light Joe Hooker advanced, Doubleday's division—formerly King's, then Hatch's—on the right, Ricketts's division on the left, and Meade somewhat to the rear in reserve. Great striking power was there, and Henderson writes of the task which confronted Jackson: "Meade's Pennsylvanians, together with the Indiana and Wisconsin regiments, which had wrought such havoc in Jackson's ranks at Groveton, were once more bearing down upon his line. . . . Meade, Gibbon, and Ricketts were there to lead them, and the battle opened with a resolution which, if it had infected McClellan, would have carried the Sharpsburg ridge ere set of sun." [13]

Concealed in the famous "East Woods" and "West Woods" and in the cornfield between them were ten brigades of the best and bravest troops of the Confederate army, under excellent commanders. Against them Hooker carried his direct frontal attack, and for nearly three hours the struggle continued, with heavy losses on both sides. In due time all of the First Corps was in the action; but though it gained ground it could not break the resolute defense.

Where was Mansfield, who according to McClellan's "plan" was also to attack? What orders he actually received cannot be told, for he was killed, and McClellan had put nothing on paper. But the Twelfth Corps had followed the First across the Antietam the night before, and had bivouacked about two o'clock "in column of companies" a mile and a half to the rear.[14] There was not time for much rest, and the old soldier, who had taken command only two days before, was moving forward soon after the sound of guns was heard. While the deployment was still going on, word was brought to Brigadier General A. S. Williams, commanding the First Division, "that the veteran and distinguished commander of the corps was mortally wounded." Thus early, McClellan's failure to have a single commander directing operations on the right had tragic consequences. Lacking such a superior, Williams did the best thing he could; he reported to Hooker to learn about the progress of the battle. Then he used his troops for the most part to carry on the attack which Hooker had commenced. The

Twelfth Corps, quite as well as the First, contained regiments which had previously handled Jackson roughly: in Crawford's brigade, the Tenth Maine, the Twenty-eighth New York, and the Forty-sixth Pennsylvania, which had smashed the "Stonewall Division" at Cedar Mountain; and in Gordon's brigade, the Twenty-seventh Indiana, the Second Massachusetts, and the Third Wisconsin, which had so well covered the retirement on that day. The Second Division of the corps also had seven regiments [15] which had fought Jackson on that memorable 9th of August when Pope's army demonstrated offensive warfare on the part of the Federals.

Hooker presently had to retire from the field with a painful and badly bleeding bullet hole through his foot, and for the most part his corps fell back to its positions of the early morning. The Twelfth Corps with remnants of the First pressed on to the vicinity of the Dunker Church, a small whitewashed structure in the southern part of the "West Woods," on the west side of the Sharpsburg-Hagerstown turnpike. From that day the modest little edifice dedicated to religious purposes became a famous landmark, for about it there raged a desperate struggle between the Union soldiers and Hood's "Texans" and other troops brought to their support. By about nine o'clock the aggressive power of the attackers had been exhausted, and the battle died away in sullen silence.

In reality the First Corps and the Twelfth had attacked in column of corps, while the reading of McClellan's "plan" would lead one to believe that it was intended that the corps should have been in line, with Sumner, and possibly Franklin, in support. Such a formation would have put pressure on more of the Confederate line, and would have prevented the shifting of troops from one place to another.

Where was Sumner all this time? He should have been on the field observing the progress of the attack, studying the terrain to see where he could go in with the Second Corps to give support; but McClellan kept him at Army Headquarters until 7:20 A.M. At 9:00 Williams was told that a part of Sumner's corps was coming. That was true, and Sumner himself led Sedgwick's division—which he should not have done—to the attack from the "East Woods." The division encountered far greater resistance than was expected, and it suffered a disastrous repulse. Presently the "first battle" of the 17th was over. Narrowly, by good troop leading and hard fighting, the Confederate line had escaped rupture. But the Federals had paid a heavy price in their attacks. Because of inadequate command arrangements, the local counterattacks of the Confederates might have thrown the right of the Federals into rout had it not been for their excellent and well handled artillery.[16]

Then came the awful fight at the "Bloody Lane." For some reason, never clearly explained, French's division of Sumner's corps, following Sedgwick, got too far to the left to help him, and started another action. Richardson's division of the same corps, detained an hour by McClellan, presently came in on the left of French, and together the two fought fiercely with divisions of D. H. Hill and R. H. Anderson, with advantage on the Federal side. Of the Confederate line, Freeman writes, "The center now was wrecked." One of Lee's artillerymen, General E. P. Alexander, put it thus, "Lee's army was ruined and the end of the Confederacy was in sight." [17]

The moment had certainly come for McClellan to carry out the final part of his plan of battle. Michie, noting that the contest up to the moment had been relatively favorable to the Union cause, observes, "Had McClellan put in his reserves across the Boonsborough Bridge at the time when McLaws was pushing Sedgwick back, there is every reason to suppose that he would have achieved a great victory." [18] Remembering how Pope strove on August 29 to get his entire army into action, one can believe that that general would have been equal to the occasion.

Of Franklin's Sixth Corps only Smith's division was in action, bringing support to Sumner at a very critical time. Slocum arrived with his division about 11:00 A.M. after marching from Pleasant Valley. Two of the brigades of the division were formed for attack by Franklin, and he was waiting for the third brigade to get into position as a reserve, when Sumner came up to him. Sumner, the ranking officer, had been fighting well, but apparently was somewhat demoralized; and he directed that the attack be postponed. Presently McClellan arrived on the scene and decided that it would not be prudent to attack because the Federal position on the right was "then considerably in advance of what it had been in the morning." [19] An amazing reason indeed. But that is just what Franklin wrote in his report on October 7, and since McClellan did not challenge the statement, one must accept it as true. In other words, McClellan did not put in all his disposable forces, precisely because he had been successful! Palfrey is even more emphatic than Michie in stating that, if the opportunity had been grasped, "the result would have been the practical annihilation of Lee's army." [20]

It may have been near 2:00 P.M. that the fighting ended on the right center and quiet reigned there, as well as on the extreme right, except for an occasional exchange of artillery fire.

The "third battle" of the hard-contested day was Burnside's, about which there has been much dispute, largely due to the absence of written orders. Burnside, a "wing" commander with only half a wing, merely passed on McClellan's orders—brought verbally by aides—to Cox, who had been commanding the Ninth Corps since Reno's death, and was himself a two-starred supernumerary. A difficult mission was given to the corps, which in addition to its own three divisions had the Kanawha Division attached. It had to force a river crossing—a touchy matter always, and something worse than that when done by daylight against the will of earnest Southern riflemen. The crossing had to be where the Antietam was deep, the banks steep, and where the hills sloped down in such a way as to make the approach to the stone bridge over the stream a veritable deathtrap. Although the defenders could not bring upon the bridge and its approaches an indirect fire from concealed weapons such as could be laid today, the attackers did not have the weapons that would now be used to carry out such a heavy task. In his final report on August 4, 1863—after Burnside had replaced him as army commander—McClellan spoke as if the crossing were not a serious matter; but in his preliminary report of October 15, 1862, he candidly admitted it was a "difficult task." [21]

Jacob Cox wrote in his report: "About 7 o'clock orders were received from General Burnside to move forward the corps to the ridge nearest the Antietam, and hold it in readiness to cross the stream, carrying the bridge and the heights above it by assault." [22]

Cox said that the order to cross the stream was received at nine o'clock; Burnside stated it came to him at ten; McClellan put the hour at ten in his first account, but advanced it to eight in his final version.[23] Covering fire was provided, but the first efforts to cross the bridge failed. Although only 403 men in the two regiments of Confederate infantry under Robert Toombs opposed the crossing, they were good riflemen and they were well placed; with supporting artillery they covered not only the bridge, but also the stretch of road which for several hundred yards ran close to the stream, and led to the bridge on the east.[24] Not till one o'clock was the crossing effected, and then the Union flags were not only on the far side of the stream at the bridge, but also at fords some distance above and below the structure. If there had been delay in making the crossing, there had been a delay also in ordering it. Why was it not ordered at five o'clock, or seven at the latest? Even the difference of two hours could have changed completely the outcome of the battle. What McClellan's actual thinking on that day was can never be divined; there is the possibility that he thought at first of the action by the Ninth Corps as merely a threat and a diversion.

Not until three o'clock was all the Ninth Corps across and formed up for advance upon Sharpsburg from the southeast; Willcox's and Rodman's divisions were in line from left to right, each with a supporting brigade of Kanawha men; the division of Sturgis was in reserve. Burnside and Cox knew what they were doing—except perhaps for one neglected point—and everything went well at first. But the cessation of fighting on Lee's left flank enabled him to bring troops to his now pressed right, just as he had moved units from his right to the left in the morning. Freeman writes: "By 4 P.M. the battle on the right was almost lost to the Confederates. The Federals had gained nearly all the high ground East and South of Sharpsburg. If they could push 1200 yards farther westward, they would be across the line of retreat the left wing of Lee's Army would have to take to the Shepherdstown Ford." Almost lost, but not quite, just as the battle on the other flank and the battle in the center had been almost lost. Perhaps Fortune had tired of having McClellan almost spurn the opportunities offered him; perhaps an answer was being made to the prayers uttered by Stonewall Jackson.

Except for the Light Division of A. P. Hill, all units of Lee's army had rejoined in time to be in the fighting of the morning and early afternoon. Stonewall had graciously released Hill from arrest after he forded the Potomac on the 12th; then he had left Hill to finish up matters at Harpers Ferry. (Moving property and stores away and paroling 11,000 prisoners required time and work.) At 6:30 A.M. of the 17th an order reached Hill from Lee to move in haste to Sharpsburg. Jackson may not have thought that Hill was a good marcher, but the Light Division was put in motion at 7:30, and relentlessly its commander pushed it over the seventeen long and dusty miles that led to battle. Some of Hill's 2,000 men may have had on stiff new shoes that hurt their feet; but some of them had put on new blue uniforms which would help them give the Federals a good surprise.

The regiments which had been hurried over the road from Harpers Ferry were in a very advantageous position to bring help to the Confederates who were being pressed back in the vicinity of Sharpsburg, and Hill lost no time in launching an attack with infantry and artillery against Rodman's vulnerable flank. The first Confederates seen by the Federals were in captured blue uniforms, and they were assumed to be friendly troops until they opened fire.[25] Rodman quickly changed his dispositions to meet Hill's attack, and in the fighting that followed he was himself mortally wounded; but no great confusion resulted from the change of command. Colonel Scammon also moved two regiments of his brigade into position to oppose the Confederates who had so unceremoniously broken into the battle, and the division of Sturgis was brought up from the bridge. Thus the attack by Hill was quickly and adequately met, but a very definite check had been given to the Federal advance on Sharpsburg, which had been going well and promised to be decisive. With the coming of darkness, Cox retired his line in excellent order to the hills above the bridge. (The criticism that one might make of Burnside and Cox was failure to foresee a possible flank attack. If the Kanawha Division, instead of being broken up and used as supports, had been advanced to the left and rear of Rodman, it could either have taken Hill himself in flank or have prevented his deployment against Rodman's flank.)

It was the last 2,000 men that Lee brought to the field that saved the day for him. After McClellan had made the strange decision against letting Franklin attack, he still had a golden chance to assist Burnside on the left, for Pleasonton's horse artillery and Sykes's fine division of regulars had already—as Palfrey puts it—"made an opening for an energetic movement to the left front of the Federal centre." [26] Though he had more than 80,000 men at his command, it is doubtful if McClellan ever actually pressed the attack with as many as 20,000 men at one time.

General McClellan observed the battle from a hill just east of the Antietam, which afforded an excellent view of much of the field. According to the detailed account of Colonel Strother, army headquarters was a place of calmness and decorum—as it should be. The records give only two messages sent during the day. One at 1:25 P.M., signed by an assistant adjutant general, was addressed to General

Meade, and it directed him to take command of Hooker's corps—
Meade was not the senior officer—and to make every effort to reorganize it. The other was essentially a repetition of this order signed
by the chief of staff at 3:10.[27] That there was at headquarters full
knowledge of the progress of the battle—as distinguished from a firm
and adequate meeting of opportunities—was shown by a long and
very remarkable dispatch written that night by a correspondent for the
New York Tribune. It was not printed until the 20th, after shorter
accounts of the battle—with gross exaggeration—had appeared beginning on the 18th. (Longstreet and Stonewall Jackson had, as usual,
been killed.) The writer stated that 200,000 men had been engaged in
the greatest battle since Waterloo, and added, "If not wholly a victory
to-night, I believe it is the prelude to victory to-morrow." An interesting and important part of the dispatch dealt with the close of the
battle:

> McClellan's glass for the last half hour has seldom been turned away
> from the left. He sees clearly enough that Burnside is pressed—needs no
> messenger to tell him that. His face grows darker with anxious thought.
> Looking down into the valley where 15,000 troops are lying, he turns a
> half-questioning look on Fitz John Porter, who stands by his side, gravely
> scanning the field. They are Porter's troops below, are fresh and only
> impatient to share in the fight. But Porter slowly shakes his head, and one
> may believe that the same thought is passing through the mind of both
> generals: "They are the only reserves of the army; they cannot be
> spared." [28]

At that time there were no Field Service Regulations, which give the
army's doctrine, with which every higher officer is supposed to be
thoroughly imbued. But combat principles and teachings were included in Army Regulations, in the passage: "The reserve is formed
of the best troops of foot and horse, to complete a victory or make
good a retreat. It is placed in the rear of the centre, or chief point of
attack or defense." McClellan's reserve consisted of Sykes's division
of regulars—good troops indeed—and Morell's division, perhaps
equally excellent, and Pleasonton's cavalry. Furthermore, the reserve
was behind the center. The book was being followed carefully except
as to one point, the purpose of a reserve—to complete a victory. And
it is to be noted that Porter's corps, though nominally the only reserve
and mustering less than the 15,000 men the correspondent mentioned—waiting, it might be noted, near Porterstown—was actually

not the entire reserve force at McClellan's command. Slocum's division of Franklin's corps had not been used, except to suppress quickly some Confederate efforts to become aggressive in their front. And by the time that the fight on the left had reached a crisis much of the First Corps should have been reorganized and in hand, in accordance with the army commander's order.

When the battle of the 17th had stopped, the two commanding generals had the hard tasks of making decisions for the next day. Much has been written about the meeting at Lee's headquarters in a field west of Sharpsburg, fabled stories with dramatic touches.[29] Present were Longstreet, Jackson, both the Hills, Hood, Early, and D. R. Jones, from whom Lee received reports of heavy losses with little said that was optimistic. The question was clear: should the army retreat that night across the Potomac, or should it remain and pretend that it was ready for another contest with its adversary? It must have been suspected that McClellan had strong units that had not been engaged— for such was his nature—and it must have been realized that the achievements of that day would be hard indeed to repeat. No A. P. Hill would arrive at just the crucial moment, and Burnside's troops were already across the Antietam in positions from which the attack could be renewed. But Lee believed that McClellan was too cautious to reengage; and, contrary to some strong opinions of his subordinates, he directed that the army remain, readjust its lines, strengthen its positions, feed its men, and care for its wounded and its dead—and on the morrow put up a bold and saucy front. Few generals have ever met a higher test of moral courage.

At McClellan's headquarters there must have been much coming and going of messengers and commanders, though Strother recorded that part at least of the staff "supped heartily and slept profoundly" in their camp near Keedysville, to which the general had returned after dark from his forward command post.[30] But what was reported by the corps commanders, or what was recommended, is of little importance. One knows what the foregone decision was: corps commanders were to do nothing in an offensive way unless specific orders were received. But at least the Army of the Potomac was not retreating, and it would work throughout the night to care for its wounded and its dead. The casualties were to set a day's record unbroken in any of the hard battles of the remaining two and a half years of bitter war. McClellan's killed totaled 2,108, and Lee's, 2,700; the wounded numbered 9,549 and 9,024.[31] The totals of 11,657 and 11,724 made it almost a case of man for man. But Lee was to have 2,000 missing as against McClellan's modest 753, and he paid dearly indeed for his great demonstration of defensive skill in a battle where the chance of changing to a vigorous offensive was nil.

A mere scanning of the losses by corps, divisions, and brigades shows how unevenly McClellan had engaged his army. The total casualties of the First Corps were 2,590, and those of Sumner's Second Corps were no fewer than 5,138—well in excess of the 4,682 men lost in the other five infantry corps and the cavalry division.

One who fell seriously injured was Private B. W. Mitchell; in 1879 McClellan wrote in a letter that it was doubtful if he had ever known the name of the soldier who had rendered the "infinite service" of finding Lee's lost order [32]—a frank admission of a strange neglect. Among the others badly wounded, who would in the future render almost "infinite service" to the country, was Captain Oliver Wendell Holmes, of the Second Massachusetts.

The hours must have dragged slowly in Washington after the receipt by Halleck at five o'clock of a message from McClellan marked 1:20 P.M.:

We are in the midst of the most terrible battle of the war—perhaps of history. Thus far it looks well, but I have great odds against me. Hurry up all the troops possible. Our loss has been terrific, but we have gained much ground. I have thrown the mass of the army on the left flank. Burnside is now attacking the right, and I hold my small reserve, consisting of Porter's (Fifth) corps, ready to attack the center as soon as the flank movements are developed. I hope that God will give us a glorious victory.[33]

It was a message which well could have raised some hopes. Then there was apparently silence until ten o'clock, when the chief of ordnance received from McClellan a message sent from Hagerstown at an unstated hour.[34] It asked that some 20-pound Parrott ammunition be sent through during the night to Hagerstown if it possibly could be done. At the same time there came from an aide-de-camp a message asking that duplicate assignments of several types of artillery ammunition and some small-arms ammunition be sent at once to Hagerstown and to Frederick.

A reply was sent to McClellan at once assuring him that a special train under charge of an ordnance officer would leave for Hagerstown, and that more ammunition would go as soon as possible to Hagerstown and Frederick. Then Assistant Secretary Watson telegraphed President Garrett of the Baltimore and Ohio about the train, asking him to make all arrangements with connecting roads. "This train," Watson said, "must have the right of way on the entire route, and must be run as fast as any express passenger train could be run." Then Watson wired the facts and the urgency to Colonel Thomas A. Scott, who had resigned from the War Department on June 1 to return to the Pennsylvania Central Railroad at Harrisburg. One would think that nothing more could be done. But at midnight Stanton—who since the beginning of the campaign had not sent a message to McClellan, nor until that afternoon to Halleck—broke into the story. In the emphatic language which the Secretary used so readily, he wrote an order "To the officers, or any of them, of the Northern Central Railroad, Pennsylvania Central Railroad, and Cumberland Valley Railroad, at Harrisburg, Pa.":

An ammunition train will leave here about 1 o'clock a.m. for Hagerstown, via Harrisburg, to be run through at the fastest possible speed, so as to reach its destination to-morrow morning early. It must have the right of way throughout, as General McClellan needs the ammunition, to be used in the battle to be fought to-morrow. It is expected that you will use every possible effort to expedite the passage of this train.

The order of the Secretary of War was itself a potent thing; but that night Edwin Stanton wrote above his name, "By order of the President of the United States."

The train did not leave Washington as early in the morning as was expected, but probably before noon Stanton received from the superintendent of the Northern Central Railroad at Harrisburg, a dispatch reading:

The ammunition train for General McClellan was delivered to the Northern Central Railroad, at Baltimore, at 6.57 a.m., and was delivered to the Cumberland Valley Railroad, at 10.20 a.m.; 84 miles—two hours and fifty-three minutes. It will be put through at all speed to Hagerstown.[35]

But the special train rushed to Harrisburg and on to Hagerstown, duplicating a train direct to Frederick, the two together supplementing 414 wagonloads of ammunition already sent to McClellan,[36] were not the only reenforcements hurried to him. The division of Brigadier

General Andrew A. Humphreys—a brilliant man, and one of the few who Palfrey said could go into battle with apparent pleasure—was also marching to join McClellan for the expected battle of the 18th. Although Humphreys had served as a topographical engineer on the Peninsula, he entered this campaign for the first time as a combat officer. On the 12th Halleck had given him command of a new division, composed of eight regiments—two brigades—of Pennsylvania infantry, with a battery from Ohio and one from New York. Inspection revealed that the troops were not ready for the field, were lacking wagons and other equipment; but, worst of all, some had unserviceable Austrian rifles. By great exertions, Humphreys's division, properly equipped, marched at daylight on Sunday the 14th. September 17 was spent under orders at Frederick, where instructions were received at 3:00 P.M. to join the army. The command toiled over the mountains during the hours of darkness, and to the general at its head came messages from the field of battle bidding him hurry, but still admonishing that his men must be ready for action. The last dispatch was signed at 5:00 P.M. by Porter, and it said briefly, "Get here before daybreak." One can imagine Humphreys, as the first touches of light came, looking back to see if his 6,000 men and eight guns were well closed up. There have been few who could equal him as a master of understatement, as there have been few who could equal him in cool bravery; and in his report he said merely: "The men were unaccustomed to marching, and were foot-sore; but I marched all night, and at an early hour the next morning was in position at Antietam, having marched more than 23 miles." [37] But when McClellan gave in his report as one of his reasons for not renewing battle on the morning of the 18th the unavailability of Humphreys's division until near the close of the day the quiet soldier's resentment was aroused, and he protested directly to the Secretary of War. Denying the charge, he said, "When I saw the long lines of the regiments as they filed into their position, in rear of Morell, I knew the kind of men I commanded." [38] The sequel will reveal how accurately the eye of Humphreys could appraise the quality of a column of troops.

On the morning of the 18th McClellan sent Halleck a brief dispatch which closed: "The battle will probably be renewed to-day. Send all the troops you can by the most expeditious route." [39] The first sentence indicated that he expected Lee to pass to the offensive, for he himself certainly had no serious intention of attacking again, though he talked about it. Palfrey wrote: "It is hardly worth while to state his reasons. . . . The fault was in the man. There was force enough at his command either day [17th or 18th] had he seen fit to use it." [40] The hostile lines were close together, and during the ensuing night the telltale noise of wheels and other sounds revealed the enemy was moving. In the morning Lee was gone—after a well planned and skillfully conducted withdrawal across the river. Under date of the 19th Strother wrote, "We are advancing this morning, but too cautiously to effect anything." [41]

Porter had the pursuit in charge, and did cross some troops, who made small captures, but which, though losses had been small, were recalled with the coming of night.[42] The next morning at seven Morell and Sykes were directed to cross their divisions; but an hour later, after the advance guard had encountered the enemy in force, Porter ordered everything back into Maryland—an operation in which one regiment had considerable losses. In his report McClellan misrepresented the affair by saying that the troops had been "attacked by a large body of the enemy, lying in ambush in the woods," [43] which was not at all in accordance with Porter's report written only ten days after the event. The facts are as follows.[44] About midnight of the 19-20th Lee received an exaggerated report of the Federal crossing, and at once sent word to Jackson to break it up—he did not want any pursuit. Stonewall had already heard about what had happened and, somewhat excited, had sent A. P. Hill back from near Martinsburg to the river, and had gone himself to the scene of action. Though tired with marching, Hill's men terminated Porter's venture in the same manner as they had changed the battle three days before.

When the last dripping soldier of Porter's corps splashed ashore in Maryland, the reverberations of the angry guns had died away, and the Maryland campaign was at an end. It had fallen short of what Lee had hoped to accomplish, though it had drawn the Federal army out of Virginia. Although it is hard to justify his accepting battle at Antietam instead of retiring across the river,[45] he had so much confidence in his army that he thought he might be able not only to repulse an attack, but also to launch a counterattack that would give him a profitable victory. His remarkable defense on the 17th and his boldness on the 18th did not conceal the fact—though Southern papers did not concede it—that he had been bested; and for obvious reasons he could not publicly plead his weak numbers as the cause. The chances of foreign intervention in behalf of the Confederacy were greatly lessened, and wishful thinking that the people of Maryland were waiting to be liberated had to be abandoned. In addition, some of the "rebel" soldiers took back to Virginia the impression that the Yankees could shoot straighter on their own side of the river, and they were not eager to engage in any more of the invading business.[46]

Halleck's actions during the Maryland campaign are difficult to evaluate. He was in a hard position. He certainly could not have been hopeful of much good from the restoration of McClellan, but he would suggest to the President no other way out of the predicament in which the High Command found itself. On the other hand his letters to Pope admitted that he knew McClellan resented his own position as General in Chief.[47] Whatever the feelings of the two men toward each other may have been, their correspondence, as McClellan moved toward the enemy, appeared to be unaffected. Not unnaturally, Halleck was concerned about the safety of Washington, thinking at first that Lee's crossing the Potomac might merely be a trick to lure the Union army away from the capital. Information from Virginia was contradictory, and he held to the belief that strong Confederate forces might be in the vicinity of Leesburg longer than was justified. (McClellan also had been much concerned about Washington in the last week of August, but he again became completely indifferent to it when he was thirty or forty miles away.) There were several other theaters of war about which Halleck had to think. In Kentucky matters were rapidly going from bad to worse; Bragg was steadily gaining ground, and Buell appeared to be unable to cope with him. It looked as if Kentucky might be lost to the Union, and an invasion of the North carried on in the West at the very time that one had been started in the East. Headlines were alarming.

But Halleck was trying to give McClellan all the aid he could, even in small ways. On September 14 McClellan said to the General in Chief in a dispatch announcing that he would soon have a decisive battle, "Look well to Chambersburg." Perplexed, Halleck replied immediately: "I do not understand what you mean by asking me to look out for Chambersburg. I have no troops to send there." The next day, however, he wired the commanding officer at Greencastle, Pennsylvania, to assist McClellan by harassing the rear of Longstreet; and directed the commanding officer at Gettysburg to move his force toward Hagerstown, harass the enemy, pick up his stragglers, and destroy his trains.[48] It is not revealed what forces may have been at Greencastle or Gettysburg, and evidently Halleck did not know: they may have been detachments of state troops. But he evidently wanted no one to be idle even if the only practical activity was to annoy or distract the enemy. In and about Washington there was an imposing number of troops—no fewer than 70,000.[49] Not all of them, however, were ready for the field, and there were not many officers like Andrew A. Humphreys, who could do wonders in a short time. In addition, the large field force that McClellan already had was creating a difficult supply problem in view of the high standard of living of the Federal army. As it moved from Washington, the army had to be supported by wagon trains alone, but after the 12th a railhead in the vicinity of Frederick was possible, supplies moving by way of Baltimore.

Three days after the battle, backbiting broke out. At 2:00 P.M. of the 20th Halleck wired McClellan: "We are still entirely in the dark in regard to your own movements and those of the enemy. This should not be so. You should keep me advised of both, so far as you know them." A bit abrupt, but Halleck was the General in Chief, and the General in Chief does not have to say "Please" unless he wants to. McClellan, replying, complained of his tone and took him to task for not having said anything pleasant about the recent victory of the army.[50] (As a matter of fact Halleck's tone was not so abrupt as that which McClellan had lately used toward his good friend "Burn" when expressing dissatisfaction with Burnside's march on the 15th.) The General in Chief was not silenced by the uncalled-for comments of a peevish subordinate; and five days later he telegraphed: "Of course, your movements must depend in a measure upon the position and movements of the enemy; nevertheless they will be subordinate to a general plan. Without knowing your plan and your views on this subject, I cannot answer the questions which are asked me by the Government. Please state your plans as fully as possible." [51]

Plans? McCellan had none. He was merely reveling in his achievement. On the 18th he wrote in a private letter, "Those in whose judgment I rely tell me that I fought the battle splendidly and that it was a masterpiece of art." This was the statement which Michie found so incomprehensible; and he wrote the calm but devastating comment, "It does not seem possible to find any other battle ever fought in the conduct of which more errors were committed than are clearly attributable to the commander of the Army of the Potomac." [52]

Each day apparently added to the satisfaction which McClellan felt for what he had done on the 17th, and on the day when he complained to Halleck, he wrote in another private letter:

I feel some little pride in having, with a beaten and demoralized army, defeated Lee so utterly and saved the North so completely. . . . Since I left Washington, Stanton has again asserted that *I*, not Pope, lost the battle of Manassas No. 2! . . . I am tired of fighting against such disadvantages, and feel that it is now time for the country to come to my help and remove these difficulties from my path. If my countrymen will not open their eyes and assist themselves they must pardon me if I decline longer to pursue the thankless avocation of serving them. [53]

And while he wrote thus there sat on the tracks in Hagerstown the cars of unused ammunition, rushed through by Stanton, because he had barely hinted that he would need and use it!

In the evening of the same day, McClellan wrote in another letter, "I feel that I have done all that can be asked in twice saving the country." Absent from his mind was the stern thought that in the grim business of war a commanding general must be judged not by what he has done, but by what he could have done if he had fully measured up to the high trust that a government and a people had placed in him. A man in his frame of mind was certainly not thinking seriously of plans for future vigorous operations; and when the General in Chief stated that he was embarrassed because he could not answer the questions of the government McClellan probably merely thought that the President and the cabinet were again becoming impertinent. And so the general again settled down to refit his army, while he listened to the flattering speeches of his favorites and wrote letters that have amazed many readers.

On the very day when he was writing the sentences quoted he signed strength returns stating that the "aggregate present for duty" in his field command was 93,149. The absentees were almost in equal number, for there were 81,538. Many were doubtless stragglers and were to be found in the region through which the army had marched. Apparently the order of the 9th had done no good whatever—as any soldier could have foretold by reading it. Presently another order was issued, calling attention to the frequent orders on the subject of straggling and pillaging. It ended, "The commanding general is resolved to put a stop to the pernicious and criminal practices of straggling and marauding, and he will hold corps commanders responsible for the faithful execution of this order." [54] This was much better than entreating general officers to stop the straggling and marauding of their troops; but a few good lusty cheers from his soldiers would probably have made McClellan forget their faults.

On October 1—the day when McClellan tried to tighten up on his army in the proper manner—Lincoln arrived for a visit. He remained for several days, and McClellan devoted a paragraph of his memoirs to the occasion. In addition to visiting the battlefields of South Mountain and Antietam and reviewing troops, the President—the Commander in Chief—and the army commander engaged in a number of confidential talks. Photographers were about, and the familiar picture of the two men seated opposite each other at a table in the general's tent was taken. Neither seemed especially at ease, and the national flag, incorrectly used as the cover for a table, looks equally unhappy. It is much to be regretted that there are not accurate and adequate records of the conversations; the few sentences which McClellan wrote late in life certainly cannot be accepted as reliable. Referring to Lincoln, he wrote: "He more than once assured me that he was fully satisfied with my whole course from the beginning; that the only fault he could possibly find was that I was perhaps too prone to be sure that everything was ready before acting, but that my actions were all right when I started." [55] McClellan was again trying to alter the record, for a famous letter which Lincoln wrote to him soon after the visit began, "You remember my speaking to you of what I called your overcautiousness." [56] He explained forcibly what he meant—as will presently be seen. In the President's mind, McClellan's overcautiousness was not something which he put aside when at last he started to move after long and careful preparation.

Without question Lincoln was much pleased to have Lee forced back across the Potomac; the entire North was. Anything which resembled a victory in the East was acceptable, when there had been another defeat at Munfordsville, Kentucky, on the 16th, in a battle which allowed Bragg to continue his march northward. Rosecrans's victory over a Confederate force under Price at Iuka, Mississippi, on September 19 and 20 was heartening, but it did not stop the threat near the Ohio River. Lincoln wanted the war pushed resolutely in all theaters, and he saw fully the unusual opportunity which had come to

McClellan with the finding of Lee's order—his telegram after South Mountain revealed that. By the time of the President's visit to McClellan the opportunity for demolishing Lee on the 17th and 18th was realized by much of the public. On September 25 a correspondent had written from Harpers Ferry, "Adieu to the drenched field of Antietam, with its glorious Wednesday, winning for our army a record than which nothing brighter shines through history—with its fatal Thursday, permitting the clean leisurely escape of the foe down into the valley, across the difficult ford, and up the Virginia heights." [57] The correspondent did not know, as Lincoln knew, about the finding of Lee's order and of the opportunities which had been allowed to slip away before the 17th. In dispatches preceding the battle, McClellan had fully revealed the opportunities that he had, and his belief that the South could not organize an army to supplement the one Lee had, so that with its destruction the rebellion would end. As late as the 12th in a moment of apparently unguarded frankness, McClellan had revealed what was probably his real thought about Lee's strength, by saying that his only apprehension was that Lee would make for Williamsport and cross the Potomac.[58] When such things are considered, it is impossible to believe that Lincoln had several confidential conversations with McClellan and yet voiced no dissatisfaction except the hackneyed one that the General was slow and methodical in his preparations. He would have been remiss if he had not gone further than that. The first sentence of his letter of October 13 shows that he did go further. But what he said was probably said in a kindly way, just as the letter of the 13th had a kindly tone, though laden with sentences such as these: "Are you not overcautious when you assume that you cannot do what the enemy is constantly doing? Should you not claim to be at least his equal in prowess, and act upon the claim? . . . It is all easy if our troops march as well as the enemy, and it is unmanly to say that they cannot do it." Not a touch of bitterness, but there could be no greater frankness.

So again in 1862, as in 1861, October with its perfect days for campaigning was lost while the army reclothed and refitted itself. Exaggerated stories leaked out that the army was not properly supplied.[59] This touched Quartermaster General Meigs to the quick, and a long letter from McClellan's quartermaster, Ingalls, reveals much of the sad story. The army had returned from the Peninsula with a superabundance of clothing. It had marched from Washington "quite well supplied with all necessary clothing and transportation." In addition, Ingalls took a wagon train loaded with extra clothing. Significantly he wrote, "It was not expected by anyone that the whole army would under any circumstances require a complete outfit at once, so soon after the opening of the present campaign." [60] The plain truth was that the army was probably wasting clothing and equipment just as it had wasted food, and had straggled on short marches. And McClellan was doing nothing about it, for there is not one order enjoining commanders to see that property was cared for and that serviceable clothing was not being needlessly replaced by new. Perhaps new shoes were not being issued because a shoestring had broken, or new pants because an essential button had come off. But any officer who has had anything to do with supply knows that unwarranted and frivolous demands for new equipment must be held down by rigid inspections and stern discipline. The low state of discipline as the men idled was shown in a general order dated October 24, after the furor about clothing was over: "Inspections in many organizations are rarely made; drills poorly attended and infrequent; cleanliness disregarded; the care of arms and ammunition but little attended to, and the instruction of officers in tactics and regulations entirely neglected." [61] It was a sad picture indeed. McClellan, listening to the flattery of those in whose judgment he relied, grumbling about his superiors, had been allowing his army to deteriorate in the prime essential—discipline.

Without success, Ingalls had been preaching the doctrine "that an army will never move if it waits until all the different commanders report that they are ready and want no more supplies." [62] As one would expect in an army where discipline was low, there had been delay on the part of officers in submitting requisitions, and Ingalls had ordered from the depots before receiving requests from troops. On October 20 he had informed McClellan's chief of staff, "The delay now for clothing is chargeable to negligence of brigade commanders and their quartermasters." Unfortunately his subsequent report— dated February 17, 1863—contained some careless sentences that McClellan seized upon and quoted in his own report, with a resulting distortion of the entire question. In the end, after all the commotion, McClellan was to march away and leave 50,000 uniforms at Harpers Ferry.[63]

Railroad congestion had developed quickly, especially on the inadequate line into Hagerstown through Chambersburg, from Harrisburg.

On September 18 Halleck directed Haupt to straighten out the tangle, and the railroader with the magic touch was at once on his way. The next day he was in Hagerstown, where he loosened a jam of five or six trains. Then he went on horseback to Frederick, visiting McClellan en route. He reported to Halleck: "At Monocacy I found about 200 loaded cars on the sidings, some of which had been standing nearly a week. General Wool, at my request, sent an efficient officer of his staff to insist upon the unloading and return of cars." There is irony indeed in that. It took one of Wool's staff officers to get McClellan's trains unloaded. Haupt was back in Washington on Monday the 22nd, and told Halleck of his activities; a written report followed on the 27th.[64]

But news of unloaded cars was not so amazing as a telegram that came to the quartermaster general on October 7, in which McClellan inquired about the availability of hospital tents, and asked, "If there are none, how long would it take to have them manufactured and delivered here in considerable amount, say three or four thousand?" The hospital tent of that day was smaller than the one with which soldiers are now familiar. Nevertheless it was a piece of canvas measuring 14 feet by 15 feet, Army Regulations stating it would "accommodate 8 or 10 patients." Three of the tents were part of the authorized equipment of a regiment, and these had been regularly supplied. Meigs replied that he had only 1,250 surplus hospital tents in the Eastern depots, that material was scarce and dear, and that it would cost between $400,000 and $500,000 to manufacture the additional ones." The next day he told McClellan that he would let him have the 1,250 tents that were available, but asked: "Is there not danger of burdening your army by care of too much property, if sent forward at this time? The railroads are now embarrassed to supply you, and here supplies wait for the return of cars detained still unloaded near your position." [65]

On the day McClellan made his strange request he received a telegram from Halleck: "The President directs that you cross the Potomac and give battle to the enemy or drive him south." Although his inquiry about tents showed conclusively that he was not thinking of immediate field service, McClellan replied to the General in Chief, "I am pushing everything as rapidly as possible to get ready for the advance." [66]

A controversy was also to be waged over the subject of horses. On October 1 McClellan had—according to Ingalls—3,219 wagons and 315 ambulances, drawn by 6,471 horses and 10,392 mules. In addition there were 8,142 cavalry horses and 7,880 artillery horses. In all, the army had 32,885 animals—one for every four men. Halleck, who naturally thought in terms of all the armies, told McClellan, "It is believed that your present proportion of cavalry and of animals is much larger than that of any other of our armies." [67] Stanton, who McClellan was still insinuating was a handicap to him, wrote to Meigs on October 13: "Complaint is made by General McClellan of the inadequate supply of cavalry horses for his command. Your authority has been for a long time unrestricted in that regard, and you are expected to spare no effort to procure an adequate supply. You will please report what efforts have been made, and are now making, by your department for that purpose, and whether any, and what, authority, aid, or instructions can be given by the Secretary of War to accomplish the object." The reply of the quartermaster general showed that 5,993 horses had been issued to McClellan in September (including the 1,500 intended for Pope), and 4,261 the first eleven days of October.[68] The weekly average had been 1,709 horses, instead of 150 alleged in a telegram received by Halleck.[69] The copy of the important message given in McClellan's report reads 1,050 instead of 150; but McClellan did not make a correction although the prompt reply from Halleck quoted the figure 150. When the matter was finally cleared up, it looked as if there had been bungling by some of McClellan's staff officers. To help with the horse situation—made worse by an epidemic of hoof-and-mouth disease—Ingalls received $200,000 to make cash purchases of animals through his own agents.[70]

McClellan again had time for "extracurricular activities." The Emancipation Proclamation which Lincoln had seen fit to issue on September 22 showed that the President had profited little if at all from the political advice McClellan had given him in the Harrison Landing letter. The War Department had promptly published the proclamation and distributed it to the army without comment. Army commanders like Grant and Buell doubtless read it and let the matter go at that, feeling they had hard work of their own to attend to; but McClellan could not allow Mr. Lincoln's errors to go unnoticed. On October 7—the hospital tent day—he published a long order explaining to his officers and soldiers the peculiarities of the American government and the respective functions of the civil and military authorities, and indicating just how far soldiers might with propriety express their views about the document which their President had recently issued. "The remedy for political errors, if any are committed, is to be found only in the action of the people at the polls," said McClellan.[71] Whether this sentence was intended for the soldiers or was a sly suggestion directed to the public in general, and was prompted by the fact that a congressional election was not far off, can be only conjecture. But one does not forget McClellan's sentence about his countrymen opening their eyes and assisting themselves, so that he would not have to go on almost singlehanded.

Lee too was rebuilding his army, but without the great resources upon which McClellan drew so lavishly. Between his gratitude for little and McClellan's ingratitude for much there was an instructive contrast. His quartermasters would probably have been jubilant if they could have had the chance to pick over the cast-off shoes and clothing and other items which were being exchanged for new issues in the Army of the Potomac. The strength return for the Army of Northern Virginia for September 22 put the present for duty at 34,418 officers and men and the aggregate present at 41,520, plus cavalry and reserve artillery. Lee wrote to the Secretary of War: "You will see by the field return this day sent to General Cooper the woeful diminution of the present for duty of this army. The absent are scattered broadcast over the land." To President Davis he stated: "Our stragglers are being daily collected, and that is one of the reasons of my being now stationary. How long they will remain with us, or when they will again disappear, it is impossible for me to say." [72] He spoke of the necessity of recruiting the army: arms he had in abundance, and if the unarmed regiments in Texas and Arkansas could be brought forward in addition to conscripts, he could with his returning stragglers rebuild his army. So far as supplies were concerned, he was well enough off, for in his location about Martinsburg and Winchester there was plenty of beef and flour for the men as well as hay and some grain for animals.

Lee's venture into Maryland had cost him more than heavy battle losses: his army had suffered in morale. On September 25 he wrote to Davis: "In a military point of view, the best move, in my opinion, the army could make would be to advance upon Hagerstown and endeavor to defeat the enemy at that point. I would not hesitate to make it even with our diminished numbers, did the army exhibit its former temper and condition; but as far as I am able to judge, the hazard would be great and a reverse disastrous. I am, therefore, led to pause." [73] In spite of this, Robert Lee could no more leave George McClellan entirely alone than George McClellan could allow Lincoln's proclamation to go unnoticed.

On October 8 Lee gave final orders to Stuart for a raid into Maryland.[74] Taking something like 1,500 selected troopers with good mounts, and four guns, the cavalier crossed the Potomac at daybreak on the 10th and rode all the way around McClellan's army—quite as he had done on the Peninsula—passing through Chambersburg and Emmitsburg. McClellan made great efforts to cut him off with cavalry and infantry; but after a number of close escapes Stuart led his command back across the Potomac near the mouth of the Monocacy on the 12th, with men and animals worn out, but without a soldier killed, and only a few slightly wounded. After some fine troop leading, Stuart tried to rival Stonewall Jackson in humility and abnegation, and wrote in his report, "Believing that the hand of God was clearly manifested in the signal deliverance of my command from danger, and the crowning success attending it, I ascribe to Him the praise, the honor, and the glory." [75]

Although Stuart spoke of "the crowning success" in carrying out the mission given in Lee's instructions, his hard ride must be regarded as largely a failure. Some stores had been burned at Chambersburg, much excitement had been caused, some Northern people had been thoroughly frightened, some Southern sympathizers had had a thrill waving at Stuart's hurrying troopers or giving them a bit of refreshment or information, and Federal forces had been futilely moved about; but the railroad bridge near Chambersburg, which Lee had set down with top priority for burning, had not been destroyed. (It had rained hard the night Stuart was at Chambersburg, just as it had rained hard the night he struck boldly at Catlett, when another bridge had refused to burn. The bold cavalryman evidently forgot such strange little coincidences when glorying in the thought that his raids met with the approval of Heaven.) A railroad trestle north of Chambersburg, not on his agenda, was found to be made of iron and beyond his power to harm. Nor could he have picked up much about the disposition of McClellan's army, intent as he was on getting away. In discovering McClellan's *intentions,* another desideratum which Lee had set down, Stuart could have had no success, because they were non-existent. Lincoln and Halleck, with a direct wire to McClellan's tent, could learn nothing about the Federal commander's plans, and Meigs was still pondering over the mystery of the hospital tents.

Fifty-three pages of the Official Records are required for the reports and messages caused by Stuart's escapade, which in the end did Lee no good and may have done him harm by damaging a little more the reputation of McClellan at a time when second thoughts about the victory at Antietam were beginning to take hold of the Northern mind.

And so the pleasant days of October passed with both armies amid agreeable surroundings. But Abraham Lincoln was growing impatient. In the West the situation had reversed itself because of substantial achievements of the Union arms. On October 3 and 4 Rosecrans with four divisions of Grant's Army of the Mississippi had handsomely defeated Van Dorn at Corinth, while Buell had driven Bragg from Kentucky after defeating him at Perryville on October 8—an action in which a young brigadier named Philip H. Sheridan had showed aptitude for command and fondness for bold fighting. The people of Kentucky had in reality revealed no more enthusiasm for Bragg's army than the Marylanders for the more renowned brigades which Lee had led across the Potomac, and Bragg fell back to the mountains of eastern Tennessee, over bad roads which prevented the removal of most of the supplies and spoils he had accumulated during the successful weeks of his enterprise.

With matters so encouraging in the West it was natural for the High Command to put the pressure on McClellan to get some good out of the remaining weeks of autumn. On the 21st Halleck sent McClellan a peremptory telegram, which ended, "Telegraph when you will move, and on what lines you propose to march." Evidently the commander of the Army of the Potomac thought his men were sufficiently used to their new shoes and their new uniforms to march, for he wired the General in Chief the next day that he had decided after full consultation to move in accordance with the plan the President had indicated in the letter of the 13th, to the south, keeping east of the Blue Ridge (but Lincoln had carefully stated that he was not ordering the line of advance); and he would need all the cavalry and other reenforcements that could be sent from Washington.

McClellan's strength return for the 20th gave 133,433 as "present for duty," with an aggregate present of 159,860.[76] In this great host were many new regiments at full strength; but the losses of the fine old veteran regiments had not been made good. Lee's army also had grown, and on the 20th he reported 68,033 officers and men as "present for duty," with an aggregate present of 79,595.[77] The cavalry divisions in the two forces were almost of equal strength: Stuart had 6,536, and Buford—temporarily commanding the Federal force— had 6,724. It is to be remembered that cavalrymen in the Confederate army usually had to furnish their own horses. This eased the procurement problem and also tended to insure better care of animals—a trooper knew that if anything happened to his mount he might be persuaded to shoulder a musket and join the infantry.

Halleck showed his pleasure and approval of McClellan's decision by telegraphing that 20,000 additional men could be sent from Washington [78]—which could have brought no happiness to Haupt, who was hard at work getting the inadequate Manassas Gap Railroad ready to supply the great army that was moving south. On the 26th the crossing of the Potomac began, and Lincoln, wiring that he was rejoiced to learn of it, showed his displeasure with McClellan's continued remarks about inadequate cavalry.[79] McClellan replied that this was unjust, and the President telegraphed back that he did not want to be unjust and regretted it if he had been; but he noted that the army had been inactive for five weeks, and that in that time every fresh cavalry horse that could be procured had been sent to the Potomac army. He asked, "If not recruited and rested then, when could they ever be?" [80]

Then things went from bad to worse, and rapidly. Later on the 27th McClellan telegraphed about the necessity of filling up the old regiments with drafted men before taking them again into action. In just twenty-five minutes there was a reply in which the President, after promising to do what he could to fill up the old regiments, wrote: "And now I ask a distinct answer to the question, Is it your purpose not to go into action again until the men now being drafted in the States are incorporated into the old regiments?" [81]

Little Mac tried to get out of his predicament by saying that a staff officer had unfortunately added the words "before taking them again into action." [82] What Lincoln thought of that explanation, it is difficult to say; what a less patient, less forbearing man would have thought is obvious. Lincoln was very careful about the dispatches he himself sent, and it was a revelation indeed to learn that McClellan allowed telegrams to be handled carelessly though they dealt with important matters. (The blunder in the telegram to Halleck about horses was

probably not known at that time.) But McClellan not only revealed a
new and serious fault; he also failed to clear himself of the main
charge, for he gave an evasive answer: he stated that he had no intention of postponing the "advance" until drafted men had been received. "Action," not "advance," had been Lincoln's word.

The first sign of weakening—which may have been all that Lincoln
was waiting for—had appeared when the army had little more than
started to cross the river. Furthermore, McClellan still mixed grumbling with his reports of progress and, what was worse, found *new
things* to grumble about. He said to Lincoln, "We need more carbines
and muskets." [83] There had been complaints about lack of horses, of
men, of blankets, of shoes, and of clothing; then there had been the
completely incomprehensible request for 3,000 or 4,000 hospital
tents. But nothing had been said about a shortage of small arms.
Some of McClellan's infantrymen perhaps had thrown away their
burdensome rifles—smoothbore muskets were practically gone from
the army [84]—and some of his cavalrymen may have lost their carbines;
but if there were sizable deficiencies they were due to lack of requisitions by McClellan's officers and should have been an occasion for
disciplining the officers and not for troubling the President. One item
in which the Army of the Potomac was certainly deficient as it crossed
back into Virginia was future Presidents. The Twenty-third Ohio was
no longer present, for the Kanawha Division had been sent back to
West Virginia on account of aggressive tendencies of the Confederates
in that region. Colonel Rutherford B. Hayes was still in the hospital
with the severe South Mountain wound, but William B. McKinley,
now second lieutenant, was in the column of six infantry regiments and
two batteries that had taken the National Road for Hancock and had
come near intercepting Stuart when he crossed the Potomac on
October 10.[85]

When McClellan reported that he had occupied Leesburg, Lincoln
replied that he was pleased and asked to be informed when the army
was entirely over the river. Surely this was not just a casual request
prompted by mere curiosity. Did it not mean that Lincoln at long last
had had enough, and that the great decision had been made? If that
is the case, George McClellan's time was rapidly running out. The dispatch was the last one which Lincoln sent to McClellan, and it ended
with a question that hit squarely at the latter's greatest weakness,
"What do you know of the enemy?" When one recalls that a modern

field order starts by giving information about the enemy, the deep significance of Lincoln's question stands out. Of all possible queries, he asked the most telling. The detailed answer that McClellan wrote at two o'clock began: "In reply to your dispatch of this morning, I have the honor to state that the accounts I get of the enemy's position and movements are very conflicting." [86]

The advance continued, and on November 4 McClellan reported from Bloomfield that the cavalry advance was at Piedmont and the infantry in Upperville and in front of Ashby's Pass, where resistance was said to be probable. The dispatch closed, "I go to the front to see." [87] That also had an old familiar sound. And it was ominous, for every time that McClellan looked at anything it grew worse.

The next day, Wednesday November 5, it came—the direction to Stanton and Halleck with the signature A. Lincoln, ordering that McClellan be relieved from the command of the Army of the Potomac and that Burnside take his place.

There was no delay on the part of Stanton or Halleck—though the President had said the necessary order might be issued "forthwith," or when the General in Chief deemed proper. On the day that Lincoln sent his directive, Stanton issued a War Department order and Halleck wrote a note instructing McClellan to turn over his command to Burnside at once and go to Trenton, New Jersey, reporting his "arrival at that place, by telegraph, for further orders." [88]

To deliver the important order, a courier with considerable rank was selected—Brigadier General Catharinus P. Buckingham, of Ohio. On the 6th Haupt at Alexandria closed a dispatch to Watson with the sentence, "General Buckingham reported at Gainesville 1:40 P.M." Though most of the message may have been routine shop talk that sentence was not, for the railroader had confidential knowledge of the mission of the high-ranking courier who was patronizing his railroad; and he probably had selected a careful engineer to run the important special train. [89] The next day, a day when it snowed very hard, Buckingham reported to Burnside near Waterloo, gave him his order, and the two officers rode to McClellan's headquarters near Rectortown, arriving well after night had fallen. McClellan read his order and the command passed at once. Details had been carefully planned, and no chance was given for any nonsense; Burnside was in command of the army before McClellan had opportunity to say a word to any of his staff. The fact that Burnside did not issue a formal order taking command until the 9th has misled some writers. Even Burnside himself, when he wrote his report some months later, apparently forgot to mention his telegram to Halleck on the 8th saying he had taken command the night before.[90]

McClellan wrote a brief address to the officers and men of the army he had commanded for more than a year. No one who has any conception of what it means to turn over the command of an army to another officer will take exception to what McClellan wrote in his

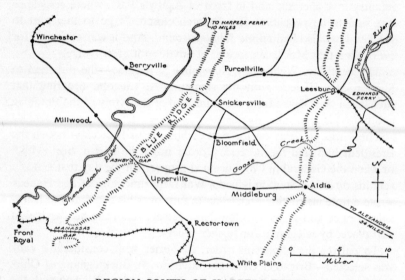

REGION SOUTH OF HARPERS FERRY

McClellan's headquarters were near Rectortown when he was relieved of command by a special messenger from Washington. En route, the messenger had picked up Burnside, who received the command.

final message, which closed with the admirable sentence, "We shall ever be comrades in supporting the Constitution of our country and the nationality of its people." [91] As the general rode away from the army where he had many devoted friends among the officers, and where he was highly esteemed by many of the rank and file, he may have softened his regrets with the thought that he could now lay aside the fear he had mentioned to his wife a year before, that he, like Winfield Scott, might "at some distant day . . . totter away from Washington, a worn-out soldier."

It has naturally been pointed out that Lincoln removed McClellan soon after election. Perhaps he had waited until the people had gone to the polls just as he waited until McClellan had the army entirely over the Potomac. An accurate appraisal of the public's judgment of McClellan at the time cannot be made; the current of opinion was against him at the end of August; South Mountain and Antietam must have restored him somewhat to favor. But, on the other hand, his inaction after the battle, and Stuart's raid, as well as reappraisal of the battle with a consequent fuller realization of the opportunities that had been missed, worked against him. A cavalryman subsequently wrote that, the very day after the battle, humble soldiers in the ranks began their comments upon the spectacle of Porter's corps being withheld when there was such a good chance to use it.[92] A change in sentiment in the army toward its commanding general would not be long in reaching the families of the soldiers.

Though he did not order McClellan's removal until after election, Lincoln acted before he knew the voting had gone quite definitely against the administration. To assess properly the various grounds of public disapproval expressed in the election is very difficult; but Lincoln's long retention of McClellan must have been the cause of some of the ballots that registered disapproval of his conduct of the war. There is no uncertainty, however, as to what Lincoln thought of the way McClellan's new campaign was beginning.

Already there was a good precedent for Lincoln's removal of McClellan on November 5, which the thoughtful people of the time could not miss. On October 30 Buell had been relieved of his command, in spite of the substantial victory at Perryville, Kentucky, and the resulting termination of Bragg's threat to Kentucky. Lincoln and Stanton not only had been displeased with Buell's actions after the battle but had thought him very slow in movement before the contest; and only the pleadings of Halleck had given him "a little more time." The grim determination of the administration was plainly revealed by the General in Chief to Major General H. G. Wright at Cincinnati on August 25: "The Government seems determined to apply the guillotine to all unsuccessful generals. It seems rather hard to do this where the general is not at fault, but perhaps with us now, as in the French Revolution, some harsh measures are justified." The President and the Secretary of War had come to see that the actions of a general reveal his character, and that it is character, not temporary success, or popularity with troops, that counts in the end. Thus, a week before McClellan gave way to Burnside, a clear precedent had been set when Buell—an accomplished soldier in many ways—turned over his army to Rosecrans. Correspondents at the headquarters of the Army of the Potomac might write that the order which General Buckingham had delivered at eleven o'clock on the night of November 7 "was entirely unexpected by all, and therefore every one was taken by surprise," but newspaper readers also had the chance to read comment which began, "The long-expected and often-rumored change has at last been made. Gen. Burnside commands the Army of the Potomac." [93]

One of the stock arguments in defense of McClellan makes the apocryphal claim that Lee said after the war, thumping the table with his fist by way of emphasis, that McClellan was by all odds the best of the Union generals. The anecdote was apparently first recorded in 1886 by Colonel A. L. Long in his well known work on Lee; and he set it down "as related by a relative of the general who had it from her father, an old gentleman of eighty years." Long himself could not accept the statement without so much qualification as practically to destroy it. He asserted that the opinion credited to his former chief could not have referred to McClellan's skill as a tactician; and he added that it was "unquestionable that Lee availed himself of McClellan's over-caution and essayed perilous movements which he could not have ventured in the presence of a more active opponent." [94]

In 1904 the son and namesake of General Lee wrote an extended account of what seems to have been the same incident, as it had been furnished to Cazenove Lee, the son of General Lee's first cousin Cassius. It began with the statement that it was "greatly to be regretted that an accurate and full account" had not been preserved of a visit Lee had made to Alexandria in mid-July, 1870. In addition to the explicit doubt thus cast upon the record by its writer, there is internal evidence of distortion, for immediately before the statement about McClellan, Cazenove Lee recorded a charge against General Richard Ewell, a very unjust part of which he put in quotations as if he were again using the very words of his famous cousin. The remark seems completely out of character for Robert E. Lee; and if he did make such a severe indictment of a former distinguished subordinate one must attribute it to the fact that he was so far from well that he complained of his condition in a letter to his wife.[95]

In order to discover what Lee thought of McClellan, it is not necessary to consult a highly dubious report of a conversation of a sick and complaining man only three months before his death. Lee's opinion of his former adversary is written in the record, clearly and unalterably. It was set forth in his famous lost order, wherein he divided his forces so hazardously; it was shown in the fact that he made no essential change in his plans when he learned that McClellan had come into possession of the order; it was shown again—and perhaps even more emphatically—by his remaining in position on September 18, when McClellan could have thrown against him a force which would have utterly overwhelmed him and probably brought ruin both to the cause he was leading and to the fine military reputation which he had built during the past three months.[96] By his acts Lee recorded his judgment, and it was essentially the same opinion that Joe Johnston put on paper when he wrote to Lee from Yorktown, "No one but McClellan could have hesitated to attack."

Surely the verdict must be: McClellan was not a real general. McClellan was not even a disciplined, truthful soldier. McClellan was merely an attractive but vain and unstable man, with considerable military knowledge, who sat a horse well and wanted to be President.[97]

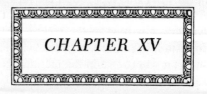

CHAPTER XV

A NEW COMMANDER MARCHES WELL

The President has just assented to your plan. He thinks that it
will succeed, if you move very rapidly; otherwise not.

Halleck to Burnside

THE severe defeat which General Burnside was to experience in
December at Fredericksburg always raises the question why he was
chosen to succeed McClellan. But it is his service previous to his selection, not the misfortunes which later befell him, that should be examined before judgment is passed upon the administration for picking
him as the new commander of the Army of the Potomac.

Ambrose E. Burnside was born in the village of Liberty, Indiana,
in 1824, and graduated from West Point in 1847. Though the Mexican
War was nearly over he had some active service as a lieutenant of
artillery in Patterson's division. He resigned his commission in 1853
and for five years was engaged in the manufacture of firearms at
Bristol, Rhode Island. Like McClellan, who was graduated from the
military academy a year ahead of him, and with whom he had formed
a close friendship, Burnside was of an inventive turn of mind; and he
patented a breech-loading rifle. Some Northern cavalry men, seated
in McClellan saddles, were armed with Burnside carbines. The friendship which had begun at school grew while the two men were connected with the Illinois Central Railroad, McClellan as engineer,
Burnside as president of the Land Office Department. After the war
Burnside was Governor of Rhode Island for three one-year terms, and
in 1875 he went to Congress; but there was never a whisper of politi-

cal ambition about him while he was in uniform. He served loyally and without more than the natural concern for his own fortunes.

As colonel of the fine regiment of Rhode Islanders that went promptly into service in 1861, Burnside rendered good service under his old commander during part of General Patterson's unhappy campaign. At Bull Run his brigade led the Federal advance from Sudley Springs and received the Confederate volleys that opened that sharp battle. Early in August he was made a brigadier general, and in January, 1862, he led an expedition of some 15,000 men against the coast of North Carolina. The successes he attained at Roanoke Island, New Bern, and Fort Macon were substantial, and they apparently showed that he had qualities needed for an independent army commander. Though his command was small, he had had to make many strategical, tactical, and administrative decisions of importance, and he had been compelled to operate without definite information about the enemy. At the age of thirty-eight he seemed to be a promising general.

The promptness with which Burnside arrived with his infantry at Fort Monroe after Lincoln had called him for the possible support of McClellan on the Peninsula, must have been pleasing to the administration. Promptness, loyalty, energy, and understanding also characterized his service at Fredericksburg while Pope's ill fated campaign was in progress. In the subsequent Maryland campaign, McClellan gave him the command of the two corps of his army which formed the right wing; and it was those corps which fought the battle at Turner's Gap on South Mountain.

On September 16 a sharp message went from McClellan's headquarters, complaining of Burnside's delay in getting into position that day, and of an alleged loss of four hours in his movement the day before. The next day Burnside replied in good spirit, and explained well his operations of the 16th, though he said nothing about the alleged delay of the 15th—a day on which he might have been in considerable doubt as to what his command was, because of a change in McClellan's orders.[1] For the delay of the Ninth Corps in getting across the bridge in the battle of the 17th, it is hard to distribute responsibility among McClellan, Burnside, and Cox, though McClellan in his memoirs decided definitely that his old friend "Burn" was the responsible party. That Burnside was not conscious of any such feeling in the period following the battle is indicated by his use of the phrase "My dear Mac" in a note of October 27 to the army commander.[2] Thus relations apparently were cordial up to the time of the passing of the command, and McClellan had no reason to believe that Burnside had any ambition to supersede him. On its part the administration knew full well that Burnside not only had served loyally, but also did not wish a higher command.[3] In addition, he had a pleasant and winning personality and had many strong supporters. His partisans were to be found in the ranks as well as among officers, and Strother records an argument between a "McClellan man" and a "Burnside man" he had heard on the march to the Antietam.[4] Newspapers reporting the change of commanders gave their readers a sketch of the career of Burnside which made a reassuring case for the new general.[5]

With commendable promptness Burnside answered Halleck's injunction of the 5th, "Immediately on assuming command of the Army of the Potomac, you will report the position of your troops, and what you propose doing with them," with a long dispatch. He gave as his purpose: "To concentrate the forces near [Warrenton], and impress upon the enemy the belief that we are to attack Culpeper or Gordonsville, and at the same time accumulate a four or five days' supply for the men and animals; then make a rapid move of the whole force to Fredericksburg, with a view to a movement upon Richmond from that point." [6]

The movement which McClellan had started to execute was designed—in accordance with Lincoln's recommendation—to cut Lee's communications with Richmond. With regard to the enemy's possible reaction, the President had said: "If he should move northward I would follow him closely, holding his communications. If he should prevent our seizing his communications and move toward Richmond, I would press closely to him; fight him, if a favorable opportunity should present, and at least try to beat him to Richmond on the inside track." Because Lee's reaction to the move of the Army of the Potomac could not yet be determined, Burnside's suggestion was a departure from the course which Lincoln had recommended, and on which McClellan had stated he had embarked. Accordingly he gave an argument for the proposed course; and, considering the time which he had had for the formulation of his ideas, one must give the paper a high rating.

Burnside's reasons for not continuing an advance toward Gordons-

MAJOR GENERAL AMBROSE E. BURNSIDE

ville were the danger to his own communications and the difficulty of supply. Advance from Fredericksburg on Richmond would have the advantage of secure water communications much of the way. The lateness of the year also influenced him, and he asserted, "A great reason for feeling that the Fredericksburg route is the best, is that if we are detained by the elements, it would be much better for us to be on that route." Burnside was soldier enough to realize that the Confederate capital was a less important objective than the main Confederate army which Lincoln was eager to have destroyed; but he believed it was a good second-best objective, and stated that the capture of Richmond "should be the great object of the campaign, as the fall of that place would tend more to cripple the rebel cause than almost any other military event, except the absolute breaking up of their army." It is particularly important to note that Burnside had already given thought to some details of the advance from Fredericksburg, and was trying to make sure that he would not be stymied. He wrote to the General in Chief, "The detail of the movement from Fredericksburg I will give you hereafter"—which should have made a good impression.

In addition to a change in the plan of campaign, Burnside recommended some changes in the organization and administration of his army. He wanted to form it into three main divisions, of two corps each, under the three ranking generals. He wished also "to do away with the very massive and elaborate adjutant-general's office" that burdened the army. He would authorize the three new commanders to carry out as much as possible of the routine administration of their own commands. Essentially, he was recommending the formation of three two-corps armies, with himself an army group commander. It was all very sensible, and it placed him in a favorable contrast with his predecessor, in spite of the frequent claims that McClellan was a genius in army administration.

In a soldierly way free of any faultfinding, Burnside noted that there were obvious embarrassments in taking command of the army, and that he would have declined the position if he had been asked rather than ordered to take it. He closed his long dispatch to the General in Chief with the sentence, "A telegram from you, approving of my plans, will put us to work at once."

There was delay in sending the dispatch, due apparently in part to difficulties in encoding, and on the 10th it was carried by special officer messenger—the only safe procedure.[7] At noon the next day Halleck wired in reply to an impatient telegram that it had been received the evening before and was in the hands of the President. Then he inquired where he could meet Burnside the next day on the railroad.[8] This was a sensible procedure, and it indicated that the General in Chief might be able to work with the new army commander much more satisfactorily than with his predecessor. With him on his trip Halleck took Meigs and Haupt, who was now a brigadier general but was still serving without pay. They must have been agreeable traveling companions, for Halleck seemed to be on the best of terms with the able quartermaster general and the energetic and competent chief of military railroads.[9]

The Official Records are contradictory about the important conversations at Warrenton on the night of the 12th and the morning of the 13th between the officer who was reluctantly General in Chief and the officer who was reluctantly commanding general of the Army of the Potomac. That army in its return for November 10 numbered 150,441 present in the field with an additional 98,738 assigned to the various defenses of Washington, and General Wool's Eighth Corps mustering an extra 15,000 men.[10] As a matter of fact, Burnside's report—dated after the war, November 13, 1865—was more favorable to the General in Chief than Halleck's own report of November 15, 1863. Burnside wrote, "General Halleck was strongly in favor of continuing the movement of the army in the direction of Culpeper and Gordonsville, and my own plan was as strongly adhered to by me." This gave the General in Chief credit for a very definite opinion on a subject where he should have had an opinion. But Halleck put the case differently, writing of the movement to Fredericksburg that he merely "refused to give any official approval of this deviation from the President's instructions until his assent was obtained." He was taking a strange position indeed, because the President in making the suggestion to McClellan on October 13, which Halleck cited, had concluded with the significant sentence, "This letter is in no sense an order." [11] Entirely in conformity with this thought, Halleck's order to McClellan on October 21 was an injunction to do something but left the army commander free to select his line of operations. And it is hard to understand just why Halleck sent the dispatch to Burnside on November 5 to report his plans, if only minor decisions about a stipulated campaign were being left to him. One must believe that

Lincoln met Halleck after reading Burnside's letter and before the conference. But it is hard to believe that he did more than reiterate what was his *view* as to the best course. He had carefully refrained from giving orders, even in a time of crisis, since the advent of Halleck in July; and it was hardly in accordance with his nature to embarrass his new army commander.

Be that as it may, Halleck should have recorded his own judgment as a General in Chief. A crucial point was up for decision: Where should the main thrust be made? Though the question was primarily one for him, Halleck does not record his own view as to the best direction for the Army of the Potomac to make its advance. In August the new General in Chief had revealed a disposition to make the decisions appropriate to his high office; but in November, though the situation in the West was no longer a cause for concern, he appears to have become nothing more than a go-between—a glorified staff officer—except for the statement in Burnside's report.

What Meigs and Haupt may have said is not recorded; but Haupt must have been a vigorous supporter of Burnside, for the poor facilities of the Orange and Alexandria Railroad made very difficult the supply of an army four times the size of the one Pope had had in the vicinity of Warrenton. There were few sidings and switches, and there was neither wood nor water at the far end of the line; and the soldiers were burning in campfires the wood hauled for the engines, and were wasting water. Haupt also had received reports that soldiers were destroying switches and switch stands. Some punishment and guards with loaded rifles should have stopped such nonsense, but the supply of the army if it advanced along the poor and exposed railroad would be a difficult problem.

Waiting and doing nothing was difficult for Burnside, aware as he was of the fact that November was advancing. At 6:50 P.M. on the 13th—the day Halleck went back to Washington—he impatiently wired the General in Chief, "If possible, can you send me to-night a definite answer as to my plan of operations?" All-night work was certainly ahead for staff officers and subordinate commanders if the telegraph instrument would only click out the release. But the hours passed without the hoped-for message, and it was not until eleven o'clock the next morning that Burnside received the dispatch from Halleck: "The President has just assented to your plan. He thinks that it will succeed, if you move very rapidly; otherwise not." [12] Again the General in

Chief failed to reveal his own thoughts; and the mystery deepens as to what he had said about his own ideas while he was at Warrenton.

Another odd feature of Halleck's version of the Warrenton meeting

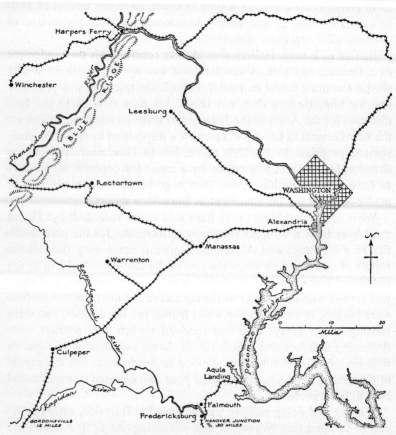

BURNSIDE MOVES TO FREDERICKSBURG

Burnside, with headquarters at Warrenton, received permission to move to Fredericksburg and advance against Hanover Junction, instead of continuing McClellan's operation toward Gordonsville. The plan facilitated supply. Jackson's corps was near Winchester; Lee with the corps of Longstreet was near Culpeper.

remains to be noted. His report states that the plan which he carried back to Washington and which was approved by the President was for Burnside to cross the Rappahannock above its confluence with the

Rapidan so that he would move toward Fredericksburg with the larger river behind him. But Burnside's record is quite different: "I was to move the main army to Falmouth, opposite Fredericksburg, and there cross the Rappahannock on pontoon bridges, which were to be sent from Washington." [13] This version seems more like the correct one, for Halleck telegraphed from Warrenton on November 12 at 7:10 P.M. to General Woodbury, commanding the Engineer Brigade in Washington: "Call upon the chief quartermaster, Colonel Rucker, to transport all your pontoons and bridge materials to Aquia Creek. Colonel Belger has been ordered to charter and send one hundred barges to Alexandria." [14] This seemed to anticipate approval of Burnside's plan, with a river crossing at Fredericksburg, though subsequent supply of the army may have been all that Halleck had in mind. Certainly the General in Chief was much at fault in not having Burnside's final plan reduced to writing, because Burnside's original letter of the 10th said nothing as to which side of the river he intended to follow in the move to Fredericksburg.

On the 14th an order directed the reorganization of the army in accord with the new commander's ideas. The Second and Ninth Corps became the Right Grand Division, under the command of Sumner; the First and Sixth Corps became the Left Grand Division under Franklin; the Third and Fifth Corps became the Center Grand Division under Hooker, who on the 12th had succeeded Porter at the head of the Fifth Corps.[15] Without delay the new grand division commanders issued orders assuming command and announcing their staffs, and the senior division commanders took over the vacated corps commands. The Eleventh Corps remained an independent reserve corps under General Sigel, with the same authority in administration and in dealing directly with Washington about routine matters that Sumner, Franklin, and Hooker had. The new chief of staff was to be Major General John G. Parke, who a year before had been a captain in the topographical engineers, and who had begun his service with Burnside on the Carolina expedition. The army, "well supplied with transportation, clothing, and forage," [16] was now organized for smooth and flexible handling, so that it only remained to be seen whether Burnside and his three senior commanders were equal to their responsibilities.

The considerable penetration of the Union army into Virginia was causing both Lee and the Richmond authorities great anxiety, and discovery of the Federal objective was the chief concern of the moment. From the time McClellan's army crossed the Potomac, a movement toward Fredericksburg must have been considered as one of the possibilities; but Burnside had considerable success in making Lee believe the Union force might continue toward Gordonsville. Lee learned of the change of commanders of the Army of the Potomac on November 10, and on the very day that Burnside received permission to carry out his proposed plan he wrote to the Confederate Secretary of War, in a long letter describing the situation as he saw it: "I thought it probable that he [the enemy] would change his line of approach to Richmond and make a sudden descent upon Fredericksburg, from which point his line of communication with Washington would be comparatively safe." Thus did the Confederate commander endorse the soundness of Burnside's proposal. With that in mind he had already ordered the complete destruction of the railroad from Aquia Creek on the Potomac to Falmouth, opposite Fredericksburg, stipulating that the ties should be stacked for burning and the rails should be piled on top, so that they would be bent and unusable. He added, "I think it would be prudent to break up the road from Fredericksburg back to Hanover Junction in the same way, and the Orange and Alexandria road from the Rappanhannock to Gordonsville." But though Lee thought it "prudent" to damage the rails so that they could not be relaid he was unwilling to order a demolition which would place additional hardships upon his countrymen. The general who twice had had the courage to divide his army for a hazardous operation, and who has been criticized for risking the complete destruction of his force on September 18, shrank from ordering railroad destruction which he described as "prudent." Not unnaturally he was willing to leave the responsibility in such a case to higher authority. Secretary of War Randolph in turn referred the matter to President Davis, who wrote on Lee's letter an endorsement containing the sentences: "Better to make the needful preparation to expedite the destruction of railroads, when necessary. Concur in reluctance stated." [17]

The cloud of discouragement which had rested on the people of the North had drifted southward to the Confederacy, where there had been so much hopefulness during the summer since the brilliant achievements which had broken the threat to Richmond. Both the Confederate invasions of Maryland and Kentucky had, however, ended in dismal failures; in battlefield defeats and disillusionment about the prospect of support for "the cause" from the border states. And farther west the scene was still more gloomy. Northern penetration along the Mississippi had reached nearly to Vicksburg, where operations were under the direction of a Northern general who, though quiet and not inclined to boast, was beginning to seem alarmingly obstinate and undismayed by great difficulties. Federal troops held firm control of northern Mississippi and western Tennessee. Great seaports had also been lost to invaders in blue, and other ports were blockaded by the fleet which flew the Stars and Stripes, and which had grown to great size by the output of the Union's shipyards. Two Confederate cruisers—efficient ships from the yards of famous builders in England—were on the loose on the high seas, doing considerable damage to Northern shipping. Their exploits might bring cheers and the raising of glasses in warm toasts; but anyone who could reason knew that eventually they would be captured or would be sunk by the vengeful guns of determined Northern sailors. The hope that foreign nations, concerned over the great and growing Republic to the west and eager to have cotton, would intervene had been held fervently throughout the spring and summer. Jackson's notable marches and battles in the Valley, Lee's defeat of McClellan before Richmond, and his victory at Second Bull Run had been accorded in Europe the praise they deserved; British soldiers had particularly acclaimed the achievements. It all tended to increase sympathy for the South and encouraged the belief that the North would fail to break the will of the seceding states. Then came Antietam and Lee's retreat to Virginia after a brief two weeks in Maryland. Almost with the announcement of his return to Virginia there had come from the White House in Washington the great document which changed the aspect of the war, and which Lincoln had correctly judged would win friends for the North among the European peoples, although it was primarily a war measure. And the Richmond administration also knew that the governments in Europe had read of the Confederate defeat in Kentucky and of Bragg's return to the fastnesses of eastern Tennessee, and that discerning advisers were evaluating the Federal penetration down the Mississippi, which halted but never turned back. And now a great Federal army, which at last had begun to show capability of offensive fighting, had again struck south across the Potomac and was gathered about Warrenton, poised to strike in a yet undisclosed direction. Federal troops were also on the coast of North Carolina, and a small column appeared to be threatening Staunton from the direction of West Virginia.[18] Though little more than distracting operations, they had an effect upon the morale of the people and could interfere with the collection of supplies for the Confederate forces.

There were efforts in the South to put a favorable interpretation upon the removal of McClellan, by acclaiming him as the best of the Federal generals. But Confederate political leaders and Confederate generals who reflected deeply must have realized how determined was Lincoln's purpose when he removed first Buell and then McClellan after each had won a battle which had turned back a Confederate army from a border state. In spite of their anger against him, many Southerners saw that Lincoln was a kindly man. Kindly too was the man in command of the Union army moving in on the great fortress of Vicksburg; but kindliness had not prevented him from demanding the "unconditional surrender" of Fort Donelson in February. So the sympathy and forbearance of the man in the White House did not mean that he would wage a war of half-measures: his removal of Buell and McClellan showed he was determined on nothing short of the destruction of Confederate armies and the conquest of the South. It was possible for "Rebels" to take considerable encouragement in the known dissatisfaction in the North, where the great cost of the war bore heavily, where the divided sentiment was clearly revealed by the recent elections, and where the draft of militia was not working well. (Nor was the draft working well in all parts of the South.) But Lincoln still had two years of his term remaining, he had the great resources of the North mobilized, he was sifting out his commanders, he had an army well advanced on the Mississippi, with one in Kentucky and eastern Tennessee, and again, after severe reverses, he had an army thrust well forward into Virginia. During the summer the defenses of Richmond had been greatly strengthened, for Lee and the authorities knew that blue-coated visitors would come again, and probably under more resolute leadership. The lateness of the season would work heavily on the side of the defenders, for many of Virginia's roads, under the rains and the freezing and thawing of winter, would become impassable. But nature's assistance, however considerable, would not be enough. Railroads would have to be torn up. Culverts and bridges would have to be destroyed, ties would have to be burned, and the rails heated and bent so that the Yankees could not easily lay them again. Such was the necessity which the Southern President reluctantly faced, as his War Secretary tried to get shoes for the few thousand men in Lee's army who were still barefoot, and as he bought 1,000 horses in Texas to sell to men in the Army of Northern Virginia who had the means to buy their way out of the infantry, which was so hard on the feet and which exacted the endurance of so much rifle fire.[19]

But horses were not the only deficiency in Lee's cavalry arm; there was a lack of appropriate weapons. On November 10 his military secretary wrote to the Confederate chief of ordnance urging the prompt dispatch of 500 carbines, and stating, "These cavalry carbines are greatly needed, in order to place our cavalry on an equality with that of the enemy which is now greatly superior to ours in sharpshooters." [20] In food the situation was quite discouraging. On November 14 Secretary Randolph passed on to Lee gloomy news that it was not possible to restore the cut in rations which had been made in April. "That regulation has not been rescinded; but, on the contrary, is more needed now than ever." Southern food production had dropped. There were 100,-000 fewer hogs than in 1861; the corn crop had failed in Tennessee and northwestern Georgia; the supply of beef was down; the wheat crop in Virginia was less than half of that of the year before. And ominously the corn crop in other Southern states was "rendered unavailable by the difficulties of transportation." Certainly there had been want of foresight, perhaps because foreign recognition had been counted on as too much of a certainty. Only recently had anyone been chosen to look after railroad transportation. William M. Wadley of Georgia was expected to arrive in Richmond on the 22nd, and the Secretary wrote, "From his experience and success in the management of railroads, I anticipate great benefit to our railroads and to the army." The local food supply was offsetting the difficulty of transportation; but it did not raise the amount to which men were entitled under the reduced ration. The commissary general of the Confederate army had also to report to the Secretary of War that some farmers were not having their grain threshed, because they hoped for higher prices; others were reluctant to take Confederate money. In an effort to increase clothing, shoes, and ordnance stores, a new agent was to be sent to Texas "with large funds for the purpose of introducing such things through Mexico" more extensively than had been done previously.[21] It was indeed a long supply route. And all the while Gideon Welles, Lincoln's Secretary of the Navy, and Gustavus V. Fox, the masterful Assistant Secretary, were adding more ships to the great blockading fleet.

Before Burnside had given a more efficient command arrangement to the Army of the Potomac, Lee's army had undergone an important reorganization. After First Bull Run, Johnston had the Confederate army at Manassas divided into two corps; but there was no legal recognition of such a unit, and it disappeared. So far as regulations were concerned, the Army of Northern Virginia was composed of divisions; but the number of divisions was too great for the army commander to handle directly, and so Lee had grouped various divisions under Longstreet and Jackson, his two outstanding division commanders, creating what amounted to a corps organization. Finally corps were authorized by the Confederate Congress and the grade of lieutenant general was created for the commanders of the new units. The new law was not far behind the similar act of the United States Congress, which legalized corps on July 17, 1862, and at the same time set forth the composition of a corps staff.* Lincoln had, however, used corps ever since March, 1862, apparently without protest from anyone. But while the South had four grades of general officers after three stars had been given to Longstreet, Jackson, and a few others, the North still had no officer higher than a major general, the General in Chief not having more rank than that appropriate to a division commander.

In Lee's reorganized army Longstreet had the First Corps with five divisions (twenty brigades) under R. H. Anderson, McLaws, Pickett, Hood, and Ransom; Jackson had the Second Corps with four divisions (nineteen brigades) under Jones, Early, D. H. Hill, and A. P. Hill. On November 10 the aggregates present in the two corps were, respectively, 38,110 and 37,049, so that the corps corresponded in strength very closely to the "grand divisions" which Burnside had formed.[22] The strength "present" in Stuart's cavalry division was 8,226, and the total present in the army (exclusive of the reserve artillery) was 83,385. As in the Army of the Potomac, many absentees were carried on the rosters, for the aggregate present and absent was set at 151,766.

There still was dissension in Lee's army, so that he had to worry about other things than shoes, clothing, blankets, carbines, and the intentions of the Federals. In spite of A. P. Hill's good work at Harpers

* See Appendix I.

Ferry and his saving Lee's army at Sharpsburg by his hard march
and timely arrival, the implacable Jackson, who now wore one more
star than Hill, pressed his charges against the commander of the Light
Division for failure to obey orders; and Lee was forced into one of the
most distasteful situations that ever confront a higher commander, for
his two subordinates wrote tart things about each other, and Hill
answered Jackson's charges with countercharges.[23] The dispute
dragged out beyond the fall, and there never was a trial; but Hill dis-
claimed that the arrest without trial which he had suffered had re-
formed him and had made him more obedient. He wrote to Lee, "Its
only effect has been to cause me to preserve every scrap of paper
received from corps headquarters, to guard myself against any new
eruptions from this slumbering volcano."

Also on November 14—a date when many important dispatches
or orders were written—Lee issued General Order No. 127, a long
document dealing with the discipline of his army.[24] Gambling had
become common, and his adjutant wrote, referring to the commanding
general's view, "He regards it as wholly inconsistent with the character
of a Southern soldier and subversive of good order and discipline in
the army." With gambling there had appeared something perhaps
worse. Because of scanty supplies, soldiers were becoming profiteers,
and imposed on their comrades by "purchasing supplies of food and
other things for the purpose of selling them at exorbitant prices to
their fellow-soldiers." Lee's order stated, "A just regard for the reputation of the army requires the immediate suppression of this great
evil." In the future none but regular sutlers or citizens having supplies
of food or other lawful articles were to be allowed to engage in barter
or trade with the officers and soldiers of the army; arrests and trials
were to follow infractions of the order. Efforts were also made to stop
unauthorized absences. Provost guards of officers and men were to
ride all trains and arrest all soldiers improperly away from their commands. All furloughs to officers and men were to be invalid from the
date, unless sanctioned by the army commander himself. Lee was
doing all he could to get his army into condition for a new contest
with the blue invaders. Though shortening days proclaimed that winter
was not far off, it looked as if the year's roll of battles was not
complete.

Information about Confederate activities was not easy to obtain in the field, and Burnside reported to Halleck that "nearly all the negroes are being run south and kept under strict guard." [25] Thus one source of intelligence—often very unreliable—had been closed up. Halleck, however, passed on to Burnside on the afternoon of the 13th a very good report from a secret agent:

> General Lee's headquarters at Orange Court-House; Longstreet at Culpeper; D. H. Hill is at Culpeper; A. P. Hill and Jackson in the Valley of the Shenandoah, part at Newtown, at Staunton, and at Thornton's Gap. A small force at Snickersville Gap and at Ashby's Gap. Conscripts and recovered sick and wounded have arrived, and about made up the loss at Antietam.
>
> Was at Culpeper Friday. No forces at Richmond; army in good condition; use carpets for blankets; have bread and meat enough for the present.[26]

The agent made no effort at giving the enemy strength, but Burnside must have felt himself sufficiently superior to Lee to warrant a thrust at Richmond, as long as he did not have to make too many detachments to cover his communications. In view of the increased defenses of Richmond [27] and the fighting quality of Lee's army, a ratio of two to one could be a conservative estimate of the strength required for the contemplated operation. The presence of Longstreet at Culpeper was a sufficient reason for Burnside not to send any of his force over the upper Rappahannock, if he had ever entertained such a thought, because Longstreet could have attacked it in flank or rear as it moved down the river.

The situation looked favorable; but Burnside could not start for Fredericksburg without considering the possibility of an offensive by the Confederates. The telegram that gave the President's assent to the Fredericksburg move called attention to a recent Cincinnati dispatch from General Wright referring to a rumored movement by Jackson upon Romney and Cumberland.[28] Wright placed Jackson in Winchester with 40,000 men—a very accurate figure; but it is clear that the "slumbering volcano," as often before, had been erupting false reports about his intentions. He was not planning any move into West Virginia or Maryland, because his orders from Lee were to unite promptly with Longstreet if a movement by the Federals toward Fredericksburg should develop.[29] General Cox, who had returned to West Virginia with the Kanawha Division about October 10, and had made Charleston his headquarters, believed the threat-

ened move by Jackson was nonsense, but President Garrett of the
Baltimore and Ohio sent apprehensive messages to Stanton.[30] The Secretary of War and the High Command evidently appraised the rumors
that Jackson sent out as Cox did. Halleck merely called Burnside's
attention to the telegram from Wright, and the new commander of
the Army of the Potomac did not alter his plans, knowing full well
that his march on Fredericksburg should cause Lee to unite his army
without delay, and that raids by Stonewall were not to be feared.
Orders to move went out on the afternoon of the 14th, and at dawn
Sumner's grand division took up the march, followed on successive
days by Franklin, Hooker, and the cavalry.[31] The promptness of it
all suggested the same Burnside who had moved so quickly to Washington from Williamsport with his regiment of Rhode Islanders in
June, 1861, and who had dispatched most of his command under
Reno in record time to reenforce Pope after the battle of Cedar
Mountain.

Fredericksburg had been in possession of the Confederates—
though lightly held—since Burnside under rush orders from Halleck
had evacuated the place early in September after Pope's defeat. So far
as possible, railroad equipment had been taken away; other property
and installations at Aquia Creek had been damaged or destroyed by
the Federals when they left, though the railroad to Falmouth had been
little damaged. Now the restoration of the port with facilities greater
than before was the primary basis for the new campaign. Even before
Burnside took command, McClellan had given some thought to the
problem, for on November 6 Ingalls terminated a dispatch to Meigs,
"Please have the road put in repair from Aquia Creek to Richmond,
via Fredericksburg." It was a casual way to refer to an extensive
undertaking, and Ingalls must have had great faith in his chief's
capacity to carry out large enterprises with little effort. Nor did he
entirely misjudge his man, for Meigs—who had borne with great
serenity McClellan's accusation that his army was not properly supplied—wrote to Halleck the next day with regard to the request,
inquiring about measures to protect his workers from "the rebels at
Richmond." He had foreseen the demand that would be made upon
him, and had materials ready for prompt starting of repairs. Burnside's
long letter had been shown to Haupt on the 11th, the day after its
arrival; and he wrote on the 12th that he concurred in general with
the suggestions it contained. Burnside suggested a way to meet his

supply problem that had not occurred to Lee when he discounted the probability of an operation from Fredericksburg. Haupt wrote to the Union general: "The floating wharf which you propose could be used very well for wagons until a new track could be graded and laid and permanent wharf erected. . . . I am preparing to commence work as soon as orders are received." [32] Meigs's question about security was not forgotten, and Burnside was asked immediately after the Fredericksburg move was approved to send a detachment of cavalry to cover the landing of stores at Belle Plain and Aquia Creek.[33] On the 17th Haupt informed him that he was just back from a personal inspection; stores were en route prepared for rapid landing, and several engineer companies had probably already gone ashore.[34] An imposing list of items was being prepared for immediate shipment, including locomotives, cars, and a complete machine shop. A historic example in army supply was about to be carried out.

Darkness came on the 17th before the head of Sumner's column arrived at Falmouth, after a march of three days over poor or indifferent roads through devastated country. The cheerless countryside was in striking contrast to the productive region of Maryland where the army had spent six weeks, and it must have been oppressive to the spirits of the soldiers. But the inhospitable country was even worse on the animals, of which Burnside had about 50,000, and he reported that many of them were without forage for two or three days, the region through which the army moved being so "completely devastated." Sumner lost no time in disposing his two corps in favorable positions opposite Fredericksburg, and quickly had a battery in a position which so commanded the railroad for a distance of two miles below the town that the Confederates were compelled to stop shipping out grain and flour.

On the 19th Burnside arrived and wrote a long and excellent dispatch which was carried to Halleck the next morning by no less an officer than Brigadier General Seth Williams, inspector general of the adjutant general's department in the reorganized army.[35] It reported Sumner's dispositions, that Franklin had arrived the night before at Stafford, eight miles north by east of Falmouth, and that Hooker was six miles northwest opposite United States Ford, near the hamlet of Hartwood. The march had been well conducted, and casualties were light. Pleasonton's cavalry had done some skirmishing and had lost two men killed and a number wounded. Through carelessness, seven men of

General Bayard's command had been captured; but the derelict officer was in arrest. When he reported the incident, Bayard, whose sense of humor was as irrepressible as his courage and devotion to duty, wrote to Burnside, "I lost 7 men yesterday, instead of 20; the rest made too good time for the enemy." Federal cavalrymen were indeed becoming better riders, and probably the initial disparity in quality of mounts between them and Stuart's horsemen no longer existed.[36]

With the pride and solicitude of a good officer for the property in his care, Burnside wrote, "All the wagons and public property have arrived." From Belle Plain and Aquia Creek—where Ingalls had been appraising facilities and giving directions—good reports had come about the landing of supplies. Burnside had made a successful change of base, without magnifying it as a great feat like McClellan in his change from White House to Harrison's Landing. Work on the wharf was progressing well, and under the vigorous direction of one of Haupt's assistants the destroyed railroad was coming back to life, so that the whistle of locomotives and the rumble of cars would soon again be heard; then extensive hauling by wagons over poor roads would no longer be necessary. About the same time Burnside would have a telegraph line into his headquarters.[87] Of the "Rebels," little had been seen—evidently they were not in force on the opposite side of the river; but their pickets could be seen curiously observing what the Yankees were doing.

Burnside had only one bit of bad news to report to his chief: "The pontoon trains have not yet arrived, and an examination of the ford here to-day demonstrated that the infantry and the artillery cannot pass." According to his final report, Sumner had suggested that some of his force cross the river for the purpose of seizing Fredericksburg, but was kept back by the decision about the fords.[38] Whatever the facts at the time the decision was made, heavy rain soon set in, and troops across the river would have become isolated. Though it was vexatious not to find the expected pontoon trains, Burnside wrote very good-humoredly to Halleck, "The delay in the arrival of the pontoon bridge, with the necessary time it will take to get our supplies, will enable the General-in-Chief to visit this place for a day, which I should like very much, as I am very anxious to have a more full consultation than we had at Warrenton." One can criticize the logic, but the attitude toward a superior was a novel one to find in the commander of the Army of the Potomac.

That day, the 19th, Burnside revealed his commendable attitude toward his subordinates as well as toward his superior. At 10:20 P.M. his chief of staff wrote to Hooker:

Your dispatch, reporting position of your command, received. The commanding general tenders his thanks for carrying out so successfully the most difficult part of the late movement—bringing up the rear. A dispatch was sent you this evening by Captain Weir, of General Pleasonton's staff. The general will communicate with you in the morning. The pontoon-train has not yet arrived, but we expect it to-morrow.[39]

A general who deals in that way with his subordinates deserves a support and loyalty from them that goes beyond the letter of Army Regulations and the Articles of War; but already Joe Hooker had transgressed against Burnside. Secretary Stanton had called on him while he was in a Washington hospital recovering from the Antietam wound in his heel; and the ambitious general, very conscious of laudatory publicity, took full advantage of the opportunity to make a favorable impression. On the very day that the cordial note just quoted was addressed to him, Hooker wrote a highly irregular letter to Stanton, which would certainly have amazed Burnside.[40] There is nothing whatever in the letter that suggests that it was in reply to a communication from Stanton, or that Stanton had in conversation extended an invitation to him to forward his views upon operations, past or current. It may not have been very bad for Hooker to take the two jabs he did at McClellan for slowness and delays, because the charges were old and common, and furthermore McClellan was gone. But it is hard to regard his comments on the current campaign as anything other than an effort to undermine the new commander of the Army of the Potomac. Hooker did not like to have many officers between himself and the top, and it is more than possible that pressure by him had caused McClellan to cancel on September 15 his order of the day before, formally placing Hooker under the command of Burnside. Now on November 19 Hooker made in his letter to Stanton—with whom he had no official reason to correspond—a sly remark regretting "that the major-general commanding did not keep up the show of an advance on the line via Gordonsville"; and he went on to say that even at the time of writing he "would recommend a demonstration, with a strong infantry and cavalry force, in that direction." Hooker was a brave officer and within limits, a good commander; but he strikingly failed in loyal support of his superior—one of the great essentials in a soldier. The criticism he passed on Burnside could not be excused even if Stanton had invited correspondence from him—and he very probably had not.

Hooker also outlined to Stanton a movement which he had just requested that Burnside permit him to make—a bold advance across the Rappahannock in the direction of Bowling Green. He had rations for three days, and he thought he could obtain forage in the region he described. Then he asked the Secretary if he could not rely on rations—sent directly from Washington—being at Port Royal three days from the morning of the 20th! It was indeed an amazing request for Hooker to make before he had received Burnside's reply to his suggested operation. But thus did Joe Hooker pile on a grave offense an offense which was still graver. What Stanton did with the very irregular letter there is no way of knowing; but it may have been part of the basis for the stinging and historic reproof which Lincoln later gave to Hooker for irregular behavior.

On the 20th Parke wrote at length in a friendly vein to Hooker about his proposal, explaining that the commanding general thought the movement premature, though he hoped that Hooker's corps might cross the river in the near future and concurred in the belief that prompt action was of great importance.[41] But already a three-day rain had commenced; streams were up; fords were unusable; roads were becoming impassable. The ambitious Hooker was probably glad he was not isolated on the other side of the river when he gazed upon the swollen stream; in a few months, as a commanding general, he would have a chance to venture across the Rappahannock.

Throughout the 20th and 21st the storm continued; but the expected pontoons did not arrive. That Burnside was doing his best to go on with a prompt advance toward Hanover Junction is shown by a circular he issued on the 20th, directing the commanders of grand divisions to enforce orders about the limitation of personal baggage and to take "whatever other measures may be necessary to enable the command to march rapidly and on an hour's notice." Pleasonton's division of cavalry, tidying up behind the army and protecting it from annoyance by Stuart's troopers, struggled through the rain and mud, and his ambulances picked up the wet and miserable infantrymen who had become sick upon the march; reasonably and in good spirit he told Parke that this was a little service that the cavalry assigned to each corps could do for their own foot soldiers.[42]

On the 21st Fredericksburg was threatened with another kind of storm, a storm of shot and shell upon the streets and against the houses associated so intimately with Mary and George Washington, James Monroe, and John Paul Jones. Shots had been fired at Sumner's troops from the cover of the houses of the town; and at the direction of Burnside he sent a note, as the commanding general of the Right Grand Division of the army, to the mayor and common council calling attention to the fact and stating: "Your mills and manufactories are furnishing provisions and material for clothing for armed bodies in rebellion against the Government of the United States. Your railroads and other means of transportation are removing supplies to the depots of such troops." Sumner demanded the surrender of the town by five o'clock in the afternoon. If an affirmative answer were not received by that time sixteen hours would be allowed for the removal of women and children, the sick, and aged before the town was shelled. In return he gave the assurance that upon taking possession of the town every means would be taken to preserve order. The message did not reach the mayor until 4:40. His reply was notable for calmness and restraint. Without denunciations or imprecations, or denials of the claims Sumner had made, he discussed the issue systematically and fully. There would be no more firing upon Federals from the town; the mills and manufactories would no longer furnish supplies; nor would the railroad and other means of transportation convey supplies to military depots.[43] Throughout the night and the next day Confederate army wagons and ambulances supplemented the transportation in the town for the removal of women and children.[44] The Federal guns did not open. A conference took place, to which word was brought that Lee would not occupy the town but would resist occupation by the Union army; and on the 22nd Sumner closed the incident with a brief note to the mayor and council stating: "I am authorized to say that, so long as no hostile demonstration is made from the town, it will not be shelled. I have also to say that there will be no firing upon the cars before 11 A.M. to-morrow."[45] The next day the mayor with some prominent citizens and Major General J. B. Kershaw crossed the river for a quite unsolicited call. The Federal blue coat and blue pantaloons which the general wore were almost concealed by "a long Rebel butternut cape," according to a newspaper correspondent who wrote, "It is very mortifying to see so many Rebel soldiers and officers dressed in our uniforms. In the next great battle many mistakes will occur through similarity in dress."[46]

A commanding general needs a stout heart in order to escape being depressed by continued bad weather, especially if he is operating in a country with few, if any, all-weather, all-season roads. Never far from his mind are his miles of infantry, heavy guns and loaded caissons, wagons and ambulances, and the added strain on the spirits of the men and on the strength of both men and animals. There was a note of discouragement in the dispatch Burnside wrote to Halleck on the 22nd. He said nothing about the rain, of which McClellan had written so constantly from the Peninsula. Rain alone might not have daunted him; but the pontoons, whose arrival on the 20th was so confidently expected as late as the night before, had not yet come. He reminded Halleck that he had been led to believe that one train would be started from Washington as soon as the General in Chief returned from the Warrenton conference on the 12th, and that prompt crossing at Fredericksburg was an essential part of his plan, and added:

Had the pontoon bridge arrived even on the 19th or 20th, the army could have crossed with trifling opposition. But now the opposite side of the river is occupied by a large rebel force under General Longstreet, with batteries ready to be placed in position to operate against the working parties building the bridge and the troops in crossing. The pontoon train has not yet arrived, and the river is too high for the troops to cross at any of the fords.

With admirable poise Burnside concluded, "The President said that the movement, in order to be successful, must be made quickly, and I thought the same." [47]

If the pontoon bridge had arrived in time for Sumner to put his strong command over the river on the 18th, a great opportunity would have been open to Burnside; for Lee had been completely outgeneraled and remained completely mystified for a number of days. In a dispatch to Jackson from Culpeper at 9:00 A.M. on the 19th Lee stated, "I do not now anticipate making a determined stand north of the North Anna." In conformity with this purpose a regiment of infantry and a battery which he had sent to reenforce the single regiment then at Fredericksburg had been instructed on the 15th to proceed to the crossing of the North Anna and the Richmond-Fredericksburg Railroad, in case the Federals had taken possession of the latter town.[48] The small reenforced regiment could have been brushed aside by Sumner's powerful command, if he had been able to cross the Rappahannock and had marched south by the pike which ran from Fredericksburg to Richmond. Just what orders Sumner had is not clear;

but the objective of the campaign was very definitely Richmond, and Burnside, like Lincoln, knew it could succeed only if moves were rapid and bold. Whether Lee could have made a determined stand close behind the North Anna as he had planned, is doubtful, for Franklin and Hooker were close on the heels of Sumner, while Lee was slow in getting Longstreet away from Culpeper and, bewildered as he was about what Burnside was doing, he allowed Jackson to remain in the Valley more than a week with very indefinite orders. It is entirely possible that Sumner could have seized Hanover with little difficulty; and there he would have been as embarrassing to Lee as Jackson was to Pope after cutting the railroad at Bristow and seizing Manassas.

The story of the pontoons is instructive.[49] Indifferent instructions and carelessness in detail were responsible for their nonarrival. All the pontoons belonging to the Army of the Potomac had been in use in the vicinity of Harpers Ferry under the command of Major Ira Spaulding, Fiftieth New York Engineers. On November 6, Captain J. C. Duane, McClellan's chief engineer, directed that most of the bridging equipment should be moved at once to Washington, where a pontoon train on wheels was to be made up. For a reason never explained the order was not received until the 12th; but Spaulding lost no time dismantling his bridges, and that afternoon and the next morning boats and material were made up into rafts and sent down the canal to Washington, the wagons going by land. On the 14th the major was in touch in Washington with Brigadier General Daniel P. Woodbury, commanding the engineer brigade, who received on that same day two telegrams from Burnside's chief engineer, Lieutenant C. B. Comstock. The second telegram showed the urgent need of a second pontoon train—in addition to the one previously ordered by Duane—fitted up to move overland to Fredericksburg. Woodbury replied that, although the order of the 6th had not reached Spaulding until the 12th, he was now on hand and thirty-six pontoons had reached the city with forty more expected the next day. He said that one train could be started on the 16th or the morning of the 17th, but that Halleck was not inclined to send a second one by land unless Burnside insisted; however, it could go by water to Aquia Creek and then be hauled to Fredericksburg by the teams which carried the first train. On the evening of the 17th Woodbury wired to Comstock that Spaulding had not yet left but expected to leave the next morning; forty-eight pontoon boats had been sent the day before to Aquia Creek. This dispatch may have been much delayed in reaching Comstock, for army headquarters were on the march. Spaulding, however, did not get away on the 17th, or on the 18th, when Woodbury wired to Comstock: "Major Spaulding has been delayed in obtaining horses [harness?] teamsters, etc., for 270 new horses. He expects to start tonight." He insisted later that "no one informed me that the success of any important movement depended in the slightest degree upon a pontoon train to leave Washington by land." Otherwise he stated that he would have seized teams and teamsters.

Not until the afternoon of the 19th did Spaulding leave with his new horses, wearing new harness that had had to be taken out of boxes and put together. But then the rain had begun, and the roads grew worse and worse, so that only five miles a day could be made, even with great labor by men and animals. Land progress looking hopeless when the Occoquan River was reached, the boats were made into rafts; and with the wagons aboard they were started down the Potomac on the morning of the 24th, the horses continuing overland.

But the great delay in starting and the unhappy ending of the land expedition would not have kept pontoons away from Burnside, if pontoon wagons had gone with the forty boats which were dispatched down the Potomac on the evening of the 16th. Whether Halleck or Woodbury was chiefly responsible cannot be said; but certainly one of them was to blame for naïvely counting on having the boats hauled away from Aquia Creek by the wagons that carried the overland train.[50] After some minor misadventures the pontoons reached Aquia on the 18th and the officer in charge, Major J. S. Magruder, having no wagons to move to Falmouth, obligingly used his boats to make wharfs for the quartermaster and the commissary. Not until the 22nd, after he had reported the nonarrival of any pontoons at Falmouth, was Burnside informed by Washington that Woodbury with forty-eight pontoons was at Aquia Creek.[51] Then Ingalls found Woodbury and obtained the story, except for the fate of the overland train;[52] information of which was received the same day in a message from Spaulding, transmitted through General Franklin's headquarters.[53] At about the same time barges with twenty-six pontoon wagons reached Magruder, and on the 24th, after a hard all-night exertion over bad roads, that officer had his boats in the vicinity of Falmouth—just a week later than Burnside had expected the arrival of a train.[54]

Halleck sought to cover up his share of responsibility, and on the 23rd he sent Burnside a telegram referring to the message he had sent to Woodbury from Warrenton on the 12th, and adding, "Immediately on my return I saw him myself, to urge them [pontoon trains] forward. He left for Aquia Creek with his brigade, to report to you; he is there under your command. If there has been any unnecessary delay, call him to an account." Burnside put the engineer officer in arrest and so reported to Halleck; but he released Woodbury after reading his explanation of what had taken place, perhaps with some doubts as to how much urging Halleck had done.[55] Both were blamed by the press; and a year later, after Halleck had said some nice things about Woodbury to the Committee on the Conduct of the War, Woodbury wrote in a letter of thanks: "When I first met Burnside at Fredericksburg, and was asked to explain why pontoons were not at hand when the army arrived, I told him that he commenced his movement before he was ready; that he ought to have remained at Warrenton some five days longer; and I added, to show that the idea was not new to me, 'I told Halleck so.' "[56] That impertinent and insubordinate remark gives an indication as to the nature of the earlier conversation between Halleck and Woodbury. The engineer may have been piqued that his days of graceful living in a comfortable house in Washington were at an end; and he probably did not know that his arrest had followed receipt of a telegram from Halleck.

Although the General in Chief and the commander of the engineer brigade did not appreciate the way in which Burnside had put the Army of the Potomac over the road, correspondents were enthusiastic and subordinate officers evaluated the feat properly. From Falmouth on the 18th there came a dispatch:

"Napoleon once told me," says Jomini, "that he knew no method of conducting a war except to march twenty-five miles a day, to fight, and then to encamp in quiet." Burnside begins like a believer in that policy. Whatever his other qualities, he is at least very much in earnest. He has already inspired the army to a marvelous extent. Officers wont to believe that a great command cannot move more than six miles a day, and accustomed to our old method of waiting a week for the issue of new clothing or a month for the execution of an order to advance rub their eyes in mute astonishment. . . . We have changed our base from the Manassas Railroad to Aquia Creek and the Rappahannock. *We have marched from Warrenton forty miles, in two days and a half.*[57]

Thus wrote one of the *New York Tribune's* war correspondents. Another reporter for Horace Greeley's great paper wrote some days later that time was everything with Burnside. He "was promised, when he left Warrenton, that the pontoons should be here before him, via the river. This delay may cost us thousands of lives, and prolong this campaign several weeks." [58] The reference which the correspondent made to the advantages of fighting at Hanover Junction is proof that Burnside had expected a considerable reward from his rapid march. The dispatch let the cat out of the bag, showing that there had been a blunder by the High Command for which payment could be expected to be great.

There has also been no little criticism of Burnside for not allowing Sumner and Hooker to cross the river; but it usually says nothing about the state of the fords and makes no reference to rain. Thus Nicolay and Hay say that Sumner had asked permission to cross and take the heights back of Fredericksburg but was refused. They assert, "Hooker in turn had asked leave to cross his corps at one of the upper fords to come in upon the left flank of Lee, but this proposition was also declined." [59] Burnside decided against Sumner after a personal examination of the ford—which would seem to have been thorough, from his comments that infantry and artillery could not cross but, by "keeping the horses well separated, the cavalry" could cross. He also stated in his dispatch of the 19th, "I have ordered a reconnaissance to-morrow morning at daylight of the United States Ford, when I hope to be able to cross some cavalry and infantry, with some light pieces of artillery." Though hourly expecting the pontoons, Burnside was not inactive while he waited. The United States Ford was above Fredericksburg, and was the one which Hooker would have used, but Nicolay and Hay do not note that the message declining Hooker's proposition—which was *not* to get on the left flank of Lee—referred to "the heavy rains of last night."

In view of the disputes that arose after the battle of Fredericksburg, any subsequent statement about the condition of the fords on the 19th is of doubtful value; and certainly any claim that Sumner could have crossed is inconclusive, unless it admits that crossing would have been slow and difficult, and that the portion of his command which reached the other bank would soon have been isolated. The statement about the weather by Burnside's chief of staff in the message to Hooker on the 20th is fully confirmed by a Washington dispatch of the 21st: "The weather is very disagreeable indeed, it having rained heavily all yesterday afternoon, swelling the streams to an unusual height." [60]

An important incident in World War II may seem to offer a comparison unfavorable to Burnside. On March 7, 1945, units of the American army unexpectedly found the bridge over the Rhine at Remagen undestroyed. It had to be decided whether the enemy had blundered in an almost inexplicable way, or whether he had laid a trap for the isolation and destruction of American troops that would use the bridge; and the decision had to be made at once. The prompt and bold use of the bridge was one of the most spectacular and fruitful incidents of a ten-months campaign full of the unexpected and the spectacular. In the Remagen case, however, it was within the power of the American command to protect the precarious connection with troops that had crossed; for antiaircraft guns and fighter planes could guard the bridge from enemy bombers while the force beyond the river was being built up and pontoons for other bridges were being brought up by motor trucks over roads that could be used in any weather. But no man can protect a ford against a rising stream—especially a ford whose practicability is even at the moment open to question. Burnside could not call on a learned meteorologist, as did General Eisenhower when he postponed the invasion of Normandy. But on the morning of November 17 there had been a rain and a lowering sky; [61] though the threatened storm did not come then, the rain began again on the afternoon of the 19th, in great earnest.[62] Burnside had observed the Rappahannock during August; he had seen it rise after a heavy rain, isolating some of Jackson's troops on the north bank—trapped troops that Pope had sought vigorously to destroy. To the judgment which he put in writing on November 19, that the ford was impracticable for infantry and artillery, he held firm; and in his final report he wrote, "It was afterward ascertained that they could not have crossed." [63]

It would no longer be easy to cross the river, and the road to Hanover was barred; still Burnside held to his purpose to cross without delay. Four hours after Magruder arrived, he received orders to prepare for throwing a bridge in the morning.[64] The army commander himself worked far into the night on the many preparations that had to be made; but like a good general he informed his superior of what was going on. At 2:20 A.M. of the 25th he wrote to Halleck that enough pontoons had arrived for one bridge, and that he hoped to have enough for two by daylight. He recounted the fate of the land train—which still had not come—and said significantly, "Had they started even on the 16th, they would have had good roads, and would have been in time." But he let bygones be bygones and closed his dispatch resolutely and cheerfully: "We are at work with preparations for throwing the first bridge over, but it cannot be done till we get more carriages, which, I hope, will be here to-day. No time should be lost. The enemy's force is constantly increasing. Will telegraph more fully soon." [65] In casting up the score for and against Ambrose Burnside that message should not be forgotten: he wanted to lose not even an hour, and he had preparations under way before all the material needed for even one bridge was at hand.

But the night passed, and additional pontoons did not arrive. Magruder's men, tired from their exertions, could lie down and sleep a little in the chill of late November, their minds filled with thoughts of the rain of bullets that would greet them when they started to put in their bridge. Farther away, infantry commanders were reconnoitering routes as their commands waited in assembly areas; artillery commanders detailed to follow the infantry were checking on their batteries, and seeing that their caissons were filled and that they had grain for their animals as well as food for their men; others were putting their guns into position to beat down some of the fire the Confederates would bring to bear upon the engineers and the crossing troops. But morning came, and still the bridge did not go down, presumably because the necessary carriages had not come. And this was an entire week after a bridge should have been ready for Sumner's 33,000 men and guns.

Early afternoon brought this telegram:

> Executive Mansion,
> Washington, November 25, 1862—11:30 a.m.
> Major-General Burnside, Falmouth, Va.:
> If I should be in boat off Aquia Creek at dark to-morrow (Wednesday) evening, could you, without inconvenience, meet me and pass an hour or two with me?   *A. Lincoln* [66]

It was the first message from Lincoln to the new army commander, and the Commander in Chief was as diffident about intruding as a schoolgirl.

Lincoln's biographers tell us nothing about the important preceding week. From the moment he assented to Burnside's plan, the President must have followed the operation with intense absorption, realizing that its success was predicated upon speed. Early reports of the movement must have been encouraging, and the long dispatch that Seth Williams brought in person on the 20th revealed that Lincoln had a general who could make the Army of the Potomac march. The situation was promising. Then Burnside wrote on the 22nd that the pontoons had not arrived, indicating that plans might accordingly have to be changed. Lincoln must have been disturbed as he waited through the 23rd and the 24th. Burnside's telegram of an early hour on the 25th, revealing the hope that two bridges would go down that morning, reached Washington at 9:30 A.M. One can only conjecture whether Lincoln saw the dispatch before he wired Burnside; it seems probable that he did. One thing is certain: the delay and the change in the program made Lincoln want to discuss the situation and the prospects with his new commander. If he had read the telegram from Falmouth and thought that Burnside might have his bridges down and his army crossing he knew the general would indeed be a busy man. He did not want to hold up for a minute any work that would help win the war; he would go at night. But even then he asked if his visit would be convenient.

Without delay Burnside wired the President that he could see him; but the dispatches in the Official Records contain no further mention of a conference, and Burnside's report does not touch on one. Washington dispatches of the 27th, however, reveal that Lincoln and Stanton returned that morning from a visit at Aquia Creek, and Nicolay and Hay somewhat inaccurately write, "The President visited the army on the 27th of November." [67] They also quote from a memorandum—not in the Official Records—written on the way back to Washington, in which Lincoln expressed to Halleck his views about future operations. He suggested the assembling of a force of some 25,000 men opposite Port Royal on the Rappahannock, some seventeen miles below Fredericksburg, where they would threaten Lee's communication and could form one part of a pair of pincers when Burnside crossed at Fredericksburg. On the 28th Burnside went to Washington to discuss further the situation that had resulted from the failure of his initial plan.

CHAPTER XVI

BURNSIDE FAILS AT MARYE'S HILL

The fire of the enemy's musketry and artillery, furious as it was before, now became still hotter. The stone wall was a sheet of flame, that enveloped the head and flanks of the column.

Humphreys

THE success which General Lee often had in anticipating his adversary's movement has given rise to an exaggerated idea of his ability to read the mind of an opposing general. Burnside's march confused him very much, and the uncertainty and indecision which he suffered for several days are plainly revealed in the dozen or so letters which he wrote to President Davis, Secretary of War Randolph, Adjutant General Cooper, and Stonewall Jackson—the latter still in the vicinity of Winchester. Lee gathered military intelligence from various sources, agents in and about Washington, at Fredericksburg, and throughout the countryside where the Federals were operating, as well as from regular military channels. Jackson was forwarding information, Stuart was searching for it, while scouts from his own headquarters were watching the Union columns on the march, and attempting to get close enough to the camps of the bluecoats to observe their actions. In addition, the Northern newspapers that were smuggled through the lines were carefully read for indications as to what the people expected from the new commander of the Army of the Potomac. It was natural that there should be contradictions and inaccuracies in the reports which came in, and the plain truth is that Lee did not make up his mind about Burnside's intentions until the situation was very clear. His record on this occasion quite disproves that he had vision which amounted to "prescience," and the confusion he revealed properly belongs in an account of General Burnside.

At first things went well for Lee, because Sumner had no more than started for Fredericksburg on the morning of the 15th when scouts reported the fact to the Confederate headquarters at Culpeper; and Lee immediately wrote to Colonel W. B. Ball, commanding the small force at Fredericksburg, "It is reported that the enemy is moving from Warrenton to-day, and it is probable that he is marching upon Fredericksburg." He repeated the instructions he had given the day before about destroying the railroad to Aquia Creek, and expressed his displeasure over some inaccurate reports received through Ball by directing, "If you find that your courier has given you wrong information, he must be corrected and punished."

Though he began with a correct deduction, Lee soon abandoned it; and it is interesting to note what led him astray. Scouts came in with the information that no preparations had been begun to rebuild the wharves at Aquia Creek, and it did not occur to Lee that the Yankees could operate without them or make some sort of hasty improvisation. On the 17th he wrote to President Davis: "I have heard of no preparation to rebuild the wharves at Aquia Creek. . . . I should think some provision would be made for subsisting a large army if a movement upon Fredericksburg was designed." To the Secretary of War he wrote on the same day in a similar vein. One sees how well advised Burnside was when he did not tarry about Warrenton for the five days that Woodbury referred to, so that things could be made ready to receive him at Aquia Creek. Knowing the sort of men that Meigs, Haupt, and Ingalls were, and confident that they would not let him down in supply, he marched, like a good field commander, and thus upset the mind of an extremely able adversary.

If the Yankees were not going to Fredericksburg, where were they headed? Lee decided they were bound for some place south of the James River, which was indeed far off. He wrote to Davis on the 17th that wagon trains were moving toward the Orange and Alexandria Railroad, and stated: "The cars on said road are in active operation. I cannot tell whether they are carrying back or bringing forward troops." Actually Haupt's trains were not carrying soldiers at all; they were either hauling supplies or just making a noise. But the thought that the trains might be taking troops back toward Alexandria had taken hold, and on the same day Lee wrote to Randolph, "I think it, therefore, *probable* * that the movement in execution is with a view of transferring the army south of James River, and the appointment of General Burnside to command favors this supposition." In believing that Burnside's operation on the North Carolina coast might be significant, Lee was forgetting that after the coastal operation Burnside had been stationed at Fredericksburg for a month and had directed a brilliant though small expedition against the Virginia Central Railroad. Although the transfer of the Army of the Potomac beyond the James River would be a great undertaking that would require time, Lee did not wait to check on the report but urged Randolph to make preparations to oppose Federal operations in North Carolina. Randolph and Davis lost no time in putting indorsements on the letter, directing that immediate attention be given to getting absentees back and calling up more conscripts.

But the unexpected message about operations south of the James, that startled the Confederate President and Secretary of War, could hardly have been dispatched before Lee received reports that there were no transports at Alexandria—a matter which he might have checked before he reported that an amphibious operation by the Federals was "probable." At 2:00 P.M. the next day he wrote to Jackson: "I learn that there are no transports at Alexandria; nothing but a few gunboats and tugs. I see, therefore, no preparation for the transfer of the enemy's troops south of the James River as yet." No wharves building at Aquia Creek; no shipping assembling about Washington; what was the Union army up to? Completely baffled, Lee wrote to Jackson, "Nor is there anything to develop their ultimate plan." The Confederate general now stopped forecasting what Burnside would probably do, and contented himself with speaking of possibilities. He wrote to Stonewall: "It is possible that they may attempt to seize Winchester, Culpeper, and Fredericksburg, which would embrace their favorite strategic plan of advancing in three columns, but I think by so doing they will much expose themselves. I hope we may be able to take advantage of it." [1]

Speed and neglect of conventions were certainly paying large dividends. For three days and a half Burnside had had his columns hurrying over the roads toward Fredericksburg, and Lee was reduced to guesses and wishful thinking.

In the evening of the 18th Lee wrote to Adjutant General Cooper,

* Italics not in the original.

giving some new information which had come in. This letter certainly did not make it easier for the Southern high command which had to collate Lee's changing views from letters addressed to three officials. In a sense he was "advancing in three columns." He told Cooper a scout had reported that it was Sumner's corps which was marching on Fredericksburg; and he expressed the opinion that if this was the only part of Burnside's army moving in that direction it could be held in check until the Federal plan was revealed. The records do not indicate whether Lee was informed that the pontoon bridges had disappeared from the vicinity of Harpers Ferry; but he certainly knew that the Union army was well equipped with them, as well as in every particular, although apparently the thought never occurred to him that the dawn of any day might reveal a bridge across the Rappahannock.[2] He had been completely outgeneraled. Though he was hoping that Sumner alone might be marching toward his right and rear, his letter itself gave evidence that this was not the case. One of Stuart's scouts was given as authority for the report that the Federals had fallen back on the 16th from Bealeton to Warrenton Junction, and that their main body had marched thence toward Fredericksburg.[3] Incredible as it may seem, Lee was not convinced by the report from the cavalry, even though he had written to Randolph on the 14th that a "sudden descent" on Fredericksburg by the Federals was probable. That Stuart himself had made a correct deduction is shown by a letter Lee wrote the next morning—the 19th—to Jackson, in which he referred to his cavalry commander and stated, "He considers the information he received as conclusive that Burnside's whole army had marched for Fredericksburg." [4]

Reports from Jackson at Winchester had added to Lee's uncertainty. In his letter of 2:00 P.M. of the 18th Lee referred to a letter (unfortunately not in the records) Jackson had written the day before, which had just come to hand, reporting that the Federal forces at Harpers Ferry were being reenforced. Lee reasoned that if this and a similar report from Middleburg were true it would indicate that the enemy was "in great force at all points from Harper's Ferry to Fredericksburg"—an assumption that was untenable. Though his letter began by stating that "there must be some mistake" about the Harpers Ferry report, it vacillated and ended by accepting everything as equally credible and equally incredible: "There must be error somewhere, and it is important to discover it."

In spite of the uncertainty which gripped him, Lee took the pre-caution on the 18th of ordering Longstreet to start some divisions toward Fredericksburg.[5] The excellent but temporary appraisal which Lee had made on the 15th could not have saved him from the critical situation in which he would have found himself if Captain Spaulding had saluted Sumner somewhere on the road on the night of the 17th and had reported that he had a pontoon train parked in the woods and was only awaiting the general's instructions. The regiment of infantry and the battery of artillery which Lee had sent on the 15th to re-enforce Ball would have added little to the defense of Fredericksburg; and Lee already had given orders that they should proceed to the North Anna rather than be sacrificed.[6] From Northern papers Lee surely learned before long the story of the pontoons, and of the conse-quent wrecking of Burnside's well conceived plans; then he must have realized how narrow had been his escape. Burnside, on his part, never had the opportunity to read the letters Lee had written from Culpeper; thus he did not know how excellently he had achieved, and was not armed with the perfect answer for crushing to earth the impertinent Woodbury—fresh from his comfortable Washington bed—when he suggested that Burnside should have waited five days longer at War-renton, so that everything could have been in apple-pie order for him at Aquia Creek.

Even the letter of the 19th, in which Lee informed Davis that two of Longstreet's divisions had started for Fredericksburg and two more were to follow that day held a distinct note of uncertainty about the Federal plans. After stating that the enemy had just burned the railroad bridge over the Rappahannock, Lee said, "I think he has abandoned his advance in this direction and west of it." He gave Davis the in-formation that there were no transports, only tugs and gunboats at Washington and Alexandria. This led him to remark, "They must expect, then, I think, to force their way from Fredericksburg." Never-theless he concluded, "I shall wait to hear again from Stuart, and then proceed as circumstances appear to dictate." [7] What more did he want to hear from his cavalry commander, after the report that he had con-clusive evidence that the whole of Burnside's army had marched toward Fredericksburg? [8]

There is no evidence that Burnside sent out false rumors about his intended moves for the purpose of deceiving Lee, after the manner of Jackson in the Valley. Perhaps the resourceful Haupt had his engines do a little unnecessary whistling, or run back and forth at night, just to make noise and seem very busy; but there is no evidence even of that. Barring such playfulness on the part of locomotive engineers, Lee was deceived though no deception was resorted to.

The appraisal just given of Lee's decisions is opposed to that of Freeman, who states that he "had anticipated the movements of his new opponent with a precision that was almost prescience." [9] Freeman makes much of the trifling reenforcement Lee sent to Fredericksburg on the 15th, but he minimizes the perplexity he revealed on the next four days. Nor does he mention the alarm in Richmond over the sudden change in the situation—an alarm which a Federal scout reported on November 20 as follows: "Great excitement among all parties was created by late information received from Fredericksburg, the Yankees having arrived at and south of Fredericksburg. The gallant little army concentrated for the defense of the place and to arrest the progress of the enemy was termed insufficient." [10] It certainly must have been conjectured in Richmond that Lee had been deceived by Burnside and had allowed the Confederate capital to be unnecessarily threatened by the detention of Longstreet at Culpeper and by the amazing delay in calling up Jackson from the Valley. Actually for a week Lee had practically abnegated command of half of his army to Stonewall, whom he allowed to disregard his repeated judgment that Jackson's command should join that of Longstreet.[11]

On the evening of the 22nd Lee wrote a long dispatch to Cooper from his new headquarters near Fredericksburg, stating that the fifth and last of Longstreet's divisions was due the next day.[12] In a mild way he conceded that the Federals had been doing very well. "Their immense wagon train is actively engaged, apparently, in provisioning their army, which, during the last three days of rain and cold, I know has been a difficult operation, and must have been attended with suffering among their troops." He intended to resist any effort of Burnside to cross the river; but he gave no assurances, and admitted that the ground was favorable to the enemy. With only half of his own army to oppose the great concentrated command of his opponent, he could indeed have been at a great disadvantage if Burnside even on that date had had the long overdue pontoons.

Although Lee could see on the 21st that Burnside's entire army was in the vicinity of Fredericksburg, Burnside at once proceeded to do some things which again cast doubt on his ultimate intentions. On the 22nd the Federal camps began to break up; their wagons and their parks of artillery could be seen moving to the rear, and when morning came the great host had gone, with only a covering force in sight. What did it mean? Was the Army of the Potomac preparing to embark at Aquia Creek? To Jackson, Lee wrote on the 23rd: "I am as yet unable to discover what may be the plan of the enemy. He is certainly making no forward movement, though he may be preparing to do so. I am apprehensive that, while keeping a force in our front, he may be transferring his troops to some other quarter, and the march of a portion of Sigel's corps to Alexandria would favor this view of the subject." [13]

By the 25th Lee was, however, putting two and two together and getting the answer. He wrote to Davis that from the tone of the Northern papers he believed an advance on Richmond from Fredericksburg was intended, and that the Northern people would regard any change of base as "almost equivalent to a defeat." He then correctly reasoned that Burnside's retrograde movement was only for the purpose of more convenient supply, and he stated, "I think they will now endeavor to get possession of Hanover Junction." That the situation had its perplexities for the Confederate commander was revealed by the way he terminated his long letter: "I need not say how glad I should be if your convenience would permit you to visit the army, that I might have the benefit of your views and directions." It would appear that Davis's military views were by no means unacceptable.

Scouts continued to bring information. The wharves at Aquia had been rebuilt and enlarged, cars and locomotives were on the reconstructed railroad to Falmouth; there was considerable shipping, but no signs of embarkation. Then word came that a large pontoon train had reached Burnside's headquarters. No exceptional general was needed to make the final deduction, and Lee wrote to his President, "Their object may be to make a winter campaign under the belief that our troops will not be sufficiently guarded against the cold for operations in the field." He was not, however, at all discouraged at the prospects ahead, for if Burnside's effort to reach Richmond could be defeated it might prove to be the last which the Federals would make. Apparently forgetting the excellent march which the Army of the Potomac had just made—and which many generals would have taken as evidence of very good morale—he wrote to Jackson, "All accounts agree that general dissatisfaction prevails in the army." [14]

Of course there was dissatisfaction in the army—soldiers are habitual grumblers. And there were reasons why the Army of the Potomac may have been doing more than the customary complaining; it had not been paid, and an order had kept away the sutlers, so that the men had not had the customary pies and cakes as well as other solaces and refreshments. Presently General Burnside took the matter up with the Secretary of War, putting it in a very tactful way, "The men are out of tobacco, and the officers are suffering for supplies." [15] What his men were to use for money, he did not explain, which may have indicated that borrowing was easy and the sutlers accommodating. When Stonewall read about the dissatisfaction in the Federal army, he may have wondered whether Lee had checked with sufficient care on his old friends in the Iron Brigade.

November was gone, and the recent storm had given a clear warning of what might be expected. It had been a great task to supply the army over the mud roads to Aquia Creek, short though they were. Although Haupt's railroad with its new trestle over Potomac Creek was in operation, and roads had been corduroyed, supply for an advance loomed as a great obstacle. Keen insight indeed had been contained in Lincoln's judgment of the 14th, that rapidity of execution was the *sine qua non* of Burnside's plan. When President and General talked together in the President's steamer at Aquia Creek on the evening of the 26th there could not have been the slightest hint by the Commander in Chief that the army commander had not literally and completely carried out the injunction to "move very rapidly," which had been contained in the General in Chief's telegram of November 14. And, what was more, Burnside could have shown Lincoln the circular which he wrote on the 20th while he waited hopefully for the pontoons already overdue, enjoining his army to get rid of surplus baggage, and be prepared in all ways to move across the Rappahannock on the anticipated bridges and on toward Hanover Junction "rapidly and on an hour's notice." [16] No commander could have stood before his superior much more in the clear than Burnside did that night; and everything in Lincoln's record makes it certain that the great President dealt sympathetically and appreciatively with the officer on whom he had forced the command of the army, an officer who had been placed in the present difficult position by the blunders of others.

No full record exists of the meetings that were held when Burnside went to Washington on the 28th; and in his final report the general did not even make note of the visit. Though both the President and the General in Chief had been doubtful about the advisability of shifting to Fredericksburg, the wishes of the field commander were carefully respected, and the conversations probably dealt chiefly with reenforcements and matters of detail. Burnside could well have had disturbing thoughts when he returned to his command on the 30th, aware as he was of the feeling of his superiors. He was going to have to make a river crossing in the face of an enemy whose fighting qualities he well knew. River crossings are not unusual, and any general must be prepared to make them; but none the less they require careful planning and good control; they are certain to give a commander many anxious moments, and they may end in catastrophe. A general who defends a sizable stream always hopes that he may throw the enemy back into the stream with severe loss. Thus Jackson had rebuffed Fitz-John Porter—who had been relieved of his corps command on November 10 and was soon to be tried for his Second Bull Run actions—when Porter crossed part of his corps over the Potomac on September 20. Such an incident, taken in connection with the way in which Lee had wrecked McClellan's campaign on the outskirts of Richmond and had bested Pope two months later, must have made Burnside think much about the dangers which would fill those hours when part of his army was on one side of the river and part on the other, separated by flimsy bridges perhaps within enemy artillery range.

No time was lost in getting reenforcements on the way. Some 15,000 of Heintzelman's Washington troops were marched down the Maryland side of the Potomac to Liverpool Point opposite Aquia Creek, whence they were ferried across and added to the field force. Wisely, Burnside delayed calling in Slocum's Twelfth Corps from the vicinity of Harpers Ferry and Sigel's Eleventh from its position about Centerville, planning instead for them to arrive after he had the rest of the army over the river; this would avoid congestion and allow Ingalls to accumulate supplies—and also help deceive the enemy as to the Federal plans. He was keeping Washington well posted, and he wired Halleck on the 5th, "Will send messenger to-morrow morning with important dispatches, giving plan of operation for the next few days." Haupt was preparing for the rebuilding of the railroad from Fredericksburg toward Richmond; and on the 6th he gave the army commander his plan with regard to railroad iron. Trains still seemed to be running to the vicinity of Fredericksburg, and the railroader was hopeful that the Confederates would not be able to do much damage when they fell back; but he refused to count on good luck. "Although we have probably iron enough, I will order 10 miles more immediately, to make sure." Ingalls on his part was loading up his wagons and preparing to get them over bad roads. He asked for more mules in order to have six animals to a team and not just four; also he wanted more horses for ambulances. Everyone was working; it was a seasoned army going about preparations for a difficult operation in a masterful way. George Bayard, on a scout mission some miles away, reported to Parke, "My rations are out to-morrow, and I have no forage to-night, and the terrible roads have thrown the shoes off a number of my horses." But he was as cheerful as he had been in the hot days of August when he was covering Pope's army, and he added the postscript, "Please reply soon. Am waiting in telegraph office." Such were the last words the brilliant young general of cavalry was to write—so far as the records show. A premature touch of real winter was adding its unpleasantness. On the 7th Lieutenant Commander Samuel Magaw, who had some gunboats below Fredericksburg, reported, "Two nights more like the last may freeze us in." Pleasonton sent word that the Potomac was frozen at Belle Plain. Apparently afraid that Burnside's chief of staff might grow complacent and believe everything was just as it should be, he added, "No hay and very little grain." [17]

Burnside's dispatches contained none of the exaggerated estimates of the enemy's strength which had been so common with McClellan, not only on the Peninsula but in the Antietam campaign. In fact, he said nothing whatever about the size of Lee's army, which he probably put at about its actual figure of some 85,000. He was well posted as to Jackson's approach, for on November 27 Sigel sent word received through scouts that Stonewall had been at White Plains and Salem the day before, both inhabitants and contrabands reporting that he would move to Fredericksburg: "His force left White Plains and Salem, undoubtedly, this morning, either for Warrenton or Waterloo Bridge." On the same day Lee reported to Davis that Jackson was halting at Orange, which was not far from where Sigel reported him. [18] An Associated Press dispatch from Falmouth on the 26th stated that A. P. Hill, D. H. Hill, and Jackson were known to be on the way to join Lee. In accordance with his habit, Stonewall spread false rumors about his activities and destination when he left Winchester, but seemed to fool no one except General Kelley at Cumberland, who on December 4 reported that he was undoubtedly in the Valley.[19] Halleck may not have been certain about Jackson's departure for a few days, but he definitely accepted it by December 4.

VICINITY OF FREDERICKSBURG

Although an extensive road network is shown, most of the roads were unimproved and were often impassable in winter. Extensive planking of the roads by the Federal army was necessary.

Burnside intended to throw his bridges about fourteen miles below Fredericksburg, at Skinker's Neck, whence he would march directly on Guinea, on the railroad to Richmond. This would compel Lee to abandon Fredericksburg quickly and force him to do a good deal of marching over bad roads in order to get into a position covering Richmond. However, preparations for the crossing could not be concealed, carried on as they were in the enemy country, and the Federal commander soon became convinced that Lee had divined his purpose and was preparing to meet him. He was aware of the fact that Jackson's corps was south of Fredericksburg, with a strong detachment at Port Royal. With the resolution of a good general, he made the quick and bold decision to cross at Fredericksburg, directly in Lee's front, believing such a move might be the least anticipated. Henderson gives no support whatever for his assertion that Burnside fell into a trap which had been laid for him when he changed his crossing place. Freeman states that Lee had to hold to Port Royal to prevent a turning movement.[20] Dispersion also made Lee's supply problem easier. But Burnside also planned to continue operations at Skinker's Neck in order to deceive his opponent and induce him to keep his force divided until a favorable position for striking a blow was seized. Maintenance of the deception for a sufficient time was the critical point of the operation. How difficult it was, was shown by the fact that on the 8th Pleasonton picked up a Confederate signal lieutenant in civilian clothes on the "wrong side" of the river. What happened to the officer is not revealed; but the Federal cavalryman was certainly moderate when he stated that Lieutenant Carey was "in an unpleasant position, and one which should be thoroughly investigated." Perhaps the incident was responsible for an order about secrecy which went out the next day.[21]

The change in plans, as well as the fact that some preparations had gone faster than had been thought possible, enabled Burnside to advance his attack to an earlier date than he had suggested as probable in his recent conference with the President and the General in Chief at the White House. That Burnside was keeping pressure on himself as well as others is shown by his record for the early morning of Tuesday December 9; dispatches to Generals Morell (on the upper Potomac) and Slocum at 3:00; to Sigel at 3:45; to Halleck at 4:05; a memorandum order to grand division commanders at 5:00. Perhaps then the army commander rested a little, but not too long, for at 10:15 a dispatch went to Halleck which ended, "Soon after 12 o'clock to-day I will send a messenger to you with definite plan of operations." [22]

The memorandum order—which would now be called a warning order—was excellent. Grand division commanders were to report at headquarters at noon, and in the meantime they were to give the orders necessary to put their commands into the positions previously indicated in verbal orders. It prescribed: "The officers and men should be provided with three days' cooked rations. Forty rounds of ammunition must be carried in cartridge-boxes, and 20 rounds in pockets. The ammunition wagons and batteries will be supplied with at least three days' forage." Brief sentences dealt with army trains, artillery, and cavalry, and there was the assurance that more would be said on these topics at the coming conference.

Burnside was too optimistic in promising to send his full plan soon after noon, for it was not until 11:30 P.M., after what must have been a full day of important decisions, that he wrote the promised dispatch; but he sent it by telegraph instead of courier. The hour was late, and so he addressed it to Halleck's chief of staff; but a copy went to Halleck, identical in all ways except for the omission of the last two words:

All the orders have been issued to the several commanders of grand divisions and heads of departments for an attempt to cross the river on Thursday morning. The plans of the movement are somewhat modified by the movements of the enemy, who have been concentrating in large force opposite the point at which we originally intended to cross. I think now that the enemy will be more surprised by a crossing immediately in our front than in any other part of the river. The commanders of grand divisions coincide with me in this opinion, and I have accordingly ordered the movement, which will enable us to keep the force well concentrated, at the same time covering our communications in the rear. I am convinced that a large force of the enemy is now concentrated in the vicinity of Port Royal, its left resting near Fredericksburg, which we hope to turn. We have an abundance of artillery, and have made very elaborate preparations to protect the crossings. The importance of the movement and the details of the plan seem to be well understood by the grand division commanders, and we hope to succeed.

If the General-in-Chief desires it, I will send a minute statement in cipher to-morrow morning. The movement is so important that I feel anxious to be fortified by his approval. Please answer.[23]

Halleck withheld the approval Burnside wished and deserved; and somewhat peevishly he telegraphed: "I beg of you not to telegraph details of your plans, nor the time of your intended movements. No secret can be kept which passes through so many hands." If he had been the General in Chief that he should have been, he would have been on his way to Aquia Creek within an hour after reading Burnside's dispatch, for there were no operations in other theaters that made his presence in Washington essential.

In the entire operation, nothing of course was more important than the instructions for the throwing of the bridges; and on the 8th C. B. Comstock, chief engineer for the Army of the Potomac though he was only a lieutenant, wrote a memorandum that was a model for adequacy and brevity, and can well bring a smile to anyone who has read the lengthy annexes to some present-day field orders. Here is how he

prepared for getting 100,000 infantry and many batteries over the
river:

Two pontoon bridges to be thrown at site of old pontoon bridge, one of
them to have approaches for artillery.

One pontoon bridge at site of old canal-boat bridge; approaches for
artillery.

Two pontoon bridges just below mouth of Deep Run, a mile below
Fredericksburg; one to have artillery approach. Major Spaulding to throw
three upper ones; Major Magruder to throw the next, and Lieutenant
Cross the lowest one.

Bridge equipage, now at White Oak Church, to move up and go into
park near Phillips' house by dark. At midnight trains to move down within
400 yards of river, and to move down and begin unloading at 2 a.m.

If enemy's fire is kept down, bridges to be thrown as soon as boats are
unloaded; if too hot, wait till artillery silences it.

Upper two bridges to be covered by two regiments of infantry; canal-
boat bridge by one regiment; two lower bridges by two regiments and a
12-pounder battery.

Corduroy at Skinker's Neck to be laid during to-morrow night; woods
to be felled, etc.

As soon as pontoons are on bank of river, all teams to be taken away.[24]

The memorandum is historic; never before had United States Army
engineers planned such an operation. An officer who could think and
write as the lieutenant had done, certainly deserved more than a bar
on his shoulders; and before the end of the war the great General in
Chief who ended it put stars on the shoulders of Cyrus B. Comstock.

Darkness came early and the tedious wait through the long hours
of a cold and cheerless winter night began. At Skinker's Neck sturdy,
skillful axmen of the Fourth Maine were felling trees and building a
corduroy road under the direction of Lieutenant Martin Van Brocklin,
Fiftieth New York Engineers. The sounds of chopping and the fires
would be noted by the Confederates, and might help confirm their
expectation of a lower crossing. In close conformity with Comstock's
orders, the heads of the bridge trains arrived at the river bank about
three o'clock, and the unloading of the boats began.[25] Over the river
there was a coating of ice about half an inch thick, which made bridging more difficult; but by 8:15 Magruder with the Fifteenth New York
Engineers was laying the balks of the last bay of his bridge. Then a
"rebel" picket came out from behind some buildings and after rubbing

the sleep from their eyes ran rapidly forward to inspect the Yankee activities. Evidently they were not only surprised but displeased, for about two companies of infantry soon appeared, deployed, and poured in a volley, wounding six of the engineers. A Federal battery promptly dispersed the Confederates, and Magruder wrote the next day, "Twice afterwards, in much larger numbers, they attempted to rally, but were each time scattered in ludicrous confusion by the accurate fire of the batteries." At nine o'clock Magruder's bridge was ready for the passage of all arms of Franklin's two corps. Lieutenant Cross with a battalion of regular United States Engineers had his bridge in at half past ten with approaches in order at eleven; he too had been somewhat annoyed by enemy skirmishers at nine o'clock, but had dispersed them by the fire of the engineer supports.[26]

Things did not go so easily at Fredericksburg, where Major Spaulding with the Fiftieth New York Engineers was to put in three bridges for the use of Sumner's grand division. The next day, with events still vivid in his mind, he wrote:

At about 6 a.m., when one of the upper bridges and the lower bridge were two-thirds completed, and the other about one-fourth built, the enemy opened a galling fire upon us at the upper bridges, from houses near the shore and from behind walls and fences, killing 1 captain and 2 men, and wounding several others. One bridge had approached so near the south shore that the men at work upon it were within 80 yards of the enemy, who were under cover, while the infantry supporting us on the flanks were at long range, and could do little damage to the enemy. My men were working without arms; had no means of returning the enemy's fire, and were driven from the work.[27]

The time had come for the use of the artillery of which Comstock had spoken. It made no difference that it was George Washington's old town; the houses were sheltering men firing upon soldiers wearing the uniform of the country of which Washington had been both General and first President; the houses would have to go. Batteries were opened and they partially silenced the fire of the enemy. But a fog hanging over the targets made the work of the artillerymen difficult; batteries at a distance could not be safely used, on account of possible damage to the incomplete bridges and to the Federal engineers. Brigadier General Henry J. Hunt, Burnside's able chief of artillery, then detached six 12-pounder batteries—six guns each—from the divisional artillery, and posted four near the upper bridges and two near the middle, and an effort was made to dislodge the Confederates from their covered positions.[28]

But the Federal gunners could neither destroy nor unnerve Barksdale's brigade of resolute Mississippians who had the task of trying to prevent the crossing. As soon as the artillery stopped so that the pontoniers could resume their work, the Southern marksmen opened fire again; and they were safely protected from the rifles of the Federal infantry on the opposite bank. Three weeks later Hunt wrote in his report:

All the batteries that could be brought to bear were now, by order of General Burnside, turned upon the town, and soon rendered it untenable by any considerable body. Again the fire of the enemy's sharpshooters was beaten down by the artillery; the work of throwing the bridges was resumed by men who volunteered for the purpose, but with the same results. A few hundred sharpshooters, scattered among the cellars, in ditches and behind stone walls, drove them from the bridges.

A preview was being given of what happened over and over again in World War I and World War II, and the Federal chief of artillery had to confess the limitation of his guns, a thing no proud artilleryman likes to do. Hunt himself pronounced the verdict; he told Burnside that nothing but infantry in close action could drive the enemy sharpshooters from their positions of immunity; and Burnside ordered that infantry be crossed in boats. Volunteers were called for from the Seventh Michigan and the Eighty-ninth New York. Again Hunt's guns beat down the Southern fire as the boats were loaded; at a signal, the batteries became quiet and the engineer crews started the assault boats across the 400 feet of intervening water as the Federal infantry took up the covering fire. The 220 volunteers lost no time in getting out of their frail assault boats, and soon cleaned the troublesome Mississippians out of their nests, taking from 80 to 100 prisoners.[29] The rest of the two regiments followed in boats, as well as the Nineteenth and Twentieth Massachusetts, and a firm bridgehead was established at the upper bridge as well as the middle bridge, under cover of which the bridges were completed. But it was now 4:30 in the afternoon and a long night was close at hand. Though Burnside could feel relieved when the pontoniers had finished their work, he was much behind his time table.

The two bridges could have been down hours before if infantry had been pushed resolutely across Magruder's bridge as soon as it was finished, and had been moved up the stream to liquidate the resistance at the middle bridge, which was only a mile away at the south edge of Fredericksburg. Then Sumner could have crossed his infantry and mopped up the town so that the upper two bridges could have been laid. The ease with which the 120 Michigan and 100 New York infantry cleared up the situation leaves no doubt as to how promptly Barksdale's relatively small command could have been driven out of the town. Responsibility for not exploiting the great advantage which was open to the Federals after the completion of the first bridge lay squarely on Burnside.

On the 10th Franklin had been directed to cross as soon as his bridges were finished and, if he thought best, to attack without waiting for Sumner.[30] Early the next morning instructions were modified a little, and he was told to move south toward the railroad as soon as he crossed, regulating his movements by circumstances. Instead, however, of carrying out the instructions Franklin merely reported when his bridges were ready, and Burnside then told him not to cross until further orders.[31] Much could be said for not crossing Franklin's entire command, because one of Burnside's chief objects should have been to leave Lee in doubt as to whether he was making a major crossing at Fredericksburg, or merely a threat. But if he had crossed sufficient troops to liquidate the resistance in Fredericksburg and form good bridgeheads and make a sufficient reconnaissance for the two grand divisions to move over under cover of night and take positions from which an attack could be launched early on the 12th, his intentions would still have remained doubtful. Actually, after the upper bridges were in, Burnside directed Franklin at four o'clock to cross his entire command, only to change the order and direct that only about a brigade be crossed to prevent the destruction of the bridges.[32] General W. F. Smith, who was crossing his Sixth Corps when the countermand came, wrote in his report that he was much relieved to receive the change of orders so that he could have daylight of the next day for crossing and taking position. It would unquestionably have been difficult to cross a large command at night and take up proper positions without previous daylight reconnaissance; but if affairs had been better handled it should have been possible for Burnside to have his army in position to attack while Lee was still doubtful as to where the main blow was to be struck, and whether he should call up his absent divisions. Although the operation was behind schedule, optimism must have prevailed at headquarters, for Parke, having in mind the railroad bridge over the Rappahannock, wired Haupt, "Our troops occupy Fredericksburg. The bridge material can now be forwarded as rapidly as possible." [33]

Fog hung over the river again the next morning, but this time it was entirely friendly, for it concealed the crossing of the great army. In perfect order, without hitch or interruption, Sumner's grand division crossed on the two upper and the middle bridges, and Franklin's on those below the town, while—according to Burnside's own account— "General Hooker's grand division was held in readiness to support either the right or left, or to press the enemy in case the other command succeeded in moving him." [34] A line of battle was established as follows: Major General Darius N. Couch's Second Corps of Sumner's command held the right and center of the town; then came Brigadier General Orlando B. Willcox's Ninth Corps, connecting on its left with Major General Smith's Sixth Corps of Franklin's grand division. These three corps held a line roughly parallel with the river. On Smith's left, but drawn back so as to be almost at right angles with his line, was Major General John F. Reynolds's First Corps. There was light infantry contact as the Federals pushed the Confederate skirmishers back; after the fog lifted and the positions of the Union troops were disclosed Lee's artillery did some firing, which Smith described as "feeble and spasmodic." The Federal batteries on Stafford Heights on the left bank of the river were quick in demonstrating their readiness to enter into action, and the enemy sensibly showed little desire to push the preliminary dispute. A correspondent who entered Fredericksburg with the Union army reported that a large number of the houses had been injured by the shelling of the day before, that all the churches showed damage, and that there was some wanton destruction by Northern soldiers.[35] He also revealed that some ardent Unionist had torn a British flag from the residence of the consul, believing it to be the "secesh" emblem; but restitution had been promptly made.

Marching to the support of Burnside's 142,551 officers and men, of whom 116,834 with 312 pieces of artillery were available for combat, were the Eleventh and Twelfth Corps, numbering 33,850 present, and bringing with them 97 guns. The advancing of the day of attack had unfortunately left Sigel and Slocum quite beyond immediate supporting distance. While his army was moving over the bridges Burnside sent a dispatch to Sigel—in temporary command of the two corps—informing him of the river crossing and enjoining him to hurry.[36] But Sigel's own corps was at Fairfax, forty miles away, with streams and indifferent or bad roads intervening, and Slocum was approximately a day's march more distant.

Lee's army occupied a ridge which encircled and looked down upon the Union troops in the plain extending a mile or so back from the river.[37] A convenient bend in the Rappahannock allowed his left to rest nicely upon the stream some three miles above the town, while his right touched the Massaponax a mile and a half above where it flowed into the river three miles below the lower pontoon bridges. Timber covered much of the naturally strong position; batteries had been carefully emplaced, and good cover had been provided for the infantry, which was located directly behind the town along the base of Marye's Hill; in addition a road had been cut along the crest to facilitate communication from one part of the line to another. Lee's strength return of the 10th gave him an aggregate present of 91,760 officers and men, of whom 72,564 were carried as "present for duty"—the equivalent of the Union "present for duty equipped." [38] Though his actual line, as laid down, was nine miles long, only six miles of it could be readily attacked; and he must have had upwards of 60,000 infantry available—about six men per yard. He had a strong line heavily manned; moreover he was satisfied with the condition of his troops, for he had written to Davis on the 6th that his army "was never in better health or in better condition for battle than now," and on the 8th that he believed the reported strength of 220,000 for Burnside's army—the part present before him—was "much magnified." Still any claim that General Lee was eager to be attacked rests only upon unsubstantial evidence; on the day of battle he wrote to Adjutant General Cooper that he wished that his army was double its size—though he could not have supplied such a force—and that any detachments from it would lay Richmond open to General Burnside.[39]

When, early in the afternoon, the lifting fog revealed the unbroken blue columns moving over the bridges and the other masses of troops already in position,[40] Lee should indeed have been again grateful for a Federal blunder. So great a general as he was must have known that if Burnside had made proper use of his bridges and of the short day and the long night that had just preceded it the Union army could have attacked him heavily at daylight on the 12th, while two of Jackson's divisions were still moving up and the other two were quite remote.[41]

Not until he was certain as to Burnside's intentions did he dare call in D. H. Hill from Port Royal, twenty miles away, and Early from Skinker's Neck. Even after Burnside had two bridges in and was laying others, Lee did no more than put D. H. Hill on the alert and instruct him to cook two days' rations. Orders for Hill and Early to march were not sent until the afternoon of the 12th, and both commands had to make night marches.[42] Lee had done remarkably well at Antietam in a situation similar to the one in which he would have been if Burnside had attacked on the 12th; neverthless, it was a great boon to be able to get his entire army in position. Just as McDowell had presented Beauregard and Johnston a day for concentrating their forces at First Bull Run, and as McClellan had given Lee the 16th of September, so now Burnside, playing high cards badly, gave his adversary the 12th of December.

Anxiously, Sumner, Franklin, and Hooker waited through the long night for orders from army headquarters. None came; and the conclusion is inevitable that Burnside was seized with complete indecision as the awful test of battle neared.[43] At 7:45 in the morning Brigadier General James M. Hardie of Burnside's staff arrived at Franklin's headquarters and explained the commanding general's plan; and presently a written order with the signature of General Parke came, showing the hour 5:55.[44] It was a strange order indeed, directing Franklin to hold his "whole command in position for a rapid movement down the old Richmond road," while he sent out at least one division "to seize, if possible, the height near Captain Hamilton's, on this side of the Massaponax, taking care to keep it well supported and its line of retreat open." Burnside seems to have believed the right of Lee's line might be lightly held, thinking perhaps that Jackson's troops had not yet arrived. Later parts of the order did, however, clear things up considerably—and General Hardie must also have been able to make some explanations that should have allowed Franklin to grasp his mission with some definiteness in spite of anything he afterward said. Sumner was being ordered to move a division or more westward from Fredericksburg up the telegraph road for the purpose of seizing a high point on either side of it. The commanding general hoped that the seizure of the heights by Sumner and Franklin would "compel the enemy to evacuate the whole ridge between these points." Franklin was told that two of Hooker's divisions were in his rear at the bridges and would be held there to support him, and that he should keep his "whole command in readiness to move at once, as soon as the fog lifts."

Without delay Franklin gave Reynolds the task of seizing the point on the ridge; and Reynolds ordered Meade to make the attack with his division, promising to support him with Gibbon's division on the right, and cover his left with that of Doubleday. Meade had to change the direction in which his line was facing and take a proper position to make a southwestward attack across the Richmond road as well as the railroad some 500 yards beyond. After he had done this, his command was taken in rear and flank by some Confederate guns posted on the road. More time was consumed in getting his batteries into position to silence the hostile fire; after that the woods in which the Federals expected to find the hostile infantry were shelled for half an hour; then Meade's infantry advanced shortly after noon. In his report the reliable John Reynolds wrote that Meade's troops "successfully carried the wood in front, crossed the railroad, charged up the slope of the hill, and gained the road and edge of the wood, driving the enemy from his strong positions in the ditches and railroad cut, capturing the flags of two regiments and sending about 200 prisoners to the rear." Gibbon in the meantime had been ordered to attack on Meade's right; he too had crossed the railroad, had driven back the first line of the enemy, and had taken prisoners; but in the dense woods he had lost contact with Meade.[45]

Actually the Federal attack broke through a gap between two brigades in the Confederate line and, rolling back the exposed flanks, reached Jackson's second line.[46] But there was not the least chance that the blue regiments could maintain themselves in a position defended by three lines of two ranks each, with D. H. Hill's division in reserve. Brigade after brigade was thrown against the Federals in strong counterattacks, and, heavily outnumbered, the troops of Meade and Gibbon were forced out of the position they had gallantly won and were driven back across the railroad; their well ordered ranks were gone, and confusion gripped them. After them came the men of Jackson, rending the air and offending the ears of the Unionists with what General Early called the "cheering peculiar to the Confederate soldier." [47] Deaf to pleas to re-form, they retired through the ranks of the division of Brigadier General David B. Birney of Hooker's command, which had been put in position to stop the Confederate pursuit.

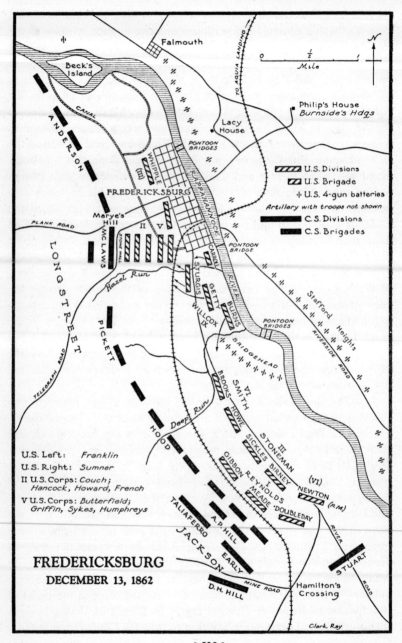

FREDERICKSBURG
DECEMBER 13, 1862

U.S. Left: *Franklin*
U.S. Right: *Sumner*
II U.S. Corps: *Couch;*
  Hancock, Howard, French
V U.S. Corps: *Butterfield;*
  Griffin, Sykes, Humphreys

U.S. Divisions
U.S. Brigade
U.S. 4-gun batteries
Artillery with troops not shown
C.S. Divisions
C.S. Brigades

Having done this, Birney counterattacked and drove the Confederates back to the woods beyond the railroad. Presently he was joined by Hooker's other division under the command of Brigadier General Daniel E. Sickles—belatedly called from across the river—and a firm line was established.

Ambition quickly stirred Stonewall Jackson, after the Federal attack had been broken and the bluecoats had begun to fall back in disorder. It would have delighted him to drive the Yankees back into the cold waters of the Rappahannock and reap some real "fruits of victory," about which he liked to talk; so, as the afternoon wore away, he planned a counterstroke. He saw it would not be easy, and in order to guard against a catastrophe he decided to push out some artillery in front. What happened is best described in his own words: "The first gun had hardly moved forward from the wood 100 yards when the enemy's artillery reopened, and so completely swept our front as to satisfy me that the proposed movement should be abandoned." [48] The "slumbering volcano" was willing to call it a day even though he had had no contact yet with his friends of the Iron Brigade, in Doubleday's division, which had not been engaged.

While Reynolds was fighting hard, Franklin allowed the Sixth Corps of General Smith to remain practically idle. In about one sentence Smith disposed of the activities of his 25,000 men who had forty rounds of ammunition in their cartridge boxes and twenty more in their pockets: "On Saturday we were subjected to severe artillery practice, and our skirmishers were hotly engaged, but we silenced the fire of the enemy, and our skirmish line was retained at its advanced position." [49] The vagueness in Burnside's original order is not an adequate excuse for Franklin's actions. General Hardie remained at his headquarters throughout the day, sending telegraphic reports to Burnside, and it would have been a simple matter for Franklin to ask some questions of Burnside; but he appears not to have done so. In the early morning order he had been told to be ready to move at once with his whole force as soon as the fog lifted, and had been informed that Burnside was beginning to attack at points distant from each other, on account of the fog and the danger of troops colliding. The Sixth Corps was deployed for battle, so that there was only one way in which it could move—toward the enemy. There is also strong evidence that Franklin received from one of Burnside's aides an order to attack with his entire force before noon, and there is conclusive evidence that such instructions were delivered to him by another aide early in the afternoon.[50] At 2:40 he revealed some irresolution in a message to Burnside:

My left has been very badly handled. All of my troops are in action at that point, and the result is so doubtful that any movement to my front is impossible at present. I have Stoneman's two divisions [Birney's and Sickles's] in action, and Burns' is the only division in reserve.* The truth is, my left is in danger of being turned. What hope is there of getting re-enforcements across the river? [51]

Apparently it did not occur to Franklin that the way to get pressure off his left corps was to attack with his inactive right corps, which was the largest in the entire army. Because this corps did nothing, Hood's and Pickett's divisions of Longstreet's corps were able to assist Jackson in breaking the attack which Reynolds made on him.[52] Franklin was in command of 60,000 men; but of his eight divisions—not counting Burns—only three were offensively engaged, those of Meade, Gibbon, and Birney. Meade's casualties alone exceeded those of all the other divisions together, except Gibbon's.[53] Franklin's actions on December 13 followed the pattern of his inadequate operations on September 14 and 15, when McClellan had told him to use all the "intellect and the utmost activity that a general can exercise."

At six o'clock in the morning an order over Parke's signature went to Sumner, directing him to prepare to push a division out of Fredericksburg by the plank and telegraph roads for the purpose of seizing the heights behind the town; but the attack was held back in the hope or expectation that Franklin's attack would quickly achieve results. Behind the town was a broken plain some 600 yards wide; then came the stone wall made famous by the battle, bordering a sunken road that ran around the base of the sharp ascent known as Marye's Hill. Halfway between the town and the road was a canal or ditch some thirty feet wide and six feet deep, which was a formidable obstacle, since attacking troops could cross it only in column at the bridges—forgotten by the Confederates or left standing as a trap—where they would be exposed to a murderous fire of artillery and infantry. There is evidence that Burnside was informed about the ditch

* The division of Brigadier General W. W. Burns belonged to the Ninth Corps of Willcox, and Franklin had authority to call upon it if necessary. Presently he did summon it to his sector, without using it.

the day before;[54] but he apparently rejected its existence, perhaps because he had learned nothing about it while in Fredericksburg during August, though one would have thought his experience in crossing the Antietam bridge would have made him sensitive to such a danger.

By eleven o'clock Burnside saw that the attack on the right could not be postponed longer in the hope of a favorable development by Franklin on his left, and the assault upon the naturally strong and heavily defended heights was ordered. Brigade after brigade of Couch's Second Corps was thrown forward; the waves of attack went forward with the greatest gallantry, but they were cut to pieces by well emplaced Confederate guns and the rifles and the muskets of McLaws's division of Longstreet's corps which was holding the sunken road and was well protected by the stone wall. Broken and driven back, some of the attacking regiments were able to find a certain amount of shelter behind little crests that intervened between canal and road. On Couch's left, Willcox threw Sturgis's division of his Ninth Corps into the attack. Carroll's little brigade of Whipple's division of Stoneman's corps—though it mustered only 600 rifles—magnificently carried a point on the crest; stubbornly it held on against repeated counterattacks, maintaining its position throughout the night and the next day. Leading two regiments that had been at Port Republic and two new ones, Carroll, though still a colonel, again showed himself worthy of a star.[55]

About two o'clock Butterfield's corps of Hooker's grand division was thrown into the assault, but the stone wall and the sunken road could not be reached. Of the many brave assaults that were made, that of Humphreys, commanding the third division of two brigades of Pennsylvania troops in heavy action for the first time, was perhaps the most outstanding. Seeing the complete protection that the enemy had against rifle fire, Humphreys rode along his lines and told his men not to fire since it was useless; nothing but the bayonet would do. Then his lines swept forward across the ranks of prostrate men who had made the previous efforts, and who now both by word and force sought to stop the regiments of Humphreys and threw them in part from line into column. Humphreys wrote: "The fire of the enemy's musketry and artillery, furious as it was before, now became still hotter. The stone wall was a sheet of flame, that enveloped the head and flanks of the column. Officers and men were falling rapidly, and the head of the column was at length brought to a stand when close up to the wall. Up to this time not a shot had been fired by the column, but now some firing began. It lasted but a minute, when, in spite of all our efforts, the column turned and began to retire slowly." Humphreys himself was again on foot, his second horse having been killed: only one officer remained mounted—the son of the dauntless division commander.[56]

At six o'clock a signal officer from an observation station on the Phillips house reported, "The fighting is about over for to-night; only an occasional gun is heard." Thirty minutes later Butterfield sent Hooker a careful account of the situation in his corps. The postscript, "What orders for the night or the morning?" was certainly that of a steady commander, unshaken by the heavy repulse of the afternoon. Presently he wrote again and stated that all agreed it would be very difficult to carry the crest in front; but, significantly, he said, "Sturgis thinks if Franklin has pressed them hard on the left, they will evacuate." The battlefield was in the grip of able soldiers—as Stonewall learned so quickly when he became ambitious and started to advance some guns. Burnside visited lower headquarters, and at 4:00 A.M. of the 14th he reported briefly to both Lincoln and Halleck: "I have just returned from the field. Our troops are all over the river. We hold the first ridge outside the town, and 3 miles below. We hope to carry the crest to-day. Our loss is heavy—say 5,000." As a preliminary report it was good enough, and it seems to indicate that Burnside had regained a grip on himself.[57]

Morning brought another fog which quickly melted before the sun. Although during the night troops had been moved up close to the enemy on the right, so that attacks could be launched more advantageously than on the day before, orders to assault previously given were countermanded.[58] The day passed uneventfully except for angry skirmish fire and annoying artillery exchanges; the Federals were readjusting their lines in order better to repel a counterattack in case Lee should risk one. Another night passed; and another day of comparative quiet, with a truce in the afternoon for the burial of the dead and for the removal of wounded not yet brought off. During the night of the 15th–16th the army was withdrawn across the river, in an operation perhaps unexcelled in military history for smooth staff work and good troop leading.

On the 14th a correspondent had contemplated with grave forebodings the possibility of a retirement. After stating that it was impossible to renew the battle, he wrote:

> To continue in the position now held cannot be thought of. An attempt to retreat to this side of the river by the precarious means of passage over a few frail bridges would undoubtedly bring the victorious hosts of the enemy at once to the attack, and might result in the worst calamity of the war. How the army is to be extricated from these predicaments I am unable to devise. I trust that those entrusted with its fortunes have the ability to do it.[59]

It was indeed no easy thing to do, with so short a time for preparation; but the army staff and subordinate commanders were equal to the emergency. In perfect order and with the utmost precision, the infantry, the artillery, the wagons, and the ambulances with the wounded went back over the six bridges then in place. At 6:20 A.M. an aide-de-camp reported to Burnside that the pickets were being called in. The engineers took up the bridges without interference or loss, and a signal officer reported with justifiable pride that he did not lose a foot of wire.[60]

Lee, Longstreet, and Jackson could hardly believe their eyes when they observed the deserted plain where the evening before a vast army had been drawn up in line of battle.[61] With their surprise there was mingled much chagrin that Burnside had been able to carry on his delicate operation without even the engineers being fired on while they were taking in their bridges. In order to explain the embarrassing escape some writers have said that during the night, in addition to the rain, there was a strong wind from the south which unhappily blew all sounds of the Federal departure from Confederate ears. Evidently D. H. Hill had not been apprised of the wind when he wrote in his report of December 24 that in no other battle had God interposed so signally for the Confederates; [62] he would hardly have made that statement if he had thought that the "infernal Yankees"—as he called them—had escaped with whole skins because of a kind wind blowing toward the north. Perhaps the industrious digging of trenches by the Federals which Lee observed on the 15th led him to sleep with so much confidence that even the hard wind did not awake him.

Desolation greeted the Confederates upon their reentry into Fredericksburg; and some of the damage had been caused by their own guns, for Longstreet had opened fire upon the town while awaiting the assaults upon his position, adding to the devastation caused by the Federal bombardment—an action which made Northern headlines.[63]

Foreseeing the possibility of withdrawing, Burnside had sent an aide to Washington who telegraphed at 9:15 P.M. of the 15th:

Saw General Halleck about 6 o'clock. He decidedly disapproved of recrossing the river. I inferred that he favored your plan of operations. He asked whether you did not think it advisable to make some use of the spade. Said he would telegraph you to-night.

The General in Chief was as good as his word, and Burnside received this dispatch:

I have seen your aide, Major Goddard. You will be fully sustained in any measures you may adopt in regard to unreliable officers. In regard to movement we cannot judge here; you are the best judge. Anything you want will be supplied as soon as possible. General Dix will assist by diversions. We have every confidence in your judgment and ultimate success.[64]

It was a message calculated to raise the spirits and sustain the confidence of a field commander; but Burnside's decision had been made before its receipt. At 4:00 A.M. of the 16th he wired briefly, "I have thought it necessary to withdraw the army to this side of the river, and the movement has progressed satisfactorily thus far." The President must have been disappointed, though he had probably passed no judgment when he directed Halleck to wire, "The President desires that you report the reasons for your withdrawal as soon as possible." Burnside replied that the army was withdrawn because he felt that the position in front of him could not be carried, and that it was a military necessity either to attack or to retire; the army had recrossed the river at night without the knowledge of the enemy and without loss of either property or men—significant facts certainly for the President to know. Already a staff officer was on the way to Washington to make a full report of the situation. On the next day, the 17th, a long dispatch from Burnside made the plan of his operations look quite plausible, and laid his failure upon the fact that the enemy had an extra twenty-four hours for concentrating his forces, due to the delay in getting in the bridges. It left entirely open the question whether he had maintained for a sufficiently long time energetic deceptive measures at Skinker's Neck, or could have crossed his army on the night of the

12th by proper management. He said, "The fact that I decided to move from Warrenton onto this line rather against the opinion of the President, Secretary, and yourself, and that you have left the whole management in my hands, without giving orders, makes me the more responsible." Critics of the administration were to charge that this sentence was suggested, if not dictated, in order to clear superiors of any responsibility for the new Northern failure. In his final report Burnside emphatically denied the charge, saying with regard to his first report, "It was written at my headquarters, without consultation with any person outside of my own personal staff, and is correct in all particulars." [65]

On the 22nd Lincoln addressed this communication to the Army of the Potomac:

I have just read your commanding general's report of the battle of Fredericksburg. Although you were not successful, the attempt was not an error, nor the failure other than accident. The courage with which you, in an open field, maintained the contest against an intrenched foe, and the consummate skill and success with which you crossed and recrossed the river, in the face of the enemy, show that you possess all the qualities of a great army, which will yet give victory to the cause of the country and of popular government.

Condoling with the mourners for the dead, and sympathizing with the severely wounded, I congratulate you that the number of both is comparatively so small.

I tender to you, officers and soldiers, the thanks of the nation.[66]

Achievements of which Lincoln was unaware can be added. From the admirable report of Brigadier General Henry J. Hunt, chief of artillery,[67] it seems probable that in no battle ever fought had artillery been handled more skillfully. In communications—always of primary importance and always difficult—the performance of December 13 seems to have been of a high order both in the telegraph and in flag signals.

On the subject of losses Lincoln said all that could be said, and he put the best face possible on the recent battle. Actually there were many fewer killed in one day's fighting at Fredericksburg than at Antietam—1,284 as against 2,108—although total casualties were about the same. But the loss inflicted upon the enemy in December was comparably much less, and the Confederates rightfully regarded it as a cheaply won victory, for their casualties in the September battle had been as grievous as those of the Union army, in spite of the fact that the latter had done the attacking. Among the Federal officers killed, none was so irreplaceable as the excellent George Bayard, who was struck by a shell while at Franklin's headquarters. Burnside's assaults on Marye's Hill have always been regarded as utterly futile; and within a few days the Committee on the Conduct of the War journeyed down the Potomac to investigate the battle, a very unfortunate procedure indeed.

The withdrawal of the entire army across the river looks very different in the light of later war experience than it did then; not only subsequent operations in the Civil War but the beachheads of Normandy, Anzio, and more especially Salerno, where American divisions were contained for so many days, come to mind. Already Sigel's division was at hand, and Slocum's was not far away. In fact, when Burnside returned to his old positions Sigel was found occupying part of the former camping ground of Butterfield's corps, which had been appropriated in the natural expectation that the Army of the Potomac was over the river to stay.[68] There would have been no point to having the two new corps cross at Fredericksburg for the purpose of hurling fresh brigades against the intrenched Confederates on Marye's Hill. But why not have sent the 33,000 men down the river for a crossing, or a threat of crossing, in the vicinity of Port Royal? This would have agreed not only with Burnside's previous intentions—but the thought of the President that an operation against Lee's communications was desirable—and Lee's supply was indeed precarious. There may not have been sufficient pontoons for another bridge at the moment, but there were six bridges at Fredericksburg and fewer would have sufficed for the supply of the army after it was in position. A smaller bridgehead could have been held if necessary, or Fredericksburg alone could have been retained and made impregnable. The canal or mill race to the west of the town, and Hazel Run and Deep Run to the south, were excellent defensive terrain features and could have been strengthened quickly by intrenchments and protected batteries. Although the Confederate guns had fired into the city it is not likely that Lee would have proceeded to reduce the houses to rubble, for his original purpose had not been to hold Fredericksburg but to retire to the North Anna River, a position which Jackson is said to have favored; and houses would have made good billets for the Federals.

Burnside's efforts at deception at Skinker's Neck had been most inadequate. How much might have been done is shown by General Eisenhower's success in May, June, and July of 1944 in keeping the German Fifteenth Army ineffective in the Pas-de-Calais region through threats of another crossing there, while the Allied force in Normandy was built up and bridges over the Seine and other means of communication were wrecked so that that army could not come to the help of the German Seventh Army. The deception was accomplished largely through shipping and troop concentrations. The same means were open to Burnside; a Potomac flotilla had previously made threats at Port Royal, but there is no evidence that it did anything to supplement the noise of the felling of trees on the night of the 10th. Burnside still had some good cards in reserve, and he would have had an additional very high one when he became master of Fredericksburg and its immediate vicinity. It is inconceivable that a resolute commander with dependable subordinates, or a general well grounded in modern doctrine, would have voluntarily given up such an advantage when two fresh corps became available, and other forces could carry on operations that would assist him. Had Burnside no more than held on to the city he had won, he would in all probability have been spared the visitation of the Congressional investigating committee. This would have been a boon indeed.

Just what Halleck had in mind that General Dix, who was in command of the Department of Virginia with headquarters at Fort Monroe, might do with the forces under him, cannot be said. His reference to using the spade, and to operations by Dix, showed that his mind was running in the right direction; but he certainly should not have contented himself with telegraphing and assuring Burnside's aide that the government would support the field commander. He should have made all haste to go to Fredericksburg, and should have been there not later than the 14th. It was a time when a good General in Chief could have done a great deal; but the bookish Halleck, who protested so much that he disliked Washington, elected to remain there instead of doing what duty indicated.

Burnside had not been back long in his old camps when he made plans to cross the river again, below the city. The day after Christmas his men were ordered to cook three days' rations; supplies for ten days were loaded, and the army was held in readiness to move on twelve hours' notice. Already the cavalry had started when he received from Lincoln the brief dispatch: "I have good reason for saying that you must not make a general movement without first letting me know of it." Orders were countermanded and the general went to Washington. There he learned that two of his subordinates, whose names were not divulged to him, had called upon the President and had made gloomy predictions about the operation that was about to begin.[69]

Burnside had indeed been caught in the middle, between his superiors and his subordinates, by surrendering his bridgehead in Fredericksburg. On the 26th Halleck telegraphed him that Kelley reported large forces of the enemy reappearing about Strasburg and Front Royal, and that it was probable that the Confederates would "take advantage of the inactivity of the Army of the Potomac to make another raid on Harpers Ferry." He found it all very disheartening, and added, "I am almost at a loss what to say or do." [70]

Matters were coming to a crisis, and the first day of the new year saw some frank writing. In the morning Burnside had an interview with the President, and later in the day he wrote in a letter that he thought it was his duty to place on paper the remarks he had made.[71] No copy of the letter was found in Lincoln's papers; but a later letter makes clear that he had offered it to the President and had himself pocketed it on seeing that he did not care to have a written record of the observations. Very candidly Burnside said that the differences of views between himself and his higher officers probably came from their lack of confidence in him. He not only suggested that it might be advisable for him to be replaced by another officer, but he wrote, "It is my belief that I ought to retire to private life." The letter had a tone of great sincerity, and no touch of bitterness toward his generals or toward the Secretary of War and the General in Chief—neither of whom, it stated, had the confidence of officers and soldiers, or of the country. As to public opinion, Burnside quickly added, the President was better informed than he himself; and it is to be noted that he did not say explicitly that Stanton and Halleck, or either of them, should be removed.[72] He probably realized fully the difficulty of selecting successors.

On the same day Lincoln wrote a brief note to Halleck stating that Burnside wished to cross the Rappahannock again, but his grand division commanders were all in opposition. Therein lay the problem; and the President said bluntly, "If in such a difficulty as this you do not help, you fail me precisely in the point for which I sought your assistance." But that was not all; the President asked him to visit the army, look at the situation, and talk with the commanders, gathering all the elements for a judgment of his own, and then tell General Burnside that he approved or did not approve his plan. He concluded, "Your military skill is useless to me if you will not do this." Halleck did not like the directive—in which Lincoln told him little more than what was his duty as General in Chief—and Lincoln indorsed the retained copy of the note, "Withdrawn, because considered harsh by General Halleck." Though perhaps not moved in the desired direction, Halleck was nevertheless moved, and wrote a letter to Stanton asking to be relieved of the duties of General in Chief. This communication also was withdrawn.[73]

Though the strange New Year's notes had peculiar fates, they and the incidental conversations cleared the air for the principal actors. They could not influence critical subordinates in the army, the investigating committee, or the public waiting for a report as to guilt and innocence in the recent reverse—a report which should not have been given to it just at that moment, however much it might be in order later. Burnside returned to his command and wrote to the President on January 5 that he was more than ever convinced that his general officers were almost unanimously opposed to another river crossing, but that he was still of the opinion that it should be attempted. He said he had already given orders to the engineers and artillery to prepare for it but, in order to avoid any embarrassment to the President, he enclosed his resignation. To the General in Chief the same messenger took a note that gave Burnside's decision, described the continued opposition of his subordinates to his plan, and mentioned his letter to the President. He explained, "I send this resignation because I have no other plan of campaign for this winter, and I am not disposed to go into winter quarters." After stating that the movement was being made entirely upon his own responsibility, Burnside said to Halleck, "and I do not ask you to assume any responsibility in reference to the mode or place of crossing, but it seems to me that, in making so hazardous a movement, I should receive some general directions from you as to the advisability of crossing at some point, as you are necessarily well informed of the effect at this time upon other parts of the army of a success or a repulse." Withholding nothing from his superior, he continued, "It may be well to add that recent information goes to show that the enemy's force has not been diminished in our front to any great extent." [74]

In making his decision Burnside may have been at least encouraged by a letter from Quartermaster General Meigs on December 30:

There are few men who are capable of taking the responsibility of bringing on such a great conflict as a battle between such armies as oppose each other at Fredericksburg. So long as you consult your principal officers together, the result will be that proverbial of councils of war. . . . Every day weakens your army; every good day lost is a golden opportunity in the career of our country—lost forever. . . . Exhaustion steals over the country. Confidence and hope are dying. . . . The gallantry of the attack at Fredericksburg made amends for its ill success, and soldiers were not discouraged by it. The people, when they understood it, took heart again. But the slumber of the army since is eating into the vitals of the nation. As day after day has gone, my heart has sunk, and I see greater peril to our nationality in the present condition of affairs than I have seen at any time during the struggle.[75]

Was Meigs slyly telling him that some of his subordinates were, in the last analysis, not soldiers? The quartermaster general had not himself had experience of field command; but he understood clearly the problem of the lonely man at the head of a great army and laid bare, in one penetrating sentence, why good commanding generals are rare. Though he may have exaggerated the extent of popular reappraisal of the recent battle, he was not the man to speak without some foundation, especially when he overstepped a little the bounds of his normal functions as he did now in writing to Burnside. The state of the "public mind" is often not easy to gauge, especially in a nation where one half is in bitter armed conflict with the other and where strong elements and groups in each half bitterly oppose the respective administrations.

Although the General in Chief would not visit the army, he wrote to Burnside on the 7th at length and in a forthright manner, definitely encouraging a further operation in spite of the season. He said, "But the chances are still in our favor to meet and defeat the enemy on the Rappahannock, if we can effect a crossing in a position where we can meet the enemy on favorable or even equal terms. I therefore still advise a movement against him." He saw many reasons why a crossing should be attempted at some point, and rejected the thought of going into winter quarters even more decidedly than Burnside: "It will not do to keep your large army inactive." He accepted—perhaps grate-fully—Burnside's view as to their respective responsibilities, and asserted, "As you yourself admit, it devolves on you to decide upon the time, place, and character of the crossing which you may attempt. I can only advise that an attempt be made, and as early as possible." [76]

A copy of Halleck's letter went to the President, who, to make certain that there would not be the slightest doubt as to his wishes and views in the entire vexatious matter, added an indorsement that re-sembles a separate communication:

I understand General Halleck has sent you a letter of which this is a copy. I approve this letter. I deplore the want of concurrence with you in opinion by your general officers, but I do not see the remedy. Be cautious, and do not understand that the Government or country is driving you. I do not yet see how I could profit by changing the command of the Army of the Potomac, and if I did, I should not wish to do it by accepting the resignation of your commission.[77]

Not often can the head of a state write thus to a general. Although Lincoln had not found the general he needed, he at least had one to whom he could speak as man to man without offending or being mis-understood. Burnside received a clear indication that the administra-tion did not want inaction if an operation were at all possible, but in a way that assured him there would be no reproaches if in his judgment the season or other circumstances caused him to decide against it; no one was driving him.

Meigs had suggested a move up the Rappahannock, a crossing of the stream, and a march toward a point on Lee's communications with Richmond. In accordance with some such idea the army moved on January 20; but even as the columns took up the march, heavy rain commenced to fall. Presently the roads became impossible and streams well-nigh impassable; two days later the army was ordered back to its camps, and the famous "mud march"—so called in the Official Records—was at an end.[78] One cannot say whether Burnside showed persistence or some unreasoning stubbornness in his efforts to drive the army on; but its performance proved both its great efficiency and its reliability under great difficulties, in spite of disaffection and many recent desertions.[79] Over twenty years later a writer stated that the army returned to its camps "desperately humiliated"—an extreme description, which has, however, been frequently accepted.[80] As important higher officers had no confidence in the operation—of which Lee seemed well informed—they probably for once looked upon rain and mud as a considerate act of Providence; [81] and the soldiers were very likely content to be back in the comparative comfort of their huts, where their efforts to amuse themselves with the assistance of the sutlers and welfare agencies would be interrupted by nothing worse than picket duty, patrolling, and some drilling.[82]

At 8:50 P.M. on the 23rd, while the army was struggling back to its camps through the mud, Burnside telegraphed to the President: "I have prepared some very important orders, and I want to see you before issuing them. Can I see you alone if I am at the White House after midnight? I must be back by 8 o'clock to-morrow morning." When the general arrived after several hours of delay he laid before the President an order that cashiered from the service Hooker and three other general officers, and relieved five officers of duty with the army, including Generals Smith and Franklin.[83]

It requires twelve lines of print to set forth Burnside's bill of particulars against Hooker, who was charged with having been unjustly and unnecessarily critical not only of his superior officers, but also "of the authorities," and of having in general created distrust on the part of those who associated with him. Summing up, Burnside declared Hooker to be "a man unfit to hold an important commission during a crisis like the present, when so much patience, charity, confidence, consideration, and patriotism are due from every soldier in the field." Two commanders of divisions and one commander of a brigade were to be dismissed, among them the officers who had gone to the President on December 29 (Burnside had of course been able to determine their identity because they had been on leave.) The officers who were to be merely relieved were pronounced as being of no further service to the Army of the Potomac.

Burnside did not have authority to dismiss an officer from the army without a trial. The President did, as part of the very broad authority to "purge" the rolls that Congress had given him in July with the request that he use it.[84] And he had used it, for under its provisions no fewer than 131 officers were dismissed in 1862, including Major John J. Key, an aide-de-camp of McClellan, who was cashiered for "uttering disloyal sentiments." [85] There was no restriction as to the rank of the officer to whom the authority of summary dismissal without trial could be applied; and it could be employed even in the case of an officer who held a commission in the regular army, as Hooker did. (He was a brigadier general in the regular army and a major general of volunteers.) Broader power could hardly have been given to the President, for he could dismiss "any officer for any cause which, in his judgment, either renders such officer unsuitable for, or whose dismission would promote, the public service."

Lincoln, however, could not delegate his unlimited authority, and Burnside certainly presumed much when he issued his order, even though it stated that, in the case of the dismissals, the order was "issued subject to the approval of the President of the United States." He knew that Lincoln, although suspicious of the conduct of Porter toward General Pope, had allowed him to be tried by a court, Burnside himself having forwarded to Washington several strange dispatches he had received from that officer. Burnside also knew that Lincoln took no pleasure in arbitrary power, and he could have expected that the use of the authority recently given him would diminish.[86] Not only was Burnside proceeding in a wrong manner, but he was violating a sharp War Department order of September 30, 1862, when he relieved officers and directed them to report to the adjutant general in Washington. That order terminated such a practice and stipulated that officers who had committed offenses should be tried and officers who were incompetent should be brought before boards or commissions; any offending or incompetent officer sent to Washington without previous sanction would be returned, and his commander would himself be regarded as having disobeyed an order.

It is possible that Burnside would never have brought the inept order to the President if an earlier clear call for assistance had received an answer. On the morning of the 22nd he had telegraphed to the General in Chief: "I am very anxious to see you. Can you come down, or shall I come up for an hour?" [87] There was nothing that Halleck could do about the rain and the mud Burnside's columns were fighting, and it is hard to believe that he wanted to discuss anything except his other and worse affliction—refractory and dissenting officers. Halleck knew perfectly well that the army was in motion, and that there were hard decisions as to operations for its commander; and he should have wanted Burnside to be at his headquarters until the venture that had started two days before was completed. But he would no more visit the Army of the Potomac on its commander's plea than he would on the President's request; and without delay he passed all responsibility back to Burnside in the brief message: "You must judge for yourself as to the propriety of your coming up. I see no objections. Please answer whether you will come, and when." [88]

Just what Halleck would have said to his subordinate if he had met the full responsibility of his high position by taking a boat for Aquia Landing, must of course be a matter of conjecture. The following May, in the course of an epistolary wrangle with General Franklin he related to that officer how the President had informed him that Burnside had submitted an order dismissing some officers "for endeavoring to create dissatisfaction and insubordination in his army." He continued, "I said immediately that if such was the case the commander in the field ought to be sustained." Strangely enough Halleck still did not know the names of the officers "charged with so high a military offense." He stated, "I have never seen that order," and added, "Moreover, I have been told by good authority that the pretended order published in the newspapers is very different from the order shown the President." [89] He would doubtless have felt that Burnside had some real and great grievances, especially since his own impression of Hooker from contact with him in California was not very favorable; he also would have realized that Hooker's superior could not continue in command without some drastic action. But it is difficult to believe that he would have failed to recommend or insist upon proper procedure and would have indorsed the issuance of a dismissal order by army headquarters, even though it was subject to the President's approval. Dismissal would have had to be by an order from the War Department, beginning with the weighty words, "By direction of the President," and not by Lincoln's writing "Approved" upon an army order ending "By command of Maj. Gen. A. E. Burnside." When commanders issue orders that they do not have the competency to give, confusion or worse is likely to follow.

The crisis precipitated by Burnside's action was dissolved in a War Department order of the 25th,[90] stating that the President had directed that General Burnside be relieved from the command of the Army of the Potomac upon his own request; that General Sumner be relieved, also upon his own request; and that General Franklin be relieved.[91] Then the order gave command of the army to "Maj. Gen. J. Hooker." Instead of hoisting Fighting Joe, bag and baggage, completely out of the army, Burnside had boosted him into his own position.

CHAPTER XVII

JOE HOOKER GETS THE ARMY AND A NOTE

And now beware of rashness. Beware of rashness, but with
energy and sleepless vigilance, go forward and give us victories.
Lincoln to Hooker

THAT an officer who had been described by his commander as so "guilty of unjust and unnecessary criticisms of the actions of his superiors, and of the authorities" that he was not fit to hold a commission during a crisis "when so much patience, charity, confidence, consideration, and patriotism are due from every soldier in the field," should be given the place of the general who had made the charge, is nothing short of remarkable, and stands in need of explanation, if indeed explanation is possible. A person's thought, at first, is that the charge itself must have been unfair and false. But such was not the case. Joe Hooker was guilty of everything that had been said by Burnside, who, in accordance with his habit, had spoken moderately. All this the President knew, and, before he read Burnside's order, he also knew that he himself was among those described by Hooker as grossly incompetent and unfit for the positions they held. Nor did he need to rely on the reports of others—on "taletelling," as some would have it—to know the habits of the colorful general. In his first interview— and perhaps his only interview up to that time with Hooker—the President had had an example of the general's propensity to belittle others and magnify himself.

Like Halleck, McClellan, Burnside, Grant, Sherman, and many others, Hooker had left the regular army, and had settled in California.[1] After failing at farming he had received a political plum as superintendent of military roads in Oregon. He foresaw the war and entered the militia of California—which Halleck commanded with the rank of brigadier general; and presently became a colonel. When the conflict came his assets were not enough for the trip East to offer his services; and his traveling expenses, including provision for some "luxuries" en route, were defrayed by friends. In Washington he was not warmly received in spite of the fact that trained officers were in demand: he had been critical of General Scott in the Mexican War, and the old General had neither forgotten nor forgiven. Scott's ideas of discipline and subordination probably gave him confidence that the army could get along without Hooker even in an emergency. After the unhappy battle of Bull Run—which he had gone to see along with other civilians—Hooker called on Lincoln and informed him: "I was at Bull Run the other day, Mr. President, and it is no vanity in me to say that I am a damned sight better general than any you, Sir, had on that field."[2] As a result of this bit of frank speech Hooker presently had a commission as brigadier general of volunteers; and within a year he had given evidence that there was much truth in what he had told the President. After the action at Oak Grove before Richmond, Heintzelman reported officially of Hooker, "Than him there is not a braver man in this army or one more worthy of promotion." Pope commended him strongly to Halleck, and McClellan wrote him a very generous letter about his fine troop leading at Antietam.[3]

The public belief in Hooker's ability was stimulated by the sobriquet Fighting Joe, which he did not like, and which was the result of an error by a typesetter and the fancy of a proofreader.[4] Many persons believed that he would eventually be in command of the Army of the Potomac,[5] and Nicolay and Hay probably put the matter well when they wrote, "There is no doubt that public opinion pointed rather to Hooker than to any one else,"[6] if a change of commanders was to be made. That all sober opinion did not, however, regard Hooker as the long looked-for general was proved by an editorial, "Have We a General Among Us?" in *Harper's Weekly,* which reviewed the accomplishments of eight generals without mentioning Hooker.[7] The editor may have had a successor for Halleck in mind, although he did not say that the General in Chief should be at once replaced; but at least he did not see in Hooker anything at this date which made him especially notable.

Burnside's dispatch at 8:50 on the night of the 23rd saying that he

had an important order to submit had a touch of urgency, for in it
the general stated that he wished to see the President alone after
midnight and must be back with his command at eight o'clock in the
morning.[8] A miscarriage in transportation arrangements kept Burnside from reaching Washington until six o'clock. By nine he had seen
the President and was at breakfast with Henry J. Raymond of the *New
York Times,* who had made the trip from army headquarters, and
revealed to Raymond that his order had struck Lincoln like a clap of
thunder.[9] It is not hard to believe, for, though the President had heard
plenty of severe criticism of Hooker, he was hardly prepared to see
written in black and white by the mild-mannered Ambrose Burnside
that Fighting Joe was unfit even to stay in the army. The general gave
him the alternative of approving the order or accepting his resignation. Thus the President had a new crisis close on the heels of the
cabinet crisis that had been precipitated when a Senate committee
brought him the resolution asking for the reorganization of the cabinet—that is, for Seward's dismissal from office as Secretary of State.[10]
By his calmness and insight in handling this emergency Lincoln had
strengthened his position, retaining advisers who were indeed quarrelsome and combative, but in whose abilities to manage their departments he firmly believed. What now could he do in the case of Burnside versus Hooker, while the general was on the way back to his
army with instructions to return the next day for the verdict?

The issuance of Burnside's order could not be considered for a
moment, on account of public opinion; and to continue him in command was equally out of the question. The only real question was the
appointment of a new commander. Here too the decision was not long
in the making, for Gideon Welles recorded January 24: "There is a
change of commander of the Army of the Potomac. Burnside relinquishes to Hooker." [11] On the manner of the decision, Nicolay and
Hay believed that Lincoln took counsel of no one after the matter had
come to an issue but acted on his own responsibility, just as he had
done when he restored McClellan to command after Second Bull Run
in spite of great lack of faith.[12] Welles's comment in his diary suggests
that there had not been anything like a cabinet meeting to consider
the question; and Halleck wrote a few weeks later to General Franklin: "The removal of General Burnside and appointment of General
Hooker was the sole act of the President. My advice was not asked
at all in the matter and I gave no opinion whatever." The General in
Chief was in a position to know something about what had occurred,

for he was summoned to meet with the President and Burnside at 10:00 A.M. on the 25th.[13] Presumably the meeting was chiefly to communicate Lincoln's decision and arrange details incidental to the transfer; but the utter candor of Lincoln makes it likely that Halleck took from the meeting a good basis for his later statement. In spite of the statements of the secretaries and Halleck, and the entry in Welles's diary, some writers—on the basis of little that can be called evidence—assert that the cabinet was definitely consulted on a successor for Burnside.[14] It can be assumed that Lincoln foresaw what their reception of the news would be—Chase would be pleased, Welles doubtful, and Stanton displeased; but the possession of such knowledge was a different thing from asking the advice of the cabinet on Hooker after the issue had actually arisen.

Though public opinion probably had great influence Lincoln had one strong military reason for selecting Hooker, in spite of the belief of some writers that either Reynolds, who probably would have declined,[15] or Meade would have been a better choice. If Burnside were to go, military custom indicated that his successor should be sought from his grand-division commanders, if some tested army commander were not transferred from another theater. Sumner of course was out of consideration, and, strangely enough, the two remaining grand-division commanders, Franklin and Hooker, though originally selections by Burnside, were indicted by him at the same time, Franklin being marked, however, with the lesser guilt. To what extent Lincoln heeded the fact that Hooker considerably outranked Meade—who was only a division commander—in type of command and in date of commission to a major generalcy, cannot be said; but one may be sure that he was not unconscious of it, though historians have been.[16] In taking Hooker instead of Meade he passed no one by; but in taking Meade he would have been very definitely passing over Hooker and would have been dipping down even below proven corps commanders. How attached soldiers are to their order of precedence perhaps cannot be appreciated by a person who has not seen evidence of it; but Lincoln had seen it, and had commented bitterly on military jealousy not many months before. In choosing between two soldiers for elevation, it may appear unfortunate to have to consider which will be the more loyal subordinate of the other; but exactly that must sometimes be done. By well established military canon, Hooker would have had a grievance if Meade had received the command—unless the President wished to take Burnside's charge as disqualifying him. Immediate decision was necessary, and so those charges had to be accepted in full or ignored completely. Before long Meade was to have command of the army, and the record he made was such as to make one say that it was a case of "six of the one and half a dozen of the other"— except in certain personal characteristics. This would be true if they had had equal military status on the day when Lincoln had to choose— as it were—an apple from a barrel where the bottom was in view.

When Burnside was informed that Hooker was to be elevated instead of debased, he was not resentful, and was induced to withdraw his resignation from the Army, with the intention of resuming command of his old Ninth Corps after a leave of absence. In the orders incident to the change of command he referred to Hooker as brave and skillful and asked the army to give him "full and cordial support and co-operation." Hooker did not go quite so far in amenities but, apparently unable to find anything in his predecessor to commend, contented himself with extending "most cordial good wishes for his future." [17] The public was well disposed toward Hooker, and received his accession to command with approval or acclaim; on his part, Burnside was rewarded by some hearty acknowledgments of his soldierly qualities that showed a real discrimination in the writers.[18]

Lincoln's part was, however, not ended when he had given the directions embodied in the War Department order of the 25th. He made an effort to point out to the new commander faults that stood in the way of his success, and that might imperil the country. Before Hooker issued his order assuming command he heard from Halleck, "The President directs me to say that he wishes an interview with you at the Executive Mansion as early as possible." [19] Whether he stood with any humility before the heavily burdened man to whom he had once blustered, cannot be said; but Fighting Joe's greatest claim for distinction is that he was the inspiration for one of Lincoln's master-pieces of writing. From the interview he carried away this letter:

Executive Mansion,
Washington, D.C., January 26, 1863

Major-General Hooker:
General:

I have placed you at the head of the Army of the Potomac. Of course I have done this upon what appears to me to be sufficient reasons, and yet I think it best for you to know that there are some things in regard to which I am not quite satisfied with you. I believe you to be a brave and skillful soldier, which, of course, I like. I also believe you do not mix politics with your profession, in which you are right. You have confidence in yourself, which is a valuable, if not an indispensable, quality. You are ambitious, which, within reasonable bounds, does good rather than harm; but I think that during General Burnside's command of the army you have taken counsel of your ambition, and thwarted him as much as you could, in which you did a great wrong to the country and to a most meritorious and honorable brother officer. I have heard, in such a way as to believe it, of your recently saying that both the Army and the Government needed a dictator. Of course, it was not for this, but in spite of it, that I have given you the command. Only those generals who gain successes can set up dictators. What I now ask of you is military success, and I will risk the dictatorship. The Government will support you to the utmost of its ability, which is neither more nor less than it has done and will do for all commanders. I much fear that the spirit which you have aided to infuse into the army, of criticising their commander and withholding confidence from him, will now turn upon you. I shall assist you as far as I can to put it down. Neither you nor Napoleon, if he were alive again, could get any good out of an army while such a spirit prevails in it. And now beware of rashness. Beware of rashness, but with energy and sleepless vigilance go forward and give us victories.

Yours, very truly,

A. Lincoln [20]

Not until 1879, a week after the death of provocative Joseph Hooker, were the American people to have the chance to read the letter that rivals the one Lincoln wrote to Mrs. Bixby.[21] There is evidence that Hooker was much affected by the manner in which Lincoln had written to him, and that he remarked, "He talks to me like a father." [22] More important than the question whether Hooker actually pronounced such words is the question whether he ever realized that he had never yet shown that he was fit to be the commander of an army. He knew he would never be frightened in the midst of personal danger, and that was good; but he had no way to tell how steady he would be when he bore the awful responsibilities of a commanding general, and had to make quick and grave decisions in the face of uncertainties. Such a doubt about their new commander must have come to his subordinates, who knew full well that his ostentatious confidence, which often manifested itself in extravagant statements, had little resemblance to the quiet sureness of a great general.

MAJOR GENERAL JOSEPH HOOKER

The army that Hooker took over was in a depressed state, though there has been considerable exaggeration about its low morale. Desertions had increased; but, for all that, the number of absentees cannot be used to sustain a charge of low morale without admitting that Burnside had taken over from McClellan an army in poor spirits, for the number of absentees on January 20, 1863, was actually smaller than it had been on November 10, 1862, having dropped from 88,823 to 86,636.[23] Nor were the complaints and criticisms of the soldiers necessarily an indication that the army lacked battle effectiveness— which is what counts. The hardships and requirements of which soldiers complain one week may be the very things of which they boast and brag the next.[24] "The history of a soldier's wound beguiles the pain of it," wrote Laurence Sterne.[25] Lee certainly learned that the dissatisfaction in the Federal army he had reported to Jackson in November was of no real significance; for never did soldiers attack more bravely than the Union forces at Fredericksburg. The smooth retreat of the army on the night of December 15 answers the question as to its efficiency on that day. There is not the slightest reason to believe that the Army of the Potomac would not also have moved out well to execute the moves that were planned to begin after Christmas—whether they were wise or foolish—had the order not been canceled. The ill-fated "mud march" demonstrated that the army was a machine that responded to orders under difficult conditions; its fighting edge was probably as good as its marching ability. One correspondent had reported on December 24: "The general tone of the army is good, far better than could be expected. There is regard for our failures, sympathy for our wounded, mourning for our honored dead; but I find little discouragement and no demoralization." It may have been the balanced judgment of an observer who saw below superficial indications. A striking evidence of good morale came a few weeks later when the Eleventh New Jersey Infantry vigorously denounced a resolution of the legislature of New Jersey that favored peace.[26]

When the temper of the army is considered it must be remembered that the men had not been paid for a number of months—six months, according to Bigelow—and that Burnside cited this fact in his report as responsible for much disaffection both in the ranks and in the families of soldiers.[27] Certainly many of the appearances of discontent would have vanished if the magical influence of pay day had been felt.

This cause was soon to disappear, for early in January a bill was introduced to raise money to pay the men in service, and before long a loan of $100,000,000 had been authorized by Congress and signed at once by Lincoln.[28] Presently the paymasters would come with bulging satchels, and there would be money to buy the "abominable gingerbread and shameless pie," [29] that the sutlers sold, or to send home to dependents who were in sore need—or to use in sundry ways that resourceful soldiers can discover.

What the people thought was determined not merely by what happened at Fredericksburg, but by the war as a whole. From west of the Mississippi good news had come in early December. Three divisions of the "Army of the Frontier" under Brigadier Generals J. G. Blunt and F. J. Herron, after some magnificent marching to effect a concentration, defeated on the 7th a Confederate force under Brigadier General J. S. Marmaduke at Prairie Grove in northwestern Arkansas. The victory not only gave security to Missouri—except for annoying raids—but opened the way for the conquest of Arkansas, no mean matter. The great "rebel" bastion at Vicksburg, however, still stood defiant against Federal approaches, and on the 28th and 29th the right wing of Grant's Army of the Tennessee, under the command of Sherman, met a severe repulse at Chickasaw Bayou. Against a position stronger naturally even than Marye's Hill, assaults of great bravery were made. Losses were heavy, and nothing at all was gained. But before the news of this reverse had time to add too much to the disappointment felt over Fredericksburg, word of another battle in the West began to arrive, much bloodier, but more cheering in its final outcome.

On December 30 General Rosecrans at the head of the Army of the Cumberland (Buell's old Army of the Ohio), marching from Nashville, came up to Bragg's position at Murfreesboro, which was protected by Stone River. The attack that Rosecrans planned to deliver the next morning was anticipated by a heavy offensive on the part of the Confederate commander; and the Union forces after heavy losses were forced back, and disaster was near. Under good generalship by Rosecrans the troops fought hard; especially against the division of young Philip Sheridan attack after attack broke. With all his brigade commanders killed, Sheridan displayed qualities which proved him to be one of the really great leaders of men in battle. Lincoln's secretaries put it thus, "The death of their commanders did not shake the constancy of his brigades who still obeyed Sheridan's orders as if on parade." [30] The Federal army seemed defeated, and Bragg sent messages of victory to his government. But when morning came the Federals were still there, and they were there again the next morning, apparently waiting to be finished off—which Bragg, however, did not attempt. Then on January 2, in the rain, Rosecrans moved his left across Stone River, precipitating another engagement, and that night Bragg retired to Tullahoma, Tennessee, leaving the final victory with the stanch Union general.

The lists of the killed at Murfreesboro that the people of the West were to read in their papers were greater than those at Fredericksburg—1,677 in contrast to 1,284—and the Army of the Cumberland had numbered only 43,000.[31] In one short winter day Rosecrans had lost as many as McClellan had lost in a week of battles in front of Richmond—with an army over twice the size of that which fought on Stone River. But the sacrifice of life in Tennessee was obviously not in vain. More important even than this, the battle had given some lessons in the way that victories are won. Although no one may have been led to change his ideas as to the futility of the assaults on Marye's Hill, it could not have escaped notice that Rosecrans succeeded in getting all his army into the battle, while at Fredericksburg a considerable part of the Army of the Potomac had—as on previous occasions —merely been spectators.

Thus the turn of the year saw a change in the over-all situation of the Federals, which well illustrated the truth of a sentence that General Meade would a few months later put in a letter to his wife, "War is uncertain in its results, and often when affairs look the most desperate they suddenly assume a more hopeful state." Still there were many people who were discouraged and many who were criticizing the administration.[32]

The first day of the new year brought the Proclamation of Emancipation that had been promised on September 22. It was by no means universally approved in the North, and many soldiers as well as civilians were disgruntled because of it. Presently, however, news came of great meetings in England where it had been generously applauded, helping to offset the word of a loan of $15,000,000 to the Confederacy.[33] But just as the way an army marches and fights is more important than the way the more vociferous of the soldiers talk, public acts that show how a country is supporting a war are more significant than the varied comments of newspapers on successes or failures in battle, or on proclamations by the President. In 1860 it had been very hard indeed for Buchanan's Secretary of the Treasury to borrow the modest sum needed for the ordinary expenses of the government, even at 12 per cent interest. After appropriate new laws were passed Secretary Chase was borrowing the great sums needed for the war at 6 per cent. Nicolay and Hay note: "At the beginning the Secretary was forced to rely more upon individual patriotism than upon public confidence; but long before the war ended he had hundreds of millions at his command." [34] Never in history had there been anything more remarkable than the increase of the credit of the United States as the war progressed, in spite of repeated and severe military defeats in the East. On Wall Street a panic resulting from the fall in the value of gold from 173 to 149 in two days ruined many speculators,[35] but proved that the people had a basic faith in the financial operations of Secretary Chase. When Europeans became doubtful about the future of the United States and offered American securities for sale, they found people in this country who were eager to purchase them.[36] The administration was not promising an early end of the war, for Chase submitted his estimates in December, 1862, with the request for $900,000,000 in order to carry on the war to the end of June, 1864. Eighteen more months of war! That surely was grim enough! "I expect to maintain this contest until successful, or until . . ." had been Lincoln's word to the governors six months before. The resolution was still there, and people close to Lincoln were conscious of it every day and every hour.

The determination of the country was shown in another tangible way. Hardly had Congress provided for paying the soldiers and sailors their long overdue wages, when it began work on a draft law. The volunteer system was clearly inadequate to keep up a steady flow of replacements for the great army of 918,191 men in service on the first day of the year,[37] and the timid draft of men in the militia attempted in the preceding August had been ineffective. Thoughtful persons had come to see that the only course was to adopt a procedure resembling that already in effect in the South, revolutionary though it might be. The opposition party in Congress contested the measure, asserting it to be unconstitutional, in spite of the fact that power "to raise and support armies" was specifically given in the Constitution. Passed after warm debate with some amendments, the draft law promptly received the President's signature on March 3.

Two provisions of the law now seem very strange. A man who was called was permitted to furnish a substitute, or he could escape service by paying $300. It was of course urged that the poor man was penalized in favor of the well-to-do; but the money clause was really in favor of the poor, and was necessary in order to offset some of the evil of the substitute provision. Evidently the "ceiling" on substitutes was $300, and a man who was willing to serve for another upon a consideration, could find no "takers" unless he offered himself for something less than the figure that would buy exemption. Already there were "bounty-jumpers"—men who would enlist because of the bounty paid, desert, and reenlist in a new community and receive another bounty. To this disgraceful group now were added those who would sell themselves as substitutes as often as they could contrive. Most revolting of all, perhaps, were the brokers for substitutes who made a livelihood out of the weakness of the law without exposing themselves to danger. But there was one redeeming feature in the bad provisions of the act. From the money that men paid to escape the army, the government largely defrayed the cost of the draft and recruiting, so those important services did not increase the mounting national debt—a consideration not without merit. Few men were to be actually drafted into service under the new law; but it was a great spur to volunteer enlistment, and the enrolling and drafting officials—under the able direction of Colonel James B. Fry, field soldier and administrator—were also effective in arresting and returning to their regiments no fewer than 76,526 deserters.[38]

With money provided to pay the men in service, the public credit improving, a conscription law upon the books, and the Military Committee of the House instructed to report on legislation to insure that the utmost skill and attention be given to sick and wounded soldiers,[39] Congress could well turn to another delicate but important question—foreign intervention. Although a year had passed without the foreign recognition that Southern statesmen had confidently expected, the possibility still existed. Sympathy for the Confederacy had been clearly expressed by leading members of the British cabinet and the influential London *Times* had irked people in the North, to put it mildly. Offers of foreign powers to mediate between the North and the South had been declined, but a new threat arose later in 1862 through the landing in Mexico of a French force. Though the occupation had made little progress by the turn of the year, the situation was full of disturbing possibilities, and in March, 1863, concurrent resolutions were reported by Senator Charles Sumner of the Committee on Foreign Affairs. Plainly it was stated that further efforts at intervention by foreign powers would be regarded as "an unfriendly act." With only five dissenting votes the resolution was approved.[40] The ambassadors in Washington could also report to their governments that upon the same day the Senate had asked the President to appoint a day of "national fasting and prayer." It was not that the senators were bumptious men: they were men of contrite spirit. That too was something to be remembered in London and in Paris.

Tuesday March 3, 1863, was indeed a memorable day. Lincoln wrote his signature to the Conscription Law. The senators revealed themselves to be humble before God, but unafraid to tell foreign countries in polite, plain words that the great war in the United States was a domestic issue. This done, they proceeded to pass a bill for the admission of Nevada as a state, and another bill that gave a territorial government to Idaho. Though the Union armies had not done much, the Congress had, and when March came many Northerners were talking less gloomily, and the President was not being advised so vociferously to drop Stanton and Halleck.[41]

The winter months also saw a return of McClellan's name to the papers. His recall to command was never entertained by Lincoln, but the thoughts that Little Mac already had about the Presidency were being capitalized by others. He was a figure to whom opponents of Lincoln's policies turned as a leader, and he became the mouthpiece for men who asserted they were supporting the government but not the administration. After calling attention to the fact that he had never spoken unkindly of McClellan, and after quoting some statements that the general had made while he was before Richmond, the editor of *Harper's Weekly* stated:

Is McClellan the only man in the country who does not know that the men who surround him, and use his name to paralyze the Government, repudiate those sentiments, and are willing to buy temporary peace with eternal dishonor?

Trading upon his military name and popularity they hope to make him President and use him as their tool. Has he asked himself at what price, and for what purpose? [42]

Many persons who were in opposition to the President found in the Emancipation Proclamation as finally promulgated a distasteful provision not foreshadowed in the announcement of the preceding September. After recommending that former slaves "labor faithfully for reasonable wages" when possible, the President concluded:

And I further declare and make known that such persons of suitable condition will be received into the armed service of the United States to garrison forts, positions, stations, and other places, and to man vessels of all sorts in said service.

An inescapable problem was being acknowledged and faced. For months Federal military commanders in the South had had the responsibility and the task of dealing with large groups of Negroes who came into their camps. Though different in many particulars, the problem was at least as vexatious as that of handling "liberated peoples" in World War II, and some historians have not had sufficient imagination to comprehend the difficulties that beset a Union commander in the field; but perhaps recent events will give a more balanced judgment on the tangled questions that confronted Lincoln and his generals. Forming colored regiments was a natural solution of part of the problem, but Lincoln had proceeded cautiously in the entire matter, with the result that he was criticized bitterly by the extreme radical as well as the extreme conservative. Against his initial and somewhat cautious step, Jefferson Davis unloosed his choicest rhetoric in his message to the Confederate Congress on January 12: "Our own detestation of those who have attempted the most execrable measure recorded in the history of guilty man is tempered by profound contempt for the impotent rage it discloses." [43] In the "raging" business, "Jeff" did not look exactly like a novice.

But it was not just the North and its President that were proving vexatious to Davis. When Washington's birthday came around he must have recalled the many disputes he had had with Southern leaders in the twelve months since he had advanced from his position as mere Provisional President to that of constitutional executive, delivering his inaugural address before a great crowd that tried to look happy as it sought to protect itself from a cold and persistent rain, by umbrellas, oilcloth, pieces of canvas or old carpet.[44] At that time it had been said that half of the people in the newly launched country condemned his policies openly; among the most outspoken was Wigfall, skillful dueler, prime mover for secession, and sword-flashing aide to Beauregard at Fort Sumter, who had broken with Davis soon after the Battle of Bull

Run. Not long after his inauguration Davis had had to face the problem of the possible secession of one of the states of the Confederacy,
for a convention held in North Carolina revealed the deep disaffection
in that state, which continued to give trouble throughout the years of
war. But in spite of many internal difficulties there had been great
achievements, and presently there came the very cheering news from
London of the $15,000,000 loan. Gorgas must have reflected the
optimism of the top-level Richmond minds when he wrote confidently
in his diary, "It is undoubtedly the forerunner of recognition." [45] The
mere fact of the loan would have been encouraging; but the Confederacy's skillful ordnance chief noted further that, although the loan
had been subscribed at 90, it had immediately risen to 5 per cent
premium—a happy omen indeed.

Hooker's written orders as a grand-division commander had shown
him to be a careful administrator with a mind for details. Without
delay he set to work to reorganize his command and to improve its
spirit and discipline. On the very day he started his task a second
heavy storm broke, which continued for three days, and left the
ground covered with six inches of snow,[46] removing all doubt that it
was well to lay aside thoughts of major operations. But Hooker was
not ordered to become inactive, or to go officially into winter quarters;
on the 31st of January Halleck sent him a copy of the directive that he
had sent to Burnside on January 7, advising a movement against the
enemy, though he indicated that everything would depend upon circumstances "which may change every day and almost every hour." [47]
In the severity of the weather there was a measure of fortune for the
new commander, for he could go about his reorganization without
being teased or fretted with the thought that he should be after the
enemy.

The new chief of staff for the army was General Butterfield, late
commander of the Fifth Corps. Butterfield while colonel of the Twelfth
New York Militia, had come to Washington almost before the sound
of Sumter's guns died away. Offering his services in any capacity, he
had soon found himself in the habiliments of a sergeant drilling distinguished citizens in the Clay Guard.[48] After some troops arrived in
the city he returned to New York, filled up his regiment, and brought
it forward for active duty. His rise was rapid, and his service distinguished. The postscript "What orders for the night and morning" to

his note to Hooker written at 6:30 P.M. December 13, from a position in front of the stone wall at Marye's Hill where so many of his men had fallen, is a sufficient indication of his military character. Temporarily Hooker continued the grand-division arrangement with Couch, Meade, and Smith at the head of the right, center, and left grand divisions, respectively; Sigel was given the grand reserve division consisting of his own Eleventh Corps and Slocum's Twelfth. On February 2 Halleck ordered the Ninth Corps to report to General Dix at Fort Monroe, with General Smith in temporary command at Hooker's request.[49] Thus was the new army commander relieved of the corps whose officers and troops were especially attached to Burnside, as well as one of the generals named with himself in the famous order that was never issued—although he no doubt thought the order was completely wrong about Hooker, he seems to have believed it *might* be correct about Smith. On February 1 the grand divisions were disbanded, the army returning to a corps organization,[50] the order for the change alleging that the grand-division organization impeded rather than facilitated administration and was adverse to the service that would be required— but distrust of the way Meade and Couch felt toward him may have had something to do with Hooker's action. The new commanders were: First Corps, Reynolds; Second, Couch; Third, Sickles (tem- porarily); Fifth, Meade; Sixth, Sedgwick; Eleventh, Sigel; Twelfth, Slocum. The cavalry was consolidated into a single corps under Stoneman. While the change made in the mounted arm was definitely for the better, the disbandment of the grand-division organization was a step in the wrong direction, though Halleck commended Hooker for both.[51] Seven infantry and one cavalry corps are too much for any commanding general to handle directly in tactical situations; and temporary groupings such as Hooker found it necessary to resort to are not satisfactory. Within a few days touchy Franz Sigel, who was Hooker's senior, peevish because his corps was not the largest in the army,[52] asked to be relieved. While Hooker was in Washington he had stated that he did not wish to be bothered with the command of the troops in that place, and on February 2 the Department of Washington was re-created, the troops in the department being consolidated into the Twenty-second Army Corps, under the command of General Heintzelman.[53]

Hooker attacked the problem of morale by leaves of absences, by improving rations and meals, by instituting insignia for corps and division, and by drills and instruction. Leaves and furloughs might seem superfluous in any army where so many were able to be away without them, and Lincoln was disturbed at first by the idea;[54] but the general understood soldiers, and was in no way lax. While he recognized the soldier's natural desire to visit home and wanted to reward faithful service and men with good records, he tightened up on unauthorized absences. To Washington there went a list of 85,123 absent officers and men, with information about them and the request that proper authorities try to have them returned to their commands. In order to make desertion more difficult, Hooker ordered the express company not to bring into camp packages containing clothing, or intoxicating liquors [55]—here he could have been accused of partiality, for excessive use of stimulants was an accepted charge against him. The wearing of an insigne that revealed by its shape and color the corps and division a man belonged to [56]—a development of the "Kearny patch" that had given a touch of distinction to that general's division—was to prove effective in creating organizational pride and esprit. It did even more; by identifying a straggler or misbehaving soldier, it made the work of the provost-marshal easier.

The cold of February and the foot of snow that had fallen near the end of the month were finally gone,[57] and a little of the sternness of war was also moderated with the approach of spring. On March 10 Lincoln promised complete forgiveness to all absentees who would return by the first of April, and at the end of the month only 51,762 men were away from their commands—though how these should be classified cannot be said.[58] When the absentees came back they unquestionably found soldiers with improved spirit and more money in their pockets. Still some things were no better than they should have been. Charles Francis Adams, Jr., then a captain, recalled later:

During the winter (1862–63), when Hooker was in command, I can say from personal knowledge and experience, the headquarters of the Army of the Potomac was a place to which no self-respecting man liked to go, and no decent woman could go. It was a combination of bar-room and brothel.[59]

With March, too, there came an innovation in the army that was less happy.[60] Hooker decided to introduce pack mules so as to reduce the amount of wagon transportation. To move a given load, pack mules take much more road space—in case they are obliging enough to stay on the road. They cannot be rested merely by stopping, but must be unpacked; in woods they scrape off their loads against the trees; and if packers are not skillful, many of the mules have sore backs. Neither Meigs nor Halleck could have thought much of the idea; but anything that the commander of the Army of the Potomac believed might help was cheerfully done. On March 19 Hooker had his 2,000 pack saddles,[61] and a lot of his soldiers had a new plaything and the chance to learn something more about the disposition of a mule. They had also to acquire a new vocabulary and learn new inflections of the voice: one does not admonish a straying pack mule in the same way he addresses the team of a wagon that is stuck in the mud.

Not only was the War Department willing to give almost everything to Hooker that he might wish, but Stanton, in spite of regretting Hooker's appointment, was as ready with commendation and encouragement as he had been for Little Mac. On March 17 Brigadier General W. W. Averell led his division of 3,000 cavalry and six guns in an engagement with Fitzhugh Lee's brigade of Stuart's cavalry in the vicinity of Kelly's Ford. It was a notable action, for it was the first purely cavalry battle east of the Mississippi in which more than small forces were engaged on each side. There were good reasons for satisfaction with some of the fighting, even though Averell failed to accomplish the mission of routing or destroying "the cavalry forces of the enemy reported to be in the vicinity of Culpeper Court-House." [62] The Confederates thought that they had come off the winner in the clash, but felt their victory dearly paid for by the death of young Major John Pelham, a very attractive and admired officer as well as an excellent artilleryman. Stanton was more than pleased with the first news that reached him and he telegraphed to Hooker on the 19th:

I congratulate you upon the success of General Averell's expedition. It is good for the first lick. You have drawn the first blood, and I hope now soon to see "the boys up and at them." Give my compliments and thanks to Averell and his command.[63]

It must have been a busy day for the Secretary, for the dispatch carried the hour 9:45 P.M. Perhaps someone had gone away from his office feeling that he was harsh and abrupt, but his army commander had tangible evidence that vigorous action would be applauded and good generals commended.

In early April Lincoln passed a week with the Army of the Potomac, enjoying a vacation from the political cares that beat constantly upon him in the White House, though his mind was somewhat preoccupied with operations then being mounted at Charleston, which it was hoped would result in the reduction of Fort Sumter. Noah Brooks, one of the close friends in the small presidential party, recorded an anecdote at the expense of Seward, whom Lincoln had resolutely defended only a few weeks before. The President was riding over a rough road in an ambulance drawn by six mules when the driver—in order to be natural both with his distinguished passenger and with his team—gave vent to some profanity. Lincoln asked him if he were an Episcopalian, and the surprised teamster replied in the negative, adding that he was a Methodist. This drew from the President the comment, "Well, I thought you must be an Episcopalian, because you swear just like Governor Seward, who is a churchwarden." Many visits were made by Lincoln to the hospitals, and the soldiers were deeply touched by his friendliness and naturalness. Throughout the camps they were eager to see him, and his appearance brought forth cheers of warmth and affection.

Before the Commander in Chief there passed in review several corps of the great Army of the Potomac—including the large cavalry corps—splendidly equipped. The appearance and fine marching of the many regiments must have stirred a man so conscious of his grave responsibility, who had himself soldiered a little and felt the cares of a captain while in the Black Hawk War. The army showed the results of the drilling that had been going on, as well as Hooker's thorough overhauling of the Inspector General's department. But if the new commander told the President that, in addition to drilling, there had been advanced instruction such as he mentioned later to the Congressional Committee, it was unwarranted exaggeration.[64] The easy confidence that Fighting Joe revealed in manner and word upset the President, who cautioned him and Couch, the next in rank, "I want to impress upon you two gentlemen—in your next fight, put in all your men." [65] The ambulance driver had at once taken Lincoln's hint and tried to handle his team without oaths; but Hooker was to pay no heed when the great opportunity came.

For a man who had spent his early years as Lincoln had, an April week in the woods and about campfires was the best of tonics; but he went back up the Potomac on the 10th with conflicting thoughts. In Washington, according to Brooks, he learned about the heavy repulse

Du Pont's squadron had received at Charleston—intimations of which had been thoughtfully released by Confederate pickets to their Union opposites. The next day Hooker ended a dispatch that he sent to the President by Butterfield: "We have no news from over the river to-day, the enemy refusing to let us have the newspapers. I sincerely trust that you reached home safely and in good time yesterday. We all look back to your visit with great satisfaction." [66] The "Rebels" had suddenly become very exasperating and very unaccommodating with their news!

A few days before Lincoln came to visit him, Hooker had received a letter from Halleck intimating that it was time to use the army that he had been polishing up for two months: dispatches from Dix, Foster (in North Carolina), and Hunter (near Charleston), as well as from the West, indicated that some of Lee's army had been scattered for the purpose of supply, as well as for operations elsewhere; and conflicts both in the South and in the West might presently attract the enemy's attention to such points.[67]

The information about the enemy merely supplemented or confirmed what Hooker already knew, for he had been gathering intelligence as usual from deserters, contrabands, and citizens, and had been watching his lines both with signal corps telescopes and with Lowe's balloon. He knew that Lee had made detachments of three divisions from Longstreet's corps, though at the end of February he had placed them wrongly in a dispatch to Washington.[68] Actually Ransom's division was in North Carolina, while Pickett's and Hood's—under Longstreet's personal command—were in front of Suffolk, Virginia. The corps commander, while he kept his eye on a Federal advance from Suffolk, was literally "bringing in the bacon" by using army wagons to gather up the rather abundant provisions that were in the country.[69] In the Fredericksburg position, Lee had only Jackson's corps of four divisions, and Anderson's and McLaws's divisions of Longstreet's command, together with Stuart's cavalry division—depleted by the hard winter—and Pendleton's reserve artillery. His 77,000 men were less than half of Hooker's great army of 163,000; [70] but they were ample to hold strongly the defensive line that had been greatly strengthened by elaborate trenches during the winter.

In addition to the sound reason of acting in consort with other Federal forces, Hooker had good reason for not delaying: he had a number of two-year and nine-month regiments that would be going

home within a few weeks. Lincoln had little more than returned to
Washington, when Hooker started to put into effect a plan that he had
guarded in his own mind even from his staff, although revealing it to
Haupt, who would have to rebuild the railroad from Falmouth toward
Richmond. On April 11 Stoneman's cavalry corps was alerted for
marching on Monday the 13th; and on the 12th a very discursive
letter went to that commander over the signature of Hooker's adjutant general, with the theme sentence, "Let your watchword be,
fight, fight, fight, bearing in mind that time is as valuable to the general as the rebel carcasses." [71] The gist of this rather unmilitary directive was that Stoneman should cross the Rappahannock above the
Orange and Alexandria Railroad crossing, get in Lee's rear, operate
against his communications and resources, and inflict all possible
damage on his marching columns. "If you can not cut off from his
columns large slices, the general desires that you will not fail to take
small ones." Assurance was given that Stuart could not bring more
than 5,000 sabers against his 11,000. Hooker evidently assumed that
Lee would quickly have to give up Fredericksburg; but Stoneman was
enjoined, "Keep them from Richmond, and, sooner or later, they
must fall in our hands." How this was to be accomplished, Fighting
Joe did not reveal.

The cavalry got away as ordered, six days' rations and five days'
short forage (grain only) in the column, supported by a train of 275
wagons with three days more of rations and grain sent by Ingalls to
Bealeton. For nine days men and mounts could eat well while they cut
slices—large and small—from Lee's columns; and, by missing an
occasional day as soldiers are constantly doing, or by taking possession of enemy supplies, they might outlast the Confederates—so perhaps thought Fighting Joe. But before the river could be crossed the
skies opened as they had done upon Burnside in late January; and
rains continued except for short intervals, for upward of two weeks.
In front of the impassable stream the operation of necessity stopped,
while Hooker devised a modified campaign—perhaps during the visit
from Lincoln, Stanton, and Halleck.[72] No one, however, was told what
he intended to do. Major General John J. Peck, commanding at
Suffolk, after quite an interchange of messages with him relative to
Longstreet's activities, asked to be informed in cipher of his own
plans. Hooker replied on the 26th:

Your dispatch received. I have been delayed in my operations by the
severe storm. I have communicated to no one what my intentions are.

If you were here, I could properly and willingly impart them to you. So much is found out by the enemy in my front with regard to movements, that I have concealed my designs from my own staff, and I dare not intrust them to the wires, knowing as I do that they are so often tapped.[73]

Matters were bad indeed if the army commander could not risk discussing his intended operation even with select members of his staff. Were leaks in information worse than they had been when he took over from Burnside? On that occasion he had had definite and striking proof that Lee remained ignorant of the change in command for several days, in spite of the fraternization of pickets and the desertions, many of which must have been directly to the enemy.[74] In early February Hooker had himself taken steps to stop the flow of information across the lower Rappahannock;[75] but he evidently distrusted his line of pickets. Before the plan locked so carefully in his mind is explained, it is necessary to look more carefully at the terrain, which played a great part in plans for the operation he was trying to mount, and in his conduct after battle in all its wild fury burst upon him.

About two and a half miles above Fredericksburg the bluffs on each side of the Rappahannock close in, rising some 150 feet above the water, with the hills on the right dominating those on the left. In general the slopes were well covered with trees, were very steep, and were cut deeply by ravines. Terrain suitable for approaching the river on both sides was found first at Banks's Ford, five miles above the town. Here the hills on the right bank were high enough to dominate much of the left of Lee's lines and thus constituted a very valuable feature, for if Hooker could gain control of them and put some of his plentiful guns in battery there Lee's position would be badly compromised. The ford had, however, been the object of much attention by the enemy, and Lee's provoking soldiers had been in position there to jeer and taunt the Federals the last week in January, when they reached the opposite bank in heavy rain. Yet Woodbury reported that he had every prospect of laying three bridges if it had not rained, and Hunt described the overwhelming artillery support he would have provided if his guns had not stuck in the mud.[76] Much digging of trenches had been done by the Confederates in the vicinity of Banks's Ford since the storm that had turned Burnside back; and Wilcox's brigade of Anderson's division, with artillery support, held the position quite securely.

Above Banks's Ford the next practicable approach to the stream was about seven miles away at United States Ford, where the river was just as unfordable at this season of the year. This possible crossing point—which Burnside had planned to use along with the other— was also securely held by the Confederates. From the Federal side discouraging intrenchments could be seen, and Mahone's and Posey's brigades of Anderson's divisions camped not far away ready to man them. A mile and a half above the United States Ford the Rapidan takes off; above the junction both rivers were less serious obstacles, and prepared defenses were not likely to be encountered, although the Rapidan lay entirely within the territory held by the Confederates.

Ten miles west of Fredericksburg was Chancellorsville, where the road reunited after dividing about halfway between the two places. It was just a single large house with a cluster of small buildings, near the eastern border of the woods that soon became known as the Wilderness. From Chancellorsville roads ran to United States Ford, to Ely's and Germanna fords over the Rapidan, and to other places. The road from Fredericksburg continued on to Orange Court House, and was almost as vital a communication line for Lee as the roads south toward Richmond.

Hooker's plan was to march three corps rapidly up the Rappahannock under cover of his cavalry, cross them at Kelly's Ford—six miles above the junction of the Rappahannock and the Rapidan—then move them with dispatch upon Germanna Ford and Ely's Ford, where they would cross the Rapidan. Moving then toward Lee's rear, they would uncover United States and Banks's fords. In order to distract Lee's attention and keep him uncertain as to where the chief Union blow would fall, a demonstration with three corps would be made below Fredericksburg near where Franklin had crossed in December, the threat involving at least the crossing of some troops and the formation of bridgeheads. As soon as the United States and Banks's fords were opened by the forced withdrawal of the enemy, two or more corps would use the shorter route to join the three already over the Rapidan. Hooker then would have in Lee's rear a force superior to the Confederates, and would have a supply route that was short and practicable. Some of the cavalry would assist with the infantry operation, but a part of it was to have a mission resembling its earlier one.

It was a brave program, but not too complex or venturesome. Hooker had good troops, and for the most part well tried corps commanders, so that he should have been able to look forward to having a superior force to engage Lee outside his well prepared position.

A modern staff would have gloried in the plan, keeping typewriters and mimeographs busy turning out pages of top-secret field orders with appropriate annexes. Hooker, however, wrote no order for his entire command, contenting himself with letters of instruction to various commanders; at the start, the right hand was not to know what the left hand was doing. On the 26th orders went to commanders of the Eleventh Corps (now Major General O. O. Howard) and the Twelfth Corps (Slocum) to march the next morning at sunrise for Kelly's Ford, which they were to reach not later than 4:00 P.M. of the 28th.[77] Eight days' rations were to be in the columns, but the main trains were to be parked near Banks's Ford—an instruction presently modified in the case of Slocum, who was told to take all his trains. Howard and Slocum were enjoined to regard the "destination of their commands as strictly confidential." At one o'clock the next morning an order went to Meade, commanding the Fifth Corps, sending him also to Kelly's Ford with only light trains.[78] He was told that he would find Slocum and Howard ahead of him, and copies of their orders were presently sent to him; but, like his brother commanders, he was directed not to tell where he was going. Later in the day a dispatch to Sickles (Third Corps) directed him to be ready to move the next morning with rations and ammunition previously prescribed; he was to wait for his mission.[79] Couch of the Second Corps was told to move at sunrise on the 28th with two of his divisions to concealed positions at Banks's Ford; because the camp of Gibbon's division could be seen by the enemy, he would have to remain in position, his men behaving somewhat as they had for days past [80]—a good deceptive detail that probably was not purposefully arranged. Couch was authorized to leave with Gibbon any of the two-year men already mentioned whom he regarded as unreliable (another sign of Hooker's mastery of detail). To Sedgwick, commanding the Sixth Corps, were assigned Reynolds's First Corps and Sickles's Third; and he was directed to put the command in position to cross the river below Fredericksburg.[81] Bridges were to go in on the 29th, and his possible operations were described briefly. The veil of secrecy about the rest of the army was lifted just a little, Sedgwick being directed to carry the enemy works "at all hazards" in case Lee detached "a considerable part of his force against the troops operating against the west of Fredericksburg."

The new commander of the Engineer Brigade—Brigadier General Henry W. Benham—was instructed about bridging below Fredericksburg, and was told to keep all his bridging paraphernalia out of sight. Comstock, now stepped up to captain's rank, was directed to throw a bridge across the Rappahannock at Kelly's Ford by daylight on the 29th; he could pick up the bridge at Bealeton Station any time after 10:30 A.M. of the 28th.[82]

A touch of secrecy permeated everything, and it was not a good thing to show a spirit of distrust toward corps commanders. One recalls the tactful letter that Lee wrote to Stonewall Jackson—who had been in the habit of keeping all his plans to himself—to take his subordinates a little more into his confidence.[83]

Into the headquarters, busy and perhaps tense, there came the dispatch—brief but eloquent—that had gone several times to McClellan.

Washington, D.C., April 27, 1863—3:30 p.m.

Major General Hooker:
   How does it look now?   *A. Lincoln* [84]

At five o'clock the general replied: "I am not sufficiently advanced to give an opinion. We are busy. Will tell you all soon as I can, and have it satisfactory." It was excellent except for the last four words; they gave a touch of the complacent confidence that disturbed the President.

CHAPTER XVIII

A BRILLIANT MANEUVER
AND A FATAL HALT

> I think we have had the most terrible battle ever witnessed
> on earth.
> *Ingalls to Butterfield*

THE turning column marched as ordered; but the day was gloomy, rainy, and cold; roads in places were almost impassable. The men, burdened with packs of fifty to sixty pounds, threw away overcoats and other things they thought unnecessary—as American soldiers have habitually done before and since. But the troops were in the best of spirits, cheering Hooker deafeningly when they saw him, and singing lustily:

> The Union boys are moving on the left and on the right,
> The bugle-call is sounding, our shelters we must strike;
> Joe Hooker is our leader, he takes his whisky strong,
> So our knapsacks we will sling, and go marching along.[1]

The lines were as good as those that had honored and praised McClellan, and show something of the versatility of the American soldier. Considering the number of knapsacks that Ingalls had to replace when the campaign was over, the reference to slinging that piece of equipment was timely and suggestive.

The march continued on the 28th through more rain; at every halt more overcoats, knapsacks, and other equipment were left behind. At all the houses that the columns passed the infantrymen saw blue cavalrymen in possession [2]—a reassuring sight, for it showed that the countryfolk were not to be allowed to carry warnings to the enemy. Hooker went forward with the column, and from Morrisville, eighteen miles northeast of Fredericksburg, he wrote a directive to Slocum,[3] who was to be in command of his own and Howard's corps, on the movement from Kelly's Ford across the Rapidan at Germanna Ford and on to Chancellorsville. For the first time there was a reference to what was "going on below Fredericksburg." Hooker was still buoyant, for his aide commented to Slocum: "The general desires that not a moment be lost until our troops are established at or near Chancellorsville. From that moment all will be ours." While he was away from his headquarters he received a long dispatch from his chief of staff, full of interesting and important details about how affairs were in the rear, which proved how thoroughly and painstakingly things were being done. The report began, "Lowe reports up to 9 a.m. that, in consequence of the wind, he is unable to ascend," and ended: "Still raining here, but not severely—slow and steady. Telegraph progressing from Banks' Ford to the United States Ford." [4]

Because of the rain, the First, Third, and Sixth Corps were considerably delayed in starting. As the columns moved to their destination below Fredericksburg, the men, like those marching up the river, threw away much of their equipment.[5]

Hooker's mind was still working well when he returned to headquarters, and he directed Professor Lowe to get a balloon up, and have some observer who knew the location of the Confederate camps look carefully for the enemy campfires.[6]

In Washington, Lincoln and Halleck had troublesome matters to think about in addition to the important operation that was beginning on the Rappahannock. Confederate forces in West Virginia seemed to be assuming the offensive, and there was an apparent threat against Wheeling. Governor Curtin of Pennsylvania again became apprehensive and wired Stanton about the danger of invasion of his state. The President took over the task of calming him and wrote:

> I do not think the people of Pennsylvania should be uneasy about an invasion. Doubtless a small force of the enemy is flourishing about in the northern part of Virginia on the "scewhorn" principle, on purpose to divert us in another quarter. I believe it is nothing more. We think we have adequate force close after them.[7]

Howard crossed the Rappahannock over Comstock's bridge on

the night of the 28th, took up a position to cover the structure, and fell in behind Slocum's column of march on the morning of the 29th, a day that was damp and misty. After Slocum the Fifth Corps of Meade crossed, and took the road to Ely's Ford. At Germanna, Slocum found

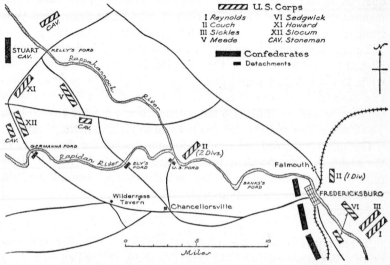

U.S. Corps
I Reynolds   VI Sedgwick
II Couch   XI Howard
III Sickles   XII Slocum
V Meade   CAV. Stoneman

Confederates
Detachments

HOOKER AND LEE AT NOON OF APRIL 29, 1863

a small enemy detachment, which was easily dislodged; but the river was up, and crossing was not a picnic; infantrymen were swept down the stream, to be rescued by cavalrymen on the largest and heaviest horses, and by boatmen. Not until after midnight did the Eleventh Corps finish crossing at Germanna. The situation was not much different at Ely's Ford, where cavalry first crossed and drove away Confederate horsemen. Of the infantry crossing, Bigelow wrote:

> The river was lighted by large fires on the farther bank, the sight of which cheered the troops forward. Out of the chilly water they climbed the slippery hillside—for it was then raining—and went to hunting firewood in the darkness, building fires, cooking suppers, pitching shelter tents, drying clothes and shoes as best they could, and finally rolling up in blankets, feet to the fire, for a comfortless night.[8]

Without too much difficulty five bridges were thrown below Fredericksburg, and Sedgwick crossed two divisions to form bridge-heads, and emplaced batteries on the left bank to give added security.[9]

In spite of low visibility, Lowe was able to make some helpful observations. Peck sent the encouraging message from Suffolk that he thought he could hold Longstreet for some time, but he said to Hooker, "You and I will have plenty of work." From the headquarters near Falmouth there came the reply: "I have fully commenced my operations here. The result may be to draw from your front, and afford you an opportunity to push or hold them." [10]

Though operations were behind the clock, much had been accomplished when dawn came on the 30th. Hooker could feel encouraged, while Lee had before him a puzzling situation. But in order to maintain the advantage Hooker had to continue resolutely; if he ceased his advance or weakened his grip the initiative could quickly pass to Lee. The Confederate commander was not one to yield to mere threats.

Optimism pervaded the turning column despite the discomfort of the night. A correspondent wrote to the *New York Herald:* "It is rumored that the enemy are falling back toward Richmond, but a fight tomorrow seems more than probable. We expect it, and we also expect to be victorious." [11]

Three squadrons of the Eighth Pennsylvania Cavalry (Arrowsmith's, Wickersham's, and McCallum's) under Major Pennock Huey moved out early on May 1 from Ely's Ford to clear the way for Meade. Favored by the fog, the advance guard of eight men surprised and captured a drowsy Confederate picket, consisting of three officers and twenty-two men, who had been making themselves comfortable in an old schoolhouse. Arrowsmith's squadron proceeded to United States Ford, which was soon secured. McCallum and Wickersham, joined presently by the rest of the regiment under Colonel T. C. Devin, moved upon Chancellorsville. An attack upon the rear guard of the Confederate brigades withdrawing from United States Ford—where their position had become impossible—was repulsed. But the Federal horse kept upon the heels of the retiring enemy, and Griffin's division of Meade's corps—followed presently by Sykes's—marching close behind the Eighth Pennsylvania, arrived at Chancellorsville about eleven o'clock, where they found the great house occupied by four ladies dressed in spring attire that was pleasing enough but plainly had not been donned to welcome them.[12] But scoldings did not drive the Federals away, and the house and porches soon were occupied by generals and their staffs, some of whom—believing that bright dresses were more significant than sharp tongues—may have used spare moments in an effort to soften the Virginia ladies.

To Meade there later came the important information from Devin that he had driven in the enemy's pickets on the road to Banks's Ford, and had advanced until he could see their line of battle.[13] From the number of wagons that were visible, he concluded that the enemy were about to evacuate the position. Meade sent to Devin, as reenforcement, Brigadier General James Barnes's brigade of Griffin's division.

Slocum, his advance covered with cavalry, and his own corps leading his formidable column, was under way about six o'clock for Chancellorsville from his bivouacs at Germanna Ford. The advance was delayed by detachments of enemy cavalry, some of which had to be driven away by infantry, and, as a result, the head of Slocum's column reached Chancellorsville about 2:00 P.M.[14]

Couch's Second Corps, which had been in waiting behind Banks's Ford to cross when that position was uncovered, had been sent up the river to United States Ford in order to expedite the movement. It was a questionable change, for it seemed to indicate that Hooker might abandon the idea of seizing the important high ground at Banks's Ford, and be content with having a strong force in the vicinity of Chancellorsville. Brigadier General G. K. Warren, his chief topographical engineer, found the approaches to United States Ford quite impracticable, and in need of considerable improvement. Nor did he know, until the mist lifted about nine o'clock and revealed some of the Federal cavalrymen, that the crossing point had been uncovered. Not until one o'clock were good approaches completed; at 3:30 two bridges were in and the band of the Engineer Brigade crossed, playing "In Dixie's land I'll take my stand." Behind the engineers followed the Second Corps, less Gibbon's Second Division. Again roads had to be built; but presently the column was on its way toward Chancellorsville, past the recently abandoned trenches of the enemy, the men in high spirits at the thought of encountering their adversary in the open.[15]

Everything was progressing favorably. Hooker had in fact accomplished one of the finest maneuvers in military history.[16] Four corps were close to concentration behind Lee, and shortly after noon an order had gone to Sickles to make a concealed march at once from his position below Fredericksburg to United States Ford and cross and join the turning column. Shortly afterward there went to Gibbon an order to be prepared to march at daylight and join his corps (the

Second). But there was one very ominous occurrence. At 2:15 there went to Slocum, Meade, and Couch through Captain Comstock the order signed by Hooker's chief of staff: "The general directs that no advance be made from Chancellorsville until the columns are concentrated. He expects to be at Chancellorsville to-night." [17] All thought of a prompt movement to uncover Banks's Ford had been given up, and Hooker was beginning to show hesitation similar to that which had seized Burnside on December 11.

Uncertainty as to what to have Sedgwick do on the left had appeared in Hooker's mind earlier in the day, probably on account of the reports of enemy activity from Sedgwick, from signal corps observers, and from the balloonist. Sedgwick's order at 8:30 to make a demonstration—but not an attack—was annulled at 11:30 for further orders. Something more than such action by him would have been needed if Hooker wished to keep Lee uncertain as to where the main blow of the Army of the Potomac was to be delivered. Later in the day—at an hour not given—there went to the commander of the "Left Wing" a dispatch telling him that Hooker would personally take up his headquarters at Chancellorsville that night, Butterfield remaining at the old post to communicate between the parts of the army. Sedgwick was told that there would be an advance from Chancellorsville the next morning, and that it would uncover Banks's Ford. The directive said: "It is not known, of course, what effect the advance will have upon the enemy, and the general commanding directs that you observe his movements with the utmost vigilance, and, should he expose a weak point, attack him in full force and destroy him." More instructions followed that seemed to indicate that if the enemy retreated Sedgwick's two corps should "destroy or capture him," the turning column having apparently achieved enough of glory. Butterfield was evidently a little worried, and after his chief had ridden away he sent a private confidential message. It said: "The general as he left expressed great anxiety for prompt and frequent reports and information. I think it would favor operations if you were to make tremendous demonstrations of camp-fires to-night. . . . He expected, when he left here, if he met with no serious opposition, to be on the heights west of Fredericksburg to-morrow noon or shortly after, and, if opposed strongly, to-morrow night." [18]

Hooker's disposition being what it was, there had naturally been mingled with the weakening displayed in his directives for the day, evidence of his confidence, that unfortunately ended in an indefensible bombastic boast. At noon Haupt was directed to be in readiness to commence work on the railroad at daylight on May 2. When Sedgwick sent word at 3:45 that Reynolds (First Corps) believed troops in his front had just arrived from Richmond, Butterfield replied, "General Hooker hopes they are from Richmond, as the greater will be our success." When Dix reported to him that the Federals at Suffolk were invested by a superior force, and that he hoped that Longstreet would not be reenforced but might be compelled to withdraw, Hooker himself wrote the reply: "The enemy has need of every man here. He has his hands full. Rely on this. I can say no more." [19]

But the General's masterpiece was still to appear. Before he started for "the front," he had written—or dictated—General Orders, No. 47, which was published when he reached Chancellorsville:

It is with heartfelt satisfaction the commanding general announces to the army that the operations of the last three days have determined that our enemy must either ingloriously fly, or come out from behind his defenses and give us battle on our own ground, where certain destruction awaits him.

The operations of the Fifth, Eleventh, and Twelfth Corps have been a succession of splendid achievements.[20]

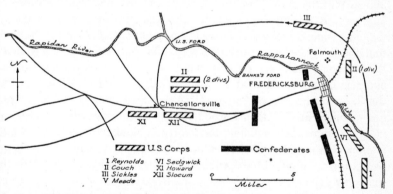

HOOKER AND LEE AT EVENING OF APRIL 30, 1863

It has been suggested that Administrative Joe would be a better label for Hooker than Fighting Joe. Optimistic Joe, or Boastful Joe, might be suggested, according to the way one reacts to such an official pronouncement as that above. Ironically, the day was one that Lincoln, at the Senate's request, had set aside by proclamation for an expression of national humiliation and the invocation of divine blessing.[21] Here and there, when there was opportunity, a chaplain had raised his voice before the bowed heads of soldiers in proper recognition of the day. But the army commander was not only insensitive to the President's appeal; he offended against taste and was tactless when he mentioned the three corps that had had the long marches. Butterfield saw the slight to the other corps that had well executed less spectacular missions, and spoke of it in his off-the-record note to Sedgwick.

The worst feature of the order was its apparent annulment of previous plans and indication of a probable passive attitude by the corps at Chancellorsville. The men were given to believe that the campaign was either won, or might be won, by defensive fighting.

At 5:30 on the morning of May 1 Butterfield sent a message to Hooker, by telegraph to United States Ford and thence by courier, saying that a deserter just in had brought word that all of Jackson's corps was opposite Franklin's crossing, that camp rumor had it that Longstreet had gone to Culpeper, and that Lee had said it was the first time that he would be able to fight equal numbers, believing that the Federals had about 80,000, with 40,000 men over the river above. Was the man a bona-fide deserter, or just one sent to deceive? Hooker was having the chance to see what the troubles of a commanding general really are. Three hours later Butterfield informed him that the telegraph was working badly, and that it was so foggy that the balloons could see nothing. Here was more trouble, such as a commander always has. At 9:30—which is really a very late hour if the day may be one of battle—Hooker sent a circular to the corps commanders in the gloomy woods about Chancellorsville. It began: "Corps commanders will hold their corps in hand, and, wherever their commands may find themselves night or day, they will keep pickets well thrown out on all the approaches to their positions. The safety of this army depends upon this being rigidly executed." [22] From lecturing experienced corps commanders about their normal duties in his first sentence, Hooker progressed in the second to "the safety of this army" —a very bad note for a commander to sound when he had started out to destroy his adversary.

Presently the sun began to melt the fog, and the day became more like what a May day should be. Hooker's courage seemed to revive a little, and at eleven o'clock he issued a circular prescribing a move toward Fredericksburg, which might be regarded as a fulfillment of Butterfield's declaration on the day before that high ground west of Fredericksburg would be seized by noon or shortly thereafter. The order specified that the Twelfth Corps should have possession of Tabernacle Church—the halfway point from Chancellorsville to Fredericksburg—by two o'clock, with proper covering detachments.[23] But the entire tactical situation had changed, and to operate against Fredericksburg on May 1 was quite a different matter from what it would have been the day before, when the seizing of the key position at Banks's Ford should have been a relatively simple matter.[24] Hooker having failed to make the necessary advance, the initiative had gone to Lee.

General Lee had not been too well served by Stuart in divining the object of the Federal movement up the Rappahannock or in reporting upon it. Stuart had posted his depleted cavalry brigades in such a way that the Federal columns had cut in between him and Lee—an error in judgment that Bigelow charitably says should not be the basis of criticism, because the best of soldiers often misinterpret enemy moves. Thus Lee did not have as full reports about what was going on up the river as was desirable; but, influenced largely by the inactivity of Sedgwick, he had decided that the Federal operations below Fredericksburg were a feint, or quite secondary, and that his main enemy was gathering in his rear. Without delay an order was issued that left one brigade of McLaws's division (Barksdale's) and one division of Jackson's corps (Early's) in the Fredericksburg lines while the remainder of the command with two days' cooked rations was to hurry westward to join Anderson's division,[25] industriously engaged in throwing up intrenchments across the road to Chancellorsville on a line through Tabernacle Church—the precise spot where Hooker in his eleven o'clock circular had stated he would open his headquarters. A clear night with a brilliant moon, and Jackson's usual forehandedness, had favored greatly the prompt execution of Lee's order, though columns were marching well into the next day.

Actually Hooker's troops were on the road at eleven o'clock, verbal orders having apparently preceded the written circular. Slocum, followed by Howard, was on the plank road on the right. Sykes's division of Meade's corps, followed by Hancock's division of Couchs's corps, used the turnpike in the center. The remainder of Meade's command—

Griffin's division, followed by Humphreys—was on the very poor river road on the left. French's division of Couch's corps was to march to Todd's tavern. Before the movement commenced Sickles had arrived with his Third Corps and had gone into position as a reserve in the vicinity of Chancellorsville. Thus Hooker had in hand five corps, totaling over 75,000 men, when he sent about 40,000 men toward approximately the same number that Lee was marching against him.[26] Lee's brigade's, however, benefited by a strong defensive position on which construction was well advanced.

The Federal columns were covered by detachments of the small cavalry brigade of three regiments and by a horse battery under Pleasonton that had been left with the main army, while Stoneman had supposedly ridden away on his independent mission to break Lee's communications as well as to gather in slices of the enemy—large and small—as occasion presented itself. Throughout the morning, the blue troopers had been in contact with Anderson's covering detachments,[27] though Hooker's circular of eleven o'clock had not indicated that enemy troops were in possession of Tabernacle Church. (If the cavalry had been remiss in making reports, Hooker had had plenty of time to inform Pleasonton, and have reports brought in.)

Jackson was in command of Lee's advancing columns and, in accordance with his aggressive nature, had stopped the fortifying of Anderson's position, and moved boldly onward. Though the country where the clash took place was less densely wooded than that about Chancellorsville, it was bad enough, with infrequent open spaces. Doubleday was to say, "It was worse than fighting in a fog." Sykes met the advance of McLaws's division and drove it back a mile, until it was heavily reenforced by Anderson, who got on Sykes's flanks, because it had been impossible for Sykes's center column to connect with either the right column on the plank road, or Meade's divisions on the river road. Sykes was driven back through Hancock's division. No line held by this general would give way easily, and he had found a ridge with open space in front that Warren thought a strong position and urged Couch not to give up, while he went to see the army commander.[28]

But other information had already reached Hooker that evidently unnerved him. At noon on May 1 Professor Lowe—both of whose balloons were working [29]—sent word that the largest column of the enemy was moving toward Chancellorsville, and that he thought the

enemy on the opposite heights was considerably reduced. The telegraph had been out of order but was now working correctly, so that the
message presumably went through. At two o'clock Hooker wired
Butterfield: "From character of information have suspended attack.
The enemy may attack me—I will try it. Tell Sedgwick to keep a sharp
lookout and attack if can succeed." [30] But Hooker did more than suspend an attack. He ordered a retirement to the position occupied the
night before; and this in spite of the fact that "the column on the

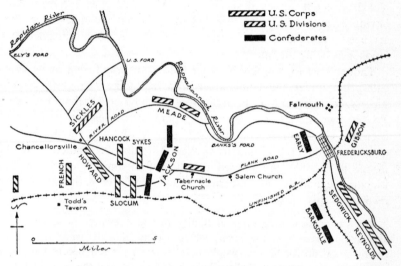

HOOKER AND LEE, MAY 1, 1863

river road was in sight of Banks's Ford, which it could have seized
and held, or have struck the right flank of the enemy with great effect."
When he received the order to retire, Couch asked permission to remain, but was informed the order was peremptory. Presently courage
came back to Hooker, and his retirement order was countermanded;
but the ridge had already been abandoned and the enemy had possession of it. [31] At 4:20 a circular was issued directing corps commanders
to put their positions in condition for a defense without a moment's
delay: "The major-general commanding trusts that a suspension in
the attack to-day will embolden the enemy to attack him." Promptly
commanders were directed to keep their pioneers at work all night
making abatis and clearing positions for artillery. To Butterfield,
Hooker telegraphed: "Hope the enemy will be emboldened to attack

me. I did feel certain of success. If his communications are cut, he must attack me. I have a strong position." [32] Was there special significance in the past tense in the second sentence?

Instructions to Sedgwick had been confusing, to say the least. Hooker had written a dispatch at 11:30 A.M. directing him to make a demonstration "as severe as can be, but not an attack." [33] It was not put on the wire until 5:05 P.M., and a failure to synchronize watches caused it to be received by Butterfield at 4:55 P.M., after the two o'clock order to attack if success were sure had been received. Not having attacked, Sedgwick decided to carry out the first order and arranged to make a demonstration; but it was countermanded by Hooker as being too late. [34]

Thoughts as to how his Number One army was faring in its new enterprise, under the commander who had talked so glibly about success, could never have been far from the mind of Abraham Lincoln. To his own desk, however, were coming troublesome points for decision. Governor Curtin was still greatly alarmed by the threat of an invasion of his state from West Virginia; he wanted Federal troops if possible and offered to call out the militia of the state. Lincoln's calmness and discernment and power of expression were revealed in his answer:

> The whole disposable force at Baltimore and elsewhere in reach have already been sent after the enemy which alarms you. The worst thing the enemy could do for himself would be to weaken himself before Hooker, and therefore it is safe to believe he is not doing it, and the best thing he could do for himself would be to get us so scared as to bring part of Hooker's force away, and that is just what he is trying to do.
>
> I will telegraph you in the morning about calling out the militia. [35]

Hooker had forgotten to take his compass when he left his old headquarters for the front. At noon on the 1st Butterfield reported that Ingalls was bringing it to him. It was not a magnetic compass that Fighting Joe was missing and suffering for. It was a drink. For four days Hooker had been subjected to a bad strain, and unwisely he had stopped his customary use of stimulants. He did not have the heart and the iron nerve of a real commanding general, but it was certainly unwise for a man who "takes his whisky strong" to become abstemious at a critical time. [36] Had not A. Lincoln written twice in his letter, "Beware of rashness"?

Under bright moonlight, the Federal position was made snug and tight. As they struggled with the tangled thickets, Federal soldiers who had already wrestled with the swamps of the Peninsula could have been pardoned if they wondered why there should be so much opposition to secession. "We're fighting for an idea," some wise soldier may have said in a way to exasperate and tease companions who were doubtful about the value of Dixie real estate. "To hell with ideas!" would be the natural reply of American soldiers as they swung their axes a little harder and shoveled more industriously.

There was also plenty of work to be done in the great Chancellor house. Excellent intelligence reports were at hand. On March 30 Hooker had appointed Colonel G. H. Sharpe of the 120th New York deputy provost marshal general, and put into his competent hands the task of forming an intelligence service.[37] Since then he had benefited from information gathered by the colonel's men; and at 7:20 P.M on May 1 Butterfield forwarded the report of an operative just in from Richmond, which was little less than amazing in its detail and precision with regard to all Confederate forces in Virginia.[38] (The marked contrast between Sharpe's reports and the information furnished to McClellan by Pinkerton shows how much was gained by putting "intelligence" into military hands.) The number of men that Lee had about Fredericksburg was not given; but it was said that 59,000 rations were going to him, and that he could receive no reenforcements except by the return of Longstreet.

At 10:30 P.M. Butterfield wrote a long dispatch with much important information, and the disturbing report that telegraphic dispatches back and forth had evidently been mutilated or misinterpreted; he assured Hooker that no word about operations had been allowed to go out to anyone—not even to Lincoln, Stanton, or Halleck.[39] It was a careful chief of staff that forwarded by special courier a copy of all his dispatches, and of everything that had come in.

Back with Butterfield at the rear headquarters, Herman Haupt was waiting, ready to throw a new railroad bridge across the Rappahannock.

Finally the messages and reports stopped coming in, as the infantry slept with the noise of both friendly and enemy axes in their ears. At three o'clock on the new day—May 2—Captain W. L. Candler, aide to Hooker, found time at last to write home. The message was brief and discreet, but contained the sentence, "To-day will tell a big tale."

Professor Lowe was up in the air at a very unacademic hour, and reported at 6:15 that the hard wind was bumping him around so much he could not use his telescope.[40] Well before this Hooker had begun to inspect his lines, and was greeted everywhere with hearty and prolonged cheers.[41] The higher officers, depressed by their commander's vacillation and assumption of a defensive attitude the day before, probably observed him carefully to see if he had recovered any degree of poise and confidence. Just what they read in his manner cannot be said; it is safe to say that some were disappointed.

The Eleventh Corps, now commanded by Major General Oliver O. Howard, held the right, reaching down the Orange Turnpike about a mile west of Dowdall's Tavern at the junction of the pike and plank

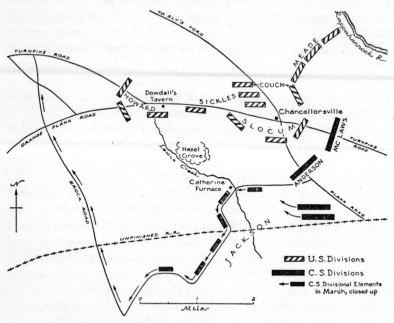

HOOKER AND LEE AT 9:00 A.M., MAY 2, 1863

roads. Then came Birney's division of Sickles's Third Corps, pushed south of the road and occupying a somewhat commanding position at Hazel Grove, behind Lewis Creek. Next came Slocum's Twelfth Corps, also advanced south of the road, and with its left turned back to the turnpike just east of Chancellorsville. Couch's Second and Meade's Fifth Corps continued the line to the Rappahannock at Scott's

Ford, a mile below United States Ford. Two divisions of Sickles's corps and part of Couch's were in reserve.

When Hooker reached his headquarters at nine o'clock he found couriers from General Birney with the information that since eight a column of the enemy—infantry, artillery, trains, ambulances—had been seen moving across his front. From his tent he could himself see a part of the column on a short stretch of road running southward. Jackson's march around Pope may well have come to his mind; for he had been with Pope, and had led the advance against Jackson's troops. Without delay a dispatch over the signature of Brigadier General J. H. Van Alen, an aide, went to Howard—a dispatch badly written, that was destined to be the basis of much bitter dispute. It directed Howard to give closer attention to his right flank than he had done, and closed with the postscript: "We have good reason to suppose that the enemy is moving to our right. Please advance your pickets for purposes of observation as far as may be safe to obtain timely information of their approach." This message is not in the Official Records, though an amplified version addressed to Slocum and Howard is.[42]

The Confederate column that had been marching west was Jackson's corps on the last march which Stonewall was to lead. A reconnaissance made late the afternoon before had convinced Lee that Hooker could not be successfully attacked from the east or the south. For much of the night he was in conference with Jackson, sitting on cracker boxes by a little fire, amid the shadows cast by the moon, near where some of his men were resting in line of battle and others were sleeping in quiet bivouacs. It was one of the great councils of war, and about it much has been written—part pure romance—in an earnest effort to reconstruct what occurred with the greatest detail and vividness.[43] To the Confederate commander—undoubtedly in a very difficult position—Stuart brought the welcome word that the right flank of the Federal army was inadequately protected, and that it was accessible. So Jackson was told to attack the Federal right. The mission was so hazardous as to be almost foolish, and would not have been confided to any other subordinate. Lee was justified in his faith that Jackson would make the most of every opportunity that he found. Whether he had reason to believe that Hooker was completely unfit for army command and would bungle all his opportunities, must be open for dispute; but he gambled on nothing short of that.

Hooker was correct in giving thought to his own flank when he saw the Confederate column; he should also have seen the great opportunity for a destructive stroke against the enemy; but it was only later, upon the urging of his more aggressive subordinates, that he considered resuming the offensive that he had just given up. At the same time that he wrote to Howard, he directed Butterfield to tell Sedgwick there was reliable information that only Early's division remained in front of him, and authorize him to attack if there was "a reasonable expectation of success"; but the operation was left, definitely, to his discretion.[44]

According to Bigelow, Hooker's order reached Howard shortly after noon, a half-hour after he had sent this dispatch to Hooker: "From Gen. Devens' headquarters we can observe a column of infantry moving westward on a road parallel with this on a ridge about 1½ to 2 m. south of this. I am taking measures to resist an attack from the west." Howard's failure to characterize his measures in any way would indicate that what he had done was mild rather than strong. If Hooker had believed that the threat to his right was great, he could have gone to the right himself—nothing was going on at the time—or could at least have sent his able engineer officer General Warren to visit Howard's position. Actually Howard, firm in the belief that the woods were so thick that a heavy attack against him from the west was out of the question, had taken very inadequate steps to protect his flank. He had three lines perpendicular to the road; but they were manned by only five regiments, and he did not have sufficiently strong covering detachments.[45]

Corps command was new to Howard—who had lost an arm at Fair Oaks, had returned to fight at Antietam, and had commanded a division at Fredericksburg—and he could well have taken more seriously his position on the flank of the army, with a command that had seen little action and contained numerous regiments displeased because their fellow German, Franz Sigel, was no longer at their head. His assignment to the flank was due to Hooker's having temporary groupings of corps rather than something like "grand divisions." [46]

Watching a parade of the Confederates across his front was more than Dan Sickles could stand, and he set forth the opportunities that were offered; about noon he obtained Hooker's permission to advance cautiously and harass the enemy movement as much as possible. Sickles stretched things as much as he could, and ordered Birney "to follow the enemy, pierce the column, and gain possession of the road

over which it was passing." [47] Whipple's division of the Third Corps
was ordered to the support of Birney, and Slocum and Howard were
asked to give necessary flank protection. Some damage was done to
the enemy, especially in the way of prisoners, but considerable time
had been spent in bridging streams and getting artillery forward, and
the enemy column, after being turned onto another road, was presently
beyond reach, except for its rear guard.

Howard's attention had been somewhat taken from his own flank
by Sickles's operation, in which Hooker had ordered him to participate.
At 4:00 P.M. he took the brigade of Brigadier General Francis C.
Barlow, which had been his corps reserve, and advanced two and a
half miles to the south to join up with Birney. In his report he stated
that there had been copious scouting and patrolling by infantry and
cavalry on his right flank, and that the reports were always, "The
enemy is crossing the Plank road and moving toward Culpeper." [48]
This was a distortion, for many reports came into Howard's headquarters that the enemy was gathering in force upon his flank, and
one imploring message, written at 2:45 by an officer in command of
pickets, stated that a large body of the enemy was forming in his
front and ended, "For God's sake, make disposition to receive him!"
Howard repulsed the appeal, with the statement that the enemy could
not penetrate the thickets. An officer who went to Hooker's headquarters fared no better.[49] The general, recently apprehensive, was
again optimistic; he concluded that the enemy was retreating, and sent
a circular to corps commanders at 2:30 P.M. telling them to load up
with forage, provisions, and ammunition so as "to be ready to start at
an early hour to-morrow," [50] presumably in pursuit of the vanishing
enemy. As the time passed he became more confident; and at 4:10 he
directed Butterfield to order Sedgwick to cross the river, "capture
Fredericksburg and everything in it, and vigorously pursue the enemy.
. . . We know that the enemy is fleeing, trying to save his trains. Two
of Sickles's divisions are among them." [51] About the time that Butterfield was forwarding this, a cruel disillusionment burst upon Fighting
Joe.

About 2:30 Jackson's leading regiment, the Fifth Alabama, reached
the Fredericksburg-Orange turnpike, turned eastward, and formed for
attack, some six miles from its starting point but twelve by the
circuitous route it had followed. In spite of the harassing he had

received, Jackson had his column well closed up, as was his wont; but time was needed for the major part of his command of upward of 30,000 men to arrive and be deployed.[52] He gave careful personal attention to details, after himself examining the Federal position from a commanding hill. Except for certain detachments he disposed his brigades in three lines of two ranks each, with a front perpendicular to the turnpike and extending approximately a mile on each side. Until the moment of attack, quiet had been observed; then, with everything ready, a calm word was passed to Brigadier General R. E. Rodes, commanding the first wave of attack, and the woods echoed with bugle calls and the "rebel yell." Preceded by startled deer and ap-

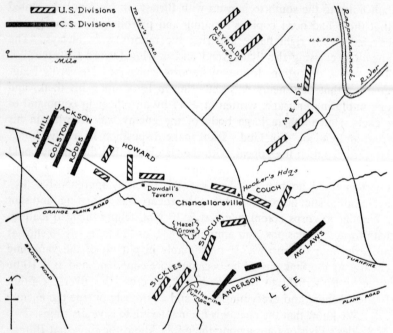

BATTLE OF CHANCELLORSVILLE, 5:00 P.M., MAY 2, 1863

prehensive rabbits, the Southern regiments, with great determination and enthusiasm, forced their way through the brush that almost tore off their clothing and soon—probably about 5:30 P.M.—were within striking distance of the very vulnerable Federal right.

Howard's men with arms stacked were preparing their supper and thinking of another moonlight night among the trees. Apparently without confusion, the units that were first struck seized their arms and quickly occupied their positions. The two regiments facing west stood their ground until they had fired three volleys; but those facing south were exposed to a murderous fire from flank and rear, and quickly broke. Two guns facing down the road got off several shots, but were captured after their horses had been killed. Colonel John C. Lee succeeded in forming something of a line with his brigade behind the disintegrating brigade of Colonel Leopold von Gilsa; but it was soon enveloped. Presently Jackson had firm hold of the high ground about Taylor's, a little west of Howard's headquarters at Dowdall's Tavern, and of the open ground about Hawkins's farm to the north, which had been occupied by the division of Major General Carl Schurz—who had spent a somewhat apprehensive afternoon.

Howard, who had just returned from Barlow's brigade over two miles away, bravely threw himself into repairing the situation for which his negligence and inflexible opinions were largely responsible. The brigade of Colonel Adolphus Buschbeck was put into line, and his four regiments were supplemented by retreating units until they amounted to about ten. In a position that was not especially strong, Buschbeck and his 4,000 men put up a stout fight until Jackson's men lapped around both his flanks; then they marched away in good order. It was not long, however, before much of the Eleventh Corps had broken into a mob of frightened, disorganized men, streaming to the rear past Hooker's headquarters, and down toward the United States Ford until they were turned back by straggler lines. Seeing what was happening, Howard wisely ordered his corps artillery back to Chancellorsville.

Amid the panic, there was leadership of the highest type by officers, and unsurpassed bravery of soldiers. The Army of the Potomac was enduring the supreme test, and it came through nobly. While some men from other corps joined those from the Eleventh who fled through their ranks, most units were as steady as if on parade, in spite of the terrible confusion, the noise of battle, the yelling of the Confederates, and the moonlit night which had settled over the forests and the few open fields. Howard had been quickly in the thick of the fight, with the national color of some regiment held beneath the stump of his right arm. Hooker was soon on his familiar white horse and among his men. There was not much that he could do. Reynolds's First Corps, which at dusk had reached the ford after an all-day march from below Fredericksburg, was marched forward, instead of being allowed to go into bivouac. Two brigades of Major General Hiram G. Berry's Second Division of Sickles's corps, which were in reserve, were sent to check the Confederate onslaught, supported by Hays's brigade of the Second Division of Couch's Second Corps. Bigelow, competent critic of military matters, wrote: "There can hardly be a severer test of discipline and *esprit de corps* than the one to which these troops were now subjected. . . . Through the surging rout of the XI Corps these sterling organizations forged their way, unchecked and unshaken, toward the mass of yelling and firing assailants." For the most part, subordinate commanders had to act as they saw the chance, and this they did. Captain C. L. Best, chief of artillery for the Twelfth Corps, began collecting all the guns he could, and before long he had a battery of no fewer than thirty-four pieces on an eminence known as Fairview, south of the road, and a short distance west of Chancellorsville. Other believers in gunfire made similar and only slightly less impressive collections of artillery. From the corps that were facing south and east not much could be done in withdrawing troops to restore the battle on the west, for Lee had opened the guns of Anderson's and McLaws's divisions and had made some infantry threats in order to immobilize Federal units, as soon as he knew that Jackson had launched his great attack.

Naturally Jackson's troops had been disorganized by their attack and advance, and it was necessary to stop for reorganization, eager as he was to keep pressing the Federals. There had also been mistakes by subordinates, who in the woods and the night had a difficult task of troop leading. Toward eight o'clock Rodes was advancing upon a rather strong Federal force west of Fairview, where Buschbeck and Schurz had posted the ten regiments that had given good service earlier in the evening. Berry was intrenching behind them, with some units of the Twelfth Corps forming on the left. About nine Jackson went forward to reconnoiter the Federal position before which his attack had come to a halt. The Confederate line was perhaps a little nervous, for a bold dash earlier by the Eighth Pennsylvania Cavalry under Major Pennock Huey had caused a warning about a possible Federal cavalry attack to be passed down the line. As Jackson returned to his lines his party was fired upon. His engineer officer was killed, and he himself was grievously wounded with three bullets. Presently Best's great battery, accepting the demand of the occasion, fired over the

Federal infantry at the Confederate lines, and in this hail of metal Stonewall Jackson was carried to the rear, while his horse "Little Sorrel" fled for safety to the Federal lines.[53] After some agonizing handling on a litter Jackson was taken by ambulance to the hospital which had been set up at Wilderness Tavern. Command of the Second Corps had devolved upon A. P. Hill, but he too was soon wounded— though not severely—in the hail from Best's guns, and Stuart was summoned from near Ely's Ford to take command. That the Confederate attack suffered from Jackson's death cannot be doubted; but it is equally impossible to believe that even he could have done much more against the accumulation of sturdy infantry and the mass of relentless guns in his front at Fairview, or on his flank at Hazel Grove, where Sickles and Barlow had finally rendezvoused, after confusing movements in the dark.[54]

Finally the noise of battle ceased, and the men of both armies, with the consuming fatigue that none but soldiers know, lay down in the shadows of the moonlight to be lulled by "the weird, plaintive notes of the whippoorwills," which seemed to outdo themselves that night.

Again the high cards were in Hooker's hands, for his army had not been destroyed, but only a little damaged. The advent of the fine First Corps under Reynolds, with the renowned Iron Brigade, more than compensated for the broken Eleventh, which was itself rather quickly re-formed to a considerable degree. Hooker had 76,000 men and 244 guns, while the separated forces of Lee and Stuart numbered only 43,000 men and 132 pieces of artillery. In order to be really successful Jackson would have had to join ranks on the right with forces directly under Lee. This was uppermost in his mind as he drove his assaulting lines onward with his customary energy. But he would not have succeeded in uniting them that night, even if he had survived.

The wind had made the day a bad one for the aeronauts, and there were times when neither balloon could be up. But they persisted and obtained considerable information about Confederate activities directly back of Fredericksburg, which was sent to Sedgwick and to Hooker.[55]

Perhaps, while things were a little slack in the afternoon, Fighting Joe had a chance to read a telegram Secretary Stanton had sent at 11:00 A.M., whose origin went back to a complaint by Hooker on April 27 about stories in the New York Times and the Philadelphia Inquirer. Stanton had replied on the 30th, assuring him that the War Department would back him in any measures taken with reporters, and suggesting that he might have to "get tough"; nothing had been allowed to pass Washington by telegraph. Then, while the battle was in progress, the War Secretary who was supposed to know no more about what was going on than the President or the General in Chief wired Hooker:

> We cannot control intelligence in relation to your movements while your generals write letters giving details. A letter from General Van Alen to a person not connected with the War Department describes your position as intrenched at Chancellorsville. Can't you give his sword something to do, so that he will have less time for the pen? [56]

It certainly was a fine situation. Hooker would not tell even his corps commanders about his plans, but his senior aide de camp was passing out information.[57] Of course someone had tattled to Stanton, and had not lost much time doing so—which suspicious persons might take as evidence of the mischievous plots in which Stanton was engaged. But those that do not like Lincoln's War Secretary should at least admit that he tried to be constructive in his criticism, and could get to the point in question without superfluous words.

At 9:00 P.M. of the 2nd, while there was still much uproar and confusion about Chancellorsville, Hooker ordered Sedgwick to cross the Rappahannock at Fredericksburg immediately, and take up the march to Chancellorsville without any trains except pack mules, carrying infantry ammunition. Any enemy that was encountered was to be attacked and destroyed; then, having reached his destination, by daylight, he was to combine with Hooker to "use up" Lee. Gibbon, who with his Second Division of the Second Corps was still at Falmouth, was also to cross the river and seize Fredericksburg.[58] The plan was good enough, but to realize the full possibilities would require that Hooker avail himself of the unusual opportunities he had at Chancellorsville, and do all that he could independently of Sedgwick, and not leave everything to that good officer.

Morning of May 3 found Sickles with Birney's and Whipple's divisions and Barlow's brigade, and some thirty-eight guns, in a commanding position at Hazel Grove effectively preventing a junction of the too widely separated parts of the Confederate army, which was in a desperate situation. This was the advantage gained by Sickles's operation against Jackson's column, offsetting the weakness that came with the gap in the Federal line resulting from Birney's movement southward from his position next to Howard—a movement severely criticized by some writers.[59] From Hazel Grove it would have been possible to sally forth and attack in flank either the portion of the Confederate army under Stuart or that under Lee.[60] Thus the tables

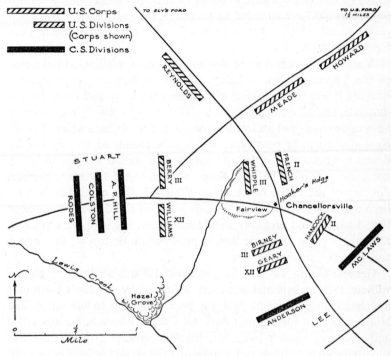

BATTLE OF CHANCELLORSVILLE, MAY 3, 1863

were very definitely again turned against Lee; but Hooker, after an early visit to the hill, ordered its abandonment, whereupon Sickles withdrew to the vicinity of Fairview. No sooner had the Confederates taken over the surrendered position than they planted a battery of thirty-one guns upon its summit. Although they were dominated somewhat by Best's great battery at Fairview, the guns were able to bring very destructive fire upon the Federal infantry. Presently, there followed assault after assault upon the log intrenchments that the Federals had thrown up, Jackson's men seeming to vie with one another in an effort to avenge their fallen leader, urging one another on with cries, "Remember Jackson." Slowly the Union troops were driven back, but not to any great degree, until a shortage of ammunition—both artillery and infantry—began to manifest itself.[61] General Berry, a promising division commander at thirty-eight, was killed by a sharpshooter's bullet while personally delivering a message which an officer more careful about himself, but less careful about his orders, would have confided to an aide.[62] Presently Sickles was compelled to ask Hooker for assistance in defending his position. Then Fate intervened.

A solid shot from a Confederate gun struck a pillar on the porch of the Chancellor house against which Hooker had been leaning, splitting it and throwing half of it against his body and head. He fell senseless, and for a few moments it was thought he was dying. Presently he was revived, but suffered great pain. The injury, which left his right side partially paralyzed, was hardly calculated to increase his fitness to conduct a battle, and whether he should attempt to was a question that both he and Surgeon Jonathan Letterman, medical director of the army, had to face. While Hooker could hardly have been expected to rule himself out, the surgeon could have pronounced him disabled, and probably should have done so, with the chance of not only winning the battle then in progress but destroying the enemy, and thus shortening the war.[63]

General Couch was next in command. He was an excellent soldier without the fundamental weakness indicated by Hooker's arrogance and boastfulness, and he had not been subjected to the strain that Hooker had felt for the past days. Of Couch, whose horse was killed and who was himself twice hit, Bigelow wrote: "His example was superb. Of slight stature, and usually of a simple and retiring demeanor, he became sublime as the passion of battle and the high-mounting sense of duty took complete possession of every power and faculty, every thought and feeling, every limb and nerve." Lincoln's admonition "put in all your men" was never forgotten by Couch, even with the passage of time, and if the command of the army had devolved upon him, that is probably exactly what he would have done. Neither Reynolds's nor Meade's corps was in action at the time; and both commanders were eager to enter into the battle, where the favorable opportunities were so great. About 9:30 Couch was summoned to a tent to which Hooker had been removed. When he came out Meade, who was waiting near by, looked at him inquiringly, hoping for two little words—"Go in." [64] But Couch could not pronounce them, for

Hooker had not turned over the command of the army to him; he had merely made him his executive, and had given him the order to withdraw to a line provisionally determined the night before. This was done. Fairview was surrendered; presently the two parts of Lee's army were united, and with the new change in the battle lines the danger to his command largely disappeared. Hooker himself did nothing after the Federal line was contracted, but waited for Sedgwick to carry out the heavy order that had been given to him.

Even if there had been no enemy intervening, it would have been difficult for Sedgwick to fall upon Lee's rear by daylight, as he had been ordered to do; and with the hostile forces interposing, it was utterly impossible. By 2:00 A.M. his column was entering Fredericksburg, arriving from his crossings below the city. By five o'clock the town was securely in Federal possession; and presently a bridge was laid, over which Gibbon passed with the Second Division of the Second Corps, bringing Sedgwick's command up to about 25,600 men and sixty-six guns. The Confederate force on the heights behind the city was much smaller, numbering about 11,600 men and forty-eight guns; but they were strongly placed. Just where an attack could be made most advantageously was hard to tell, and Sedgwick was under pressure to get things done. A turning movement appeared impracticable, and it was decided to storm Marye's Hill, in spite of the futile efforts and heavy losses of the preceding December. Now the heights were not so strongly held, and under superb leadership the Seventh Massachusetts and the Sixth Wisconsin carried the wall and, halting for a moment, swept on to the top. Reserves followed without delay, and the hold upon the crest was made secure. Still Sedgwick had done no more than make a penetration, Early's division remaining in force upon his left, and Barksdale's brigade upon his right. Only the brigade of Wilcox—which had just joined the Fredericksburg force—fell back toward Chancellorsville. Sedgwick's order prevented him from stopping long to "mop up," and he had to push to the relief of his commander, though he was leaving an energetic enemy in his rear. Gibbon was left behind to make Fredericksburg secure, and by 2:00 P.M. Sedgwick—whom Butterfield three different times had started to remove for imagined slowness [65]—had his three divisions (Brooks's, Howe's, and Newton's) at the Guest house, two miles west of Fredericksburg. He undoubtedly would have felt more comfortable with the support of Reynolds's sturdy corps; but that command had been marched around to join "Fighting Joe," who allowed it to stand by with unused rifles and artillery. Rapidly the campaign that had begun so well was becoming ludicrous. If Letterman had only taken the hint from the cannon ball and had counted Hooker out! Not often does a surgeon have the chance to do so much.

Realizing that his communications with Fredericksburg would probably fail, Sedgwick at once tried to get into communication with Benham at Banks's Ford, so that a bridge could be thrown for him. The first messenger never came back, the second came back three months later by way of Richmond exchange, the third got through and returned within an hour.[66] With less apprehension Sedgwick continued upon his succoring mission, Brooks's division leading. Near Salem Church and School the division of McLaws—which had been sent back by Lee—and the brigade of Wilcox were found deployed in a strong position. Brooks attacked promptly and at first with success; then numbers told against him, and he was forced back. Newton's division, with Burnham's light division attached, stabilized the action, Howe being kept in column. Word came that Benham had a bridge in at Scott's Ford about a mile below Banks's and that a brigade of the Second Corps had crossed to the south bank to make things tight. Yet Sedgwick had plenty to think about, and a discerning soldier wrote:

We slept in line that night with the dead of the day's battle lying near us. The stretcher bearers with their lamps wandered here and there over the field, picking up the wounded, and the loaded ambulances rattled dismally over the broken plank road. The pickets were unusually still, for the men of both armies were tired, and went willingly to rest. . . . Sedgwick scarcely slept that night. From time to time he dictated a dispatch to General Hooker. He would walk for a few paces apart and listen; then returning would lie down again in the damp grass, with his saddle for a pillow, and try to sleep. The night was inexpressibly gloomy.[67]

At 8:45 in the morning Butterfield had received from Ingalls, who was with Hooker, a message that showed that his clear mind had taken in more than matters of supply. He reported:

A most terribly bloody conflict has raged since daylight. Enemy in great force in our front and on the right, but at this moment we are repulsing him on all sides. Carnage is fearful. General Hooker is safe so far. Berry is killed. I return to the front, but will keep you advised when in my power. Our trains are safe, and we shall be victorious. Our cavalry has not come up.

It took the chief of staff only five minutes to address to Abraham Lincoln, President of the United States, this message: "Though not directed or specially authorized to do so by General Hooker, I think it not improper that I should advise you that a battle is in progress." Butterfield probably was glad he had said no more when he received Ingalls's 12:45 P.M. dispatch:

I think we have had the most terrible battle ever witnessed on earth. I think our victory will be certain, but the general told me he would say nothing just yet to Washington, except that he is doing well. In an hour or two the matter will be a fixed fact. I believe the enemy is in flight now, but we are not sure.

Doing well! Even Ingalls was becoming too optimistic, though at the end he drooped a little. Butterfield's conscience was troubling him, and he could not keep away the thought that the man in the White House was entitled to know, and should know something about the battle. The man of indomitable will and inflexible purpose! So at 1:30 Butterfield wired His Excellency Abraham Lincoln:

From all reports yet collected, the battle has been most fierce and terrible. Loss heavy on both sides. General Hooker slightly, but not severely wounded. He has preferred thus far that nothing should be reported, and does not know of this, but I cannot refrain from saying this much to you. You may expect his dispatch in a few hours, which will give the result.

Grateful indeed was Lincoln for the thoughtfulness of the chief of staff, and in accordance with his habitual kindliness he expressed his appreciation through the Secretary of War (harsh, unfeeling, radical Stanton): "The President thanks you for your telegrams, and hopes you will keep him advised as rapidly as any information reaches you."

Hooker himself had not been entirely remiss in the matter of communicating, for at 1:30 he wrote, in a dispatch which was not received in Washington until four o'clock, because it had to be carried by courier to United States Ford:

We have had a desperate fight yesterday and to-day, which has resulted in no success to us, having lost a position of two lines, which had been selected for our defense. It is now 1.30 o'clock, and there is still some firing of artillery. We may have another turn at it this p.m. I do not despair of success. If Sedgwick could have gotten up, there could have been but one result. As it is impossible for me to know the exact position of Sedgwick as regards his ability to advance and take part in the engagement, I cannot tell when it will end. We will endeavor to do our best. My troops are in good spirits. We have fought desperately to-day. No general ever commanded a more devoted army.

Though this confirmed the quality of the army, a thing which needed no confirming in the mind of the President, and revealed a somewhat humble man, the message certainly was not very encouraging; and it lacked definiteness. As usual, Lincoln sought to go through to the essential facts. He wired Butterfield: "Where is General Hooker? Where is Sedgwick? Where is Stoneman?" Like a competent, experienced general, Abraham Lincoln thought in terms of personalities and positions. His dispatch is one to be studied by soldiers. By now he was seeing military matters in a clearer way than many of his generals; and one must believe that there was another question in his mind, though it was one that he knew Butterfield could not answer: Had Hooker put in all his men?

The chief of staff made the best reply he could at 4:40, and at 8:00 P.M. he telegraphed:

I have had no time to advise you. We have to-day here over 800 prisoners; six guns handsomely taken at the point of bayonet. I can give no general idea of how affairs stand. Last reports all quiet in front of Chancellorsville, and Sedgwick fighting at 6:15 p.m. Will try after a while to advise you if an interval occurs.[68]

There was a touch of cheer in the message: guns had been carried at the point of the bayonet; and more important, someone was still *fighting*. In spite of that, Lincoln's rest and sleep were probably as fitful as John Sedgwick's.

A helpful dispatch came to Sedgwick at 6:30 on the morning of the 4th from General Warren, who, after having spent the preceding afternoon with the Sixth Corps, returned to Hooker's headquarters. The message was dated midnight, and began: "I find everything snug here. We contracted the line a little and repulsed the last assault with ease. General Hooker wishes them to attack him to-morrow." [69] Here, alas, was the clear announcement of the continued abandonment of aggressive action; but Sedgwick did have his own mission of saving the main body somewhat relaxed, for Warren directed him to look to the safety of his own corps, and gave him permission to go either to

Banks's Ford or to Fredericksburg if the necessity arose, the former having the advantage of putting him within supporting distance of the main body. That he would have to take advantage of the permission soon became clear, for Lee had correctly interpreted Hooker's quiet nonaggressive lines, and had turned to crush Sedgwick. At seven

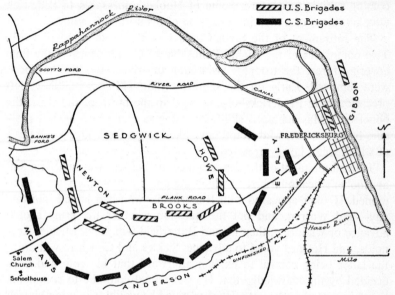

SEDGWICK'S BATTLE, MAY 4–5, 1863

o'clock the evening before, he had directed Early to bring forward his 10,000 men from Fredericksburg and join with McLaws: "See if you cannot unite with him and, together, destroy [the enemy]. With his five brigades, and you with your division and the remnant of Barksdale's brigade, I think you ought to be more than a match for the enemy." [70] In the morning, fearing nothing from Hooker and hoping to destroy the Federal corps, Lee added Anderson to the force that was to attack Sedgwick; but it was not until 5:30 P.M. that the assault of about 21,000 against Sedgwick's 19,000 was launched. Bigelow wrote:

All this time Hooker with his 75,500 men, and the sound of Sedgwick's guns ringing in his ears, was held in check by Stuart with his 25,000. . . . Behind his intrenchments bristling with cannon and swarming with men, he waited supinely for Stuart to attack him or Sedgwick to attack Stuart.

Sedgwick held his own, and after dark retired to Scott's Ford, which he crossed before dawn of the next day, after an exchange of contradictory and confusing dispatches with Hooker. Ever since his injury Hooker "had been almost continuously alternating between sleep and stupor." [71] Letterman's failure to act, though understandable, was becoming subject to censure. Some of Hooker's messages to Sedgwick were not those of a man in possession of his normal faculties.

The retirement of the Sixth Corps was a smooth piece of work. Two companies of the Eighth Pennsylvania Cavalry formed the final covering force, the troopers swimming the river after the pontoons were removed. Early on the same morning—May 5—Gibbon, left precariously in Fredericksburg, crossed to the north of the river, the Nineteenth Massachusetts skillfully acting as rear guard against pressure by the enemy, who would have liked to get the bridges—all three of which were, however, saved. [72]

Toward midnight of the 5th–6th a council of war was held in a tent at Hooker's headquarters, to which the corps commanders were summoned. Hooker appeared with Butterfield—who had joined him that day—and Warren, and put the question whether the army should advance or withdraw; then he and Butterfield withdrew. Meade, Reynolds, and Howard voted to advance; Sickles and Couch to withdraw, the latter being careful to explain afterward that his vote had been decided by the knowledge that Hooker would continue to command. When informed of the vote, Hooker stated he would take upon himself the responsibility of withdrawing. As they left the tent Reynolds—who had difficulty staying awake—remarked, "What was the use of calling us together at this time of night when he intended to retreat anyhow?" To cover the withdrawal, Warren and Comstock selected an inner line three miles long with the ends resting on the river, a mile distant from the two bridges that had been thrown at United States Ford. During the night this line was occupied by the Fifth Corps, the others being massed near the river, and the army started crossing in a drenching rain, the artillery leading. Hooker himself crossed early, and a rise in the stream of six feet soon stopped the movement. Couch, finding himself in command on the south bank, said, "We will stay where we are and fight it out"; but a peremptory order arrived from Hooker for the crossing to be continued. One of the bridges was sacrificed to piece out the other, and the movement in the heavy rain was continued. Barnes's brigade of Griffin's division had the honor—and the responsibility—of being the last to cross, throwing behind it a rear guard composed of detachments from the Eighteenth Massachusetts and the 118th Pennsylvania.[73] The Confederate pickets felt the retiring Federal pickets only lightly as they withdrew behind the rear guard.

Some nonsense has been written about the damage that would have resulted if Lee had launched an attack while the corps were massed for passing over the river, or if some guns had swept the bridges, and it has been repeated since Bigelow competently disposed of the question.[74] Lee would have needed a number of hours to make dispositions for a heavy attack against the Fifth Corps, even if there had been no rain. As to effective artillery fire upon the bridge, that was an utter impossibility. With the Fifth Corps in position in the line covering the bridgehead, and others near at hand, there was no more danger that the crossing would be molested by Lee's forces than that the columns would be bombed from the air while passing over the bridge. Unfortunately, trained soldiers discussing such situations have sometimes let their imaginations run away with them, and have forgotten the realities of the "time and distance" factors or ignored the state of exhaustion or the ration situation of an opposing force. Lee did not have unused divisions to throw against the Federals, and his 10,293 killed and wounded was comparably a far more grievous loss than Hooker's 11,549.

Although the retreat of Sedgwick on the previous night had left Lee free to give full attention to Hooker's main force, he was in complete ignorance of the Federal withdrawal when he wrote to Secretary Seddon on the 6th:

General Hooker did not recross the Rappahannock after his defeat on Sunday, but retreated to a strong position in front of the United States Ford, where he is now fortifying himself, with a view, I presume, of holding a position this side of the Rappahannock. I understand from prisoners that he is awaiting re-enforcements, and that among others, General Heintzelman is expected.[75]

It was embarrassing to have this statement turn out to be wrong, and Lee, in his report the following September, forgot what he had written earlier and gave another version, which likewise bristled with inaccuracies: "Preparations were made to assail the enemy's work at daylight on the 6th, but on advancing our skirmishers, it was found that under cover of the storm and darkness of the night he had retreated over the river." [76] This was a disingenuous fabrication, for when daylight came even the Federal artillery had not quite finished its crossing; and six corps of infantry remained to pass, while the Fifth Corps was in position to receive a real and not just a mythical assault. Lee's achievement in the campaign had been remarkable, but his record would have been better if he had not tried to deny the skill of the Federals and the smooth working of the Army of the Potomac in the last as well as the first phase of the operation. Probably the Confederate commander never realized that while Hooker retreated it was he who probably escaped on May 6. Bigelow—the most painstaking and objective student of the campaign—has expressed the view that if Hooker had remained in his strong position, Lee, in attacking him, would have played into his hands and would probably have been unable to make his venture into Pennsylvania a few weeks later. He might even have suffered such losses as to advance the end of the war.[77]

Hooker had allowed the instructions he had given the cavalry for their intended operation in mid-April to remain in effect as a suitable accompaniment for the infantry campaign, though it is questionable whether he should have. Leaving Averell's division, which had been guarding the bridges at Kelly's Ford from the brigade of W. H. F. Lee at Culpeper, Stoneman struck south without a wheel in his column except the essential ones on his guns and caissons.[78] Some difficulty arose in crossing the Rapidan; and, knowing that Stuart with Fitzhugh Lee was not far away, Stoneman had his men pass a most uncomfortable night standing to horse in a cold rain. Many troopers, reins in hand, sank exhausted in the mud beside their saddled animals. Stuart evidently did not know just what was going on, and the next day the Federal horse passed nearly behind his column on its way to Fredericksburg. Instead of adhering to his old orders, Stoneman broke up his command into detachments of various sizes after reaching the Virginia Central Railroad, for the purpose of destroying track, bridges, and supplies. It cannot be denied that he wrought considerable havoc, for at one place he burned twenty-one wagonloads of bacon—which was a great quantity of bacon—and at another place, 50,000 barrels of corn and wheat, as well as other commissary supplies and clothing. Numerous bridges were burned or wrecked, and both the Virginia Central and the Richmond and Potomac railroads were broken below Hanover Junction in two places—to remain out of operation, however, for not over two days. The bold and close approach of some of

Stoneman's horsemen to Richmond caused no little alarm in that capital, and was in part responsible for the recall of Longstreet's divisions from before Suffolk.[79]

Stoneman was of necessity out of touch with Hooker, and lack of knowledge about his cavalryman's work may have influenced the army commander's surrender of the initiative about Chancellorsville. On May 2 Butterfield sought information from General Keyes at Yorktown, without success. Two days later, however, Halleck wired, "Major-General Dix telegraphs that Longstreet is in full retreat from Suffolk," which was very good evidence that Stoneman's operations were having some effect, though it might not have been what the confused Hooker wanted.[80] Hooker had perfect proof that none of Longstreet's troops had rejoined Lee, for although he had a good many prisoners none were from the divisions of Hood, Pickett, or Ransom up to early morning of the 5th.[81]

A part of Stoneman's cavalry crossed the lower Rappahannock and found safety at Gloucester Point opposite Yorktown, but the main body returned by the route it had followed outward. Early on the 7th Stoneman crossed the Rapidan at Raccoon Ford into a position of comparative safety. Fires were allowed for cooking the meager rations that were left; worn-out troopers who had done most of their sleeping in the saddle had the chance to stretch themselves upon the ground and sleep. Upward of 1,000 horses had been abandoned, replaced when possible by farm animals; but many a luckless horseman had been left to follow as best he could on foot or be picked up by the enemy. From the week of hardship and adventure enough solid material had been secured for a long life of story-telling—and many of the troopers who rode behind Stoneman had one or two years in the saddle before them, if they were lucky.

Lieutenant E. V. Sumner—proud bearer of his father's name—was sent by Stoneman to report to Hooker. After miraculously swimming the swollen Rappahannock in the dusk with bullets from an enemy patrol striking about him, he was borne unconscious by a horse that seemed to understand what was expected of his rider, to the tent of the commanding general. When he was taken from his mount the dispatches in his boot were found.[82]

Stoneman would have performed more valuable service if he had adhered to instructions, had kept his command together, and had struck hard at Guinea, close in Lee's rear. Much of Lee's transportation was there, and the supplies he needed for current use. A blow at that spot while he was fighting at Chancellorsville would have been paralyzing. Hooker himself should have seen that one cavalry division—which would have been Averell's—took post upon his right flank. If Averell had been in possession of the road to Germanna Ford, Jackson could not have made his advance to the turnpike and the consequent attack—as Stonewall himself said before he died. But the Union cavalryman, apparently not understanding orders or the situation—the latter is not strange in view of Hooker's great secretiveness—loitered about in the vicinity of Rapidan Station until May 1, when Hooker called him in and relieved him of command.[83] To the adjutant general of the Army Hooker wrote, "If the enemy did not come to him, he should have gone to the enemy." [84] It was a fine pronouncement indeed for a general who several times had said that he hoped the enemy would come and attack him.

Hooker's efforts to put responsibility for his defeat on Stoneman, on Averell, on Howard, and on Sedgwick make very unpleasant reading, especially when one recalls the favorable situation in which his army was placed as late as the morning of May 3, and that he himself then ruined everything by ordering the abandonment of Hazel Grove early on that day. There is fairly good evidence that Hooker, when asked by Doubleday a few weeks after the battle what had ailed him, replied, "Doubleday, I was not hurt by a shell, and I was not drunk. For once I lost confidence in Hooker, and that is all there is to it." [85] He was intimating that he had not been his usual self; and that was true. But the explanation might be put otherwise; heavy responsibility, fatigue, and nervous exhaustion had stripped away the mask of personal bravery, ready confidence, and boastfulness which he had always worn, and had left the real Joe Hooker—unprepared by previous contemplation and humble self-examination for the terrible ordeal of a commanding general opposed by a very able adversary, who had several times been through that trial.

With its swiftly changing aspects, culminating in the strange finale of Sedgwick's engagement at Salem Church, while Hooker sat idle near United States Ford with a fresh army of 35,000 men, the battle is full of interesting and instructive lessons. Although the week of operations can be satisfactorily understood now, it is not strange that at the time the campaign seemed utterly bewildering. Morgan Dix, with lightness of touch, wrote in his diary:

It would seem that Hooker has beaten Lee, and that Lee has beaten Hooker; that we have taken Fredericksburg, and that the rebels have taken it also; that we have 4500 prisoners, and the rebels 5400; that Hooker has cut off Lee's retreat, and Lee cut off Sedgwick's retreat, and Sedgwick has cut off everybody's retreat generally, but has retreated himself although his retreat was cut off; that Longstreet has not left Suffolk at all, and again that he has never been there. In short, all is utter confusion. Everything seems to be everywhere, and everybody all over, and there is no getting at any truth.[86]

Very properly Stanton had sought to control the news that was passed to the public while the army was on the south side of the Rappahannock.

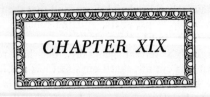

CHAPTER XIX

GOOD MARCHING
AND QUARRELSOME NOTES

*If you and he would use the same frankness to one another,
and to me, that I use to both of you, there would be no difficulty.*
Lincoln to Hooker

A PARTIAL record of events at the White House on Wednesday May
6 has been made by Noah Brooks, who spent a portion of the day at the
home of the President.[1] When Brooks arrived Mr. Lincoln had had no
recent official news, but nevertheless was certain that "Hooker had
been licked." In the early afternoon he came into a room where
Brooks was visiting Dr. A. G. Henry, another friend; and with ashen
countenance he handed Brooks a telegram from Butterfield that had
been received a short time before—written "In the Field" on Tuesday
at 11:00 A.M. The delay testified that matters were badly dislocated.
After stating that Hooker was too busy to write, the chief of staff said
rather ominously: "He deems it his duty that you should be fully and
correctly advised. He has intrusted it to me. These are my words, not
his." The President was told that the cavalry apparently had not
carried out instructions, and that Sedgwick had "failed in the execution of his orders"; but the reason for the retirement of the main army
was left for future explanation. After stating that the army might
recross the river that night the dispatch closed with what from
April 30 had become the tiresome theme song of the campaign—
Hooker's hope to be attacked in the position which he held.[2]

Just before receiving the fateful message Lincoln had wired to
Hooker the contents of Richmond papers of the 5th, as received by
him from General Dix by telegraph.[3] They announced that Jackson
had been severely wounded, and Heth and A. P. Hill slightly. Equally
important was the word that Federal cavalry had been at Ashland,
Hanover, and other points, and had destroyed several locomotives and
other property, as well as "all the railroad bridges to within 5 miles of
Richmond." The Commander in Chief was doing excellently in the
important matter of passing down information to his field commander,
and Dix was showing both enterprise and intelligent cooperation.
That the news was not sent by Halleck appears to have been acci-
dental; two days before, the General in Chief had forwarded news
received from Dix.[4]

Only five minutes after reading Butterfield's ominous message at
12:30 P.M., Lincoln telegraphed Hooker again, stating that he already
had sent information which showed that the cavalry had not failed,
and he was in hope that the rain of the day before had changed the
situation for the better, since it might have made Hooker's flanks
secure—a matter of which Butterfield had spoken with apprehension.
Still—as usual—Lincoln was most careful to leave all decisions with
his general.[5] A half-hour later Butterfield replied that the army was
over the river with bridges up, and that the President's messages were
on the way to General Hooker. At 4:30 Hooker telegraphed:

Have this moment returned to camp. On my way received your telegrams of 11 a.m. and 12.30. The army had previously recrossed, and was
on its return to camp. As it had none of its trains of supplies with it, I
deemed this advisable. Above, I saw no way of giving the enemy a general
battle with the prospect of success which I desire. Not to exceed three
corps, all told, of my troops have been engaged. For the whole to go in,
there is a better place nearer at hand. Will write you at length to-night.
Am glad to hear that a portion of the cavalry have at length turned up.
One portion did nothing.[6]

Fighting Joe seemed indeed to be himself again. Not only did he
have an explanation for the President, but he published the same day
a General Order to the army, in which he had a surprising amount to
say. Actually there were of course definite accomplishments—as there
had been at Fredericksburg—for both officers and men to feel proud
of, and these were listed. In explaining the defeat, another line was
used than with the President. The reasons, he began, were well known

to the army. "It is sufficient to say they were of a character not to be foreseen or prevented by human sagacity or resource." [7] Was he referring to the pillar that had struck him—an accident which Surgeon Letterman had not seen fit to turn to the advantage of his country? To the corps commanders there went a circular bidding them to have their commands well in hand, arms inspected, and everything in readiness—including dry ammunition—for action the next afternoon.[8]

While Hooker was looking to his army, Lincoln was thinking about the public's reaction to the new defeat. "What will the country say! What will the country say!" were the anguished words that Brooks recorded.[9] With the lifting of censorship the news had broken quickly, and at 3:00 P.M. former Governor Morgan of New York wired the President, "Nothing will so cheer the hearts of all good men as the immediate re-enforcement of General Hooker by troops from around Washington, Fort Monroe, and Suffolk." Not often did Lincoln call upon Secretary Seward to handle matters of a military nature; but to that diplomat, and not to the sometimes brusque—or on occasion, ironical—Stanton, he now turned. The Secretary of State—himself a former governor of New York—graciously but effectively told Morgan to keep his fingers out of affairs, and not to get excited, in a dispatch worthy of full quotation:

General Hooker has had, has now, and will have everything he asks for by telegraph, which is always in full connection with the War Department. He knows best what he wants, and when and where, and directs everything according to his own plans. He reports confidentially that only three corps of his army, all told, have been engaged. You need not be told that this is less than half of the army in his command and actually with him. Further accumulation of troops, not called for by him, would exhaust his supplies and endanger his plans. Be patient.[10]

It was not strange that Lincoln had refused to part with a Secretary of State who could handle a disturbed ex-governor so adroitly.

Stanton too had a little task for his pen, and he wired Hooker: "The President and General-in-Chief left here this afternoon at 4 o'clock to see you. They are probably at Aquia by this time." The War Secretary is often pictured as a man who went into panics in emergencies. Perhaps he did at times—most persons do. The casualness of the message just quoted in full would, however, suggest that it had to do with anything but a crisis in the history of a nation.

While at the headquarters of the army Lincoln wrote a note to

Hooker that probably contained the essence of his conversation with the general:

The recent movement of your army is ended without effecting its object, except, perhaps, some important breakings of the enemy communications. What next? If possible, I would be very glad of another movement early enough to give us some benefit from the fact of the enemy's communication being broken; but neither for this reason or any other do I wish anything done in desperation or rashness. An early movement would also help to supersede the bad moral effect of the recent one, which is said to be considerably injurious. Have you already in your mind a plan wholly or partially formed? If you have, prosecute it without interference from me. If you have not, please inform me, so that I, incompetent as I may be, can try and assist in the formation of some plan for the army.

In reply the general abandoned the explanation for his failure at Chancellorsville that he had put into his telegram of the day before, and followed the line set out in his General Order, stating it had resulted

from a cause which could not be foreseen, and could not be provided against. . . . I have decided in my own mind the plan to be adopted in our next effort, if it should be your wish to have one made. It has this to recommend it: it will be one in which the operations of all the corps, unless it be a part of the cavalry, will be within my personal supervision.[11]

Here was the promise that Hooker might paralyze seven corps by his presence instead of only six!

Lincoln and Halleck evidently tried to be hopeful, and after their return on the 7th Stanton wired to six generals and twenty-five governors what might be called an official communiqué on the recent unhappy battle, stating that the efficiency of the army had not been impaired, and only one third of it had been engaged. Stoneman's operations were described as "a brilliant success," and it was stated that the Army of the Potomac would "speedily resume offensive operations." [12]

Probably Ambrose Burnside, who was then in command of the Department of the Ohio, with headquarters at Cincinnati, and John Pope read the dispatch with special interest, though their feelings about Joe Hooker were very different.

To Hooker himself the War Secretary sought to send good cheer and ended a dispatch about Stoneman's raid as portrayed by Richmond papers: "The result at Chancellorsville does not seem to have produced any panic. Gold has only risen 6 per cent. in New York, and at the close to-day had gone down 4. The public confidence seems to remain unshaken in the belief of your ultimate success." [13] The next day he forwarded reports he had received from Generals Curtis and Rosecrans which he thought would please Hooker, just as "the cheering voice of brother soldiers" would be welcome. Also he sent a dispatch in which Governor Seymour of New York thanked him for his official account of the recent battle and stated that the information was "most acceptable and encouraging."

It would be idle to say whether Chancellorsville depressed and discouraged the North more or less than former defeats. Was it better or worse to lose a battle that should have been won than a contest like Fredericksburg that had seemed to most people to have no chance whatever of success? Between such alternatives it is indeed hard to choose. Once more there was striking evidence of the fighting qualities of the army; and this time the losses of the Confederates were known to have been essentially as great as those of the Federals except in the number captured. (Excluding the "missing," the Union casualties numbered 11,368.) [14] Transitory though it was, Stoneman's raid was an achievement, and the papers not unnaturally made much of it. On May 13 the people read that Stonewall Jackson had died on the 10th from pneumonia that followed the amputation of his arm; and they knew well it was a loss to the enemy hard to overestimate. Many stanch soldiers, hearing of his death, must have bowed their heads in tribute to a great American general, even while taking hope from the thought that Lee no longer had a lieutenant to whom he could confide a march like that to the rear of Pope at Manassas or the one to the flank of Hooker at Chancellorsville. Among the last words that the dying Stonewall uttered were: "Order A. P. Hill to prepare for action. Pass the infantry to the front. Tell Major Hawks . . ." [15] Even when losing consciousness Jackson knew how to give orders. As General Sir Neill Malcolm writes of Foch, he had "the fire in his belly." [16]

But Chancellorsville was forgotten as Vicksburg burst onto the front pages of the papers, and people who had begun to despair about the capture of that great fortress were electrified with the story of the new campaign that had begun on the very day that Hooker had laid his restraining hand on the corps moving to the rear of Fredericksburg.

They were to read of blow following upon blow with amazing rapidity, and though they were one day deceived by the false report that the great citadel had fallen, their disappointment gave way to the knowledge that it was completely invested by a strong force whose flanks rested securely on the great Mississippi both above and below the town. Thereafter its fall was merely a question of days. Also there came at last the delayed news of the brilliant cavalry raid of Colonel B. H. Grierson from La Grange, Tennessee, to Baton Rouge. The quiet hard-working general who for months had striven to capture Vicksburg had grown tired of the raids of Morgan, Forrest, and Van Dorn, and he had mounted one of his own. For audacity and skill of execution Grierson's exploit exceeded in many ways anything that Stuart had done; he traveled six hundred miles in sixteen days.

Burnside also was back in the news and in a way to provoke controversy almost equal to that raised by his December battle. He had no more than taken command of the Department of the Ohio when he issued a General Order announcing that "all persons found within our lines, who commit acts for the benefit of the enemies of our country, will be tried as spies and traitors, and if convicted, will suffer death." A large number of specific acts were listed as constituting a basis for the extreme penalty, and provision for milder punishment for less serious offenses was announced in the statement: "The habit of declaring sympathy for the enemy will not be allowed in this department. Persons committing such offenses will be at once arrested, with a view to being tried as above stated, or sent beyond our lines into the lines of their friends." Ohio happened to be the home of one of the most outspoken critics of the government, Clement L. Vallandigham, who had failed of reelection to Congress the preceding fall, in spite of the fact that the voting, taken in the large, had been against rather than for the administration.[17] He had then become a public speaker, and as his appearance was imposing and his rhetorical powers considerable, he had become the outstanding support of the "Copperheads" and had been made president of the "Sons of Liberty." An officer from Burnside's headquarters, dressed in civilian clothes, heard Vallandigham address an enthusiastic crowd at Mount Vernon, Ohio, on May 1, in which he spoke without restraint. The officer reported that there had been a clear violation of Burnside's order by Vallandigham, and on the evening of the 4th a company of soldiers went by special train from Cincinnati to Dayton, arrested the great orator, and brought him to military headquarters. Two days later he was tried by a military commission, was found guilty, and was sentenced to confinement for the period of the war.

Both approval and denunciation of what had taken place was expressed, and in answer to protests from a meeting at Albany on May 29 President Lincoln wrote in one of his great state papers:

Must I shoot a simple-minded soldier boy who deserts, while I must not touch a hair of a wily agitator who induces him to desert? This is none the less injurious when effected by getting a father, or brother, or friend, into a public meeting, and there working upon his feelings till he is persuaded to write the soldier boy that he is fighting in a bad cause, for a wicked Administration of a contemptible Government, too weak to arrest and punish him if he shall desert. I think that, in such a case, to silence the agitator and save the boy is not only constitutional but withal a great mercy.[18]

Nevertheless he mitigated considerably the sentence given. Taking the cue perhaps from Burnside's order, he directed that the Copperhead orator should be sent within the Confederate lines. On May 26 the people read that the former congressman, after a trip in a special train with carefully selected and accoutered companions, had arrived at Murfreesboro. There the journey was resumed on horseback. What the cavalry escort thought of the equestrian ability of the orator is not in the record; nor is there any receipt from a Confederate officer attesting that there had been delivered to him one Clement L. Vallandigham, complete and in serviceable condition. But when the escort returned, one trooper had a led horse; and the case which had been a diverting incident for three weeks dropped out of the news as a national issue.

There was no uncertainty about the effect of the victory at Chancellorsville upon the South. Fredericksburg had been a comparatively easy victory; but the brilliance of the battle fought in the thickets of the Wilderness was apparent and was stirring. It did much to offset the discouragement over Vicksburg's apparent doom, and helped remove the recollection of the mob that had formed in Richmond in March, and of the guns that had been unlimbered in the streets to hold in check the riotous citizens.[19] With two of his best divisions absent, Lee had driven the numerically superior Federal army back over the Rappahannock after Hooker had executed his brilliant maneuver and had gained a position of great advantage. Perhaps Lee and the Army of Northern Virginia were invincible; perhaps Antietam had not been an adequate test of what could be done on the other side of the Potomac; perhaps, if better preparations were made, the Army of the Potomac could be defeated on Northern soil. Such an achievement would provide the Confederates with a substantial foundation in bargaining for peace.

Probably no sentences in the Official Records have been pondered over more than those in which Robert E. Lee sought to explain and justify the Gettysburg campaign. Writing on the last day of the month in which the great battle was fought, with its many incidents fresh in mind, the Confederate commander stated:

The position occupied by the enemy opposite Fredericksburg being one in which he could not be attacked to advantage, it was determined to draw him from it. The execution of this purpose embraced the relief of the Shenandoah Valley from the troops that had occupied the lower part of it during the winter and spring, and, if practicable, the transfer of the scene of hostilities north of the Potomac. It was thought that the corresponding movements upon the part of the enemy to which those contemplated by us would probably give rise, might offer a fair opportunity to strike a blow at the army then commanded by General Hooker, and that in any event that army would be compelled to leave Virginia, and, possibly, to draw to its support troops designed to operate against other parts of the country. In this way it was supposed that the enemy's plan of campaign for the summer would be broken up, and a part of the season of active operations be consumed in the formation of new combinations, and the preparations that they would require. In addition to these advantages, it was hoped that other valuable results might be obtained by military success.[20]

The generality and vagueness in some of Lee's statements keep them from being entirely satisfactory, but his wish to pass over the whole unhappy enterprise as hastily as possible is readily understandable. Doubtless foreign recognition or even intervention was among the "valuable results" that it was believed might accrue from a heavy defeat of the Union army on Northern soil. This had indeed been a keystone of all Confederate hopes. The chance of recognition had almost disappeared on the day when Lee wrote, so that one can comprehend why he only hinted at it now. Foreign intervention was like a disappointing relative of whom one did not speak too openly.

Another "valuable result" of a severe Federal defeat north of the Potomac might have been stimulation of the Copperheads and other political malcontents and pressure upon the plain non-courageous persons who had lost heart, to terminate the struggle on generous terms. Vallandigham is reported to have warned that an invasion of the North would tend to unite opposing parties; [21] but whether unity so created would long survive a severe Northern defeat was quite another question. A decisive victory over the Army of the Potomac outside Virginia must have seemed to Lee worth half a dozen Fredericksburgs and Chancellorsvilles.

The question of supply also entered into the picture. The winter had been a hard one on Lee's troops and animals, in a region which showed everywhere the exhaustion of war, and which was served by a poor and inadequate railroad. But in contrasting the supply situation of his army with that of the Federals across the river one must not forget that organization and administration also were involved. Richmond, with the largest flour mill in the world, was in fact served by five railroads and the James River Canal,[22] while into Washington there came only the one railroad from Baltimore, and the canal from up the Potomac. Furthermore the Baltimore and Ohio line to the west from Baltimore was constantly threatened with being cut, and was cut from time to time. Although supplies could reach Hooker's depots at Aquia Creek by water from ports other than Washington, it is nevertheless true that the achievement of the railroad into Washington —double-tracked in 1863—was striking, and Stanton's praise of Northern rail management was well deserved.[23] Whatever Lee may have thought of the efficiency of his government and its railroads contrasted with that of the war administration of Lincoln and Stanton and the Northern railroaders, he knew that his men and his animals had poor prospects for a season of good eating, and that, only about a hundred miles to the north, there was a land of plenty untouched by war. From the farms of Maryland and Pennsylvania he could easily gain subsistence if his army were properly situated—at the cost of some perplexing problems for his supply officers; and from the shelves of the stores in prosperous towns and cities it might be possible to obtain shoes and clothing. Furthermore there was always the chance of capturing well stocked Federal supply depots and railroad or wagon trains of excellent Federal equipment. Supply was undoubtedly important in Lee's mind; but to say, "He had to invade the North for provisions, regardless of all else," [24] is to pay too little heed to the unequivocal first sentence in the quotation from his report, as well as to a dispatch that he sent early in the campaign, which will be cited.

Just how much thought Lee may have given to an invasion of the North before the conferences of May 14–17 in Richmond cannot be said with certainty.[25] The question that the High Command was wrestling with was whether to dispatch some of Lee's divisions to aid the Western Confederate armies while the rest of the Army of Northern Virginia continued a defensive attitude. The decision was against this course and strongly in favor of the invasion plan, though no clear written directive or order appears to have been given to Lee at the time. But in his headquarters he encountered strong opposition from Longstreet, the commander of his First Corps, who was back from ration-gathering exploits south of Richmond and threats to the Federal force about Suffolk. Longstreet did not like the invasion plan at all, and was strongly in favor of transferring offensive operations to the West with aid to Bragg for an attack on Rosecrans that might cause a withdrawal of forces operating against Vicksburg. This was merely reopening a question already decided by the cabinet, and so he directed his efforts to persuading Lee to adopt a "tactically defensive" attitude after crossing the Potomac.[26] He believed that Lee could take an advantageous position which the Federals could be induced to attack with possibly disastrous results to themselves. Doubtless Longstreet recalled both the losses that Lee had sustained when he attacked the Federal army in a good position at Malvern Hill and the heavy defeat he had himself done so much toward administering to Burnside. Did Lee make any commitment to Longstreet as to the general character of the approaching campaign? That is a vexing question over which there has been much dispute. Freeman clears Lee of even the most minor violation of any promise, by describing the discussion between Lee and Longstreet quite as if he had been present and made notes, and states that Longstreet mistook courtesy for consent to some of his proposals.[27] While it is impossible to believe that a soldier of Lee's ability and nature would ever commit himself to abstention from attack under all circumstances, it cannot be believed on the other hand that Longstreet wholly imagined his story. Longstreet's claim was not put forward only in his later years when time might have been playing tricks with his memory; before the war was over a year he had told a distinguished Northern war correspondent that Lee had "expressly promised his corps commander that he would not assume a tactical offensive, but force his antagonist to attack him." [28] Lee was guilty of too much vagueness at times in written orders to assert that he could not have contributed to misunderstandings in verbal conferences. If he thought that there could be any misconception by subordinates, because of assertions he had made at any time concerning objectives or conduct of the campaign, he should have removed it before he started to march.

Though Lee's subordinates may have been left with some misunderstanding, his superiors were not, for shortly after the movement of his army toward the North began he wrote to Seddon revealing his purpose. He stated that unless the Federal army were drawn out of its strong position opposite Fredericksburg into some region where it could be attacked, it would take its time to make preparations, and be on the way to Richmond, and he would be forced back into the intrenchments about that city. In order to avoid this "catastrophe" he thought his movement worth the "hazard" he knew it entailed. He hoped, however, that during the coming "sickly season" on the Southern coast the unacclimatized Northern troops could be held in check by local troops, and that all available regular forces would be thrown to his aid. Not a word was said about the *necessity* of invasion as a means to subsistence; and in accordance with his usual cordial acceptance of the instructions of his superiors he stated: "Still, if the Department thinks it better to remain on the defensive, and guard as far as possible all the avenues of approach, and await the time of the enemy, I am ready to adopt this course. You have, therefore, only to inform me." Was this a hint for reconsideration, or only the wish to have the War Department commit itself on paper? Seddon met the issue unequivocally two days later, June 10, writing to Lee: "I concur entirely in your views of the importance of aggressive movements by our army. Indeed, in my present judgment, such action is indispensable to our safety and independence, and all attendant risks must be incurred." As to reenforcements he could give no promise, stating that he had already sent the regular covering forces from Richmond, leaving that place much exposed.[29]

About twenty-five years after the event D. H. Hill wrote, "The drums that beat for the advance into Pennsylvania seemed to many of us to be beating the funeral march of the dead Confederacy" [30]—a pronouncement that one cannot dismiss as just an afterthought. Undoubtedly many persons in the South looked with alarm upon Lee's invasion of the North; and Hill may have been one, for in June, 1864, he wrote to Beauregard of one of Lee's views as "arrant nonsense." [31]

The army with which Lee was starting forth on his great adventure had recently been reorganized into three corps of three divisions each. Longstreet had the First Corps, with the divisions of McLaws, Pickett, and Hood. Ewell, back with a wooden leg after tiresome months of recovery, but with three stars on his shoulders, had the Second Corps, composed of the divisions of Early, Johnson, and Rodes. A. P. Hill, also a new lieutenant general, had the Third Corps, comprising the divisions of Anderson, Heth, and Pender. In Hill's promotion several senior officers had been passed over, apparently because they were not Virginians; and some discontent resulted.[32]

With the exception of Rodes's division, there were four brigades in each division; Rodes had five. Each division had its own organic battalion of artillery; and each corps had in addition two battalions of corps guns. A better and more flexible army organization could hardly be imagined, and there was only one bad feature: Stuart's cavalry division was rather clumsy with its six brigades. The strength return for May gave Lee an aggregate present of 88,735 officers and men, with 206 field guns. The cavalry had increased very much since Chancellorsville, and stood at 11,922, though probably not all men were mounted—the return for May 20 showed Stuart had 6,216 officers and men as "effective mounted," and 2,162 as "non-effective." The loss of Stonewall naturally rested very heavily upon Lee, and he wrote to Stuart with regard to a "successor of the great and good Jackson," saying, "Unless God in His mercy will raise us up one, I do not know what we shall do." [33]

Apparently Lee was completely unaware of the inadequacy of his staff for an operation such as he was beginning. Above everything else he needed a good chief of staff with sufficient ability and rank to command respect and to handle the multitudinous details that were certain to arise. At his headquarters there was little more than high-ranking clerks and letter writers. There was no one who could do responsible planning other than himself, and this fact threw him back too much upon his corps commanders for suggestions. Although the Confederates had full four-star generals and lieutenant generals, while the Federals had no officer higher than a major general, the Union armies had staffs presided over by suitable chiefs of staff. Hooker had a

major general in that important position and an excellent brigadier
general for adjutant; his chief engineer also was a brigadier general,
and his fine quartermaster would soon be wearing a star. Lee on the
other hand had no general officer upon his staff. Although he probably was compelled to depend upon Providence to "raise up" another
Jackson, he might have done something for himself in the matter of
staff officers. When tables of organization and regulations do not
provide proper personnel, commanders are in the habit of making up
for deficiencies by assigning officers to special duty.

On May 27 Colonel Sharpe turned in to Hooker an excellent intelligence summary of the enemy situation, which stated that Lee's army
was under marching orders, and that an order had recently been read
to the troops announcing that a campaign was about to start that would
require long marches and hard fighting. The general forwarded the
document to Halleck at once; but for some reason it did not reach the
latter for ten days. Its contents were, however, somewhat indicated
in a telegram to Stanton announcing that information—derived from
deserters—in which Hooker said he placed "a good deal of confidence," indicated that Lee would soon be in motion. Now, whatever
may have been the duties which had chiefly occupied Lincoln during
this day, his mind was evidently upon the Rappahannock when the
day's work was over, for at 11:30 P.M. he wired Hooker: "Have you
Richmond papers of this morning? If so, what news?" It was brief and
to the point as usual, but it also indicated something about his idea
of efficiency. Fighting Joe was not doing so well as the President
hoped; but he was doing well, for twenty minutes later he replied that
although he did not have that day's paper from Richmond he had one
of the day before, and it was disappointing in the matter of news. The
next day he was not so certain as to a probable move by the enemy,
for he wired Stanton that everything looked uncertain and spies that
he had sent across the river had failed to return. On the 28th the
New York Tribune, however, carried a dispatch about Lee's intended
invasion, and Governor Curtin, no longer hopeful of results from
telegrams, was on the way to Washington to see about protecting the
frontier of his state.[34] Lee on his part was quite uncertain as to what
Hooker might be intending to do, as he revealed in a dispatch to Stuart
(near Culpeper) on the 27th, and in a letter to Secretary Seddon on
the 30th.[35] The fog of war was heavy indeed along the Rappahannock,

where Hooker with his awkward army of seven infantry corps and a cavalry corps, mustering 122,046 men present, faced Lee's army of 88,736 men. Although in addition to heavy casualties in the recent battle, Hooker had also sustained extensive losses due to the expiration of enlistments, he had as large an army as he wished, according to a report that Halleck made to Stanton on May 18. It is also to Hooker's credit that the General in Chief reported that he had not claimed that he had been outnumbered at Chancellorsville, and had never put Lee's force above 70,000. But the Army of the Potomac faced future weakening, for 16,000 men were scheduled to go home before the end of June.[36]

The situation, however, presently began to clear. On June 2 Keyes wired Hooker from Yorktown that rumors all concurred in indicating that enemy troops were moving from the south to the north, "and that the idea prevails over the lines that an invasion of Maryland and Pennsylvania is soon to be made." [37] There was nothing definite, but that was the way that the wind seemed to him to be blowing. Professor Lowe's aeronauts also were watching enemy activities from their elevated positions, and on the 4th some of the enemy camps appeared to have been abandoned. This fact, added to the information recently obtained from deserters that the divisions of Hood and Pickett had rejoined the army, led Hooker to conjecture that Lee might indeed be preparing for a movement such as the one he had attempted the year before. The next morning more camps were gone, and at noon Hooker wrote a long dispatch to Lincoln asking if his instructions allowed him to cross the river and assail Lee's rear. He also spoke of the desirability of having one commander over all the troops that might operate in any way against Lee's army.[38] It is to be noted that he had declined the general control of Dix's troops when Stanton offered it to him before the battle of Chancellorsville, and that Halleck had afterward offered to move Dix to any point that Hooker would suggest.[39] Hooker's charge that he was ignorant of the operations of other forces was also not accurate. Just as he forgot on the 28th having wired the day before to Stanton that he had reliable information that Lee was about to move, so he forgot the various messages received from Peck, and the efforts of the President and the War Department to keep him informed.

Lincoln digested Hooker's long dispatch in a remarkably short time. Within an hour of its receipt he had filed a reply stating that

Halleck would answer the main questions; but he advised against crossing to the south of the Rappahannock if it should be discovered that Lee was moving westward with the probable intention of crossing it to the north: Lee should be fought on the north of the river if he would be so accommodating as to cross. No order, however, was given, and the decision was to rest solely with Halleck and Hooker. Within a short time, the General in Chief sent a telegram endorsing the President's view: it was not wise to cross the river and attack the very strong Fredericksburg intrenchments even if they were occupied by only a part of Lee's army; rather Hooker should conform to the movement of Lee's main body with a view of striking a blow at it. Halleck thought that troops had come to Lee from North Carolina, but not from Charleston, as Hooker had surmised: Army Head-quarters in Washington believed that any troops that could be spared from South Carolina had been hurried West to bolster the deteriorating situation of Joe Johnston. Halleck promised to have other forces cooperate with Hooker as much as possible and ended with a suggestion or caution that showed that in spite of his many failings he could give sound advice: "Lee will probably move light and rapidly. Your movable force should be prepared to do the same." [40] Already Hooker's thoughts were running in the direction that Halleck suggested, for early on the 5th a circular from his headquarters directed that the army be made ready to move on short notice with three days' cooked rations. Surplus baggage was to go to the rear, and no more leaves of absence and furloughs were to be given. Fighting Joe was about finished with pack saddles, but not completely; they were now to be carried in wagons, so that they could be used if the situation were propitious.[41] Secretary Stanton too was worrying over the excess impedimenta that Hooker usually had about his camps; and the next day he broke into the beginning campaign with the vexed dispatch:

I have been trying hard to keep the women out of your camp, but finding that they were going in troops, under passes, as they said, from your provost-marshal and commanders, I have given up the job. I think no officer or soldier should have his wife in camp or with the army. In other military districts, the order of the Department excludes them. If you will order them away, and keep your provost-marshal and other officers from issuing passes, not one shall be issued here, and all that profess to come from the Department will be forgeries.[42]

If, as some denunciators of the War Secretary claim, he wanted the war to continue until the South had been sufficiently conquered, it is hard to see why he combated a practice that would help immobilize a field force. He may not have been fully informed about conditions in more remote theaters, and perhaps elsewhere everything was not quite as he indicated. But his sharp note to Hooker was no more calculated to increase his popularity than his stern dealing with officers who were careless with government property, his watchfulness over contractors, or his censorship of the press. While Stanton was trying to get Hooker to "crack down" on his army a little, a Southerner was suggesting that Federal forces occupying Southern territory should become harsher. This resident of Mount Jackson, south of Winchester, wrote to the Secretary: "Increase the ill-feeling between the rich and the poor in your occupation of all towns in the Valley; . . . impress the poor with the idea that the rich are the cause of all their miseries, and divide the wealth of the rich with the poor." The Confederates already thought the Union army was too tough, and presently Lee wrote to Seddon that its conduct was "unworthy of a civilized nation," while Ewell in an order to his troops branded the men in blue as "a band of robbers." [43]

Stanton's telegram doubtless caused some profanity at Hooker's headquarters, but full and adequate comment must have been prevented by new developments. With commendable promptness Hooker had had bridges thrown on the 5th at Franklin's old crossing and had ordered Sedgwick to cross a sufficient number of his corps to make a reconnaissance that would reveal whether the enemy had withdrawn heavily. Meade, whose corps was holding the line farther up the river, was instructed to feel the enemy and find out as much as possible about his strength and position. The "approach," however, was to be friendly and conversational, for Hooker's chief of staff wrote, "Let your pickets chat enough not to tell him anything, but to find out his regiments." Seeing the possibility of moving, Hooker directed the commanders of the Second and Eleventh Corps to be ready to move the next morning—the 6th—with their trains. The Confederate reaction to Sedgwick's partial crossing on the 5th was prompt and decisive. He reported that he could not advance far without bringing on a general engagement; it was unsafe to cross all his corps, and both a contraband and prisoners had given the information that Lee and Longstreet had been in the vicinity the night before. [44] It is not likely that anything worthwhile was obtained by the pickets who attempted the fraternization approach.

The disappearance of camps that had been noted on the 4th had indeed been real, for Lee had started withdrawal on the 3rd; and on the 6th only the corps of Hill remained in the Fredericksburg lines. The new corps commander had managed things so adroitly that Hooker was more doubtful after Sedgwick's reconnaissance of the 6th than he had been before; but by the 10th he was aware, from cavalry activities higher up the Rappahannock, that some of Lee's infantry was at Culpeper and some at Gordonsville. In a long dispatch to the President he said there was a "manifest tendency of other corps to drift in that direction." Once more he brought up the question of moving toward Richmond, stating that this was the course he would follow if left to himself, and that he considered it "the most speedy and certain mode of giving the rebellion a mortal blow." Again the President replied without delay, saying that he did not think it wise for Hooker to move south of the Rappahannock if Lee were moving north of it. With perfect clearness he announced the correct governing principle: "I think Lee's army, and not Richmond, is your sure objective point." Hooker was playing with the thought of first taking the Confederate capital, and then going after Lee, but Lincoln said to him, "If you had Richmond invested to-day, you would not be able to take it in twenty days; meanwhile your communications, and with them your army, would be ruined." [45] The next day, a brief dispatch from Halleck informed Hooker that he agreed fully with the President. In view of the decisive way in which Fighting Joe had been defeated a month before by a force about half the size of his army, it would have been utter folly to start on an adventure such as he proposed, even if the correct objective had not been the one so clearly set forth by the President. It is true that by this time Richmond had become a great arsenal for the Confederacy, far exceeding Atlanta in importance, and Fayetteville, North Carolina. [46] Thus its loss would have crippled the war effort of the South. None the less Lee is supposed to have stated that he would be willing to "swap queens" with the North—sacrificing the Confederate capital for possession of Washington. Though none of the great factories that were producing so abundantly for the Union was located in the national capital, the security of Washington was essential; and Lincoln would not risk the exchange that Lee would have been willing to make. He also knew that if the Army of Northern

Virginia could be destroyed or heavily defeated, the taking of Richmond would be relatively simple.

The first real clash of the great campaign had already taken place when Lincoln told Hooker in clear terms that Lee's army and not Richmond was his true objective, and the battle had ended in great humiliation for Jeb Stuart. On the 5th the show-loving cavalryman—with a staff resplendent in new uniforms—had reviewed his troopers on a great open plain near Brandy, before many enthusiastic spectators who had come from the surrounding towns for the great occasion.[47] Lee was to have taken the review but could not be present; and so Stuart had the imposing show repeated on the 8th for the benefit of the commanding general, who rode around lines of troopers three miles long, and then took post and watched the skillful regiments pass by at a gallop. So absorbed had Stuart been in arrangements for his show and in preparing for a march that was to start on the 10th that he had all but forgotten that there was an enemy; but it happened that Alfred Pleasonton had been directed to cross the Rappahannock and find out what was going on in the vicinity of Culpeper.[48] Early on the 10th his columns started across at Kelly's Ford below and Beverly Ford above the railroad crossing. Buford's smart regiments of the First Division were well over at Beverly Ford before the Confederates were aware of what was going on. The Southerners were forced back, but Stuart called up supporting brigades, only to find himself taken in the rear by the column that Gregg had led across the river at Kelly's. The battle that ensued was the largest cavalry encounter of the war, and it shifted back and forth in a confusing manner still not completely understood. Confederate infantry was encountered, and, using authority he had received during the day, Pleasonton had his command back over the river when night came with total casualties of 866—including those in an attached infantry brigade—and two or three guns.[49] But comparable losses had been inflicted on the enemy, and Federal troopers reaching Stuart's headquarters had seized valuable papers—well worth a few guns—from which it was learned that he was to have started a march that very morning. Pleasonton interpreted it as a raid and told Hooker he believed he had prevented it—at least temporarily. Most important of all, the Northern cavalrymen returned with the knowledge that they had become the equal of the proud cavalry of the South, and they were to start the very heavy work that lay ahead with high morale and an eagerness to engage the enemy that they had never known before. At noon two days later Pleasonton wired Hooker: "Have just reviewed my cavalry. They are in fine spirits and good condition for another fight." [50]

Correspondents worked hard by candlelight and with pencil, and typesetters worked equally hard with their type and their sticks, to put before the Northern people the story of the battle. The *New York Tribune* on the 11th gave four closely packed columns on the front page to an account of the engagement, under the headlines: "The Cavalry Fight on Tuesday—River Crossed in Face of Enemy—A Brilliant Dash into His Lines—Severe Hand-to-Hand Fighting—The Rebels Driven Six Miles—A Successful Achievement—Heavy Losses on Our Side—Slaughter of the Enemy Fearful—Highly Important Work Accomplished—An Extensive Rebel Raid Foiled." Armchair strategists disposed to complain that Pleasonton had returned to the north of the river, and that nothing permanent was accomplished, lost all ground for objections when they learned—if they learned—that not far behind Stuart were heavy masses of infantry which were marching to the front when Pleasonton broke off the engagement. Though Stuart had fought well and had done much to restore a battle that was going against him, he had been completely surprised—an early message from Pleasonton to the contrary notwithstanding; and against him the *Richmond Examiner* directed a bitter criticism that made pleasant reading for Northern officers when the papers came into their hands.[51]

It is sometimes stated or insinuated that Hooker tarried too long at Fredericksburg. Usually such judgments are based upon after-knowledge of the situation of Lee's army and of his intentions, and not upon the information that Hooker had or could be expected to obtain, while important considerations to which he was compelled to pay heed are conveniently forgotten. The days that followed the battle of Brandy are among the most interesting of the entire war for the military student, and Hooker did very well indeed so far as his movements are concerned, though he did reveal some of his weakness of character, in a way which must have disturbed the President, the Secretary of War, and the General in Chief. Hooker's staff and subordinate commanders likewise acquitted themselves very creditably. Though Lee was forced to watch carefully what Hooker was doing, he could in general execute moves in accordance with his own wishes, which is one of the great advantages that come to the commander who plays an offensive role. The Federal general on the other hand faced the task of divining the intentions of a very able adversary who understood well how to mask his plans, and who always moved rapidly and struck hard.

For the most part Hooker had to rely for information upon Pleasonton, with whom he had telegraphic communication by way of Washington and Alexandria. From Warrenton Junction the cavalryman reported on the evening of the 10th that there had been no infantry in Stuart's recent big review, but that there were five or six divisions in the vicinity of Culpeper and Orange. This took no account of Hood's Texans, who had been spectators at Stuart's show, ready to jeer mounted troops after the manner of good foot soldiers. Two hours later Pleasonton informed Hooker that he had encountered some infantry the day before: "I am satisfied the enemy have a strong infantry force at Culpeper. I am also satisfied their cavalry was crippled yesterday, while mine was not." [52]

Unfortunately the papers found in Stuart's camp revealed nothing whatever about projected infantry moves, and as usual there were contradictions in the accounts of captured men, deserters, and contrabands. One informant asserted that Hill would cross at Fredericksburg and attack Aquia Creek after Hooker had been lured up the river. Some support was given to his story by the activities within the Fredericksburg lines, which may in part have been planned to deceive the Federal balloon observers. At least Fighting Joe became impressed with the extensiveness of reenforcements from Richmond, and he presently—for the first time—made the mistake of somewhat over-estimating the size of his adversary's command. [53]

Although Hooker could not give up his position opposite Fredericksburg too quickly because of the great supply base and the hospitals with 11,000 sick and wounded, he did on the 11th begin to slip more of his infantry up the Rappahannock; and at the same time he sent out a warning order preparing the rest of the command for rapid movement. [54] But even if it were assumed that A. P. Hill's corps was merely a force with both a covering and a deceptive mission, and that Lee's aggressive plans were directed elsewhere, Hooker still was not certain where the blow would come. Would Lee move through Thoroughfare Gap, seize the Orange and Alexandria Railroad, and interpose himself between Hooker and Washington, as he had done the preceding

August? Or was he this time really bound for the Shenandoah Valley, as Pope had thought ten months earlier when Jackson's turning column was observed? On June 12 General Reynolds was put in command of all the forces that Hooker had shifted up toward the railroad; [55] and Pleasonton's reports went to him as well as to Hooker. At 6:20 in the

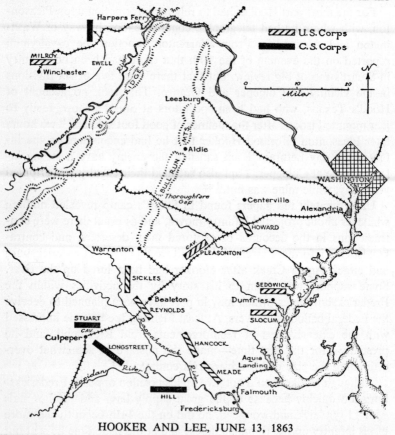

HOOKER AND LEE, JUNE 13, 1863

evening a telegram from Hooker to the President indicated that the rest of his army would probably be moved within a few days. The army was indeed being made ready for combat, and a long General Order— to be read to every company and battery—not only tightened discipline, but prescribed constant instruction of both an elementary and an advanced character during all intervals between active operations.[56] It was an army of veterans; but even veterans could improve.

The next day—the 13th—was a busy and decisive one. At eight o'clock Pleasonton wired that a Mr. Smith had just reported that Ewell had marched away from Culpeper on Sunday the 7th and Longstreet had followed him on Monday and Tuesday, both bound for the Shenandoah Valley—although the fact was that Ewell left Culpeper on the 10th.[57] Butterfield told the cavalryman to ascertain speedily the road the Confederates had taken, and Pleasonton replied at once that Negroes stated that Ewell had taken the route to Sperryville, and that all columns had gone in that direction. It looked indeed like a move toward the Valley, but Butterfield continued to press for more information. Reynolds was told that the indications were that the enemy planned to turn the right of the Army of the Potomac or to go into Maryland. The Navy Commander was at once requested to get all his shipping into Aquia Creek, and at noon Reynolds and Pleasonton were directed to plug up Thoroughfare Gap through the Bull Run Mountains.[58] Lincoln had been planning to come down in the afternoon to witness the demonstration of a new incendiary shell; but, sensing the posture of events and not wishing to intrude at a critical time, he wired at 11:30, "I was coming down this afternoon, but if you prefer I should not, I shall blame you if you do not tell me so." The reply was, "It may be well not to come." [59]

Probably by the middle of the afternoon Hooker had made his decision. It was embodied in an excellent Circular, whose preparation must already have been well advanced, for the multitudinous details could not have been drawn up on short notice. Though present-day arrangement and paragraphing was not followed, the order would meet the high standards of modern field orders. Except for the omission of information about the enemy, everything was in the directive that one would expect to find. There were no if's or ambiguous statements to confound subordinates and puzzle the student as to what Hooker intended, nothing to produce volumes of debate and charges against subordinates for disobeying or doing what was not contemplated. The crisp, stirring first sentence, "This army will be transferred from this line to the Orange and Alexandria Railroad," revealed a commander who had made up his mind and a staff that could write. (The order was signed by Seth Williams, but Butterfield certainly had a great part in its formulation.) The vicinity of Centerville was given as the place of concentration, with appropriate instructions for all elements of the command. Sedgwick, whose corps was still across the river, was to start withdrawal as soon as it was dark, protect the engineers as they took up the bridges, and then start for his new location. Hancock, who had succeeded to command of the Second Corps after Couch had asked to be relieved, was to remain to keep A. P. Hill on his own side of the river and to cover the withdrawal of supplies and equipment. Headquarters were to close the next morning, and to open in the afternoon at Dumfries. The quartermaster, commissary, ordnance officer, and medical director all had heavy assignments, and the order closed with a distinct touch of the modern, "The chief signal officer will cause a detail to report to Generals Hancock and Sedgwick for duty during the withdrawal." [60] To the civilian in charge of various telegraph offices, instructions were sent that would insure the use of wire circuits during the movement without leaving anything of value for the enemy. [61]

The amount of material to be removed was enormous, including locomotives and cars; but Ingalls, the great quartermaster, already had things well under way. In the morning he had telegraphed Washington asking for the immediate removal of the 11,000 sick and wounded—a procedure that would put a great strain upon the hospitals in the city as well as upon the transportation facilities. He asked the quartermaster in charge at Aquia Creek if he could not have all the invalids on the way by the next morning, and told him that everything valuable about the wharf and buildings must go to Washington, and that nothing was to be destroyed without orders. At 8:00 P.M. he reported to the quartermaster general that the army was moving and concluded his dispatch: "I shall go with the trains when not with General Hooker. Though the movement will be hurried, and our forces somewhat scattered at first, I still apprehend no loss. I will keep you advised." [62]

The orders referred to are sufficient to disprove Sandburg's statement that the staff of the Army of the Potomac had never worked as smoothly as that of the Army of Northern Virginia. [63] The best order that Lee had issued up to this time may have been the famous lost "Special Orders, No. 191" of the preceding September, but it had dealt with a far less complicated situation than that which faced Hooker on June 13, and the latter's Circular had more of the "modern" than anything that ever came from Lee's headquarters. There can be no doubt as to which staff a present-day commander would prefer: that presided over by Major General Butterfield, with Brigadier

General Henry J. Hunt for chief of artillery, Brigadier General Seth Williams for adjutant, Brigadier General Rufus Ingalls (his star not a month old) for quartermaster, Brigadier General Gouverneur K. Warren for chief engineer, and Colonel George H. Sharpe for intelligence officer, or the militarily undistinguished and inadequate staff of Lee.

At Washington preparations had been under way to meet an invasion before Pleasonton and Stuart clashed on the 9th. The preceding day, Major General Robert C. Schenck, commanding the Middle Department with headquarters at Baltimore, forwarded to Halleck a significant dispatch just received from Major General Robert H. Milroy, who was garrisoning Winchester with some 5,000 men. Milroy stated that a "mighty raid" of some kind was undoubtedly in the making, and he advised that the militia of Maryland, Pennsylvania, and Ohio be called out. Halleck soon had General Barnard, senior engineer officer in Washington, on the way to Pittsburgh to prepare that city against a raid.[64] On the night of the 10th a dispatch from Pleasonton stated that Stuart's raid had been intended for Pennsylvania and Pittsburgh, and Secretary Stanton at once passed the word on to Major General W. T. H. Brooks, commander of the newly formed Department of the Monongahela.[65] Pittsburgh was a long way off, but the Secretary evidently thought well of the endurance of Stuart's troopers and their horses, for he said the Pittsburghers must expect the Southern horsemen daily and should get to work. Halleck sent another engineer to Pittsburgh who could stay and supervise the digging of trenches. No money was available and no field forces could be sent, but the General in Chief believed the city could be held by the Department Corps of the Monongahela that Stanton had ordered created on the 9th.[66]

The eastern half of Pennsylvania was made into the Department of the Susquehanna, and General Couch, who had lost confidence in Hooker and had asked to be relieved from duty with the Army of the Potomac, was sent to Harrisburg to take command. The possible theater of operations was being broken up into a good many compartments, but efforts at cooperation were to be made and were to be quite effective. Stanton evidently was not too hopeful about the militia as secondary forces; he sought to create a reserve force more under Federal control that could be called out in an emergency, and Couch

was given the task of forming the Department Corps of the Susquehanna, into which it was hoped men who had seen field service would
enter.[67] At first Governor Curtin demurred, thinking the time not
propitious for such an innovation; but when Stanton stood firm, he
fell in step and issued a good strong proclamation urging support of
the two corps then being formed by Brooks and Couch.[68]

Nor were efforts to distract Lee forgotten. As early as the 9th
General Halleck instructed General Foster at New Bern, North
Carolina, to resume offensive operations if it were possible on account
of the dispatch of Confederate troops to the West and to Virginia.
The next day General Dix reported from Fort Monroe that he would
start a movement up the Peninsula from Williamsburg on the 11th, and
would at the same time have the forces at Suffolk begin to move forward. He did not have many troops, but he would do what he could.
On the day mentioned he informed Hooker that the movement from
Williamsburg had started, but stated that Peck at Suffolk was temporarily held up.[69]

Milroy, at Winchester, presented a problem. Much effort had been
expended on fortifications, and there was quite an armament as well as
much other property and supplies in the historic Valley town; but a
single division was inadequate to defend the place against a serious
attack. On the 10th Schenck, on Halleck's direction, ordered Milroy
to remove his command to Harpers Ferry, thus getting rid of his
heavy guns and surplus stores at once, and retaining only a light
"lookout" force that could decamp quickly. Milroy, however, im-
prudently tarried, and on the afternoon of the 12th Ewell's corps
began to invest him. The next day Schenck passed on to Couch the
news of Ewell's activities and stated that he had no way to stop the
Southerner in a northward movement and was therefore concentrating
his small forces to hold Maryland Heights.[70] Lincoln was disgusted
with the news, and on the 14th wired Schenck, "Get Milroy from
Winchester to Harper's Ferry if possible. He will be gobbled up if he
remains, if he is not already past salvation." To Hooker he telegraphed
that it looked as if Milroy were surrounded at Winchester and Tyler
at Martinsburg. It was the dispatch in which he used one of his famous
homely but apt remarks, "If the head of Lee's army is at Martinsburg
and the tail of it on the Plank road between Fredericksburg and
Chancellorsville, the animal must be very slim somewhere. Could you
not break him?" [71] Of course no "breaking" operation could be under-

taken, especially since Hooker had begun to overestimate the enemy strength, as shown by his telegram to Lincoln that Lee had between 70,000 and 80,000 men in his advanced force while Hill with 30,000 more was preparing to make a river crossing in the vicinity of Fredericksburg.

The situation had cleared a little the next morning—the 15th— when Hooker reported to Halleck that a dispatch just in from Hancock revealed that Hill had moved off toward Culpeper. Presently Butterfield sent word that the Richmond papers of the 13th were laying it on Jeb Stuart heavily for having been surprised at Brandy and were exhorting him to redeem his reputation. He also reported that Dix's movement up the Peninsula was causing anxiety.[72]

Bad news began to arrive at noon, when Tyler, after making good his escape from Martinsburg, wired Halleck from Harpers Ferry: "Officers and men just in from General Milroy show that he is wiped out. I doubt if 500 will escape." Twenty minutes later he wired that Milroy himself would arrive within an hour: "Not nearly so bad as I had feared." But the better news did not atone for Milroy's disobedience, and Halleck wired Schenck: "Do not give General Milroy any command at Harpers Ferry. We have had enough of that sort of military genius." Distrust of the discomfited general was not anything new, for on January 6 Halleck had telegraphed to Burnside: "I do not rely much upon General Milroy's statement of the enemy's movements. He cries 'wolf' so often that he may be caught." [73] Though he had directed the abandonment of Winchester, the General in Chief did not want Harpers Ferry given up. Instructing Schenck to concentrate all available troops there, he said bluntly, "That place must be held." [74] By squads and depleted regiments a part of Milroy's command arrived in a demoralized condition, and Tyler, who ranked Kelley, moved everything to the strong position of Maryland Heights, reporting 4,000 effective men, not counting those who had made the hasty trip from Winchester. General Kelley being a supernumerary, Schenck shrewdly ordered him to New Creek in the vicinity of Cumberland, with instructions to concentrate all the small forces available for the purpose of holding as much as possible of the important Baltimore and Ohio east toward Martinsburg. Averell in West Virginia was instructed to cooperate. The hospital and hospital stores were removed from Frederick, where something of a panic had broken out.[75]

The harvest at Winchester was considerable for the Confederates—

3,358 prisoners, and 28 pieces of artillery; but Milroy's train of 500 wagons made good its escape to the north, and did not stop until it reached Harrisburg.[76] Thus Ewell missed a good deal of booty after all. Nevertheless the general with a new star on his collar and a new wife was doing well in spite of his new leg. By using a buggy at times he got over the road without difficulty; with a led horse near at hand he looked at least as martial as a modern general in a jeep.

Hearing that some of Milroy's men had escaped with the wagons, Schenck sent the general to gather them up, and on the 22nd Couch reported that Milroy had 2,800 of his command at Bedford.[77] Halleck was still angry, and ordered Milroy's arrest; but Couch interceded on account of his present usefulness.[78] Milroy, who had come into the service at the head of an Indiana regiment, and who believed that West Pointers had it in for him, made an appeal to the President; and on a crucial day in the campaign, June 29, Lincoln sought to assuage the grieved commander by a very frank letter in which he said: "I have never doubted your courage and devotion to the cause. But you have just lost a division, and *prima facie*, the fault is upon you; and while that remains unchanged, for me to put you in command again is to justly subject me to the charge of having put you there on purpose to have you lose another." Very discerning and just was the indorsement which Lincoln added to the findings of the commission that soon examined Milroy's actions.[79]

The route into Pennsylvania was open, and on the 15th Jenkins's brigade of cavalry, attached to Ewell, crossed the Potomac, to be followed soon by Rodes's division, which halted at Williamsport while the troopers rode on.[80] It was a busy day in the War Office, and a calm and clear-headed Secretary was sending dispatches to mobilize emergency forces. His reserve army corps idea, sound as it was in many ways, had to be scrapped, and Lincoln called for 100,000 militia to serve for six months, unless sooner discharged: from Maryland, 10,000; from Pennsylvania, 50,000; from Ohio, 30,000; and from West Virginia, 10,000. To the governors of other states Stanton telegraphed that the movement of the "rebel" forces was sufficiently developed to show that Lee with his whole army was moving into Maryland and Pennsylvania. The governors were asked if they had any organized forces they could send. A special telegram went to Governor Seymour inquiring if New York might not send 20,000 men. That state was far ahead of others in organized militia. Although Seymour had been bitterly opposed to the draft he responded wholeheartedly to the emergency, and by evening Stanton had the assurance that the New York City and Brooklyn regiments would soon be on the way.[81] There would be in these regiments from 8,000 to 11,000 men, some of them without arms; but the deficiency could be made up quickly when they reached Harrisburg from stocks sent to Couch. Secretary Stanton informed the general of the coming of the New Yorkers, with the assurance, "Every exertion is being made by the Department to support you"—which Couch could well believe because he already had authority to take military possession of the railroads for the movement of troops and supplies. Remembering that Hooker would want all possible information of the enemy, Stanton directed Couch, "Please keep me advised of the position of the enemy, that I may communicate with General Hooker." [82]

States other than New York had nothing to contribute, and Governor Richard Yates of Illinois had the most melancholy report: "Day after tomorrow the Democratic Convention for the Northwest is to be held here, and it is supposed by some that it will inaugurate direct opposition to the Government, if not Revolution in our midst. . . . Should the convention prove harmless, then Illinois will do her full share." However, the Democrats were not as violent as Yates had feared, only adopting peace resolutions.[83] Pennsylvania herself had few troops organized to assist in home defense and her apathy was commented upon in the New York press.

The story broke on the 16th, when the people learned that Winchester was lost, and that Lee was advancing into Pennsylvania. While in some papers, at least, the Army of the Potomac had dropped out of existence, others complained of the existing rules of censorship, loose though they were. Probably everyone knew by this time that Aquia Creek had been abandoned—knowledge from which surmises could be drawn. But as Lee rode into the zone of Northern newspapers he certainly did not get too much information—as events were to show.

To Hooker at Fairfax there came a dispatch from Warren at Alexandria, informing him that everything was out of Aquia Creek on the evening of the 15th except a little rolling stock that soon would follow. Nor had the enemy crossed the Rappahannock at Fredericksburg. Presently Hancock, whose corps had remained behind while the army moved away, reported from Dumfries. He had marched the Second

Corps hard in order to catch up; the heat had been terrific; men worn out from loss of sleep fell victims of sunstroke; some had died. But all his stragglers were up, and he had sufficient forage for his artillery—that was what counted. In forty-five minutes he wired again; his divisions were already on the move; he himself was about to start; no public property would be left; the telegraph office would be dismantled.[84] Winfield Scott Hancock, who had distinguished himself as a brigade commander, and then as a division commander, was handling a corps with the hand of a master. The famous old general of the Mexican War who was in retirement would have been thrilled at the messages received from his namesake.

The whole army had done well, and the concentration about Centerville had apparently been perfectly executed in all particulars. A directive of the 16th stripped the army of further unnecessary baggage in order to shorten its great trains.[85]

But Joe Hooker was becoming a little peevish—in part, it can be assumed, on account of uncertainty as to the enemy's intentions. At 11:00 A.M. on the 16th he addressed a peculiar dispatch to Lincoln in which he stated:

You have long been aware, Mr. President, that I have not enjoyed the confidence of the major-general commanding the army, and I can assure you so long as this continues we may look in vain for success, especially as future operations will require our relations to be more dependent upon each other than heretofore.

Lincoln had not been giving any directions; and when Hooker had addressed direct questions to him he had been punctilious to turn them over for answer to Halleck, expressing merely his own view but never in the form of an order. But there was no hesitation in meeting squarely the situation that Hooker brought up. That night Lincoln telegraphed:

To remove all misunderstanding, I now place you in the strict military relation to General Halleck of a commander of one of the armies to the general-in-chief of all the armies. I have not intended differently, but as it seems to be differently understood, I shall direct him to give you orders and you to obey them.[86]

In order to soften a little this blunt statement a messenger was already carrying a letter to Hooker that was written in the friendliest fashion but nevertheless went to the heart of the matter with the fullest candor. In part the President wrote:

> When you say I have long been aware that you do not enjoy the confidence of the major-general commanding you state the case too strongly. You do not lack his confidence in any degree to do you any harm. . . .
> I believe Halleck is dissatisfied with you, to this extent only, that he knows that you write and telegraph (report, as he calls it) to me. I think he is wrong to find fault with this; but I do not think he withholds any support from you on account of it. If you and he would use the same frankness to one another, and to me, that I use to both of you, there would be no difficulty. I need and must have the professional skill of both, and yet these suspicions tend to deprive me of both.[87]

Here the President proclaimed his belief that honest candor must be the basis for successful action by men in high authority. In a way, Hooker was outspoken enough; but instead of having a dispassionate and objective attitude toward others, he was contentious and snappish to a degree that increased rather than lessened misunderstandings. Lincoln all but passed over the amount of *confidence* that Halleck had in Hooker, and that had been the word Hooker had used in his letter. So long as Hooker was in command this was not exactly the issue; the issue was *support*. Certainly no one could have had full confidence in Hooker after the battle of Chancellorsville. But there remained the question whether he would be aided or impeded in carrying out the wide range of decisions open to him under the mission assigned him by the High Command on June 10 and previously. Whether Fighting Joe saw that it was Lincoln and not he who had employed the really relevant word, can be only a matter of conjecture.

The 16th revealed some of the difficulty that Halleck and Hooker had in working together without misunderstanding. After telegraphing to Hooker that there was no evidence that Lee was over the Potomac in any force, the General in Chief wired at 3:50 P.M. that it was certain that Harpers Ferry was being surrounded, and he stated that no relief could be expected except from Hooker's command. The message was certainly open to misunderstanding, but Hooker went the limit in misconstruing it. He issued an order putting the First, Fifth, Eleventh, and Twelfth Corps in motion at 3:00 A.M. on the 17th for Leesburg; the Second, Third, and Sixth to follow the next day; and he reported to Halleck at 7:30, "In compliance with your directions, I shall march to the relief of Harper's Ferry." Now Halleck had given no directions whatever for Hooker to march to the vexatious old town, and it was of course foolish for Hooker to start all his army for that place. Already Halleck had another message on the way stating that the report about Harpers Ferry was false, and that the situation there was as uncertain as it was in Hooker's own front. To the unexpected telegram from Hooker the General in Chief replied that he had given no order to march to Harpers Ferry and that all he wanted was that some force be pushed up toward Leesburg so that it could provide relief if necessary.[88] The rest of the army, he stated, should be put in position to support such a detachment, while the cavalry was pushed out to "ascertain something definite about the enemy."

Halleck of course knew of the blunt telegram that had gone from Lincoln to Hooker just fifteen minutes before he sent his own dispatch, and as if to make clear their relations he said: "You are in command of the Army of the Potomac, and will make the particular dispositions as you deem proper. I shall only indicate the objects to be aimed at."

Hooker had plenty to sleep over after the General in Chief's message arrived at 1:00 A.M. of the 17th, and when normal breakfast time came he seemed to be in a quarrelsome frame of mind. After he had countermanded his march order with the assignment of new movements for his corps, he sent a long dispatch to Halleck listing the contradictory or confusing reports that he had received from Washington. He ended, "I should very much like to have reliable and correct information concerning the enemy on the north side of the Potomac." Naturally he would. But had he any right to expect it? Halleck replied that he regretted that reports were so unreliable and contradictory: "So far, we have had only the wild rumors of panic-stricken people." On the 16th Stanton, fully aware of Hooker's perplexities, had informed him that he would have to exercise his own judgment as to the credibility of reports sent to him: "The very demon of lying seems to be about these times, and generals will have to be broken for ignorance before they will take trouble to find out the truth of reports." As a matter of fact Hooker had no "reliable and correct information" about the enemy situation in his own front, and there were contradictions in reports coming from Pleasonton just as much as there were in those from Washington. He was as much out of humor at 9:20 P.M. as he had been in the morning, and he closed his last dispatch to Halleck with the dig, "Has it ever suggested itself to you that this cavalry raid may be a cover to Lee's re-enforcing Bragg or moving troops to the

West?" [89] It would of course have been possible for Hill to entrain at Culpeper or at Gordonsville; but whether he had or had not done so was something for Hooker's cavalry to find out. After Lee should break connection with the railroad, there would no longer be the possibility that his move to the Valley was merely a trick to cover such a move as Hooker suggested, and the general's remark must be put down as part of the kickback of a tired officer who was chafing under a reprimand.

Halleck kept his temper—as befitted his position—and came off ahead in the exchange of repartee with Hooker. His reply, after referring to inquiries from officers and citizens, commented: "They are asking me why does not General Hooker tell where Lee's army is; he is nearest it." After this sharp little prick, he put the problem directly up to the field commander, "I only hope for positive information from your front."

The next day—the 19th—Fighting Joe made some good suggestions about establishing signal stations at Crampton's Gap and on South Mountain which would allow observation of the country north of the Potomac, and Halleck replied that he had given the necessary directions. Then Hooker complained about reports in the *New York Herald* as to the movements of his army. Three days previously he had asked Stanton to have the newspapers announce that he was moving his army to the James River.[90] Such an announcement would have been little less than silly and would have fooled no one; the Confederates knew that Hooker was not marching toward Richmond, and to assemble shipping to transport his great army by water would have required weeks. Halleck commiserated with him about the newspaper reports, but told him the way to stop them was to bar offending reporters from his lines. As to enemy plans, he ventured the statement that it looked as if Lee had been trying to draw Hooker's right across the Potomac so as to attack his left.[91] But in order to predict what Lee meant to do, it must be discovered where his army was. So said the General in Chief. However, he was helpful to the extent of saying that no large body of Confederates had appeared either in Maryland or in West Virginia. Perhaps in exchange for this bit of knowledge Hooker, who had apparently mellowed a bit, gave the position of his army as of 7:30 P.M., June 19: Twelfth Corps, Leesburg; Eleventh, four miles from Leesburg; Fifth, Aldie; First, vicinity of Herndon; Third, Gum Springs; Second, Centerville; Sixth, Germantown; Pleasonton resting and feeding his horses—and their riders—at Aldie. He shared Halleck's doubt as to whether Lee intended throwing any considerable force into Maryland. Pleasonton, who had been trying to break through Stuart's cavalry (skillfully screening the Confederate army by holding the passes in the Bull Run Mountains), went further in his views. From questioning of prisoners he believed that Lee's infantry was still for the most part on the west side of the Blue Ridge—which was the truth—and that the Confederate commander intended to attack eastward toward Hooker's present position. But Pleasonton was soon to change his views and change them radically. At 3:00 A.M. of the 21st he wrote, "My opinion is, that Stuart's force is kept in our front as a blind until their main force is thrown across the Potomac; they will turn westward toward Pittsburgh." [92] On what did Pleasonton think the Confederate army would subsist after it reached the Pennsylvania mountains?

Efforts at coordinating all forces so as to disregard department lines and give Hooker control over all disposable field forces had been made since the 18th, when Halleck directed Hooker to communicate directly with Heintzelman and Schenck. Then provision was made for Hooker to give orders direct to the subordinates of those commanders; but this was not accomplished without confusion. [93] Hooker, whose headquarters were at Fairfax Station, was in Washington on the 23rd conferring on the question. [94] The next day he learned that his command did not extend to troops inside Washington and Baltimore, and that a good portion of the troops given him was militia. [95] To obtain full information, Butterfield went to Baltimore; and at an early hour on the 25th he sent a long report to Hooker, in which he set at 26,000 the total of reenforcements—including the Harpers Ferry garrison but excluding the militia—which, added to the 80,000 that Butterfield had set down for the Army of the Potomac, apparently put Hooker in command of a force of 106,000. [96] But Fighting Joe was not satisfied. On the 25th he stated to Halleck, "You will find, I fear, when it is too late, that the effort to preserve department lines will be fatal to the cause of the country." [97] It was an unfair attack: he saw only part of the problem that faced the High Command. Halleck, though he may have made mistakes as to procedure, was not trying to preserve department lines. In addition to putting at Hooker's disposal troops that he thought could be spared, or that were fit for field duty, he was trying to increase the threat to Richmond by bringing some troops from North Carolina to augment the force that Dix had. [98] No General in Chief should tolerate talk such as Hooker's from a general who had such a poor record for using troops under his command.

The War Secretary had continued giving special attention to the guarding of the formidable Susquehanna River as a limit to Lee's invasion. On the 20th he asked Couch whether he had sufficient powers for the emergency. Briefly the general replied, "My powers are ample. I require nothing more." Two days later he reported at length upon his situation: From New York 13,000 men had arrived, or were to arrive, with orders to remain for thirty days; they looked very well but had little confidence in themselves. His artillery was raw and likewise his cavalry; but he believed he could prevent a crossing of the Susquehanna above the Maryland line.[99] Like any soldier he would have been glad to have some seasoned regiments, and some batteries that had fired their guns in earnest. But Couch was not inclined to threaten his superiors with disaster if he did not receive everything he wanted.

On the 20th Hooker had wired to John C. Babcock of Frederick directions about procuring information for him, and the same day a detailed dispatch concerning the first crossings of the Confederates at Williamsport was received in reply. Ewell was over the river and the division of Rodes was identified; but the main body of Lee's army was said to be not even within supporting distance of the force that had crossed. On the 23rd Babcock was again appealed to, and the next day he paid off with a big story. There was no doubt that the last of Lee's army had passed through Martinsburg; from the mountains the main body could be seen crossing at Shepherdstown, where scouts reported that a pontoon bridge was being built. Nine thousand men and sixteen guns had passed through Greencastle the day before.[100] At Antietam Furnace a large force could be seen. A patrol from Maryland Heights brought in two prisoners from the Eighteenth Georgia who confirmed the fact that Longstreet was crossing at Shepherdstown.[101] A dispatch from Couch, in reply to a query from President Lincoln, brought the word that deserters said that Hill and Longstreet were over the river with 40,000 men and that Ewell had 30,000 in the advance.[102] The report was forwarded at once to Hooker.

A glimpse at Hooker's headquarters on the afternoon of the 24th reveals an incident important in the history of staff work. The competent General Warren, as engineer officer, had presented on the 16th an excellent report on roads and all possible fording places of the Potomac.[103] Hooker now gave him the task of presenting an "estimate of the situation," such as might be prepared at present by an operations officer and an intelligence officer. In well organized and convincing form Warren set forth the reasons for moving the army to the vicinity of Harpers Ferry. He began: "The whole of Lee's army is reported to be on the Potomac, above that place, part of it across the river, and

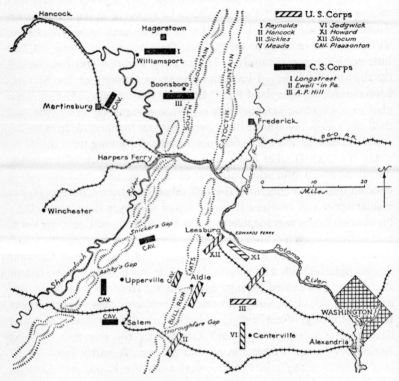

HOOKER AND LEE, JUNE 24, 1863

threatening an advance upon Harrisburg." No staff officer of Lee could have put the situation more accurately, and perhaps none so concisely. After considering the mission that had been assigned to the Army of the Potomac, Warren stated that it should march to the neighborhood of Harpers Ferry, where it could paralyze the movements of the enemy army by threatening its flank and rear as it advanced, while time was gained for collecting reenforcements so as to make the Federal army the stronger of the two, if it were not that already.[104]

The period of uncertainty was over at last, and the great army was ready to move.

On the 25th, the First, Third, and Eleventh Corps, with the Artillery Reserve, crossed the Potomac on pontoon bridges at Edwards Ferry with General Reynolds in command.[105] The rest of the army was put in motion for the river at 3:00 A.M. of the 26th, the Sixth Corps and the cavalry forming the rear guard.[106] On the evening of the 26th Hooker had his headquarters at Poolesville, Maryland, and he wired Halleck, "I desire every facility to be in readiness for supplies to be thrown to Frederick by rail." Fighting Joe should have felt a comfortable assurance in the fact that Herman Haupt was in Washington; and an order from Halleck the next morning put upon the able railroader the responsibility of transportation of troops and supplies for the field armies.[107]

In the last ten days the cavalry had written a splendid record in the many skirmishes it had had with the horsemen of Stuart, who had had slight success in determining what Hooker was doing. Their exploits made encouraging reading for the people of the North. With regard to one action, Buford—who had an eye for good fighting whether done by his own men or by the foe—wrote, "The enemy then came up in magnificent style from the direction of Snickersville, and for a time threatened me with overwhelming numbers." But the carbine fire of the Eighth Illinois and the Third Indiana broke them and drove them back, and under pressure the enemy retired over the mountains into the Valley. He continued: "I saw most of the engagement from the start to the end. I cannot conceive how men could have done better." [108] High praise indeed from an officer whose standard seemed to be perfection! As he led his troopers over the pontoon bridge Buford may have been very tired, but he had what does most of all to set the mind of a commander at ease—perfect confidence in the will to fight of the men who followed him. And a few days later he would show his assurance by dismounting his troopers and throwing them in front of an entire corps of Lee's infantry.

Some infantry and all the cavalry—that of Major General Julius Stahel—from the Washington defenses had already joined Hooker; and Heintzelman—in command at Washington—reported that if the enemy moved upon the capital from the Virginia side he would not know it until they appeared before his works. In all, 30,000 veteran troops had been lost from the city defenses, either to Hooker or to

Dix.[109] The city was almost wide open to a hostile raid; but fortunately there was no Confederate force that could threaten it as Dix was to threaten Richmond—though Lee sought to assemble one at Culpeper.[110] The passage of the "rebels" over the Potomac had of course been prominently proclaimed by the papers, but the story of the developing invasion was sometimes pushed into second place by the more encouraging news from Vicksburg. It was seen that Lee intended to subsist his army on the country to an extent that no Federal army had done in the East, and it was reported that Ewell was sending immense quantities of supplies and goods southward. Governor Curtin burst forth with a somewhat panicky proclamation containing the exhortation, "Do not undergo the disgrace of leaving your defense mainly to the citizens of other States." [111] Well indeed might he feel chagrin that it was regiments from New York that had taken over the mission of defending Pennsylvania's capital! A few days previously Couch had reported to Stanton, "Most of the men that rushed to arms at Altoona and south are rushing home." [112] Frightened citizens of Pittsburgh besought Lincoln to put General Frémont in command, at whose word 10,000 men, according to one dispatch, or 20,000 according to another, would spring to arms.[113] But the President had no more intention of putting Frémont back on duty than he had of restoring Little Mac, and the messages from Pittsburgh apparently received no reply. The dispatches had arrived on the 27th, which was to be a momentous day, and one when Lincoln could give little attention to the suggestions and supplications of alarmed citizens. It is quite possible that he had also read the dispatch from Couch, reporting the homeward trek to Altoona.

CHAPTER XX

A COURIER FROM WASHINGTON
AT THREE A.M.

You need not believe any more than you choose of what is
published in the Associated Press dispatches concerning this
army to-morrow. *Hooker to Lincoln*

Rumors and false reports of all sorts were everywhere, and on almost
everybody's tongue. Someone reported to the President that Hooker
had been in Washington on the night of the 25th. The rumor may have
originated with a person who wished to lower still more the standing
of the general with the administration, either for selfish personal reasons or from an honest lack of faith in him; or it may have arisen from
no more than a simple mistake in identification. A few days later
General Couch, who was very steady and paid little attention to idle
gossip, was to make the amazing report to Secretary Stanton that
Jefferson Davis had *undoubtedly* been in Greencastle, Pennsylvania.
If someone of standing sufficient to impress Couch could "see" the
President of the Confederacy on Northern soil, certainly someone could
"see" Fighting Joe at his old familiar haunt in Willard's Hotel—where
wise Assistant Secretary Watson had sought him the preceding August.
Lincoln did not like the report about Hooker, and he made inquiry of
the general himself as to its authenticity. Hooker, unable to be objec-
tively candid and direct, replied to Major Eckert, who was in charge of
the Washington telegraph office: "Dispatch received. My compliments
to the President and inform him I had not that honor." However, he
could not let the matter rest there; curiosity about the rumor intruded

[643]

upon his thoughts, and two hours later—at 8:00 P.M. of the 26th—he telegraphed directly to Lincoln: "You need not believe any more than you choose of what is published in the Associated Press dispatches concerning this army to-morrow. Was it from the newspapers that you received a report, or an idea, that I was in Washington last night?" Was this the General's conception of the frankness that Lincoln had asked for ten days previously? Even McClellan at his worst had not been much more condescending: the President need not believe any more than he chose! Not frankness, but swaggering impudence, was what was required to ask the direct question that Hooker asked. At 8:00 A.M. the next day Fighting Joe had his answer, simple, direct, unevasive: "It did not come from the newspapers, nor did I believe it, but I wished to be entirely sure it was a falsehood." [1] Five months before—at the time he elevated Hooker to the command of the army—Lincoln had told the general there were qualities in him he did not like; his reply to Hooker's query said he still was not sure of him. Fighting Joe let the President off without further cross-examination.

On the evening of the 26th, between his messages to Eckert and Lincoln, Hooker asked Halleck, "Is there any reason why Maryland Heights should not be abandoned after the public stores and property are removed?" He intended to visit the place the next day on the way to Frederick, in order to satisfy himself on this point; and he lectured the General in Chief a little: "It must be borne in mind that I am here with a force inferior in numbers to that of the enemy, and must have every available man to use in the field." The next morning he wired again, stating that his force of enlisted men for duty would not exceed 105,000 men; and a few illuminating remarks led up to another little lecture for the scholarly Halleck: "I state these facts that there may not be expected of me more than I have material to do with." [2] It is the business of the High Command to assign missions in accordance with its own judgments. The words indeed ill became the general who on May 4 had assigned to Sedgwick the task of taking the intrenchments overlooking Fredericksburg and then of marching with his one corps to the relief of the six corps that Hooker had near Chancellorsville. It was evident that the same hesitancy was coming over Fighting Joe that had paralyzed him in that battle.

Just how the estimates of Lee's strength on file at Hooker's headquarters at that moment may have looked, cannot be known. But now that the Confederates were over the river men devoted to the Union

cause, eager to aid its armies, were coolly watching the Southern
columns, were counting guns and men, and were sending messengers
through the day and through the night to Federal officers. At 5:30 P.M.
of the 26th Howard, commander of the Eleventh Corps, sent from
Middletown to General Reynolds a dispatch remarkable for the extensiveness and the precision of its information. It gave extensive identifi-
cations of Confederate units, their camping places, and their routes.
Not only was there much about Ewell, but the corps of Hill and Longstreet were definitely stated to be over the river. Also: "Lee in person
crossed the Potomac last night. His entire force on this side up to
yesterday reported to be between 60,000 and 70,000 men." [3] It was
not likely that Howard's fresh news was passed on that night from the
bivouac of the First Corps at Jefferson to Hooker, who was twenty-five
miles away at Poolesville, with the Catoctin Mountains intervening.
But it is equally unlikely that Hooker could have offered any substantial backing for his positive assertion that Lee was leading a force
larger than his own command of 105,000 men. Just as Fighting Joe
followed McClellan's example in lecturing the High Command on what
could be expected of him, so too he followed his predecessor—whom
he liked to criticize severely—in exaggerating though less extravagantly
his opponent's strength.

But it is not at all unlikely that good staff work at Hooker's headquarters was in part responsible for the information Howard sent in
from Middletown. On the 25th Colonel Sharpe telegraphed Babcock
at Frederick, "General Reynolds goes to-day with three corps to hold,
if possible, the South Mountain Gap and Crampton's Pass. Report to
him, and remain with his advance." [4] Perhaps Babcock was not disposed to diaries; perhaps he was too busy to write— but a full diary
by John C. Babcock covering the last ten days of June would have been
of much value and interest.

June 27 was a momentous day for both Hooker and Lincoln. From
Point of Rocks at 10:00 A.M. the general sent a brief dispatch to
Butterfield, then en route to Frederick with army heaquarters: "Direct
that the cavalry be sent well to the advance of Frederick, in the direction of Gettysburg and Emmitsburg, and see what they can of the
movements of the enemy." [5] It was to be Hooker's last operation
directive for his army, and it was excellent. He kept clearly in mind
the true mission of the cavalry, covering his army and gathering in-

formation; and he did not allow himself to be distracted by secondary possibilities. When Hooker reached Harpers Ferry he probably received the dispatch that Halleck had written at 10:30, which stated: "Maryland Heights have always been regarded as an important point to be held by us, and much expense and labor incurred in fortifying them. I cannot approve their abandonment, except in case of absolute necessity." [6]

On the 24th Hooker heard from Halleck that Schenck had been notified that all troops in Harpers Ferry and the vicinity would take orders directly from him; the next day he directed General French— in command at the ferry—to have three days' cooked rations "on hand for the present," and to prepare his command "to march at a moment's notice." [7] The rest of the dispatch showed that his scheme was not to have French's force join his main army, but rather "to make a dash" at any enemy force above Harpers Ferry that had not yet crossed the river. This would not have left Harpers Ferry open to enemy occupation, and Hooker's inquiry on the evening of the 26th showed plainly that he knew Halleck had not given him authority to order the total abandonment of Maryland Heights. During Hooker's Washington visit on the 23rd the Harpers Ferry question must have been discussed, so that he could supplement Halleck's dispatch of the 24th with additional knowledge as to the wishes and views of the General in Chief.

Though Halleck had telegraphed in good temper and did not say that under no conditions should Maryland Heights be abandoned, and certainly did not even intimate that the force there might not be diminished, Hooker lost patience—like a peevish child with an unsatisfactory parent. He ceased being a disciplined soldier and was not equal to showing the attitude to his superior that he without question would have expected from one of his own corps commanders. He telegraphed that he had found at Harpers Ferry 10,000 men fit to take the field, and added: "Here they are of no earthly account. . . . All the public property could have been secured to-night, and the troops marched to where they could have been of some service." Of the fitness of the entire command for field duty General French, its immediate commander, thought differently—as will soon appear. Just why did Hooker not state where he wanted to move the command? Would not Halleck want to know, and would it not influence his decision? But it was not in Hooker to be so thoughtful, so considerate, so balanced. Nor was he content with bluntly giving his superior a dig and weaving an insinuation of poor judgment into his message. He made a clear-cut issue with the General in Chief by closing his dispatch, "I beg that this may be presented to the Secretary of War and His Excellency the President." [8] The first question which "His Excellency the President" would have asked would probably have been where Hooker wanted to march the garrison: Lincoln had a penchant for figures and precise knowledge, as witness his dispatch of a few weeks before with its three *where*'s.

Although Hooker was either so careless or so angry as not to put the hour of writing on his dispatch—an important item in view of the fact that Butterfield had been careful to inform Halleck that after 11:00 A.M. messages for the army commander should go to Frederick —Halleck's headquarters fortunately put the hour of receipt upon the message that was to be so important on this crucial day. It arrived at 2:55 P.M.

There was far more wisdom in Halleck's attitude and judgment with regard to the holding of Maryland Heights than Hooker and many subsequent writers have seen: the general, because of his unbalanced temperament and lack of willingness to see a superior's problems; the latter-day critics, because of a tendency to dismiss Halleck with a superior and disdainful shrug of the shoulders, as well as a complete neglect of certain important facts. In the Maryland campaign of the preceding September it had been Halleck's refusal to withdraw Colonel Miles from Harpers Ferry that led Lee to divide his army, giving McClellan the chance to destroy half of his adversary's force that he had thrown away. The loss of the garrison to one half of Lee's army would have been a small price to pay for a crushing victory over the other half. Halleck's refusal had been based chiefly upon the impracticability of withdrawing the command of Miles because of the position of Lee's army; furthermore he believed that McClellan, if energetic, could free the position from all danger—and the Commission that examined the surrender of the position concurred fully in his view.[9] But one must believe that the General in Chief fully understood the great importance of the Harpers Ferry position, and would not have ordered Miles out of it even if he had been able to join McClellan without any difficulty.

There were two principal reasons why Maryland Heights—dominating the town of Harpers Ferry—was an important position for the Federals to hold. In the first place it gave control of the single water-level gateway into the strategically important Shenandoah and Cumberland valleys—the gateway through which in earlier days so many settlers had passed on their way to Kentucky and Tennessee. Nothing could have pleased Lee much more than to learn that this important door had been stupidly surrendered, and that his precarious line of communications was not to be threatened by it. Here—as in other places—World War II helps one make a reappraisal of the Civil War. By seizing inconspicuous and apparently unimportant Kiska in June, 1942, the Japanese caused the United States much trouble indeed. It was an unknown name when it first appeared in headlines, and Americans turned to their atlases or studied the maps in the papers and looked incredulously at the tiny island which for months was to distress them because the enemy had seized it. It had great strategic value, and one writer lists no fewer than six unhappy consequences that resulted from the fact that the Japanese recognized its importance and occupied it. So too Maryland Heights, dominating with its majestic bulk the water-level gap into the great valley beyond the South Mountain and Blue Ridge Range, had substantial *strategic* value.

Through Harpers Ferry there also ran the Baltimore and Ohio Railroad, a vital supply road and artery of communication. Several times it had been cut, and soon after Lee broke it again in June, 1863, the *New York Tribune* informed its readers that it had become necessary to divert supplies for Grant's army at Vicksburg to the Lake Shore Railroad, increasing the time of transit from about ten to as many as twenty days.[10] Not only was Harpers Ferry the natural point on which to base the essential protecting forces that the Federals had kept at Martinsburg and Winchester—when they could seize and hold those places— but there the railroad crossed the Potomac on a great bridge. A saga of stirring perseverance and accomplishments can be told about this structure; for floods on the river conspired with Confederates in repeatedly destroying it![11] At the time of Lee's first invasion of Maryland in September, 1862, an iron bridge had replaced the former wooden structures, but on the 24th it was blown and lay a complete wreck upon the river's bottom, and for the fourth time in fifteen months traffic across the river was interrupted. On October 31 the president of the railroad wrote to McClellan that the masonry for a new iron span had been completed. Remembering perhaps that the general had been chief engineer for the Illinois Central and then president of the Ohio and Mississippi, President Garrett wrote, politely but pointedly:

"You are aware of the large losses heretofore and of the heavy cost of the proposed iron structure. . . . Do you think the prospects of permanent military protection at this point are sufficiently favorable to justify us in again incurring this large expenditure?" [12] Lincoln saved McClellan the necessity of writing another of his meaningless notes, and by the middle of April, 1863, a new bridge was in position—the sixth in the history of the railroad. Justifiably the historian of the Baltimore and Ohio writes: "Damaging and pillaging and rebuilding. Faith never lost. Nor heart." [13]

Since Maryland Heights was essential to holding Harpers Ferry, is it strange that the man on whom rested the responsibility for operations in the whole gigantic theater of war, who was aware every day of the importance of the railroads, would not approve of its abandonment, except in case of necessity? It was important to hold Maryland Heights and Harpers Ferry in 1863, just as it was necessary to seize Guadacanal and hold Malta in World War II; and Halleck would certainly have been shortsighted and derelict in his duty if he had written to Hooker otherwise than he did. It is hard to believe that Hooker did not understand the importance of the railroad; but he was not an officer to be much disturbed by the responsibilities of others. He would not have minded giving Halleck a heavy future problem by losing another bridge if he could add a few thousand men to his field force, even though in the end he might have allowed them to sit a battle out, as he had allowed so many of his brigades to do at Chancellorsville.

World War II should have caused a reappraisal of the value of Harpers Ferry in the Civil War. But in 1945 a historian of the period, apparently forgetting that Hooker may have seen the entire situation only from the standpoint of a somewhat inconsiderate subordinate, wrote that Hooker had "correctly" asked for the "abandonment of Maryland Heights"; and he seems to place no value upon the often destroyed bridge, making no mention of it. His discussion does not intimate that the railroad and the bridge, as well as the holding of an easy entrance into the Cumberland-Shenandoah Valley, entered into Halleck's evaluation. He states that Halleck had the old obsession of guarding Washington by a scattering and immobilizing of Union forces, and replied he could not approve the abandonment. [14] Where in Halleck's dispatch to Hooker is the word Washington? Not only is the qualifying part of Halleck's reply to Hooker ignored, but the first part of what he said is interpreted from a much too restricted point of view.

It will be seen in due time that Halleck—who, in spite of limitations, had both military experience and knowledge—was right with regard to Harpers Ferry in June, 1863, just as he had been in September, 1862.

It is hard indeed to straighten out Hooker's mental processes on June 27; but he apparently decided to deliver a virtual ultimatum. At 1:00 P.M. he wired the General in Chief:

My original instructions require me to cover Harper's Ferry and Washington. I have now imposed upon me, in addition, an enemy in my front of more than my number. I beg to be understood, respectfully, but firmly, that I am unable to comply with this condition with the means at my disposal, and earnestly request that I may be relieved from the position I occupy.[15]

Hooker's original instructions had not unequivocally specified covering Harpers Ferry, and his unqualified assertion that the enemy's force exceeded his own was very inaccurate. The entire presentation of his case was characteristic of his unprecise and none too scrupulous mind. The real question, however, is whether Hooker—perhaps as the result of a bit of stimulant—was or was not just bluffing. Nicolay and Hay, who must have heard much discussion pro and con, could only write, "It will always be impossible to say whether General Hooker intended to be taken at his word." [16] But certain it is that he sent the request to be relieved before receiving an answer to his earlier dispatch, for the later message was received at three o'clock, five minutes after the one sent earlier. It is perfectly possible that the two were handed to Halleck at the same time.

But there is the best of evidence that Hooker, before he started on his twenty-mile ride to Frederick, did one thing proving that he did not believe the administration would part with him, and that he had no intention of insisting that he be relieved of command, in spite of the impressive word "earnestly" in his telegram. He must have directed General French to have two brigades "victualed" and ready to join a corps from his army at 6:00 the next morning in an expedition up the river toward Lee's communications, for at 8:00 P.M. an order went to Slocum to have the Twelfth Corps ready to march light—with ambulances but little or no train—at 4:00 A.M. Though a mission was not actually given to Slocum, it being said that more explicit orders would follow during the night, he was told that two brigades of French's force would join him when he went through Harpers Ferry; and so there is no doubt as to where he was to go. The contemplated use of the two brigades from French's command would not have been in any way an "abandonment" of Maryland Heights, and Hooker might well have ordered them away under the authority given him on the 24th. However, he was still suffering from indecision and told Slocum a half-hour later that his march toward Harpers Ferry was countermanded. Instead of going westward he was directed to march his command to the vicinity of army headquarters. Simultaneously there went to French this order:

Colonel Lowell, with a regiment of cavalry, is ordered to report to you at 7 a.m. to-morrow. The general directs you to send all your cavalry to make a reconnaissance in the direction of Williamsport. The general suggests that you cross at Keedysville, looking into the rear of Sharpsburg. Acknowledge.[17]

The sending of infantry up the river was a questionable move; but a good commander weighs all possibilities, makes his decision, and then tries resolutely to carry it out. There is no evidence of any new information reaching Hooker in the period 8:00 to 8:30 P.M., and his significant change of plans merely proves that he was suffering from the same sort of irresolution that seized him in the early days of May. It is sometimes incorrectly stated that Meade changed the orders for Slocum's corps after he had assumed command.[18]

Hooker's request to be relieved made Lincoln's problem very easy; in fact he had few easier decisions in the entire war. He did not have to either sustain or override his General in Chief in the matter of Harpers Ferry, as he would have been compelled to do if Hooker had not sent his second message. He had only to deal with an army commander in whom he had never had too much confidence, who had now lost the confidence of most of his leading subordinates and of the public. Hooker's conduct of his army from the time he began to move its first units from the Rappahannock opposite Fredericksburg until its last elements crossed the bridges at Leesburg had been excellent, except in secretiveness toward his corps commanders. In this regard the habit that he had revealed before the battle of Chancellorsville was persisting, and on the 25th General Meade closed a long letter to his wife with the complaint:

I hear nothing whatever from headquarters, and am as much in the dark as to proposed plans here on the ground as you are in Philadelphia. This is what Joe Hooker thinks profound sagacity—keeping his corps commanders, who are to execute his plans, in total ignorance of them until they are developed in the execution of orders.[19]

It can be assumed that Lincoln realized that the army had been maneuvered skillfully, and that its crossing the Potomac so soon after the main body of Lee's force was very creditable. But the coming battle would be the pay-off; excellently conceived and well executed marches would no more win the campaign under way than they had won that of Chancellorsville. This also the President knew full well. In addition there had been the tone and temper displayed in Hooker's dispatches, qualities a superior might bear from a subordinate who had recently won a great victory, but must find hard to overlook in one who had ingloriously failed. From still another point of view the situation was easy: there was no question at all about Hooker's successor. It would be General Meade. Thus an important part of the problem involved in a change of commanders stood already solved.

It was not until 8:00 P.M. that Halleck wired Hooker: "Your application to be relieved from your present command is received. As you were appointed to this command by the President, I have no power to relieve you. Your dispatch has been duly referred for Executive action."[20] Certainly Halleck was not in a state of collapse at the thought of losing Hooker; he was no more upset than he would have been if he had received a dispatch from his wife announcing that she would have to substitute boiled for baked potatoes for his supper. The General in Chief seemed to be shrugging his shoulders and saying: "It's quite agreeable to me; but the chief will say the word."

As a matter of fact the President must already have said the word, and it is quite possible that Colonel James A. Hardie of Halleck's staff was already on the way with War Department orders relieving Hooker and putting Meade in command of the army, and a letter of instructions to Meade from Halleck.[21] A more prompt acknowledgment of Hooker's request would have saved Halleck from speaking as if the matter were still under consideration; but certainly the vital question was the decision, the issuance of orders, and the dispatch of the messenger. Halleck was a busy man and should not be criticized too severely if he treated his old "friend" of California days a little disingenuously. As when McClellan was replaced by Burnside, an officer of some rank was chosen to carry the fateful orders.

The episode was made to order for a person who likes to embellish records, add fanciful details, and write knowingly of what went on behind closed doors. Such a person was Charles F. Benjamin, who pretended to know the tone of voice in which Stanton and Lincoln gave their instructions to Hardie, and who even described what went on in the War Secretary's mind when a remark of Meade's was reported to him.[22] Like Benjamin's very pretty story of the trip Lincoln and Halleck had made to Hooker's headquarters on May 6, his story of this event has the fault of not being true, for it disagrees with the Official Records (which had not been published when he, without citing a single document, wrote twenty years after the event on which he gave so much "inside information").

Benjamin, regarding Lincoln as now merely a sort of mouthpiece for the decisions of Secretary Stanton, put responsibility for the removal upon Stanton, who was determined that Hooker should not be allowed to fight another battle. The War Secretary was "master of the situation," but "Hooker was so full of hope and energy that severe measures had to be resorted to in order to wring from him that tender of resignation deemed to be necessary to enable his supporters at Washington to keep on outward terms with the Administration." But there had been no tender of resignation, and just how Hooker's warning to Halleck not to expect too much from him fits in with the buoyant "hope" mentioned by Benjamin is hard to see.

It is one thing to assert that the High Command—Lincoln, Stanton, Halleck—was very hesitant about allowing Hooker to fight another battle and would welcome his request to be relieved as a simple solution of its problem. It is quite another to suggest that the Harpers Ferry incident was a neatly contrived trap into which Hooker obligingly stepped. Benjamin missed one little touch that he might have added. He could have stated that the deeply plotting Stanton sent an officer to Harpers Ferry to assure that such refreshment would be available for Fighting Joe as would increase the combativeness of his humor. But one thing Benjamin did do to involve Stanton just a little more: he created a new office, and asserted that messenger Hardie was chief of staff to the Secretary of War, when in reality he was assistant adjutant general to the General in Chief. At least that is the way Hardie signed a telegram; and General Meade's son, who as his father's aide was with Hardie, refers to him as Colonel Hardie—Benjamin had him a general—and states that he was on Halleck's staff.[23]

It is surprising to find that a professional historian should have for the Benjamin story anything but distrust, and should refer to it except by way of warning against its acceptance.[24] The one sentence that Benjamin wrote about the actual battle of Gettysburg is so laden with distortions as to be additional proof that he was too careless to be trusted.

Toward three o'clock in the morning of the 28th General Meade heard an inquiry for his tent, and presently Hardie entered with the important dispatches. Every commanding officer of much experience has been waked at all hours of the night to receive disturbing news; but not many have had thrust upon them at such a time the command of an army in a critical phase of a great campaign. Meade wrote the next day to his wife that his first thought was that he was being put in arrest or relieved of the command of his corps. That may be true. But in his last letter to her, on the 25th, he had discussed at length the possibility of being given command of the army, in reply apparently to some things that his wife, ambitious for his advancement, had said. He was not hopeful, and he wrote, "I do not stand, however, any chance, because I have no friends, political or others, who press or advance my claims or pretensions, and there are so many others who are pressed by influential politicians that it is folly to think I stand any chance upon mere merit alone." [25] Meade's good record of tending to business, his brave and skillful handling in battle of a brigade, then of a division, and finally of a corps—though at Chancellorsville he was little more than an observer—coupled with the preference which had been expressed for him by officers who were his seniors, had brought about his selection.

Anxiously Washington headquarters now waited for the word from the field army. It came in a brief message that Hardie sent at 5:30 A.M.: "I have accomplished my mission. Will telegraph again in an hour or two." Actually it was not until 2:30 P.M. that the important messenger reported again. He had been waiting, he stated, "for the formal issue of the order of the late commander before telegraphing." Hooker's order of farewell had at last been written; it spoke very highly of Meade and was in a tone very proper throughout. Halleck and Lincoln must have read with satisfaction these sentences from their courier: "I have had a chance to ascertain the state of feeling and internal condition of the army. There is cause for satisfaction with it." To Quartermaster General Meigs too there came a report from the ever watchful Ingalls that may have reached the President and in-

MAJOR GENERAL GEORGE G. MEADE

creased his hopefulness: "General Meade is in command. The army has confidence in him. We must all support him." [26] But Ingalls never could forget he was a quartermaster; he put a price on his report: 10,000 pairs of bootees and the same number of socks, not at some distant time, but *at once*. That evening a special train took him not 10,000 but 20,000 pairs of bootees.[27] Evidently Meigs did not regard socks as so essential for soldiers as bootees; he let the number of socks stay at the figure Ingalls had requested.

Meade could not have permitted much more delay than the eating of a good breakfast—one of the first obligations of a soldier to his government—before telegraphing Halleck at 7:00: Like a soldier he would obey the order he had received, and would execute it to the utmost of his ability. Without full knowledge of the situation as yet, it seemed to him that he must move toward the Susquehanna, at the same time keeping Washington and Baltimore well covered. If the enemy were checked in the attempt to cross the river, or turned toward Baltimore, he would give battle. He hoped that every available man would be sent to him because of reports about Lee's force. He closed by promising to report again as soon as he knew the situation.

In the letter handed him by Hardie, the new army commander had found his mission stated in these words:

You will not be hampered by any minute instructions from these headquarters. Your army is free to act as you may deem proper under the circumstances as they arise. You will, however, keep in view the important fact that the Army of the Potomac is the covering army of Washington as well as the army of operation against the invading forces of the rebels. You will, therefore, maneuver and fight in such a manner as to cover the capital and also Baltimore, as far as circumstances will admit. Should General Lee move upon either of these places, it is expected that you will either anticipate him or arrive with him so as to give him battle.[28]

Not a word about Philadelphia! Not a word even about Harrisburg! It was a good thing that neither the trembling citizens of those places nor Governor Curtin could read the directive of the General in Chief. Evidently Halleck saw that a serious threat as far up as the Susquehanna by an army of the size Lee could muster, which had to live off the country and depended on a long and very precarious route for ammunition supply, was not likely if the Army of the Potomac was properly handled.

Very sensibly Meade allowed himself the day of the 28th to get a grasp of the situation; he did, however, issue an appropriate order assuming command, and direct some changes of station. The Sixth Corps, bringing up the rear from Poolesville, had its march objective changed from Frederick to New Market—later to Hyattstown—and

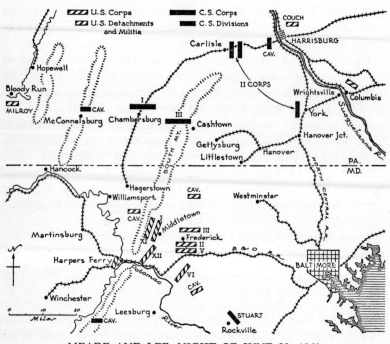

MEADE AND LEE, NIGHT OF JUNE 28, 1863

the three corps over which Reynolds exercised command were concentrated near Frederick.[29]

General French's cavalry reconnaissance up the Potomac certainly did not take place, though just when it was called off is not clear.[30] But what about Harpers Ferry itself, the point that had been so much in dispute? In his directive to Meade the General in Chief had said, "All forces within the sphere of your operations will be held subject to your orders," and as if this were not sufficient, he added specifically, "Harper's Ferry and its garrison are under your direct orders." Did that mean that Halleck at once gave Meade what he had denied to Hooker? It is often asserted that he did; and that thought may have been what caused Benjamin to charge that Hooker's "resignation" had been wrung from him.

Halleck's language was hardly satisfactory; but it was quite similar to that he had employed in telling Hooker on the 24th that the troops at the old ferry were under his command—words that Hooker did not understand as authorizing him to order the *abandonment* of the place. Moreover it is proper for a superior to give to one officer authority he would not think of conferring upon another. Certainly to no other subordinate would Lee have entrusted the march to Pope's rear or to Hooker's flank that he confidently gave to Jackson. And later Grant was to write to Sherman that to no other living soldier would he have given the mission of marching from Atlanta to the sea. Meade clearly realized the value of Harpers Ferry, and later wrote of his wish to hold it as a *débouché* into the Cumberland Valley.[31] In accordance with this thought he wired Halleck soon after noon, "Am I permitted, under existing circumstances, to withdraw a portion of the garrison of Harper's Ferry, providing I leave sufficient force to hold Maryland Heights against a *coup de main*." Like many engineer officers, he could not get along without French words, though he was not so fluent in French as Irvin McDowell. His dispatch furnished clear evidence that he could be trusted to take a more comprehending view toward the entire situation than Hooker. Without delay Halleck replied: "The garrison at Harper's Ferry is under your orders. You can diminish or increase it as you think the circumstances justify." [32] Though a mathematician might contend that one can diminish a thing to zero, even an engineer might say that abandoning the ferry would be not diminishing its garrison but obliterating it. Presently Meade asked the really pertinent question of General French: How many men did he think were sufficient to hold Maryland Heights against a *coup de main*? French replied: "Five thousand reliable men could make a practicable defense. I do not consider the force here stronger than that." [33] Thus according to their own commander the garrison did not have 10,000 men fit for heavy field duty, as Hooker had asserted. Accepting the statement of General Butterfield—whom he had retained as chief of staff—that the subsistence stores of the garrison were low (Butterfield afterward denied that he had ever made such a representation), Meade later in the night ordered French to bring 7,000 of his men to Frederick and use the rest to move and escort equipment and stores to Washington.[34]

Meade's first day of command included one very upsetting incident that gave him a prompt initiation into the trials ahead. Early in the afternoon he received intelligence from Halleck that Fitzhugh Lee's brigade of enemy cavalry had crossed the Potomac a few miles above Washington, and that apparently another brigade was about to follow. He must have read the dispatch almost with unbelieving eyes, for, on the basis of a report from Howard [35] and perhaps other unrecorded reports, he had just telegraphed Halleck that "reliable information" led to the belief that Stuart's cavalry had crossed the Potomac at Williamsport in the rear of Lee's army. How then could Jeb's horsemen be between the Federals and their capital? But any doubters at army headquarters must soon have been stilled by another telegram from the General in Chief stating that 150 wagons en route to the army from Washington had been captured by F. Lee near Rockville. Two brigades and a battery of horse artillery were sent in pursuit of the ambitious and disconcerting "rebels," but both Washington and Meade were troubled over the prospect of serious interruption of communications. [36] With Washington completely stripped of cavalry, it was up to Meade to combat the sudden threat. The captured wagons had been loaded for the most part with oats and corn, though a few were filled with ham and whisky and other delicacies that relieve the drabness of soldiering. The wagons were new, the mules were well fed, and the harness had never been used before, and so Jeb Stuart, who was personally in command of the raiding force of three brigades, took the Federal train with him. [37] But the wagons slowed his march, and eventually he, the whole Confederacy, and subsequent apologists were to regret their capture. Nor did the feed that Stuart diverted cause Federal animals to suffer, for at 7:00 P.M. on the 28th a Washington quartermaster telegraphed Ingalls that 600,000 pounds of oats—more than twice the load of the 125 escort wagons—were already on railroad cars and would go forward on the special train with the bootees and the socks. [38] Would the train get through before the Confederate troopers struck the railroad? That question must have filled the minds of railroaders and army officers alike. The next morning was well advanced when Stuart hit the Baltimore and Ohio, to tear down telegraph wires, tear up a little track, and fire a bridge—but to miss the trains that alerted engineers briskly ran out of his way. [39] Even after a good supper the night before, Stuart's horses could not catch the trains; so no railroad cars of supplies for the Army of the Potomac went up in smoke.

In taking the captured wagon train with him, Stuart was of course

merely following the explicit order in Lee's letter of the 22nd to "collect all the supplies you can for the use of the army." What occurred
was a striking illustration of the danger in a commander's giving secondary tasks that can lead to the defeat of the primary mission. In his
letter Lee should in fact have cautioned his subordinate not to en-
cumber himself with any kind of booty, for he could have known that
in riding around the Federal army Stuart would almost certainly be in
a position to make captures.

On his first day of command Meade had a bit of good fortune that
compensated for the unexpected threat caused by three brigades of
enemy cavalry between his army and Washington. There was brought
to him a remarkable document based upon the observations of Union
men in Hagerstown, covering the period from the first appearance of
troopers of Jenkins's cavalry brigade, on the 15th, to the passing of the
last units. Trained intelligence officers could not have done better or
given more essential information. The observers, some of whose names
were given, had counted the troops; then they had met at night and
discussed results. They could not make Lee's force more than 80,000.
That was the figure they set down for the sum total of all the "rebels"
—and it was extremely accurate. They put the number of guns at 275,
which showed they were very good counters, for the actual number
now given is 272. The writer of the report had himself seen two regiments containing only 150 men each; the largest he had seen, a Maryland regiment, mustered about 700. The average strength of a regiment
was given as probably less than 400. The hostile army had abundant
transportation, and men and animals were in good condition. Lee also
had brought plenty of money—Confederate money. It was carried in
flour barrels. The Southerners preferred giving $5 of secession money
for cleaning a horse, or putting on two shoes, to paying fifty cents of
United States money. Nor did the reporter fail to tell what the Confederates said about their own strength and their mission. A leading
Confederate sympathizer, whose name was given, had told of hearing
Confederate officers say that their whole army numbered 100,000
men, and that they were going to Philadelphia. The strength the Confederates boasted was the strongest sort of corroboration of the 80,000
limit that the Union enumerators had given. The statement about
Philadelphia was merely silly, unless it was accompanied with the
assertion that Lee first proposed to destroy the Army of the Potomac

as an effective field force, accomplishing such annihilation without seriously crippling the Army of Northern Virginia.

At 4:45 P.M. of the 28th Meade put the splendid report he had received on the wire to Halleck, preceding it with the very significant sentences: "The following statement has been furnished me. It is confirmed by information gathered from various other sources regarded as reliable. I propose to move this army to-morrow in the direction of York." [40] The long dispatch was in Washington at 6:05, and it should have helped the President, the Secretary, and the General in Chief to eat their dinners with enjoyment.

The 80,000 limit for Lee's army was not too far out of harmony with the 60,000–70,000 that Howard had sent in two days before, which was doubtless one of the corroborating reports that Meade had in mind. In transmitting the statement to Washington with the endorsement quoted, Meade was virtually making it his own intelligence summary, and saying to Halleck, "The enemy force does not exceed 80,000 men and 275 guns." But the general was to forget all about this before many months had passed, and when he appeared the next March before the somewhat inquisitorial Congressional Committee on the Conduct of the War he stated, when speaking of his assumption of command, "I had no information concerning the enemy beyond the fact that a large force under General Lee, estimated at about 110,000 men, had passed through Hagerstown, and had marched up the Cumberland valley." [41]

It should not have been difficult for Meade to estimate the situation and come to a sound decision. Three courses were open to Lee: (1) He could continue up the Cumberland Valley in order to join Ewell's corps, which Meade knew was making for Harrisburg. (2) He could bring the other two corps of his army through one of the gaps in the mountains that formed the eastern barrier of the Valley, recalling Ewell, and with his concentrated army threaten Baltimore and Washington and force the Army of the Potomac to battle. If this maneuver were adopted the march toward Harrisburg would be of a diversionary nature, meant to frighten Washington and lead the authorities to waste some good field forces by sending them to defend the Pennsylvania capital. (3) He could halt his main body under the protection of the mountains and let Ewell return from his raid toward the Susquehanna.

Of the three possibilities the last seemed the most unlikely because

Lee was living off the country and could not stay long in one position. Furthermore, what satisfaction would this procedure have given to the men who had marched so hard and to the people at home who were expecting so much of their invincible brigades? There would be nothing for the army except some days of good living and the chance to see what the Yankees were like at home; for the people at home there would be nothing but the stories their soldiers told in their letters. Nor would this course stimulate foreign recognition. Nevertheless from "opposite Williamsport" Lee wrote to Davis the night before he crossed the river that he might have to return without any other achievement than forcing the Federals to cross to the north bank of the Potomac, and thus delaying any plan that they might have for a summer campaign.[42]

On the other hand, if Lee adopted the second plan he would certainly come through the Cashtown Gap, because it led to Gettysburg, where several important roads converged.

Thus Meade's proper decision would seem to have been this: to move northward, keeping his army well in hand, so as to be able to fall upon any part of Lee's army that might venture through the Cashtown Gap and destroy it before it could be supported, and to engage Lee beyond the termination of the mountains if he continued toward Harrisburg. The movement toward York that Meade reported to Halleck that he would start on the 29th was not out of harmony with such an operation, except that it tended to take the Federal army toward the east and might forfeit the opportunity to strike Lee before he could concentrate east of the mountains after coming through the Cashtown Gap.

A warning order went out for all corps to be ready to march at daylight, followed presently by a march order that put the army on the road at four, which meant early reveilles and breakfasts in the dark.[43]

It had been a busy day and a hard day—without time for a letter home—for the new commander of the Army of the Potomac. Though George Gordon Meade was born in Spain, his father was a Pennsylvanian, and his wife was from Philadelphia, and he had served in that city as an engineer officer. His friends and home were not forgotten when the general said in his first order to his officers and men, "The country looks to this army to relieve it from the devastation and disgrace of a foreign invasion." And through the mind of Lincoln the thought that Meade was a Pennsylvanian certainly passed as he wondered how well his new general would meet the test immediately ahead.

The rain of the past days continued on the 28th. Speaking of wet bivouacs and three o'clock reveilles in the rain, one regimental commander wrote in a letter, "Well—that is soldiering, and it is a great deal more comfortable soldiering, than to march through suffocating clouds of dust under a hot sun. In the dust, men are dogged and silent. In the rain they are often even hilarious and jolly." [44]

How did it happen that three brigades of Stuart's cavalry were between the Army of the Potomac and Washington? How indeed? That is one of the top questions of the Civil War, about which there was bitter verbal debate in the South for years, and concerning which many pages have been written. With the location of Lee's army it was certainly not the place for Jeb Stuart and three of his best brigades to be on June 28. He had disobeyed orders, some have charged; his action was in harmony with his orders, his defenders have asserted with equal fervor. Fortunately the orders were written and can be studied.

Stuart had been smarting under the attacks of the Richmond press for being surprised at Brandy on June 9, and it was only natural that he wished to reinstate himself. Though he had handled his brigades very skillfully in screening Lee's army as it moved toward the Potomac, the South as well as the North saw that the Federal cavalry, with its feeling of inferiority overcome, had won some of the encounters over the gaps in the Bull Run Mountains and west toward the Blue Ridge. Jeb was probably in the mood to seize an opportunity to top off steady substantial achievement with something spectacular, something like the two rides around the Federal army that he had made the year before. Even though such a raid might have little real military value, the people would talk about it and the Brandy record would be forgotten.

On June 22 Jenkins's brigade of cavalry was in the advance with Ewell, and Imboden's regiments were westward on the Baltimore and Ohio Railroad, destroying the tracks toward Cumberland and sending in cattle and sheep so effectively that Lee the next day wrote and thanked him. [45] These two commands were not normal parts of Stuart's cavalry division, and Jeb himself was south of the Potomac with his five regular brigades, holding back Pleasonton and trying himself to get a peep at Hooker's army. On that day Major Charles Marshall, aide to Lee, wrote the first of the fateful and much debated letters of instructions to Stuart. Of Hooker he wrote in a letter that Lee read and signed:

> If you find that he is moving northward, and that two brigades can guard the Blue Ridge and take care of your rear, you can move with the other three into Maryland, and take position on General Ewell's right, place yourself in communication with him, guard his flank and keep him informed of the enemy's movements, and collect all the supplies you can for the use of the army.[46]

There was not a word as to timing and nothing about Stuart's route into Maryland. Three missions were given to him, of which collecting supplies—"all the supplies you can"—was likely to interfere with the other two. Furthermore he was not directed to keep *Lee* informed about Federal movements; he was to attach himself to *Ewell*. In a letter to Ewell the same day—the 22nd—Lee instructed the Second Corps commander to be sure to have Jenkins cover his flank and keep him informed about the Federals. Sending in enemy information is one of the things even a good commander, absorbed with his own decisions, may sometimes forget. So Lee made the excellent suggestion that Ewell attach one of his own staff officers to Jenkins's headquarters; then there would be constantly with the cavalryman someone whose first thought was always about corps headquarters. The letter to Ewell gave no intimation that Stuart was being ordered to help protect Ewell's right; but it did state that Lee was invoking God's protection for the exposed Second Corps.[47] Perhaps he remembered that Stonewall Jackson, who could be relied upon to do his own praying, had been replaced by a general more inclined to rip out an oath than to intone a prayer —the third star, the wooden leg, and the wife, were all too new to have made a dependable reformation. "Old Baldhead" could be trusted to march hard, but not to pray hard.

At 5:00 P.M. of the 23rd Lee's aide wrote to Stuart the second of the historic letters. After a poorly worded description of a contingency in which Stuart was to cross the Potomac *west* of the mountains and then move to Frederick, Maryland, it stated: "You will, however, be able to judge whether you can pass around their army without hindrance, doing them all the damage you can, and cross the river east of the Mountains. In either case, after crossing the river you must move on and feel the right of Ewell's troops, collecting information, provisions, etc." [48] This letter, like the former, bore the signature R. E.

Lee. Now a *fourth* mission had been given to Stuart—to damage the Federal main body as much as he could if he rode around it.

It has been argued with vehemence that Lee's meaning was known to Stuart, and that the latter should never have done the things he did do. But the directive was as bad as the one with which Winfield Scott —great general though he was—had confounded Patterson two years before. Not for one moment should passing around the Federal army have been considered, for no one could foresee what delays might be encountered in such an operation, or what hazardous situations might arise. It was perfectly possible that Stuart's three brigades would be boxed in and completely destroyed. It has been emphasized by way of excuse for Lee that feeling Ewell's flank was a must for Stuart; so too was collecting provisions a must. As in the first letter, not a word was said about keeping *Lee* posted on Federal movements; Stuart was to function *only for Ewell* in the matter of information, in spite of the fact that Ewell was already amply provided for in orders to Jenkins and prayers to God. Stuart was, however, to be a quartermaster for the *entire Confederate army*. Is it conceivable that any command or staff school would use the letter that Lee read and signed as anything but an example of a bad order certain to bring undesired consequences? Lee's faults in orders and command have often been attributed to his amiability and courtesy. Exactly on account of those qualities he should have had an adequate staff constantly at hand, with sufficient rank and experience to raise searching questions about what was done, and perform other duties of higher staff officers. He was planning too many things for his cavalry, and was dangling before Stuart—eager to reinstate himself in popular esteem—an opportunity that should have been denied. A good operations officer or chief of staff would certainly have challenged the entire cavalry instructions.

Brave and resourceful, and with recollections of extricating himself from many tight places, Stuart rode *eastward* at 1:00 A.M. of the 25th from the vicinity of Salem, at the head of the brigades of Fitzhugh Lee, Wade Hampton, and W. H. F. Lee—the last under the command of Colonel John R. Chambliss since the action at Brandy, where "Rooney" Lee was wounded and captured.[49] The inevitable happened. Stuart encountered Federal troops and had to halt until the roads were cleared. Perhaps in fulfillment of his *fourth* mission he opened up some guns on the blue columns; a little gunfire was, however, nothing to worry Hancock, whose corps was in the way. After his first loss of time, Stuart had to halt in order to graze his horses, there being no forage to be found anywhere. Naturally there was none: the Federal army had been in this region for ten days, and it had many thousands of horses and mules. Both Lee and Stuart should have known what would happen. Finally he had to search for a practicable ford, and he was very fortunate indeed in finding one. Not until the morning of the 28th did he have his command across the river, with both men and horses tired. Without the least idea where Ewell was—or General Lee —he struck northward, and fortunately encountered nothing more formidable than the Federal wagon train without an adequate escort. In accordance with his orders to gather all the provisions he could, Jeb took the wagons along as he continued his hunt for Ewell.

That night—the 28th—Lee was at Chambersburg with the corps of Longstreet and Hill, completely ignorant of the Federal movements of the past few days; and he would have continued in that state if it had not been for the thoughtfulness of Longstreet—who later was made a scapegoat for the campaign by many Southerners, though not by Lee himself. Lee had sent a scout named Harrison—with pockets heavy with gold coins requisitioned from Richmond—to Washington at the time the campaign started, under instructions to report back to the First Corps after the Confederate army had crossed the Potomac. To Lee's tent an officer of Longstreet's staff brought Harrison about ten o'clock; and the scout imparted the unexpected information that the Federal army had been over the river two to three days and was now in the vicinity of Frederick, and that Hooker had been replaced by Meade. Lee is reported to have spoken with some distrust of the scout's story, adding, "I do not know what to do, I cannot hear from General Stuart, the eye of the army." [50] Why should he have expected to hear from that officer when he had directed the cavalryman—with a well known penchant for spectacular raids—to put himself on the right of Ewell and "keep him informed"? Already Stuart had a good load of provisions—in accordance with orders—and was on his way to find Ewell. True, he had used up a good deal of time—but not a single date had been mentioned in Lee's last letter to him, on the 23rd, which said only, ". . . but I think the sooner you cross into Maryland, after to-morrow, the better." Rather indefinite and rather inflexible, that was. Quite as unprecise as the words "without hindrance."

In an effort to clear Lee of responsibility for Stuart's spectacular ride it has been stated that the cavalryman had clear orders to cover the movement of the main body of the army. Thus Colonel William Allan of Lee's staff wrote, ". . . Stuart had been specially ordered to cover his [Lee's] movements, and keep him informed." [51] No such statement is justified by the written orders that Stuart received. That Lee should have left it open to him to ride around the Federal army becomes harder to understand when one recalls the use of the Federal cavalry in the Chancellorsville campaign. The wounded Jackson had remarked that he could not have attacked the Federal right flank if Hooker had not made the mistake of sending his cavalry away.[52] Surely this criticism must have been echoed by others at Lee's headquarters; but he repeated Hooker's error, which according to Stonewall had brought ruin to a brilliant Federal operation.

It is equally difficult to understand Lee's reported surprise when Harrison told him on the night of the 28th that the Army of the Potomac was well over the river whose name it bore. According to the second order to Stuart, he was not to ride around the Federal army unless that army was moving northward.[53] Thus as soon as Lee learned that he had moved eastward—which he certainly must have learned early on the 25th—he should have expected that the Union army would soon be over the Potomac. There still were three cavalry brigades near at hand that he could have called upon for mounted service: Imboden's operating toward the west, and those of B. H. Robertson and W. E. Jones guarding the passes below the Potomac that soon needed little or no guarding. There seems to be no excuse for Lee's finding himself at Chambersburg on the 28th without a single regiment of cavalry, or his surprise at the move of the Federals.

Much of that crucial 25th—when Hooker crossed three infantry corps and the artillery reserve to the north of the Potomac—Lee must have devoted to composing two important but long letters to Jefferson Davis. After that he was compelled to act as a public relations officer for his army, receiving requests for locks of his thinning hair from admiring Maryland ladies, and talking pleasantly to persons who called upon him. On the 27th he wrote a General Order for his army—excellent, except that it was lengthy—commending his soldiers for good behavior, exhorting them to behave like Christians, and laying it onto the Yankees pretty heavily for their "atrocities," which he said must not be copied.[54] But he did nothing to summon the needed horsemen from the brigades of Imboden, Robertson, and Jones. Again Lee was badly in need of a good chief of staff who could present him with well digested summaries of the situation such as Warren had recently presented to Hooker.

Could Lee's invasion force have been increased? Did Jefferson Davis keep in other places men who could and should have been in the columns that crossed the Potomac? A recent writer has stated confidently that 30,000 more men could have been with Lee in the great offensive, without telling from where such a great reenforcement—greater than any of Lee's three corps—could have come.[55] Useless dispersion of troops is always a constant danger in war, and it is an easy and cheap charge to make against a High Command. The criticism is usually based upon afterknowledge, and the causes that led to certain dispositions of troops are forgotten, for it is impossible to restore a past situation exactly as some commander envisaged it. Certainly in World War II American forces were scattered to the four corners of the earth to the bewilderment of the layman—and that at a time when there was a cry for a second front in Europe. The question of weighing one theater of war against another was always present in Civil War, just as it was in the great conflict of the 1940's. Scouts of the Army of the Potomac captured two long and extremely important dispatches from President Davis to Lee in which the question of available forces was gone into in detail;[56] and the Southern President's analysis and estimate must be refuted point by point before one can soundly claim that Lee might have been significantly reenforced.

Although General Halleck thought that the expedition sent out by Dix from Fort Monroe failed to accomplish much of value, Dix did not agree;[57] and it was certainly true that there was plenty of alarm in Richmond, and that the Federal operation in that vicinity resulted in the detention of some regular Confederate brigades in the city. In the Department of North Carolina commanded by D. H. Hill, with headquarters at Petersburg, Virginia, there were six brigades, with an effective strength of about 18,000.[58] Three of the brigades had been moved to Richmond, where the brigade of Henry A. Wise, properly belonging to Lee's army, was also being detained.[59] On the 25th Hill wrote to Seddon that he was prepared to move more of his men to Richmond in case of need, and he thought the city could be held against 40,000.[60] Hill was a hard fighter, but a good deal of a boaster, in spite of the fact that he spoke piously about the "Merciful Father," who had been showing him some favors. How many of the regular brigades would Davis have been justified in sending to Lee when he probably knew that Dix had upwards of 30,000 men at Fort Monroe and the White House, and that Major General John G. Foster had upwards of 12,000 in North Carolina, with headquarters at New Bern? [61] The Richmond defenses had been made very formidable, and, knowing that four regular Confederate brigades were present, Dix and his subordinate commanders did not feel like undertaking an attack; [62] but he probably would have thought differently had the city been defended only by militia and companies of clerks.

Lee had already drawn troops from West Virginia to such an extent that Major General Sam Jones was troubled about his ability to protect from possible Federal raids the all-important saltworks and line of railroads for which he was responsible. With the force left at his disposal he felt unable to carry out the diversionary operation that Lee had suggested, unless some one else looked after the saltworks or the railroad, or unless they were left without guardians, and only hope that no harm would befall them. [63]

And it must not be forgotten—though frequently it is—that every time a rifle is added to the firing line, a stomach and two more feet are added to the trials of the quartermaster. Every time a gun is given to the artillery about ten men and ten horses are added—and artillerymen and their animals are proverbially hungry. It may have been supply considerations in part that led Lee on the 23rd to suggest that a force be built up at Culpeper to threaten Washington, instead of having the troops sent to him. [64] If fear for the capital led the Federals to withhold troops from the field, the plan would have the same result as an augmentation of his own command. However, the Culpeper suggestion was altogether too late, and Lee's letter did not reach President Davis for five days. But a much worse misfortune was ahead. Bold and alert Federal scouts relieved the returning Confederate dispatch rider of Davis's reply—including a long explanation of the Richmond forces—and delivered them without delay to Meade, who forwarded them to Halleck. [65] The difficulties of conducting operations in the enemy's country far off from one's base were beginning to present themselves. Lee's defense of Virginia in 1862 had been a masterpiece, full of bold conceptions and fine execution. Offensive warfare is quite another matter.

June 28 was a busy day for Darius Couch at Harrisburg. New York had sent him seventeen regiments of National Guard, and the invaded

Keystone State had given him seven regiments of militia.[66] Some of his regiments had been at York, Carlisle, and elsewhere as covering forces, but his chief force was held at Harrisburg, organized as a division under Brigadier General W. F. Smith, with four brigades of the New Yorkers, and one of the Pennsylvanians. Early in the afternoon a dispatch from Halleck notified Couch of the change in commanders of the Army of the Potomac, and instructed him that he was under Meade's authority; to Meade the General in Chief said all information would be forwarded that Couch could send to Washington. Careful instructions had gone for the detachment guarding the Wrightsville-Columbia bridge over the Susquehanna about destroying that structure when the proper time came.[67] All boats and rafts were to be taken to the left bank of the river; the bridge at Harrisburg was prepared for burning.[68]

Couch was well informed about the northward advance of Ewell, though some of the dispatches he received contained notable inaccuracies—one, for instance, said that Ewell had a pontoon train.[69] But he could never have suspected the Southern general had a map that not only showed every farmhouse, but gave the owner's name.[70] Lee also had a copy of the remarkable drawing that had been compiled from county maps by Jackson's able engineer; so, although he did not know where his own cavalry was, he could call the Maryland and Pennsylvania farmers by their correct names. At 2:30 P.M. on June 28 Stanton received this message from Couch:

By night the rebels will have possession up to my defenses on the river. My information is that there are 15,000 in or near Carlisle, and 4,000 or 8,000 from Gettysburg to York and Hanover. Their advance has just opened artillery 4 miles from my defenses.[71]

The strength report was excellent, but the reference to artillery firing perplexed Lincoln. With his irresistible desire for precision in information, he wired Couch at four o'clock, "What news now? What are the enemy firing at 4 miles from your works?" That was a question the general had no answer for. But he could give some good news and at 7:40 he reported, "They have not up to this time made any show of attack in force. They are burning bridges on the Northern Central road. I have lost 400 men in the vicinity of York and Gettysburg. Probably 15,000 men are within a short distance of my front." [72]

Encouraged perhaps by the handsome performance of New York,

Governor Curtin called upon his next-door neighbor, Governor Joel Parker of New Jersey, for some troops. Obviously it was better for Jerseymen who loved their firesides to help stop the Confederates at the Susquehanna than to have the men in shabby gray and butternut peering wistfully across the Delaware. New Jersey's perplexed governor asked Stanton what he should do.[73]

Earlier in the day the Secretary had received a report from Postmaster C. A. Walborn of Philadelphia that was hard to evaluate,[74] and shows what a variety of things were continually being tossed at the bespectacled Secretary. Walborn himself at the Pennsylvania Railroad outer depot had observed four men—whose names he gave, and one of whom he pronounced "a noted rebel sympathizer"—making arrangements to send one of their number to New York by the first train "to request Major General McClellan to resign his position, and come to Philadelphia and take military charge of things generally." He had tried to get the conspirators to desist, by informing them that he would make a report of what he considered to be "an attempt to usurp the powers of Government."

As Couch wondered how his raw regiments would behave when under fire, as Lincoln wondered what the "rebels" had been shooting at, as Stanton wondered about the emissary dispatched to see McClellan, as Halleck pondered the intelligence summary that Meade had forwarded, and studied on his map the road net that led north from Frederick—the people everywhere throughout the North were waiting anxiously for news from Vicksburg as well as from Pennsylvania. About the outcome at Vicksburg there was no uncertainty, for the unbreakable line of blue that had at last been forged about the great stronghold by the general who said so little but never turned back was slowly starving the great stronghold into unqualified surrender. All that was in doubt was the day, the hour when the good news would come, and the feelings and emotions long held under control in the war could be released in rejoicing over a truly great victory. But the issue in Pennsylvania—that was different. From Vicksburg there would not be the great casualty lists in the papers that families throughout the land read with fear. The fighting there was over. But the Army of the Potomac—which had all but dropped from the news—was marching, marching no one could say where, but certainly to battle. So there was anxiety, anxiety both for the nation which had existed only a brief "fourscore and seven years" and for the men in the long columns of infantry, the drivers handling the reins of the artillery teams, the cannoneers on the limbers and the caissons, and the troopers in the squadrons of cavalry that the people were so proud of after the battle at Brandy and the clashes beyond the Bull Run Mountains.

CHAPTER XXI

THE FIRST TWO DAYS OF GETTYSBURG

A tremendous battle has been raging since 9.30 a.m. with varying success. . . . The enemy's line is a semicircle on the height from north to west. . . . In my opinion there seems to be no directing person. . . . We need help now.

Buford to Butterfield

For two days the army marched, and on the evening of the last day of that momentous June it stood with about half of its corps in Pennsylvania, and the remainder not far below the border: First Corps, five miles north of Emmitsburg on Marsh Creek; Second Corps, at Uniontown; Third Corps, southeast of Emmitsburg; Fifth Corps, at Union Mills; Sixth, at Manchester; Eleventh, north of Emmitsburg; Twelfth, at Littlestown. Buford was at Gettysburg with his cavalry division—less Merritt's brigade; Gregg, at Manchester; Kilpatrick, at Hanover. Army headquarters were at Taneytown, where the reserve artillery was parked. On the 30th a regimental commander wrote home: "We have marched through some beautiful country. It is refreshing to get out of the barren desert of Virginia into this land of thrift and plenty." [1] After their tedious winter in the bleak surroundings of Falmouth, their battle in the tangled thickets of the Wilderness, and their recent march to Edwards Ferry through the poor and now war-devastated counties of northern Virginia, the mere appearance of the fields, the villages, the farmhouses, and the barns north of the Potomac must have been a tonic to the Federals. If the very landscape smiled at the soldiers, the inhabitants did more. They waved their hands, they cheered the long blue columns, they stood with uncovered heads as bullet-riddled colors passed before them. The 30th of June was also a day when regimental commanders—busy though they were—found time to muster for pay, a spirit-elevating procedure in a soldier's life.

Not until the 30th did the papers report that Hooker had been

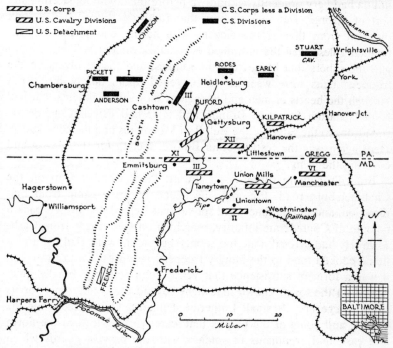

MEADE AND LEE, NIGHT OF JUNE 30, 1863

superseded by Meade; but the word had spread through the country-side. People stood upon the streets and at their doors to watch for the new commander upon whom a great responsibility had suddenly been placed; they also sought glimpses of the corps commanders: Reynolds, Hancock, Sickles, Sykes (well known since First Bull Run, now in command of Meade's Fifth Corps), Sedgwick, Howard—riding with one sleeve pinned up—Slocum, and Pleasonton. The names of many of the division commanders were also by this time household words: Wadsworth, Doubleday, Gibbon, Hays, Birney, Humphreys, Wright, Newton, Barlow, von Steinwehr, Schurz, Williams, Geary. Happy must the people of Gettysburg have been upon that last day when their town was a place dear only to those who called it home, on seeing John Buford ride down the street at the head of the brigades of Gamble and Devin. The Gettysburgers had already seen the invading Confederates, for a few days before some of Ewell's regiments had passed through on the way to York, and a regiment of Pennsylvania militia had very prudently withdrawn before them without starting any sort of dispute. But the troopers that followed Buford had a look different from that of the citizens who hastily had picked up unfamiliar rifles; even the untrained eye could distinguish. The carbines and the sabers that hung from the saddles, and the revolvers on the troopers' belts were weapons to be relied upon. Surely thrills ran through the hearts of men and women as they saw regiments that had helped chasten Stuart at Brandy and later had driven Confederate squadrons to the safety of the Bull Run Mountains and the Blue Ridge. Here again was the restless John Buford, feeling for the enemy and covering the army.

Buford's column turned west toward the Cashtown Gap on the Chambersburg road. Presently the sound of firing came from that direction, and in due time word spread that Buford had turned back a column of Confederate infantry, marching on Gettysburg from Cashtown. He had arrived none too soon. The people were glad to furnish home-cooked food to the hungry troopers who drifted into town; but it was a form of subsistence that vexed John Buford.[2] Finally quiet settled on the town, known that night beyond the county only for its little college and its small Lutheran seminary. Quiet except for the coming and going of the patrols that were working toward the north and east, and arguments of soldiers with the provost guards which Buford, knowing well the ways of troopers, had probably thrown into the town. The retiring Confederate infantry had left pickets behind, and it looked as if there would be work to do the next day. Buford would want no absent men if the enemy infantry came again.

The army had been well concentrated on the evening of the 28th of June; Meade had succeeded in scattering it by night on the 30th. His mind was filled with conflicting ideas, and he did not hold steadfastly even to good decisions which he announced from time to time. General Lee was counting upon the difficulties his new antagonist would find with army command; as his military secretary wrote later:

The change he [Lee] considered advantageous to the Federal cause, as he had always held Meade in much higher estimation as a commander than

Hooker. But he was of the opinion that the difficulties which would beset Meade in taking command of an army in the midst of a campaign would more than counterbalance his superiority as a general over the previous commander. He was, therefore, rather satisfied than otherwise by the change.[3]

Meade was not bothered by the many details involved in handling a large army, for these could be well taken care of by the adequate and excellent staff of the Army of the Potomac. His problem was fundamental—whether he had the great moral courage that the new position required, or would fall a victim to vacillation. Writing to Mrs. Meade on the 30th from Taneytown that all was going encouragingly, he added frankly: "I continue well, but much oppressed with a sense of responsibility and the magnitude of the great interests intrusted to me. Of course, in time I will become accustomed to this." [4] There was no lack of sincerity or honest piety in his request for prayers in his behalf. There was, however, too much certainty in Meade's "Of course"; it would have been better if he had used the word "perhaps." Though experience and familiarity with heavy responsibility would without doubt have a steadying effect, it was not at all certain that George Meade had the necessary quality for a good army commander. In the letter then only five days old in which he had discussed the possibility of the army command coming to him, he had come nearer to the point when he wrote, "It remains to be seen whether I have the capacity to handle successfully a large army." Although "capacity" was a good word, "high moral courage" would have put the matter better.

At 10:00 A.M. on the 29th Meade revealed his analysis of the situation and his purposes in a long dispatch to Halleck: "While I move forward, I shall incline to the right, toward the Baltimore and Harrisburg road, to cover that, and draw supplies from there, if circumstances permit it, my main objective point being, of course, Lee's army, which I am satisfied has all passed on through Hagerstown toward Chambersburg." Contradictory thoughts were intruding; Lee's army was on the left, and Meade's inclining to the right did not look as if he were making the columns in gray his objective point, in spite of his assertion. Actually, railroads had been built as if with an eye on the needs of the Union army in this campaign, for branch lines ran to Westminster and to Hanover and Gettysburg. Thus it was not necessary to use railheads on the North Central Railroad as Meade had in mind. Furthermore he seemed to be forgetting about Meigs, Haupt, and Ingalls, as well as ignoring the capacity of his great supply trains. Excellent, however, were the following sentences in the dispatch: "My endeavor will be in my movements to hold my force well together, with the hope of falling upon some portion of Lee's army in detail. ·. . . My main point being to find and fight the enemy, I shall have to submit to the cavalry raid around me in some measure." [5] Surely the enemy was not to be found over toward the railroad from Baltimore to Harrisburg—except in small fragments—but toward the left; and if Meade had been moving in accordance with his fine words he would have had his army ready to concentrate rapidly toward the left, and would not have ordered the Sixth Corps to Manchester, thirty miles from Gettysburg.

Telegraphic communication with Washington had been cut and Meade said to Halleck, "I send this by courier, with the hope and expectation that it will reach you safely." The message did indeed reach the General in Chief; but the courier was the victim of an enemy bullet, for above the letter in the Official Records there appears the sentence, "Dispatch found on the body of a soldier, killed June 30, 4½ miles from Glen Rock." Who was the dispatch rider? What were the circumstances of his clash with some enemy detachment? Who took the important message from the fallen courier, looked at him for a moment with the deep feeling that one soldier has for another, and then sped the note to its proper destination? These questions cannot be answered; but of delay there could have been little, for on the 30th Halleck wrote: "Your plan of operations is approved. I have just received your second dispatch by the hands of an orderly. I write no fuller for obvious reasons." [6] Since he later warned Meade against getting his army too far to the east, it is possible that Halleck saw the danger in Meade's plan, but let it stand because he feared to discuss it. "By the hands of an orderly." Adroitly the General in Chief thus told Meade that his dispatch rider had been killed.

It is impossible to put any coherence and sense into the dispatches, circulars, and orders that Meade issued on the 30th. They show a vacillating, disturbed officer, from whom all resolution and clear purpose had departed. No longer could Meade add 2 and 2 and be certain of the result. June 30 was as bad a day for him as the day Burnside threw the bridges over the Rappahannock had been for that general.

Reynolds was directed to assume command of the left wing of the army, consisting of the First, Third, and Eleventh Corps; but it was a strange sort of command indeed, for Meade continued to give orders to Sickles and Howard instead of assigning a general mission for the "wing." A circular for the army began with the positive assertion, "The commanding general has received information that the enemy are advancing, probably in strong force, on Gettysburg." Then the general who had said so positively the day before that his main point was to find and fight the enemy, and that he hoped to fall upon a part of Lee's army in detail, stated, "It is the intention to hold this army pretty nearly in the position it now occupies until the plans of the enemy shall have been more fully developed." [7] The initiative was entirely surrendered, and Lee, whose army had been dangerously dispersed, was to be allowed to come through the Cashtown Gap and assemble it unopposed.

The order for the next day's movements—July 1—revealed Meade's change of heart even more clearly:

> The commanding general desires you to be informed that, from present information, Longstreet and Hill are at Chambersburg, partly toward Gettysburg; Ewell at Carlisle and York. Movements indicate a disposition to advance from Chambersburg to Gettysburg.
>
> General Couch telegraphs, 29th, his opinion that the enemy's operations on the Susquehanna are more to prevent co-operation with this army than offensive. The general believes that he has relieved Harrisburg and Philadelphia, and now desires to look to his own army, and assume position for offensive or defensive, as occasion requires, or rest to the troops.[8]

But the worst remains to be related. After having told his corps commanders that the enemy was "advancing, probably in strong force, on Gettysburg," Meade ordered the First and Eleventh Corps to Gettysburg, the Third to Emmitsburg, with Reynolds—a hard fighter —in command of all three corps, and did not know that he was giving orders certain to cause a battle. By concentrating his whole force he would evidently have had the chance to strike an isolated portion of Lee's army—an intention he had announced—for it was plain that two of Lee's corps would have to move toward Gettysburg by a single road over a mountain pass. But though he had given orders that were sure to cause a battle in view of his own statements about the enemy, Meade allowed the Sixth Corps—the largest in his army—to remain at Manchester, thirty miles away.

As if in a dream Meade wrote to the General in Chief, after posting him about Longstreet's position and Hill's eastward movement: "I shall push on tomorrow in the direction of Hanover Junction and Hanover, when I hope by July 2 to open communication with Baltimore by telegraph and rail, to renew supplies." Of his first clash with the enemy Meade reported briefly, "Our cavalry engaged with Stuart at Hanover this a.m. Result not yet known." In this clash with the troops of Brigadier General Judson Kilpatrick's division, the Southern cavalier for the second time narrowly escaped capture, his fine horse Virginia taking a wide ditch that was too much for the mounts of his pursuers.[9]

Even before late afternoon brought a dispatch from Couch, stating that Ewell had hastily fallen back toward Chambersburg and Gettysburg, and that his own cavalry might already have reoccupied Carlisle, Lincoln had become actually optimistic. At 10:55 A.M. he wired Governor Parker of New Jersey: "I really think the attitude of the enemy's army in Pennsylvania presents us the best opportunity we have had since the war began. I think you will not see the foe in New Jersey." [10] "The best opportunity we have had since the war began." Strong words these were for a man who did not speak carelessly, and one wishes there was a full indication of what the President had in mind as he noted the shifting position of the Confederate forces; but certainly he was thinking differently from his new field commander, who had apparently succeeded in convincing himself that relief of a threat to the Susquehanna was the sole reason for the marches he had been exacting of his men.

As soon as General Early occupied York he demanded $100,000 in money and supplies of food and clothing. Though he marched away with well filled wagons, he took only $28,000 of the cash he sought to levy. In exchange for what he was given the general left a very nice proclamation, explaining that he had refrained from burning railroad buildings and the car shops through fear the flames would endanger the town. He seemed to feel some pity for the people in his closing words, which urged them to "make an effort to shake off the revolting tyranny under which it is apparent to all you are yourselves groaning." [11] Advice like that was surely a bargain at $28,000.

As Lincoln waited hopefully, and as Meade continued in the throes of indecision—failing to get the sleep he should have had—the momentous first day of July arrived. Most of the soldiers were probably well refreshed by a good night's rest, in spite of the army commander's implication that they were tired—a claim he was beginning to use as an excuse for inaction.[12]

During the night a special messenger brought to Taneytown the dispatch from Couch that had reached Washington at 5:30 P.M. Although he spoke of some Confederate troops falling back toward Chambersburg as if to seek protection of the mountains, Couch also said, "My latest information is that Early, with his 8,000 men, went toward Gettysburg or Hanover, saying they expected to fight a great battle there." [13] Then there came a dispatch Stanton had sent just before midnight, passing on a late message from Haupt, who was at Harrisburg:

Lee is falling back suddenly from the vicinity of Harrisburg, and concentrating all his forces. York has been evacuated. Carlisle is being evacuated. The concentration appears to be at or near Chambersburg. The object apparently a sudden movement against Meade, of which he should be advised by courier immediately.

As source for his statement Haupt gave Colonel T. A. Scott, formerly with the War Department, now back with the Pennsylvania Central Railroad. [14] That there was some disagreement between Couch and Haupt as to the point of concentration was immaterial; the most significant point in the two messages was the assertion of Couch—who had better sources of information than Scott—that Early was moving to a concentration point east, not west, of the mountains. Hanover was quite out of the question as a gathering point for Lee's army, and he could be intending to unite his corps nowhere else than near Gettysburg, where Meade himself had virtually reported an impending concentration the day before when he informed his corps commanders "that the enemy are advancing, probably in strong force, on Gettysburg."

In the dispatch to Halleck at 7:00 A.M. acknowledging receipt of the messages of Couch and Haupt, Meade gave the positions of his corps, and added: "These movements were ordered yesterday, before the receipt of advices of Lee's movements." There was a touch of the disingenuous in this, in view of what he had written the day before about the enemy's movements and his statement that Couch believed the Confederate movement toward the Susquehanna was largely diversionary. In spite of the confirmation of the enemy movements that early morning had brought, he made no change in his orders of the day before, which moved two corps to Gettysburg, and he said, "The point of Lee's concentration and the nature of the country, when ascertained, will determine whether I attack or not. Shall advise you further today, when satisfied that the enemy are fully withdrawn from the Susquehanna." [15] He might as well have stated, "I shall write you again when *really* satisfied that 2 and 2 make 4."

The message did not reach Washington until four o'clock in the afternoon; but the General in Chief had already become somewhat alarmed by Meade's dispatches of the day before, for at 10:45 he had sent the brief note: "The movements of the enemy yesterday indicate his intention either to turn your left, or to come himself by the South Mountain and occupy Cumberland Valley. Do not let him draw you too far to the east." [16] It was a pronouncement that goes very definitely on the credit side of Halleck's record.

Meade's purpose of June 29, *to find and fight* the enemy, had been entirely forgotten. Instead of viewing the removal of Lee's threat to the Susquehanna as merely incidental—the Confederate army being his "main objective point"—he had argued himself into a strange state of mind, full of contradictions and impossible clearly to describe. His circular of the 30th had directed corps commanders to hold their commands in readiness to march against the enemy with three days' rations in the haversacks and sixty rounds of ammunition on each soldier, entirely as if he were still wishing to find and fight the enemy. But at the same time officers, on his order, were reconnoitering a defensive position to the rear along Pipe Creek, near Westminster. Now on the morning of July 1, while the First and Eleventh Corps were carrying out their fateful orders to march to Gettysburg, he was drawing up a long circular that provided for the occupation of the Pipe Creek position. The complete reversal of his previous purpose was candidly announced in the opening paragraph:

From information received, the commanding general is satisfied that the object of the movement of the army in this direction has been accomplished, viz. the relief of Harrisburg, and the prevention of the enemy's intended invasion of Philadelphia, etc., beyond the Susquehanna. It is no longer his intention to assume the offensive until the enemy's movements or position should render such an operation certain of success.

Then he asserted that if the enemy assumed the offensive and attacked he would withdraw to the Pipe Creek position. But he went further. He virtually surrendered command of his army, authorizing any corps commander to initiate the retirement toward the rear position in this amazing sentence:

Whenever such circumstances arise as would seem to indicate the necessity for falling back and assuming this general line indicated, notice of such movement will be at once communicated to these headquarters and to all adjoining corps commanders.[17]

The entire army would retire if one corps commander thought things *seemed to indicate* it should be done—a definite change indeed from the previous purpose to *find and fight the enemy.*

The strange circular was issued so late that it had no real influence on the outcome of the day; but it was afterward to plague Meade, much as he sought to explain and justify it. It was one thing to have officers reconnoiter a position in the rear to which the army could retire in case of defeat; but it was quite another thing to abandon a plan, on which he had obtained the approval of his superior, to attack part of Lee's army before he could concentrate the whole of it. At noon, however, he did inform the General in Chief of his new intentions in a message blandly stating that his advance had accomplished its full purpose, and that a position was being prepared on Pipe Creek where he intended to accept battle. Still for the sake of appearance he made this slight promise of an offensive: "If I am not attacked, and I can from reliable intelligence have reason to believe I can attack with reasonable degree of success, I will do so." Significant too was a change in his report of the enemy situation, for now he wrote: "Ewell is massing at Heidlersburg. A. P. Hill is massed behind the mountains at Cashtown. Longstreet somewhere between Chambersburg and the mountains." [18]

Meade knew that Buford had driven Confederate infantry back toward Cashtown the day before.[19] What caused him to change so significantly his view and have Hill "massed behind the mountains"? Apparently, only wishful thinking. But, quickly, he was undeceived a little, for the message he began at noon was concluded at one o'clock with the sentence, "The enemy are advancing in force on Gettysburg, and I expect the battle will begin to-day." But not for three hours and a half was an order sent to the far-away Sixth Corps!

Unfortunately John Hay was away from Washington, and so we do not have the significant entries that might have gone into his diary about what Lincoln thought when he read Meade's statement that the purpose of his advance had been achieved. Halleck replied at 9:15 P.M., immediately upon receipt of the dispatch. He stated that Meade's tactical arrangements for battle seemed good, so far as his knowledge of the character of the country enabled him to judge; but from a strategic point of view he again raised the question whether Meade was not too far to the east, opening up to Lee the chance of turning his left.[20] Within an hour a message that went through much faster was to bring to Washington some information about the events of a very stirring day.

In his subsequent report John Buford wrote: "The night of the 30th was a busy night for the division. . . . By daylight of July 1, I had gained positive information of the enemy's position and movements, and my arrangements were made for entertaining him until General Reynolds could reach the scene." Between eight and nine o'clock Colonel Gamble, commanding the First Brigade—Eighth Illinois, Twelfth Illinois, Third Indiana, Eighth New York—sent in word that the enemy was advancing from Cashtown in force. Said Buford, "Colonel Gamble made an admirable line of battle, and moved off proudly to meet him. The two lines became hotly engaged, we having the advantage of position, he of numbers." For more than two hours the dismounted troopers held on against some of Lee's best infantry, and they "had to be literally dragged back a few hundred yards to a position more secure and better sheltered." [21] There they fought waiting for the arrival of Reynolds and the infantry. Probably at a fairly early hour there came to Buford an order from cavalry headquarters—also at Taneytown—that if he were too hard pressed he should fall back to Taneytown and then to Middleburg. But the order said, "The cavalry will dispute every inch of the ground," and, as if that were not enough, a postscript added that the retirement would be made only "in case of great necessity." [22]

Under such orders John Buford began the Battle of Gettysburg—a battle in which the name of the first Union soldier to fire a shot, the first to kill an enemy soldier, the first to be killed, the first Confederate to be captured, are all in the record.[23]

Here is the first message from the field of battle which Buford sent to the army commander, who was still at Taneytown:

Headquarters First Cavalry Division
Gettysburg, July 1, 1863—10:10 a.m.

The enemy's force (A. P. Hill's) are advancing on me at this point, and driving my pickets and skirmishers very rapidly. There is also a large force at Heidlersburg that is driving my pickets at that point from that direction. General Reynolds is advancing, and is within 3 miles of this point with his leading division. I am positive that the whole of A. P. Hill's force is advancing.

Jno. Buford,
Brigadier-General, Commanding

General Meade,
Commanding Army of the Potomac.[24]

The hour could hardly have been as late as Buford indicated, though there is great disagreement about time on that eventful day; that many watches were incorrect seems certain. Soon Reynolds, who had ridden ahead of his troops, joined Buford in the belfry of the Theological Seminary on a ridge a mile west of the town, to watch the battle. Gamble's brigade was in action along a second ridge beyond Willoughby Run, a stream that flowed in the little valley between the ridge where the fighting was going on and the one on which the seminary stood. Devin's brigade was across the roads north of the town, whence Buford knew that Ewell would be coming from Heidlersburg. Now the responsibility for decisions rested with Reynolds. He had not received the Pipe Creek circular; his quick eye saw some good terrain; Pennsylvania was his state; he would fight where Buford's troopers were disputing "every inch" of the ground. Orders went to hasten his own column, and a staff officer from the Eleventh Corps, who presently arrived, at once rode back with orders for Howard.[25]

The division of Brigadier General James S. Wadsworth was leading the First Corps in its march north on the Emmitsburg Road, the brigade of Brigadier General Lysander Cutler heading the column, followed by the Iron Brigade, now commanded by Brigadier General Solomon Meredith. To the four regiments—Second, Sixth, and Seventh Wisconsin and Nineteenth Indiana—which had composed the Iron Brigade when it won renown at Groveton, there had been added the Twenty-fourth Michigan. On other heads the peculiar black hats the men of the Iron Brigade were wearing might have caused opprobrious remarks; [26] but they could have worn ruffles on their trousers without being laughed at. Cutler's brigade, with the Sixth Wisconsin attached, supported by the Second Maine Battery, was thrown in on the right of the Chambersburg Road, and Meredith's remaining regiments were put in on the left. Cutler fell back at first under heavy pressure, then threw himself on the enemy that was following, and captured two regiments—the Second and Twenty-second Alabama—complete with their flags. Not to be outdone, the Iron Brigade attacked Archer's brigade of Heth's division, and captured several hundred prisoners, including General Archer himself.[27]

Thus was the course of the battle quickly changed as Reynolds's infantry took over the front from Gamble's troopers, though according to Buford some of the men of the Third Indiana, apparently not having had enough, or being unreasonably angry, picked up infantry rifles and joined one of the Wisconsin regiments, proud indeed to be shoulder to shoulder with some of the black hats—as was John Burns, the seventy-year-old inhabitant of Gettysburg, armed with an old musket.[28]

A heavy price had, however, been paid: General Reynolds had fallen with a bullet from a sharpshooter's rifle through his head. The command of the First Corps fell upon Major General Abner Doubleday, who benefited from a lull in the fighting after the repulse of the

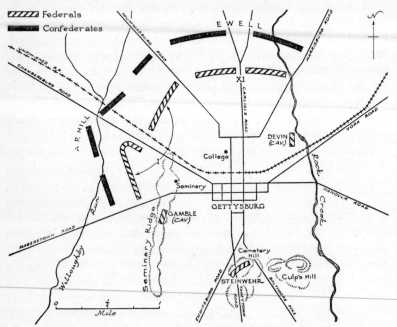

GETTYSBURG, FIRST DAY, JULY 1, 1863, 2:30 P.M.

Confederates by organizing a good defense with his own division—now under Brigadier General T. A. Rowley—and that of Wadsworth in the first line, the division of Brigadier General John C. Robinson being in reserve at the seminary.[29] Toward noon General Howard arrived ahead of his corps; and in view of his seniority the command of the field fell upon him. Buford gave ample warning of the attack that could be expected from the north, and Howard placed the Eleventh Corps—now under Major General Carl Schurz—to meet it. Schurz's own division—now under Brigadier General Alexander Schimmelfennig—and the division of Brigadier General Francis C. Barlow were deployed north of the town, and von Steinwehr's division was put in reserve at Cemetery Hill, a commanding position south of Gettysburg, where Howard also established his own headquarters.[30] (The thanks of Congress which Howard received for the early seizing of Cemetery Hill were thought by many in the army to be an unnecessary tribute.)

Without delay Howard sent word to Sickles at Emmitsburg and to Slocum—only five miles away at Two Taverns—to come to his assistance, and by two o'clock he had a report on its way to Meade.

By three o'clock two of Ewell's divisions—those of Rodes and Early—had appeared in heavy force in front of Schurz, and shortly thereafter Hill had his corps reorganized and was attacking heavily. The fury of the onslaught developed rapidly, and Buford, using his troopers to help the Federal infantry as best he could, wrote the most remarkable of his many unusual messages; this time he addressed the cavalry corps commander, and there was a touch of informality in his note:

> Headquarters First Cavalry Division
>
>   July 1, 1863—3:20 p.m.
> I am satisfied that Longstreet [Ewell?] and Hill have made a junction. A tremendous battle has been raging since 9:30 a.m., with varying success. At the present moment the battle is raging on the road to Cashtown, and within short cannon-range of this town. The enemy's line is a semicircle on the height, from north to west. General Reynolds was killed early this morning. In my opinion, there seems to be no directing person.
>
>   *Jno. Buford,*
>   Brigadier-General of Volunteers
> General Pleasonton.
> P.S.—We need help now.[31]

Help, the two heavily outnumbered and outflanked Federal infantry corps did indeed need; but none was close at hand, and so, after they had broken repeated attacks and had caused heavy losses, Howard ordered them to withdraw to a position on Cemetery Hill. It was a difficult movement, and some of the covering work that was done by both infantry and artillery during the withdrawal appears to have been of the highest order. Already Buford had disengaged his division—which, since being relieved in the morning by the First Corps, had come in on its flank to pour a devastating carbine fire on a Confederate attack; and he reassembled his men east of the Emmitsburg Road at the base of the ridge that ran south from Cemetery Hill, where the troopers now standing to horse, ready to mount and strike with their sabers, presented a heartening sight to the heavily pressed First Corps men.[32] The Confederates saw them too, or knew they were there, and Hill wisely ceased pursuit—perhaps at the direction of Lee—not wishing a cavalry charge upon his flank. But the First Corps had left many of its men in the woods and fields to the west of Gettysburg, Wadsworth reporting that over half of his division had been killed or wounded.[33]

The withdrawal of the two divisions of the Eleventh Corps was also attended with heavy loss, for Early had come in upon their right flank from the direction of York, and while the corps was falling back through the town several hundreds of its men were made prisoners, raising to 3,672 the total thus lost by the First and Eleventh Corps.[34] Probably on account of the manner in which the Eleventh Corps had given way at Chancellorsville, some unjust accusations were made against its behavior on July 1; [35] and an unjust statement by Howard that the First Corps had given way was sent by Hancock to Meade.[36] Among the men left desperately wounded on the field north of the town was Francis Barlow. With no previous military training Barlow had enlisted as a private in a New York regiment, and by sheer fighting ability and the revelation of a battlefield valor akin to that of General Humphreys, the "boy general" had risen to the merited command of a division composed principally of regiments from New York and Ohio.

About 4:30 P.M., while Howard was trying to get his command reorganized on Cemetery Hill and its vicinity, General Hancock arrived and announced that Meade had sent him forward to take command—a strange procedure indeed, little less than a shirking of responsibility by the army commander, who should have been present himself before that hour. Howard was senior to Hancock, and he was justified in not surrendering without a written order authority—and responsibility—that was his by Army Regulations. From this ambiguous situation, some confusion resulted; but for the most part the two officers worked together rather harmoniously, though each considered himself to be in command.[37]

Under the directions of Howard, Hancock, and Warren, who also was present, the new position was rapidly organized, and the moment of danger passed: a matter of great importance, because it has been claimed that if Ewell had acted resolutely the Confederates could have seized Cemetery Hill. But von Steinwehr's division was already in position with batteries well placed, and Howard's report states that when the enemy promptly tried to turn the Federal right "his line was instantly broken by Wiedrich's battery, in position on the heights." [38] This little incident was conveniently overlooked by the Confederates who spoke of Ewell's "lost opportunity," and intimated that Jackson would promptly have captured Cemetery Hill, forgetting how quickly that general desisted from following the Federals at Fredericksburg after a blast from their artillery. It is also frequently overlooked that Culp's Hill, a key eminence to the east of Cemetery Hill, was seized at once by the Federals, and that it was none other than the Iron Brigade that was sent to hold it.[39] Though only 700 men of the 1,800 that had entered combat in the morning remained, they occupied a strong position, which they immediately began to improve for defense. Seeing the importance of Culp's Hill, Wadsworth at once sent the Seventh Indiana of Cutler's brigade, which had been on duty in the rear as train guard, to join the Iron Brigade; it took to the heights of Culp's Hill 500 fresh rifles just as reliable as those that remained from the other Hoosier regiment that had fought so well that day. The artillery of the First and Eleventh Corps was brought off with remarkable success, only three guns having apparently been lost in addition to five that had been disabled in action; the batteries were quickly put in position again on the hills where they were practically immune to enemy gunfire. Skirmishers from the retiring divisions of the Eleventh Corps located themselves in houses at the base of Cemetery Hill, and had very discouraging effect upon enemy reconnaissance, one of them putting a bullet into Ewell's wooden leg.[40]

Fresh troops were rapidly nearing the field. At 3:15 Sickles informed Army Headquarters that in response to Howard's request he was moving the Third Corps to Gettysburg at once, by two roads, and wrote to Howard acknowledging receipt of his two dispatches with the cheering statement, "I shall move to Gettysburg immediately."

He left two brigades and two batteries to hold Emmitsburg, and so notified Meade. At 3:35 Slocum addressed to "General Hancock, or General Howard," the brief but important message, "I am moving the Twelfth Corps so as to come in about 1 mile to the right of Gettysburg." [41] General Geary, commanding the Second Division of the corps, stated that he was in position on the left of the Federal line at five o'clock, having been shifted there from the right by General Hancock, who regarded the right of the line as perfectly secure since the arrival of the First Division of the Twelfth Corps. The hour may have been later than Geary asserted, but certainly not a great deal later; a dispatch from Hancock to Meade at 5:25 stated that Slocum was going into position on the right. The reports for the First Division of the corps, written by Williams and Brigadier General Thomas H. Ruger, do not give hours, but leave no doubt of its rapid movements. More important than this, Williams stated that his command had actually started preparations for an attack when it learned that the First and Eleventh Corps had fallen back; and Ruger stated that the division took a position "threatening the left flank of the enemy," and expressed the view that its mere appearance had had a salutary influence on Confederate actions.[42]

Though his two divisions had gone into position, General Slocum himself declined to go forward, being senior to both Hancock and Howard and apparently not wishing to assume command of the mixed-up situation that the army commander was himself so patently avoiding. In all probability he had received the "Pipe Creek Circular"; and well could he feel uncertain as to what Meade's latest intentions were. One of Howard's aides brought him word that Slocum was only about a mile away, but declined to come forward, and in his five-o'clock message Howard wrote to Meade, "Slocum is near, but will not come up to assume command." Slocum, who was second in command after Reynolds's death, was certainly "on the spot" in view of the haziness of the commanding general's purposes; and Howard, though clearly provoked at the time, wrote in his report that Slocum afterward explained that it was his view that Meade did not want to bring on a general engagement at Gettysburg. Anyone who had read Meade's long circular of the morning—Howard presumably had not—could hardly have thought otherwise. Howard gave 7:00 P.M. on July 1 as the time when Slocum arrived at the cemetery and took over a situation that had worked itself out and had become well stabilized; Sickles reached the field at the same time, and Hancock returned to report to Meade about the battle that part of his army had so valiantly fought.[43] Yet even after night had fallen there was uncertainty as to the "directing person," for at 9:30 Sickles, wondering whether his action in moving to support Howard was approved, wrote to Butterfield, "General Hancock is not in command—General Howard commands." Very important was the ending: "This is a good battle-field." [44]

After reviewing the Confederate situation as well as that of the Federals, General Hunt made the pointed summary:

In fact an assault by the Confederates was not practicable before 5:30 p.m., and after that the position was perfectly secure. For the first time that day the Federals had the advantage of position, and sufficient troops and artillery to occupy it, and Ewell would not have been justified in attacking without the positive orders of Lee, who was present and wisely abstained from giving them.[45]

Freeman entitles a chapter "Ewell Cannot Reach a Decision"— when Ewell very definitely did make a decision—and also makes strong statements against him based in large part upon detailed but debatable incidents recorded after the event; yet he virtually absolves him of any charge of having lost an opportunity, without apparently realizing it.[46] He notes that Johnson's division of Ewell's corps would not arrive until about dark, and that Ewell knew that Rodes had suffered heavily in the afternoon attacks. "Still again, the force with which Ewell could attack immediately was small. . . . Two brigades of Early, then, and the tired survivors of Rodes's confused charges—these were all Ewell had for the attack till Johnson arrived." Nothing more need be said if one takes cognizance of the Federal reports; but Freeman did this inadequately, for he makes no mention of the attack that Howard stated was broken by Wiedrich's guns. The battery commander himself reported the action—officially in 1863, not subsequently as part of a dispute—as follows: "And after our infantry was driven out of the town, and the enemy made his appearance in our front, I received him with canister, which checked his progress, and gave our troops time to rally in rear of the battery, to advance on the enemy again, and to drive him back into town, when the fire was kept up until late in the evening." [47] Just as, earlier in the day, two Confederate regiments had been captured when they pushed retreating Yankees too closely, so also in the afternoon, Confederates were driven back into the town by counterattacking Federals, and it is quite safe to say that any eagerness they had in pursuing had been well satisfied. Freeman likewise does not refer to Buford's 2,000 troopers (probably more) waiting for call with their carbines and sabers; nor does he note that Culp's Hill had been quickly seized by the Iron Brigade and the fresh Seventh Indiana, the colonel of the latter regiment reporting that he immediately began throwing up temporary breastworks, and easily beat off a Confederate effort to penetrate his lines during the night.[48] In fact, Freeman states that Culp's Hill was unoccupied by the Federals even after night had fallen, apparently accepting inadequate Confederate reconnaissance without consulting Federal reports. Inconspicuously, in a *footnote* at the end of the chapter wherein he pictures Ewell as unable to reach a decision while fateful seconds were ticking away, Lee's biographer informs the reader that Slocum's corps had left Two Taverns as soon as news of the battle was received and "had advanced to the town." [49]

The reports of Ewell and Lee [50] when studied in connection with those of Federal commanders dispose of the question and make one wonder why the debate has been seriously continued after Hunt had so effectively described the situation. General Early, who had the only two fresh brigades to make an attack, finally concluded that Ewell's decision had been correct in view of the caution that he had received from Lee about not bringing on a general engagement.[51] Lee was present on Seminary Ridge and assumed full responsibility for what was done when, after stating that it was known from Federal prisoners that the rest of Meade's army was approaching, he wrote in his report, "Without information as to its proximity, the strong position which the enemy had assumed could not be attacked without danger of exposing the four divisions present, already weakened by a long and bloody struggle, to overwhelming numbers of fresh troops." [52] Both Lee and Ewell knew that it was not a question merely of what troops the Federals had close to the brow of Cemetery Hill, but of the reserves that were close enough at hand to counterattack. A couple of brigades might valiantly reach the top of the hill. But could they stay? That was the question which a responsible commander had to consider. One can put the case more strongly than Hunt put it, and assert that by 4:00 P.M. the position was secure; for by that time the Twelfth Corps was within reach as a strong counterattacking force, and under the direction of Hancock and Howard it could have smashed any regiments that Ewell could have placed on the brow of the hill, quite as effectively as the First Corps had thrown back the advance of Heth in the morning with very heavy captures from the brigades of Davis and Archer.

A French general has written, "The greatest difficulty is not in piercing the front, but really in progressing beyond it to a sufficient depth and with such rapidity that the decisive victory may be obtained, before the hostile strategic reserves come into the picture." [53] By the time the First and Eleventh Corps began to form on Cemetery Hill the Twelfth Corps was a "strategic reserve" very much "in the picture." And Buford—himself on "Cemetery Hill for observation"—had not put his men in position so that they might observe the sunset, but to "fight the enemy should he make another attack." [54]

In closing his chapter against Ewell, Freeman states that Federal prisoners had said there were two Union corps around the town, but omits the more significant fact—which Lee noted, and which Ewell certainly knew—that they also asserted that the remainder of the army was approaching Gettysburg.[55]

A full moon was near the meridian when at last General Meade dismounted at the great entrance portal to the cemetery, where he found Generals Slocum, Howard, Sickles, Warren, and other officers.[56] Even a note from Slocum written "Near Gettysburg" at five o'clock, stating that matters did not appear good and that he hoped the work of the day was nearly over, had not brought him forward to get a look at the battlefield by daylight. At six o'clock he sent a message to Hancock and Doubleday (why include Doubleday and omit Howard?): "If General Slocum is on the field, and I hope he is, of course he takes command. . . . It seems to me we have so concentrated that a battle at Gettysburg is now forced on us, and that, if we get up all our people, and attack with our whole force to-morrow, we ought to defeat the force the enemy has." [57] At the same hour he informed Halleck of events, writing: "A. P. Hill and Ewell are certainly concentrating; Longstreet's whereabouts I do not know"—although at noon he had reported Longstreet as between Chambersburg and the mountains. "If he is not up to-morrow," Meade continued, "I hope with the force I have concentrated to defeat Hill and Ewell. At any rate, I see no other course than to hazard a general battle. Circumstances during the night may alter this decision, of which I will try to advise you." [58] A remnant of Meade's earlier intention to fall upon a portion of Lee's army was reappearing. It could still have been realized if he had ordered forward everything he had when he received the dispatches from Couch and Haupt; for the Second, Third, and Twelfth Corps could have then arrived in time to defeat the four divisions that Lee had concentrated; but now it was too late.

At seven o'clock Sykes, who had made a hard day's march, was ordered to move to Gettysburg at once with the Fifth Corps, Butterfield ending his dispatch, "The general had supposed that General Slocum would have ordered you up." Things were certainly mixed up, with Slocum fearing to go personally to Gettysburg because he was not certain of Meade's purposes, and Meade believing that he had given Slocum authority to order Sykes into battle. Even then, however, Meade himself did not go forward, but remained at Taneytown harassed by his uncertainties. Some explanation of his behavior seems to be given later in a dispatch to Sedgwick, to whom an order had been sent at 4:30 for a night march to Taneytown. At 7:30 another message from Butterfield told Sedgwick that his march would have to be a forced one, and terminated significantly: "The general desires you to report here in person, without delay, the moment you receive this. He is waiting to see you here before going to the front." [59]

Plainly the awful responsibility of army command as battle approached was resting very heavily upon Meade. Reynolds, his close friend and former superior, upon whom he had been counting heavily, had fallen quickly in the day's battle, as if by special act of an unkind Fate. No other commander in the Army of the Potomac was more respected than "Uncle John" Sedgwick, and no one else could by his mere presence or by a word have given greater encouragement or greater support to Meade. So believing that night must have brought an end to the combat of the day, and hoping that Slocum—who had met a heavy test at Chancellorsville—had arrived and had his hand upon affairs at the front, Meade would wait for consultation with John Sedgwick. Matters were working somewhat in reverse, for it is from the quiet sureness and equanimity of an army commander that corps commanders should derive a feeling that all is well. So the hours passed—about five of them—with Meade doubtless fretting too much to relax and sleep, but finally summoning courage to join his army without first seeing "Uncle John." [60]

It must have been an eerie place on Cemetery Hill that night, with clouds floating over the moon from time to time, soldiers sleeping among the suggestive tombstones, the great somber portal, and the

groups of talking officers waiting for the coming of the army commander. The day before, the battle had begun along a stream with an
enchanting name—Willoughby Run—and in the woods about a
seminary of religion. Many men now lay in those fields, either dead or
suffering from their wounds, but the battle was to be renewed on terrain
where even the names were rugged or had an alarming sound:
Cemetery Hill, Culp's Hill, Rock Creek, Spangler's Spring, Little
Round Top, Round Top, Ziegler's Grove, the Devil's Den, the
Codori house, the Trostle house. When Howard informed Meade that
night that the position was very favorable for a defensive battle, he
probably did not say, "And what is more the leading terrain features
bear names that make the place seem foreordained to be a battlefield,"
for he had been too busy posting troops to post himself on local names.
Accompanied by Howard, Hunt, and other members of his staff,
Meade finally set out—at an hour when he could have been asleep if
he had reached the field when he should have—to see in the moonlight the field that now is the great memorial park which many
thousands of Americans visit every year, some in uninformed curiosity,
others with deeply stirred humility and reverential understanding.[61]
Now guns stand to mark the places where the batteries fought in the
great battle; but on that night there were the caissons too, and about
the carriages the sleeping cannoneers. Not far away in sheltered places
were the teams, unhitched probably, but perhaps not unharnessed, the
drivers sleeping after they had done all they could for the comfort of
their animals. That night there were the lines of sleeping infantry, depleted but reorganized portions of the First and Eleventh Corps, as
well as the four fresh brigades of Sickles's Corps and the two divisions
of Slocum's Twelfth. Out in front of the sleeping men were the
pickets, watching and listening as they struggled with the all but
irresistible desire to sleep. As for Buford's cavalry, in one sentence the
cavalryman disposed of what he did, "My division bivouacked that
night on the left of our position, with pickets extending almost to
Fairfield." [62]

Throughout the night supply trains were moving, and miles away
the Sixth Corps was on its way to the field of battle, the discomfort
of a forced night march much mitigated by the moon, and by the
morning rain that had laid the dust.[63]

After a heavy march the day before and a rest of only two or three
hours after midnight, two divisions of the Fifth Corps began to arrive

about six o'clock on July 2, and went into position on the right, the third division arriving at noon.[64] The Second Corps had bivouacked only a few miles away, and at three o'clock the men were roused; after a short march they were in an assembly area close at hand by six. Colonel Frank A. Haskell of General Gibbon's staff wrote to his brother: "The morning was thick and sultry, the sky overcast with low vapor clouds. As we approached all was astir upon the crest near the Cemetery, and the work of preparation was speedily going on. Men looked like giants there in the mist, and the guns of the frowning batteries were so big, that it was a relief to know that they were our friends." [65] The two brigades of the Third Corps that had been left at Emmitsburg had been ordered up by Meade and were approaching the field.

After day had come Meade quickly took things in hand and began a skillful disposition and rearrangement of the six corps that he now had at hand. The line he was to hold, which has often been likened to a fishhook, ran westward from its strong anchorage on Culp's Hill to Cemetery Hill and the less conspicuous East Cemetery Hill, where it turned southward, following a ridge—Cemetery Ridge—that died away into low ground at the base of Little Round Top, which in turn was well dominated by Round Top, a thousand yards farther south. From Culp's Hill to Little Round Top the line measured about three miles and constituted a strong defensive position—though Cemetery Ridge is less of an elevation than many may suppose—with both flanks secure and the possibility of moving troops rapidly from one part of the line to the other. The Confederate deployment on the other hand was to be concave; considerably longer in extent, it was to pass through the town—a magnet for stragglers—and was not to lend itself to a quick transfer of troops from one extreme flank to the other.

After some shifting of divisions the Army of the Potomac was deployed as follows:[66] Slocum's corps—Williams's division on the right, then Geary's—held the wooded ground sloping down south-easterly into the valley of Rock Creek from Culp's Hill. Wadsworth's division of the First Corps occupied the summit of the hill; next on the left came the Eleventh Corps—first Barlow's division (now commanded by Brigadier General Adelbert Ames), then Schurz's division and von Steinwehr's division with its left resting in Ziegler's Grove, a spot to become famous in the battle. Doubleday's and Robinson's divisions of the First Corps—now commanded by Brigadier

General Newton, whom Meade had summoned from the Sixth Corps the evening before for that purpose—were in reserve behind the Eleventh Corps. Connecting with the Eleventh Corps was Hancock's Second Corps—first Hays, then Gibbon, then Caldwell. Next came Humphreys's division of the Third Corps, followed by that of Birney, whose left rested near the base of Little Round Top. The Fifth Corps, after being withdrawn from the extreme right, was held in reserve nearer the center of the line; the reserve artillery was parked between the Baltimore Pike and the Taneytown Road. Buford's division, still depleted by the absence of the brigade of Brigadier General Wesley Merritt in the vicinity of Emmitsburg, covered the left flank of the army, while Gregg's division—less Huey's brigade—gave protection to the right flank. Kilpatrick's brigade was en route from Abbottstown, six miles north of Hanover.

The dispositions were virtually complete by 9:00 A.M.[67]—an important fact, for it disposes of the unjust accusation made for years against Longstreet that he wasted time while the Federal corps were concentrating. About this more will be said. But it is to be noted that Little Round Top was not occupied. During the night it had been occupied by troops of Geary's division of the Twelfth Corps—which may also have occupied Round Top [68]—due to directions given by General Hancock in the afternoon. Early in the morning, however, Geary's troops marched away to join the Twelfth Corps on the extreme right of the Federal line, in accordance with orders from Slocum, and Little Round Top was forgotten. It was left unoccupied except for some signal-corps men who set up a station there. Because artillery could—with great exertion—be moved to its summit, where they could render untenable the Federal line running to the north, it was of priceless value. The sister eminence farther south—Big Round Top—was too high and too rugged for the emplacement of guns, except mountain artillery that neither army had. Furthermore, infantry on its summit could not reach Little Round Top effectively with their rifles, so that guns placed there would be immune.

Here and there along Cemetery Ridge were clumps of trees, but generally the gentle slope in front of the Second and Third Corps was covered with fields of wheat about ready for the reaper, with grass and pasture land and some fields of corn. Orchards and farm buildings filled in the picture of prosperity and comfort. But beyond the Emmitsburg Road lay Seminary Ridge, occupied now by the

Confederates in gathering strength, and the peaceful little valley lay in the path of death and devastation.

In the modest little Leister house on the Taneytown Road, near the center of the Federal line, General Meade set up his headquarters; and from it he sent orders verbally or at times "written on little slips of paper," no copies of which were kept.[69] Perhaps this bad practice resulted from the fact that Butterfield had been left behind at Taneytown, for no other apparent purpose than keeping in touch with Sedgwick.[70] Somebody of much lesser weight than a two-starred general could have attended to that and other minor matters, and obviously the place for the army chief of staff was the battlefield headquarters.

Meade was still torn by a conflict of purposes. A desire to assume an offensive role manifested itself in a brief note at 9:30 A.M. which directed Slocum to examine the ground in his front and report "as to the practicability of attacking the enemy in that quarter." Probably before a reply was received, a more positive tone was taken in a second dispatch—signed by the chief of staff, who arrived at about ten o'clock—that told him to make preparations for an attack with his corps, supported by the Fifth. The army commander, Butterfield wrote, "wishes this a strong and decisive attack, which he will order so soon as he gets definite information of the approach of the Sixth Corps, which will also be directed to co-operate in this attack." [71] Here there seemed to be some firm resolution, emphasized by the statement that an officer had been sent to learn the position of Sedgwick's approaching column.

At eleven o'clock Slocum's reply to the first message was received. It was not favorable to an attack: there was heavy enemy strength on the Federal right, but the ground the Confederates held did not give them any particular advantage.[72]

Already, however, thoughts of a retreat had entered Meade's mind, for he had put Butterfield to work in the low upstairs of the Leister house, preparing an order for a retirement. It was never issued and even disappeared from the headquarters files, but it was destined to annoy Meade as much as the Pipe Creek order of July 1. Testifying before the Committee on the Conduct of the War, he attempted to minimize its significance and even asserted that Butterfield could have drawn it up in ten to fifteen minutes—which certainly was not true if it was written with the care and thoroughness that such an order requires, and that Butterfield said he gave to it.[73] Whatever Butterfield may have said in later years, he told the committee that Meade "may have desired" the order "prepared for an emergency without any view of its excution, or he may have had it prepared with a full view of its execution"; and Gibbon, one of the officers to whom he had submitted the order for criticism, testified: "General Butterfield did not say General Meade did intend to leave; he merely said something to the effect that it was necessary to be prepared in case it should be necessary to leave, or some remark of that kind." [74] Seth Williams, the adjutant general of the Army of the Potomac, could give the committee no light on what had become of the order, though he stated that copies might have been made for corps commanders and other officers: it had never been issued, and therefore could with perfect propriety have been soon destroyed.

Whatever may have been Meade's purpose in having the retirement order written, his decision to do nothing offensively after he received the report from Slocum was certainly wise. He held a good defensive position and, as Lee asserted in his report, there was nothing that he himself could do but attack the Federals. Meade stressed this fact in his testimony the next spring before the Congressional committee, saying that the enemy would either have to attack him or retire, and he knew "that it was not within his [Lee's] power to wait any length of time in my front and manoeuvre, and that the chances of victory on my side were greater if I acted on the defensive than they would be if I assumed the offensive." [75] However, he was about as fickle in some of his post-battle statements as in his pre-battle messages and orders. When in 1870 the war was being fought over again, and the Pipe Creek Circular and the retirement order of the 2nd were being criticized, he wrote that Longstreet's recommendation to Lee to move around the left of the Federal army "was sound military advice, . . . and it was the step I feared Lee would take." [76] Obviously this contention gave more color to the retirement order and the prearranged position along Pipe Creek; but it was also a flat contradiction of the testimony that Meade had given in March, 1864, that Lee could not maneuver and had no choice but to attack him or to retire.

Good as the Federal position was—especially because of the commanding ground on either flank—it had one bad feature, the low

and somewhat marshy ground just north of Little Round Top where
Birney's division of Sickles's corps was located. The proud and able
commander reported that his division had marched "with enthusiasm
and alacrity" the afternoon before from Emmitsburg over a road
heavy with mud; but it was not pleasant to take up a position in low
ground commanded by the ridge along which the Emmitsburg Road
ran, though temporarily his skirmishers were occupying the ridge.[77]
Disturbed over the position, especially because of lack of possible
artillery locations, General Sickles had asked Meade personally and
through staff officers for permission to adjust his lines by departing
from the position assigned—in orders concerning which there has
been warm debate.[78] Meade did not visit the left of his line after
daylight—though there was no reason why he could not have done
so—but, perhaps about noon, he sent General Hunt to examine the
position that Sickles was proposing to occupy. This the chief of
artillery did; he found that the Third Corps commander wished to
occupy a ridge that ran from the Devil's Den—a rocky locality west
of Little Round Top—generally along a road to a peach orchard on
the Emmitsburg Road, thence northward along that road.[79] Hunt's
trained eyes saw immediately that the enemy could secure the position with advantage, and that it had some distinct virtues for the
Union army. But the gain would be at a price, because the line would
have a salient at the peach orchard that could be enfiladed on both
sides. Worse than this, however, was the fact that a larger force than
the Third Corps would be needed for occupying it, and the only
available addition was the Fifth Corps; and use of this would leave
the army without any strong general reserve until the arrival of the
Sixth Corps. Though Sickles's proposed line seemed tactically better—if properly occupied—than the one in which he had been placed,
Hunt could not of course sanction a change; he stated he would report
to Meade for instructions. Sickles, however, would not wait, for he
knew that Buford's division, which had been protecting the Federal left,
had been sent away; and reconnaissances that Birney had sent out,
after driving in the covering skirmishers of the Confederates, uncovered three enemy columns moving toward the left; [80] so, assuming
responsibility—as he had done the day before when he moved to
Gettysburg upon receiving Howard's call for help—Sickles moved
into the advanced position, Birney's division taking the line from the
Devil's Den to the peach orchard, while that of Humphreys held the

Emmitsburg Road northward about three-fourths of a mile to a point
a little south of the Codori house.

The new position had more than a "tactical advantage" for the
First Massachusetts, which was on the right of Humphreys's line.
Within the lines of the regiment there stood the Roger house, and
a visiting granddaughter, Josephine Miller, set to work industriously
to bake biscuits for the men in blue. Her stock of flour being presently exhausted, six Massachusetts men made a raid on Sickles's
commissary stores, and returned not only with flour, but with raisins,
currants, and a whole sheep.[81] Not even tactical virtues in a position
will make soldiers hold on to it more stubbornly than hot biscuits,
especially when produced by a comely cook; in due time Josephine
became the only woman member of the Third Army Corps "Veterans'
Association."

In amazement the men of the Second Corps watched the forward
movement of their neighbors on the left.[82] Their own arms were
stacked, and anyone who knows soldiers can picture the scene; many
men were catching up on lost sleep; many were smoking pipes; some
were writing letters; others were playing cards or other games, or just
idly conversing. Of course they wondered as to what might happen
within a few hours; and doubtless many thought their Third Corps
comrades were inviting trouble, not knowing that the men in one
lucky regiment were fortifying themselves with hot biscuits. The
Second Corps had an entire brigade of four Pennsylvania regiments,
and six other regiments from that state, while Graham's brigade of
Birney's division was solidly Pennsylvanian. Some of the Pennsylvanians were actually not far from their homes, and that they were
feeling deeply need hardly be said. Also watching the advance of
the Third Corps were the Nineteenth Maine and the First Minnesota. The soldiers from the remote Northwest must have felt far
from their homes indeed; but before the battle was over they were
to give evidence of their attachment to the Union by valor which cost
them grievously. Calm and cheerful the sturdy veterans were, quite
as if nothing unusual were about to happen; at last the days and
nights of heavy exhausting marches were at an end. Once more the
situation was normal; for, after the many weary miles, there again
in the woods, and behind the opposite ridges, was the same old Army
of Northern Virginia, with which they had been in close contact for
six months along the Rappahannock. To march that far just to fight

another battle! But the scene on which they gazed was at least pleasant—the well cultivated fields and the orchards in the little valley
in front of them. On Little Round Top and about the Devil's Den
was thick and bad terrain; but the men along the ridge had something
more important than pleasing vistas—they had open fields of fire,
and in the neatly piled stone walls they saw virtues the builders had
never contemplated. Calmly they rested, and amused themselves,
with their rifles stacked.

At times throughout the morning of July 2 there had been an
exchange of artillery fire, and it can be assumed that the gunners
laid their guns carefully, not firing just to pass the time, nor to amuse
themselves. They were shooting themselves into their positions and
discovering the ranges to possible future targets. Angry exchanges of
musketry also broke out between the skirmish lines of the two armies.
After the Confederates had driven Federal pickets from a house in
his front, Hays sent out a regiment that seized the place, took some
prisoners, and then burned the house and other buildings. War had
begun to strike the quiet little valley. The story of the battle the day
before, of the heavy fighting of the outnumbered First and Eleventh
Corps spread throughout the lines, and all the men in blue knew
that the Southern infantry, though now an invader and not a de-
fender, still struck with its customary spirit. But for the enemy
artillery the Northern soldiers had no great respect, and within recent
weeks their feeling with regard to Stuart's horsemen had changed.
Wrote Colonel Haskell: "And, of late, we have begun to despise the
enemies' cavalry too. It used to have enterprise and dash, but in the
late cavalry contests ours have always been victor, and so now we
think about all this chivalry is fit for is to steal a few of our mules
occasionally, and their negro drivers." [83] There could be no better
source of morale for the Northern infantry than belief that their own
artillery and their own cavalry were better than those of the enemy.
Then it was up to them to show that they could match the courage
and tenacity, as well as the marching ability, of the superb though
shabbily dressed brigades that followed Longstreet, Ewell, and Hill.

But though the infantrymen and the artillery lounged about as the
sultry day wore one, with the sky overcast and a "mizzling effort at
rain," there still was activity of a kind. Surgeons were setting up hospitals, and were searching for streams, springs, and wells. Ambulances
were being put in position behind the lines, and stretchers were being

made ready. Groups of stragglers were being brought in by the provost guards, and were being distributed to their regiments. But the men loitering about the long lines of stacked rifles took all this as commonplace, or as a topic for jest.[84]

Farther behind the lines men were also working hard, for a new railhead had to be established in order to restock with food and ammunition the now-filled wagons and caissons of the infantry, the cavalry, and the artillery. Into the railhead there soon would also come from the front the long columns of wagons and ambulances filled with the wounded; and these would go back in the emptied cars to the great hospitals in Washington, where preparations also were going ahead.

At 12:45 A.M. of July 1 Haupt in Harrisburg had wired to Halleck that he believed the enemy concentration would be at Gettysburg instead of Chambersburg as he had previously predicted, and that Meade should be advised and be prepared for a sudden attack from Lee's entire army; but for some reason there was a twelve-hour delay in forwarding the message to Meade by courier from Frederick.[85] Though there is no reason to believe that Haupt's appraisal would have had any influence upon Meade, the dispatch is of importance as showing Haupt's correct views. At six o'clock the energetic railroader sent a longer intelligence summary, and a message to Stanton about the general tone of things and about the Harrisburg situation.[86] Then he returned to Baltimore, having to take the long route through Philadelphia because the enemy had destroyed many bridges and culverts on the Northern Central Pennsylvania. After he reached Baltimore miracles began to happen.

Westminster would have to be the railhead, for the Western Maryland was open to that place; but a wretched little road it was, with no telegraph line to help in handling trains, no sidings, and a normal running time of five hours for only twenty-six miles. From Alexandria, Haupt called up Adna Anderson, directing him to bring carloads of railroad iron, bridge material, and even wood for engine fuel, as well as workmen. Water for the engines would have to be dipped from streams in buckets, but on the afternoon of the 2nd he reported to Stanton that fifteen trains a day would be put into Westminster, and that the 150 cars, in returning, could carry from 2,000 to 4,000 wounded. At the same time repair crews were working on the Northern Central, and he promised that as soon as operation was militarily safe he would have the line into Gettysburg in operation. Though the map showed a railroad from Hanover to Littlestown, his information indicated that the track actually was laid only a few hundred yards beyond Hanover.[87] As Ingalls had informed Meigs on the 1st that he thought he had enough of everything "until after a fight," [88] the battle of Gettysburg from a supply point of view was something to go into the textbooks.

Into Westminster on the morning of July 3 would come Buford with the brigades of Gamble and Devin, the cavalryman consoling himself for missing the last part of the battle he had so valiantly begun with the thought that there was plenty of oats at the railhead, as well as rations, so that the men and horses that he had worked so hard could be rested and fed.[89]

Private enterprise and initiative were also helping greatly in the important matter of keeping messages flowing back and forth between Washington and the army. On the 1st Haupt informed Meigs that the Adams Express Company, working with General Schenck, was starting horse expresses every three hours from Baltimore to Westminster, with relays every seven miles, day and night, with a running time of three hours.[90]

The afternoon also was half gone when Meade wrote to Halleck at three o'clock:

I have concentrated my army at this place to-day. The Sixth Corps is just coming in, very much worn out, having been marching since 9 p.m. last night. The army is fatigued. I have to-day, up to this hour, awaited the attack of the enemy, I having a strong position for defensive. I am not determined, as yet, on attacking him till his position is more developed. . . . If not attacked, and I can get any positive information of the position of the enemy which will justify me in so doing, I shall attack. If I find it hazardous to do so, or am satisfied the enemy is endeavoring to move to my rear and interpose between me and Washington, I shall fall back to my supplies at Westminster. I will endeavor to advise you as often as possible. . . . I feel fully the responsibility resting upon me, but will endeavor to act with caution.[91]

The dispatch said—though Meade probably did not know it—that unless he was attacked he intended to fall back, in spite of having a strong defensive position; for attacking Lee's concentrated army would indeed have been hazardous. In this message there is not the least intimation that Meade then believed—as he later assured the Congressional committee—that Lee had no choice but to attack him or retire. Candidly he was admitting that he was not enough of a general to attack his opponent, if the latter indulged in the very risky operation of a flank movement around the Federal left. The new commander of the Army of the Potomac would have allowed such a maneuver to proceed without molestation, and after falling back to his Pipe Creek position he would in the same way have allowed himself to be turned out of it, and so on back into the defenses of Washington, "fully" feeling at each stage the responsibility resting upon him, and determined "to act with caution." It is quite appropriate for a commander to speak of his consciousness of responsibility at the time he is placed in high position, but hardly appropriate to emphasize it in battle communiqués.[92]

The message did not reach Washington until 10:20 the next morning, July 3, and it could not have been too encouraging to a person with Lincoln's ability to read the character of men. Doubtless he realized that the fact that Lee had no supply line and was compelled to pick up his food here and there would prevent him from maneuvering Meade from one position to another.

At about the time the message to the General in Chief was dispatched the corps commanders began to assemble at headquarters for a conference. Whether it had been intended to consider the retirement order that Butterfield had drawn up can never be known, though statements to Halleck make it appear that the order might well have been on the agenda. The intended conference never even began, for as Sickles—who had reluctantly left his command—arrived, a heavy cannonading was heard on the left, and Meade, meeting Sickles, told him he need not dismount.[93] Back to the Third Corps its commander rode in haste, knowing full well that the attack that he had been looking for had at length broken against his lines. After giving Sykes orders to move the Fifth Corps to the support of the left flank, General Meade himself went in that direction, and he was much amazed when he discovered the very advanced position into which the Third Corps had been moved, though a report from General Warren that the corps had moved forward prepared him a little for what he was to see.[94] There was no chance of withdrawing the corps—that Meade saw at a glance —and so his whole effort was devoted to saving the left of his line by bringing up reenforcements. Sickles's troops were compelled to bear

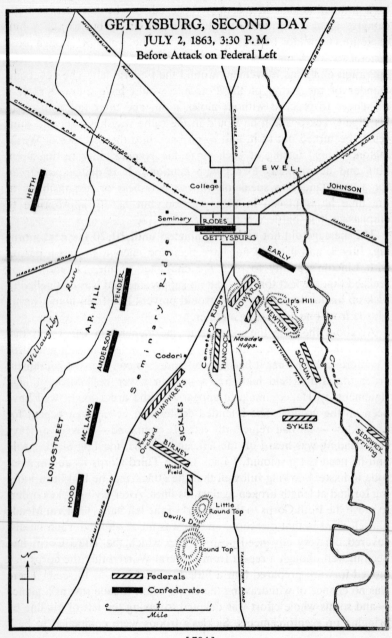

GETTYSBURG, SECOND DAY
JULY 2, 1863, 3:30 P.M.
Before Attack on Federal Left

MUMMASBURG ROAD

CHAMBERSBURG ROAD

CARLISLE ROAD

YORK ROAD

HETH

EWELL

JOHNSON

College

Seminary

RODES

GETTYSBURG

HANOVER ROAD

EARLY

HAGERSTOWN ROAD

A. P. HILL

PENDER

Seminary Ridge

Willoughby Run

HOWARD

Culp's Hill

NEWTON

Cemetery Ridge

Meade's Hdqs.

Rock Creek

ANDERSON

Codori

HANCOCK

SLOCUM

BALTIMORE PIKE

McLAWS

LONGSTREET

HUMPHREYS

SICKLES

SYKES

SEDGWICK arriving

Peach Orchard

BIRNEY

HOOD

Wheat Field

EMMITSBURG ROAD

Little Round Top

Devil's Den

TANEYTOWN ROAD

Round Top

N

▨▨▨ Federals

■■■ Confederates

0   ½   1
Mile

the brunt of the heavy onslaught, and even the severest critic of Dan Sickles never denied that he fought hard and skillfully, or that he exacted heavy losses from his assailants. The assault upon the Federal left was made by Hood's and McLaws's divisions of Longstreet's corps, but the attack was soon taken up by Anderson's division of the corps of A. P. Hill, who was holding the center of Lee's line.

Soon new names had been added to American history: the Devil's Den, the Peach Orchard, the Wheat Field, about which the battle raged furiously. By the heavy attack of Hood, Birney's division was broken; while under the terrific blows of McLaws and Anderson, Humphreys, after some brilliant handling of his division, was forced back. About 6:00 P.M. Sickles himself received a grievous wound that resulted in the loss of his right leg, command of his corps devolving upon Birney until, at Meade's direction, Hancock took it over. Not only was the Fifth Corps thrown into the battle to stop the assaults of the three divisions of Lee's army, but a large part of the Twelfth Corps was brought from the Federal right to be ready for action on the left. Units of the First Corps as well as some of the Sixth, after it arrived in midafternoon, were also moved to places where they could be used if needed. On the left of the Confederate attack, Wright's brigade of Anderson's division actually broke the line of Hancock's Second Corps and reached a line of Federal guns. But the Confederate hold of the prize was very short, for Wright was soon forced out of the position he had seized, and under heavy artillery fire he was driven back practically to the position from which he had led his regiments.[95]

Not long after the battle had broken out, General Warren made the appalling discovery that Little Round Top was not occupied, and from the Fifth Corps which was then approaching he secured Vincent's and Weed's brigades and Hazlett's battery—D, Fifth United States— and hurried them to the threatened key to the Federal left flank.[96] Only a determined battery commander, skillful drivers, and cannoneers ready to put their shoulders to the wheels of their pieces and their caissons, could ever have taken six guns to the top of Little Round Top; but there Hazlett got his battery. Men from Hood's division stormed the hill, and there was bitter hand-to-hand fighting; in the terrible struggle Weed and Hazlett were killed and Vincent was wounded. But Little Round Top was held. By dark on July 2 the contest had closed upon the left, with the Federals strongly holding the line that they had occupied in the morning.

After Longstreet's guns had proclaimed his attack upon the Federal left, Ewell opened a heavy cannonade at the other end of the line; but it was soon overpowered by the Federal guns on Cemetery Hill.[97] Presently, however, Johnson's division of Ewell's corps advanced against the position which had been practically vacated when all but Greene's brigade of the Twelfth Corps had been moved to the support of the Federal left flank. Some abandoned trenches were captured easily by the Confederates, but Greene, fighting hard with his brigade, and some 700 or 800 men sent from the First and Eleventh Corps, held his own intrenchments. On Johnson's right, Ewell threw the divisions of Rodes and Early at Cemetery Hill, and in places they reached the top; but a counterattack by Carroll's brigade of the Second Corps, launched after night had begun to close in, drove from the hill all the Confederates who were not captured, and regained the batteries that had been momentarily lost.[98]

It had been a hard battle indeed that had raged over the three-mile front, and Meade was entitled to feel that he had handled with marked success the many crises and swift developments requiring quick decision. The thought should have given him a measure of sustaining confidence. At eight o'clock he wrote to Halleck, "The enemy attacked me about 4 p.m. this day, and after one of the severest contests of the war, was repulsed at all points." A more modest, fitting, as well as accurate description of the four hours of fierce fighting could hardly have been written. He once more spoke of a possible offensive—which had become something of a habit with him—and closed his dispatch with the statement: "I shall remain in my present position to-morrow, but am not prepared to say, until better advised of the condition of the army, whether my operations will be of an offensive or defensive character." [99] Although his dispatches had generally contained plenty of "escape clauses," it is to be emphasized that his statement about remaining in the position he then occupied was not conditional in any way. Yet, in spite of that, Meade called a council of war on that same evening, for the specific purpose of submitting to his corps commanders precisely the question that he had just reported to the General in Chief had been decided. That perhaps is the most serious charge that can be made against him, about which there can be no argument. Surely an army commander should not regard his word on a vital question, that he had just given to Supreme Headquarters—and thus to the President —as subject to the nullifying votes of his subordinates. But that is exactly what Meade did on the night of July 2, 1863.

In a modest room in the Leister house, containing a bed in one corner, a small plain table in the center with a wooden pail of water and a tin cup, and some five or six chairs, General Meade assembled his corps commanders to deliberate upon the morrow.[100] Three questions were formally proposed: Should the army remain where it was or retire to a position nearer its base of supplies? If it remained where it was, should it attack or await the attack of the enemy? If it waited for the enemy to attack, how long should it wait? [101] As is the custom in military deliberations, replies began with the junior member of the council, General Gibbon, and the answers are recorded in the Official Records. The vote of all nine officers (in addition to Gibbon, another division commander—Williams—was present) was to remain, and to stay upon the defensive, but the answer to the third question was indecisive.

The mere fact that he had called the council of war and had submitted the question about retiring would have proved an embarrassment to Meade, especially because he was to have difficulty enough explaining the Pipe Creek order, and the retirement order that Butterfield prepared on the morning of July 2. But the rumor soon spread, and in due time appeared in the papers, that Meade's own views had not agreed with those of his corps commanders as expressed in the evening meeting.[102] His own denial that he favored retirement was supported by a number of his officers, but Slocum subsequently wrote that Meade said after the formal voting was finished: "Well, gentlemen, the question is settled. We will remain here, but I wish to say that I consider this no place to fight a battle." [103] Whatever the facts may be, it is clear that Meade's statement to the Congressional committee, "I utterly deny ever having intended or thought, for one instant, to withdraw that army, unless the military contingencies which the future should develop during the course of the day [July 2] might render it a matter of necessity that the army should be withdrawn," [104] cannot be accepted as entirely true, in view of the first question he submitted to his subordinates on the evening of the 2nd. That question envisaged a voluntary withdrawal in order to be nearer the base of supplies.

CHAPTER XXII

THE BATTLE ENDS;
THE ARGUMENTS BEGIN

We turned the charge; nine acres of prisoners!
An unnamed orderly

IT WAS about midnight when the Twelfth Corps returned to the right of the Federal line; but the men were not given a long rest, for Slocum ordered his command to attack at daylight and drive the enemy from the intrenchments that Johnson had found so easy to occupy the night before.[1] At 4:00 A.M. the artillery preparation opened, and the Confederates were subjected to a heavy shelling for an hour.[2] Geary was ready to advance, when Johnson, who had been reenforced, seeking to exploit the advantage gained a few hours before, made a vigorous attack all along the line of his division in an effort to extend the advantage he had gained the night before. Attack after attack was made against the strong position that Slocum held, with heavy losses to the Confederates and small loss to the Federals; it was a case of Marye's Hill but in reverse. Until after ten o'clock the battle raged, and when it was over the Twelfth Corps held all its old intrenchments again; Johnson was back in the position from which he had started the day before, and there he remained quietly throughout the rest of the day, including the very eventful hours of late afternoon. All the smashing power of the Second Corps of the Army of Northern Virginia was gone, except for the sting of the bullets from its sharpshooters, especially those lodged in houses in the town. Bravely it had fought, and heavy had been its casualties, but not one foot of conquered ground lay within its grasp.

Wisely enough Meade did not devote too much attention to what was going on upon the right flank, feeling certain that Slocum would prove a master of the situation there. Shaler's brigade of the Sixth Corps was marched at Meade's orders from the left of the line and took position in a woods behind Geary's division on the extreme right; [3] but Slocum got along very handsomely without it, though he probably felt a little more comfortable knowing it was waiting for his call. At 8:00 A.M. Meade got off a dispatch to Halleck, an excellent message that seemed to indicate a composed and rested army commander, a message that was purely factual—without *if*'s, and without highly qualified talk about attacking Lee. The dispatch is worthy of full quotation on account of its tone, the conclusive evidence it affords of good intelligence work, and the rather amusing last sentence. Truly the Federals were being supercareful about their code—a code the Confederates never did break.

The action commenced again at early daylight upon various parts of the line. The enemy thus far have made no impression upon my position. All accounts agree in placing the whole army here. Prisoners report Longstreet's and A. P. Hill's forces much injured yesterday and many general officers killed. General Barksdale's (Mississippi) dead body is within our lines. We have thus far sent off about 1,600 prisoners, and a small number yet to be started. I have given certain instructions to General French, which he will telegraph you. The dispatches from you yesterday, owing to the disappearance of Caldwell, telegraph operator, are here in cipher, unintelligible.[4]

The message was in Washington at 5:10, after a day of nervous and anxious waiting filled with alarms and rumors. As if to make the tension greater, the entire day passed without Meade's message of the evening before being received, and it came to hand actually five minutes after the fresher one of the morning. It was another one of those little mishaps—like the mystery of Caldwell—connected with communications in time of war that will never be explained.

As dawn came, with a breaking of the clouds after a sultry, starless night, there was only some skirmish fire upon the left. But there was no oversleeping, and Haskell wrote: "But one could not have told by the appearance of the men, that they were in battle yesterday, and were likely to be again to-day. They packed their knapsacks, boiled their coffee and munched their hard bread, just as usual." [5] Probably many letters were written in which something of the day before was told, and in which there was a prophecy, such as that which a Confederate officer, seated beneath a tree on the opposite ridge, was soon to put into a letter: "This will be a great day in history." [6] By ten o'clock it could be seen plainly that the Confederates were making a heavy concentration of artillery along Seminary Ridge, reaching nearly all the way from the town to the Peach Orchard. Battery after battery went into position until over a hundred guns could be counted; it looked as if Lee were planning an artillery preparation such as the continent had never seen, as a prelude to a grand infantry assault against Cemetery Ridge. No one watched the gathering Confederate guns with closer analysis than Hunt, and the fine Union gunner began to shift the Federal batteries, and to call up new guns from the reserve park between the Taneytown and Baltimore roads.[7] Along the ridge he rode, instructing the corps chiefs of artillery and the battery commanders to withhold their fire for fifteen or twenty minutes after the enemy had opened, then to concentrate it with all possible accuracy on the enemy guns that seemed to be doing the most damage to the Federals, but even then to fire slowly so that plenty of ammunition would be left to meet the infantry assault.

Hancock was in command of the center of the Federal line, which consisted of his own corps—temporarily commanded by Gibbon—and parts of the First and Third, and some smaller units. Meade discussed with him the likelihood that the enemy would launch an attack against the Union center, and it seems that it was tentatively decided that if such an assault were made and were repulsed, then the Fifth and Sixth Corps would be advanced in a counterattack.[8] Sykes's Fifth Corps was occupying the left of the line, reaching as far as Round Top. Sedgwick's men, who had made such a long and hurried march to reach the field, constituted Meade's greatest potential striking force, for only a few of them had been used, and that only lightly. But Meade had dissipated them in driblets, sending a brigade here and a brigade there, in order to strengthen his line; and except for two brigades of the corps, which were behind the left of his line, it could not be said that he had an army reserve. The test of Meade's generalship was at hand and lay in what he did with the Sixth Corps. He should have told Hancock that he *must* hold and break the coming Confederate assault with the Second Corps and the parts of the First and Third Corps that were in the center, while the Sixth Corps and part of the Fifth were made ready to deliver a counterstroke. At Second Bull Run,

Lee had Jackson withstand assault after assault while he withheld
Longstreet from battle in order to launch him in a counterattack at the
moment when the Federal attacks had exhausted themselves. Hancock,
with his striking military appearance, was a more inspiring commander
in many ways than Stonewall, and he had unexcelled brigades at his
command, occupying strong positions. He could have met a harder
task than breaking Lee's last effort proved to be.

If most of the Sixth Corps had been reassembled early, it appears as
if there would have been an unusual opportunity to place it well on the
Confederate right flank, for by noon a Federal cavalry brigade was in
position squarely across the Emmitsburg Road and compelled Longstreet to bend his line to protect Lee's rear. The horsemen would have
screened and protected a movement of the Sixth Corps to a position
from which the strong body of fresh, well commanded men might have
struck a devastating blow. But even if Meade did not have the heart
to move Sedgwick away from behind the line he held, and had wished
to play safer and launch his intended attack in a more frontal manner,
the powerful Sixth Corps should still have been reassembled in part at
least. At the meeting the night before, the total number of "effectives"
was reported to be 58,000, so that for the active front of three miles
Meade had about ten rifles per yard. In addition, he had an abundance
of guns, and parts of his line were so strong by nature that they could
be lightly held. If 15,000 men had been held out as a striking force,
the Federal commander would still have had more than eight rifles per
yard; and with that power he should have been able to withstand an
enemy already much weakened by attacks. Yet in spite of all his advantages, and in spite of any understanding with Hancock, it does not appear that Meade made any preparations whatever for launching a
counterstroke; and without careful preparations it might not be possible
to make one with the promptness essential for success.

In some particulars, however, Meade was undoubtedly thinking
ahead, though not in an unqualified manner. Doubts like those which
prevented preparation for a counterstroke were also revealed in a
message to General French at Frederick at 7:00 A.M.,[9] to which he
referred in his dispatch to Halleck. Stating that he had held his position after the enemy renewed the conflict the day before, Meade
ordered French, if the outcome of the 3rd were a retreat by Lee toward
the Potomac, to reoccupy Harpers Ferry and do all that he could to
annoy and impede the enemy's retreat. It might be possible, Meade

said, to operate against Lee's communications at once with cavalry and light marching infantry. This was all very much to the point; but there was also the sentence, "If the result of today's operations should be our discomfiture and withdrawal, you are to look to Washington, and throw your force there for its protection. You will be prepared for either of these contingencies should they arise." It looked as if Meade feared he might be completely wiped out, and as if the saving of Washington were to depend upon the 5,000 to 7,000 men that French had. How could French start at once operating effectively against Lee's communications if he were also to hold himself ready to fall back hastily to Washington?

Other efforts were being prepared to put a "squeeze" on Lee and gather fruits of victory. At nine o'clock Couch sent a dispatch to Colonel Lewis B. Pierce at Bloody Run, Pennsylvania, with some fragments of the Winchester garrison and a little militia, informing him of the battle in progress, and adding, "So far, our people have the advantage." He asked Pierce if it were not possible for him to move toward Chambersburg and do a little harassing. Later he wired: "I think Meade will whip them tomorrow, and we must help him every way. Push on at all hazards." Pierce replied that Couch's orders would be obeyed, and he added some good news: "My scouts in from the Potomac. Same high and rising." At 1:00 P.M. Halleck directed Couch to throw forward all the force he could, saying that the best assistance could be given to Meade by moving against Lee's left flank. Already General W. F. Smith was getting ready to move forward from Carlisle, but he reported he could not get away by noon. That the militia which he had at his disposal was not all that could be desired was indicated by the statement, "My ammunition has not yet come up, and I don't know if my ordnance officer knows enough to bring it." He also feared that some of the wagons that had been furnished him had deserted.[10]

Of all the dispatches that reached Washington that day none could have been more surprising than one that Stanton received at 10:30 A.M. from Couch, "Jefferson Davis was undoubtedly at Greencastle yesterday." [11] Greencastle, halfway between Hagerstown and Chambersburg, was squarely on Lee's line of communications, and was fifty miles from Harrisburg, but some scout or other person in whom Couch had confidence had evidently brought a message that the general accepted. How the strange report was evaluated in Washington cannot be told.

Noon had little more than passed when the commander of the Twelfth Corps wrote:

July 3, 1863—12.20 p.m.

General Meade:

I think I have gained a decided advantage on my front, and hope to be able to spare one or two brigades to help you on some other part of the line.

Slocum, Major-General [12]

In one sentence John Slocum had revealed the sort of thoughtfulness a subordinate is likely to forget. As he watched the enemy preparations for assault, nothing could have been more heartening to Meade than to know that the battle on his right—which had been a bitter contest—was completely under control, and that troops could be withdrawn if the need were great elsewhere. (Shaler's unused brigade should have been returned to Sedgwick.) Close upon the receipt of Slocum's message there drifted across the valley—sharp on the stroke of 1:00—the sound of a single gun. Everyone knew it was the signal gun. Instantly the great concentrated mass of Confederate guns broke out in a furious cannonade, which was taken up presently by batteries of Hill's corps and of Ewell's. The firing was not too accurate, and Hunt noted that a former artillery pupil of his seemed to have forgotten the lessons he had given him.[13] At 2:15 Howard reported to Meade that little damage had been done to him: "The batteries on our right do not reach us, and in center invariably overshoot us." [14] But though the shorts were innocuous that was not true of the overs, for some of them fell among artillery teams and others drove Meade's headquarters away from the Leister house. The shells that struck near their true targets dismounted some guns, blew up caissons, and gave some of the Federal infantry a rough time.

Slowly, as Hunt had ordered, the Federal guns began to answer—with great precision, he discovered to his satisfaction when he later inspected Cemetery Ridge.[15] Presently, at his direction, the batteries on the left ceased fire, for the master gunner knew that the true target for artillery was the greatest threat to the friendly infantry, and that would be the hostile infantry. Hunt wanted long-range projectiles ready to take the advancing Confederates under fire from the moment they started their march for the Union lines. He knew that his cannoneers would be subjected to a great ordeal after they had stopped their fire, for then the Confederate gunners could serve their pieces undisturbed

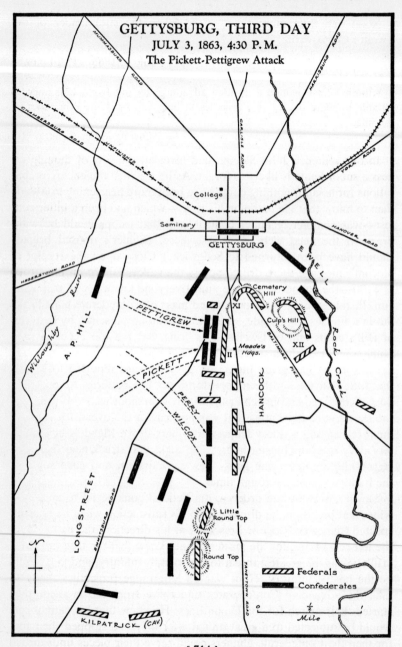

GETTYSBURG, THIRD DAY
JULY 3, 1863, 4:30 P.M.
The Pickett-Pettigrew Attack

by shells bursting about them; but he had as much confidence in the fire discipline of the Federal artillerymen as he had in the lines of waiting infantry. Some of Hancock's batteries on the right did not cease fire and used up most or all of their long-range projectiles. The diminution of the fire from Cemetery Ridge caused hopefulness among the Confederate officers anxiously studying the effect of the cannonade upon which so much depended: perhaps there was some demoralization in the Union lines; perhaps the powerful Federal guns had been effectively silenced. The moment of supreme opportunity appeared to have come.[16]

It was almost 3:00 P.M. when the Confederate guns ceased fire, and Warren, watching from Little Round Top, wigwagged to Hunt, "They are moving out to attack." [17] Then the smoke cleared, and from all along the Union line the Confederate infantry could be seen as it moved out of the woods and formed quickly for the assault. The attacking troops were under the command of George Pickett and consisted of his own three brigades—which had arrived late the day before—and eight brigades from Hill's corps, six of which were under the command of James J. Pettigrew, while two directly supported Pickett. In all no fewer than forty-two regimental colors floated over the three great lines of 15,000 infantry that started their magnificent and steady march of nearly a mile toward Cemetery Ridge, stopping to climb the fences along the Emmitsburg Road, and then re-forming carefully. At the Union left, McGilvery's concentration of forty guns along the ridge and a six-gun battery on Little Round Top, served with great precision, opened at long range. They enfiladed Pickett's division and helped cause the right of the Confederate attacking force to move toward the left,[18] intensifying the weight of that part of the formation. The batteries on the Union right, having spent their long-range projectiles, were compelled to stay out of action and to withhold their fire until the target was within the range of canister. Hancock's chief of artillery reported that when at last he reopened his silent guns it was with devastating effect.[19]

Onward the great attacking force came, in spite of the gaps torn in the ranks by the Federal guns. The well disciplined Union infantry, protected in part by crests of the ridge and by stone walls, held their fire, watched admiringly, and waited. Gibbon—former teacher of ordnance at West Point, author of a long treatise on the subject—reared in North Carolina—whence came fifteen of the regiments that were marching against the Union center, saw that his brigades were destined to receive the greatest shock, and he did just what he should have done. Wrote Haskell: "General Gibbon rode down the lines, cool and calm, and in an unimpassioned voice he said to the men, 'Do not hurry, men, and fire too fast, let them come close before you fire, and then aim low and steadily.' The coolness of their General was reflected

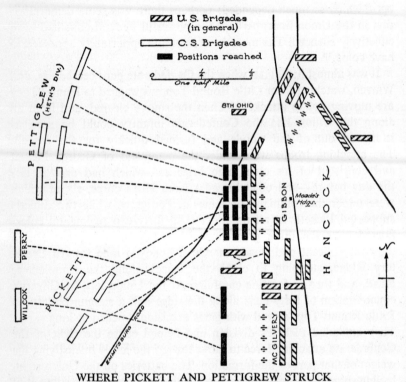

WHERE PICKETT AND PETTIGREW STRUCK

The Union line was momentarily broken at Ziegler's Grove, marked X; but the attacking force was soon in bewildered retreat, leaving many dead and wounded, as well as prisoners.

in the faces of his men." [20] Along the line of infantry there was clicking of locks as hammers were drawn back; cap boxes were slid to the front of the body, cartridge boxes were opened, officers opened their revolver holsters. Everyone waited. It was an example of what every infantry officer wishes to have in battle—perfect fire discipline.

Although there were plenty of "good yelling regiments" in the attacking force, the lines came on quietly without the customary "Rebel yell," [21] and they had probably closed to about 100 yards before Gibbon's brigades opened fire with their rifles, the attacking ranks halting and returning the fire, though they were now so deep in places on the left of their line that only a part of the men could use their weapons. In front of Hall's brigade the decision was over in a moment, for the Confederates recoiled and fell back in disorder, leaving a line of dead and wounded to mark the limit of their advance.[22] But it was not so in front of Webb's brigade, the left of which rested in Ziegler's Grove. Upon his three Pennsylvania regiments a great and overwhelming force was descending, for there the Confederate tendency to congregate had been encouraged by an attack that the Eighth Ohio—of Carroll's brigade—had made upon the left of the assaulting lines while George J. Stannard's brigade of Vermonters—fresh from the defenses of Washington, and never before in battle—was skillfully attacking the right flank. Webb's lines fell back from the wall; but Hall, his own front no longer threatened, brought his men to Webb's support, and after a period of desperate and confused fighting, with units badly intermingled, the great masses of the enemy fell back in precipitate retreat. Many dead and wounded lay on the field; hundreds of the attacking force were marched to the rear as prisoners; and Federal soldiers held in their hands many battle flags that for a few moments had floated triumphantly over the stone wall. In the small group of Confederates to cross the wall was intrepid Brigadier General Lewis A. Armistead, soon killed with his hat raised aloft upon his sword, his hand upon a Federal gun in demand for its surrender.

Actually the great assault by 15,000 was broken by the Federal artillery and 9,000 to 10,000 steady disciplined infantrymen, with great unneeded reserves near at hand.[23]

The time for a counterstroke had arrived; and if plans had been made, and if the Sixth Corps and part of the Fifth had been prepared and in position to launch one, it is possible that a great victory might have been won. Such was the view of Hancock as his conversation with the army commander came to his mind. He had been wounded; but he remained on the field to see the attack broken, and as soon as he reached a place where some attention could be given to his injury— which was by no means minor—he wrote to Meade: "I have never seen a more formidable attack, and if the Sixth and Fifth Corps have pressed up, the enemy will be destroyed. The enemy must be short of ammunition, as I was shot with a tenpenny nail." [24] It was exactly as the wounded Hancock believed, and the opportunity was great indeed. From Colonel Fremantle, the British observer who watched Lee carefully at different times during the great battle, we have a good description of the manner in which Lee and his staff threw themselves into the work of halting and reorganizing the thousands of men streaming back across the fields toward Seminary Ridge.[25] The Confederate commander exhibited his customary calmness and control, but the very business in which he was engaged was eloquent proof of the magnitude of the disaster and of the alarm which he felt but did not reveal. However, the counterstroke which Lee expected his opponent would launch, and which he made such efforts to prepare for, was not delivered. Meade, dominated by the caution he had promised the day before, was indeed perfectly content with passively repulsing an attack. Hancock's conjecture about the Confederate ammunition, communicated to him in such a painful way, was entirely correct. Their batteries were low indeed, and anyone who considered the great amount of firing that Lee's guns had done for three days should have realized that the store of ammunition he had with him had been very heavily drawn upon. On the other hand, Hunt still had fresh batteries in his artillery reserve, and a good supply of ammunition in his train.

While the great conflict for Cemetery Ridge was going on there was also cavalry action on both flanks. Stuart with his three brigades had reached Lee on the afternoon of the 2nd, having been as far north as Carlisle, where he had burned the cavalry barracks; and after a night's rest he had moved to the left of Ewell's position, Jenkins's brigade being added to his command. He hoped to get to the Federal rear and cause damage there, but his movement was discovered by his old West Point friend David Gregg, who was covering the Federal right with the Second Cavalry Division, to which George Custer's brigade of the Third was attached. Both sides had horse artillery batteries and may have numbered 5,000 sabers each, Stuart perhaps having more.[26] A sharp contest lasting several hours, with varying fortune, took place; but Stuart certainly did not fulfill his mission of annoying the Federal rear. Entirely forgetting this, one of his officers wrote later in a patronizing manner, "The cavalry of the enemy were steadily improving, and it was all we could do sometimes to manage them." [27] July 3, 1863, was certainly one of the "sometimes."

Kilpatrick's other brigade under Brigadier General Elon J. Farns-

worth was on the left, west of the Round Tops, watching and annoying Longstreet's right flank, with the help after 3:00 P.M. of Wesley
Merritt's brigade of Buford's division.[28] (Buford was guarding West-
minister with his other two brigades.) Kilpatrick learned of the failure
of the Confederate infantry attack from an orderly who dashed up
shouting: "We turned the charge; nine acres of prisoners!" Believing
that by a cavalry offensive he could cause confusion that would aid
the counterattack that he took for granted, he ordered both his brigades to attack. Farnsworth apparently remonstrated that it was futile
to charge well placed infantry through bad terrain, but led his men in
a gallant dash from which he and many others did not return.[29] Nearly
every word that a soldier could value as a tribute was applied by
Pleasonton, in his report, to this officer who had begun service as adjutant of the Eighth Illinois: "Gifted in a high degree with a quick per-
ception and a correct judgment, and remarkable for his daring and
coolness, his comprehensive grasp of the situation on the field of battle
and the rapidity of his actions had already distinguished General
Farnsworth among his comrades in arms." Kilpatrick's report expressed the opinion that the confusion into which Farnsworth's and
Merritt's attacks threw the enemy would have helped to create a rout if
an infantry attack had been launched by Meade at the opportune
moment.[30]

Though he made no counterattack, Meade pushed forward an
"armed reconnaissance" from the left and found that the enemy was
in force, as he noted in the dispatch sent to Washington at 8:35 P.M.[31]
The statement was peculiar in view of the fact that units sent on reconnaissances never go barehanded; and there was no reason to suppose that Lee's army had suddenly evaporated. Nevertheless it was a
very welcome message that arrived in the nation's capital bright and
early on its birthday—6:10 A.M., July 4. Meade ended his report of
the day: "At the present hour all is quiet. My cavalry have been engaged all day on both flanks of the enemy, harassing and vigorously
attacking him with great success, notwithstanding they encountered
superior numbers, both of cavalry and infantry. The army is in fine
spirits."

Thus ended the great three-day battle. Rain had begun to fall, adding to the discomfort of the wounded and to the difficulties of those
who worked to bring them in.[32] On this day the Federal wounded, with

the exception of Farnsworth's men, were in better fortune than their enemies, because they were within their own lines and accessible to help. Heavy indeed had been the casualties on Seminary Ridge, north of Gettysburg, on and about Culp's Hill, on Cemetery Hill, in the Devil's Den, in the Peach Orchard, in the Wheat Field, along the Emmitsburg Road, and in the final swift and awful moments about Ziegler's Grove. The battle really was a succession of engagements, as great battles often are. Accurate revised figures are available for the losses of the Army of the Potomac, which remained in possession of the field, permitting an accurate separation of the killed, the wounded, and the captured or missing—except the lightly wounded who were captured and marched away. There were 3,155 killed, 14,529 wounded, 5,365 captured or missing, giving a total casualty role of 23,049.[33] But one who examines the status in which the army stood when quiet came on the night of July 3, in order to estimate how nearly it may have come to losing the great contest, must look at the figures for the different corps. Of Meade's seven infantry corps, four— the First, Second, Third, and Eleventh—had sustained 80 per cent of the killed, 81 per cent of the wounded, 94 per cent of the killed and missing, and 84 per cent of the total casualties. Officer losses were high: one brigade of the First Corps lost six commanders; the Eleventh New Jersey, of Humphreys's division, lost five, entering action under its colonel and coming out with a lieutenant in command. The Fifth, Sixth, and Twelfth Corps were not comparably engaged; and it was almost literally true that the Sixth Corps—the largest in the army— was not in the battle. It had only two officers and twenty-five men killed, ten of these being in a single regiment, the 122nd New York, which was in line with the Twelfth Corps for a few hours on the morning of the last day.[34] After having demonstrated their fine marching ability, Sedgwick's troops were not called upon to show their fighting prowess.

The reported Confederate casualty total was 20,451,[35] a figure that cannot be accepted without question, in view of the fact that Lee was the attacker and therefore should have had heavier losses than the Federals. Livermore put the Confederate killed at 3,903, the wounded at 18,735, the missing at 5,425, which raises the total casualties to 28,063. Of each 1,000 men, the Federals—according to Livermore— had 200 hit; the Confederates, 301. On the other hand, each 1,000 Yankees hit 256 "Rebels," while each 1,000 "Rebels" hit 235 Yankees

—figures in harmony with the respective offensive and defensive roles
the two armies played. The "efficiency figures" of Livermore were
based upon the strengths he used for the two forces, figures fairly close
to those arrived at by several other writers. As to "effectives"—real
fighting men—Livermore put the figures at 90,626 for Meade, and
75,000 for Lee.[36]

The guns had not been silent long before the controversies started
about the battle. Laying aside the Pipe Creek order, the retirement
order, and the council of war, they centered on the Federal side
chiefly around Sickles's forward movement, against which Meade spoke
in very harsh terms.[37] Many persons were unquestionably influenced
by the fact that Sickles a few years before, while a member of Congress, had killed Philip Barton Key, son of the highly esteemed com-
poser of the National Anthem, because of his affair with Mrs. Sickles.[38]
In the sensational trial, which led to Sickles's acquittal, Stanton was one
of the leading attorneys for the defense.

But quite apart from these incidents there would certainly have been
a dispute about the move that Sickles had made on July 2 entirely upon
his own judgment, like that of the day before when he had marched
promptly to Gettysburg in response to Howard's call for help—a soldierly act for which nothing but commendation has been given to
him. Though the Third Corps lost very heavily in the exposed position
to which he had moved it, it did much to shatter the terrific Confederate assaults thrown against it by Longstreet, preventing them from ever
reaching the main Union line.[39] An officer of Humphreys's staff, who
saw the fury of the fighting along the Emmitsburg road and became
one of the most careful students of the battle, believed that if Sickles
had not moved forward Longstreet would have broken the Federal
line and would have reached the Taneytown road—a view that Longstreet himself expressed in a letter to Sickles.[40]

But of one contribution that Sickles made to Gettysburg there can
be no dispute, for it deserves nothing but esteem from North and South
alike. Dan Sickles more than any other man was responsible for the
battlefield becoming the great memorial park that it is today. After
achieving much in the matter of erection of suitable monuments to
New York troops, he won election to Congress for the express purpose
of rescuing the field from vandals and souvenir hunters and turning it
into the most impressive of shrines of the reunited nation.[41] Dan Sickles

certainly did not cease battling for the field of Gettysburg when he was carried away in a litter badly wounded in the early evening of July 2, 1863.

In the mid-eighties another dispute, less bitter and less noticed, but in a way deeply significant, broke out, when General Hunt published the article in which he asserted that the Federal artillery alone would have broken Pickett's charge if Hancock had not countermanded his order to stop counter-battery fire against the Confederates so as to preserve long-range ammunition for the charge. There was no question about the right of Hancock to overrule the order that had been given to his corps chief of artillery by General Hunt, for it had not been specifically an order from the army commander. The batteries of the Second Corps were *organic*, and Hancock had authority to give directions about their fire, provided only that he did not go counter to instructions that he knew came from Meade.[42]

Hancock, however, should have been slow to set aside instructions of Henry Hunt, for that superb artilleryman understood his guns. As a colonel he had become chief of artillery in the Army of the Potomac less than two weeks before the Battle of Antietam, and he was responsible for the effective long-range support that batteries had given the Federal infantry. Wearing a star on his shoulder, he performed distinguished service with his guns at Fredericksburg, and wrote a report that is a military classic. In those first two battles he was using his batteries in offensive action. Then on May 2 and 3, in the woods at Chancellorsville, he had the chance to demonstrate how gunfire could intervene when disaster threatened an army. There was innovation and a breaking of artillery tradition after Jackson had rolled back the Federal right flank; Captain Best's aggregation of thirty-eight guns went into action from a slight elevation and fired into the enemy infantry, over their own troops, 500 yards away. That was new, but the master artilleryman in his report put the matter very simply, with great pride in his blue-clad gunners: "The use of the guns was imperative. The firing was very effective, and, as far as known, without accident to our own troops."[43]

Men thought and acted in a hurry on that night of May 2. There was more time to think and plan as afternoon approached on July 3, and Hunt rode along the Gettysburg ridge, surveying the batteries with an expert eye and talking to the corps chiefs of artillery. Two sentences in Army Regulations announced the doctrine for the guns: "In the attack, the artillery is employed to silence the batteries that protect the [enemy] position. In the defense, it is better to direct its fire on the advancing troops." It was the second sentence that Hunt was following when he ordered the batteries to become silent after they had fired for a while at the Confederate guns. Although the enemy shells were not doing the Federal infantry too great damage, they were rather effectively harassing artillery positions and interdicting routes of approach for ammunition vehicles from Hunt's reserve train.[44] The best way to have long-range projectiles available to break the infantry assault seemed to him to be to stop his fire. Hancock had died when Hunt made his assertion that Pickett would not have reached the Federal line, if his order had not been countermanded. In defense of Hancock, Brigadier General Francis Walker asserted that the Federal infantry's morale would have suffered if their own guns had ceased firing. Hunt had a ready retort: on the left of Hancock, where his orders were followed, the morale of the blue riflemen was unaffected, and the enemy infantry did not reach their line.[45] Walker did not question what Hunt said his guns could have done, which seems to leave the argument with the artilleryman, although he had not advanced the claim in his official report of the battle.

Hunt's statement did more than challenge the legend that Winfield Scott Hancock had never made a mistake on the field of battle. It announced that artillery had developed to such a point that tactics must be adjusted to take account of its new power. Guns could break an infantry assault even before the attackers had come to a range where they could be met with canister and accurate rifle fire. Few could have known of the page of military history that Best had written in the early hours of darkness of May 2; but if Hunt's instructions had been followed on July 3, the utter folly of having infantry march in close formation upward of a mile against guns and artillerymen such as the Federals had, would have been revealed to everyone.

Hunt knew that turning back the Confederates would have been a barren thing, and he said that there would have been an opportunity for a successful counterattack. Of course the Federal infantry would not have been heavily engaged, but whether Meade would have been equal to the occasion and whether he had sufficient control of his line to pass to the offensive is uncertain. Unless he could have promptly sent his infantry forward against the retiring Confederates, it was perhaps better for the Federals that the attack ran its course in the way it did; for the casualties of the enemy were greatly increased by the temporary dent they put in the Union line.

Among the Confederate participants and Southern commentators, the disputes were even more bitter and more lasting than those waged by Northerners over some of the orders and actions of Meade and the movement of Sickles. It seemed to many who had given their all to the "lost cause" that a battle narrowly lost might have been won. The high esteem in which Lee was justifiably held caused many to assume that he could not have made bad errors, or suffered from indecision, or issued poor orders. Thus there was a tendency to claim that Gettysburg would have been a Southern victory if Lee's subordinates had done better, even though this has resulted in bitter accusations against all three of his corps commanders as well as the commander of his cavalry, each of whom holds a firm place in military history. As Stuart was blamed for the absence of the cavalry, and as Ewell was criticized severely for failure on the first day of battle, so A. P. Hill has been reproached for bringing on the battle contrary to Lee's express wishes or even orders, while Longstreet has been held responsible for the Confederate failure on July 2, and to a less extent—but in company with Hill—for the disaster on the last day. Stuart was killed a year before the end of the war, Hill fell during its last days; thus two who were criticized were unable to utter a word in defense of themselves. Ewell was handicapped by his wooden leg, and did not get around as nimbly as Dan Sickles. Longstreet was hale and hearty physically; but he consorted with Republicans, and this caused him to lose caste with his former comrades.

There has been intimation, if not assertion, that Lee intended to concentrate about Cashtown, close to the mountains, and that it was only Heth's and Pettigrew's adventure to get a stock of shoes that was reported to be at Gettysburg that caused Confederate troops to approach that town. But within a month of the battle Lee wrote officially, apropos of his decision to move east of the mountains: "Accordingly, Longstreet and Hill were directed to proceed from Chambersburg to Gettysburg, to which point General Ewell was also instructed to march from Carlisle." Hill reported in November, 1863, that on the 29th of June he was camped at Fayetteville, six miles east of Chambersburg on the road to Gettysburg, and was directed to move on that "road in the direction of York, and to cross the Susquehanna, menacing the communications of Harrisburg with Philadelphia, and to co-operate with General Ewell, acting as circumstances might require." [46] This indicates that at the time he took the road his orders had not been changed as a result of the report that Lee had received from Longstreet's scout Harrison on the night of June 28, though Freeman implies that they were promptly altered.[47] Lee made no indorsement on his subordinate's report indicating that it was in error; but the following January he submitted a new report of the campaign, which not only was fuller than his first report but contained a significant alteration in the important matter of the move toward Gettysburg. Whereas in July he had taken full responsibility for the movement to that place, he wrote in January, "Hill's corps was accordingly ordered to move toward Cashtown on the 29th, and Longstreet to follow the next day." [48] There is no doubt that orders were handled very carelessly at the headquarters of the Army of Northern Virginia in the last days of June, just as they had been a few days before when the ambiguous directives to Stuart were evolved. The order to Ewell recalling him from Carlisle is described as having been copied in Lee's letter book "from memory." [49] There must have been great eagerness to get a horseman riding northward, and also uncertainty about the calendar as well as the locations of Stuart and the Federals, for the order as recorded must have an erroneous date. This little fact has added some pages to the abundant literature of controversy over the campaign.[50] According to the memory version of the order, General Ewell was informed that Lee thought it was "preferable" for him to keep to the east side of the mountains, and he was told, "When you come to Heidlersburg, you can either move directly on Gettysburg or turn down to Cashtown." It seems that Lee was not certain just where he wanted the Second Corps to go, though the word "directly" must suggest to Ewell that sooner or later he would march to Gettysburg. Indecision in an army commander is likely to breed hesitation in the leaders of his corps; but Ewell is severely blamed for indecision on July 1 by writers who have failed to look for a measure of responsibility in his superior. If the written order that he received was indefinite, what is one to think of some of the verbal orders that were given to him or sent to him by staff officers?

Hill also stated in his report that he had informed Lee on the evening of the 30th that Pettigrew had had contact with enemy cavalry near Gettysburg that afternoon; [51] and this is a crucial fact in the campaign. Making use of a record by Colonel Allan of a conversation with Lee in 1868, Freeman states that Lee could hardly believe Hill's report, and he adds that even if it were true there was nothing he could do until morning.[52] It seems very strange indeed that Lee should find it hard to believe Federal cavalry was at Gettysburg, after learning two days before that the Army of the Potomac was in the vicinity of Frederick. And there was much, very much indeed, that he could have done that night. It was only five miles from Greenwood, where he had stopped, to Cashtown, where Hill was; and he could easily have reached Hill with an order not to send any troops back to Gettysburg until he himself arrived the next morning. He missed Stuart and his cavalry badly; but he was sufficiently close to where a suspicious contact had been reported to take personal supervision, without compelling a subordinate to read his mind and guess at his purposes. There was still time to make a concentration at Cashtown, if that is what he wanted; but what he wanted is as uncertain as what he ordered. Lee could not even have told on the night of June 30 just where Ewell would show up, unless he sent him a new order, for he had only a memory version of the last order, which left it to Ewell to decide upon his destination. One reason for limiting the discretion granted to a subordinate is the commander's need to know at times exactly what the situation is. After allowing Stuart to get away from him, Lee left it to Ewell to decide whether he would march to Gettysburg or Cashtown! With enemy cavalry reported at Gettysburg it was evidently important for Lee to know where his Second Corps was going.

There is no question that Longstreet disapproved of Lee's plan to attack the Federals on July 2; he plainly tells us so himself, saying that he urged a movement around Meade's left flank so as to interpose between the Union army and Washington.[53] Such an operation would have dangerously exposed Lee's flank, and probably was made impracticable by lack of suitable roads and Lee's supply status. Longstreet's dissent from the plan Lee described to him on the night of July 1 has brought accusations against that very able corps commander of sulking, and vehement charges that it was only because he spent so much time in getting into position to attack on July 2 that the Federal army had time to assemble on Cemetery Ridge. Believing that Freeman's first account of Gettysburg was very unfair to Longstreet, Lieutenant Colonel D. B. Sanger made probably the first adequate investigation of the disputed question. He measured distances, computed lengths of columns and marching times, and—knowing from experience the difficulties and delays in moving forward when a large army has a single axial road, as well as the slowness of marching across country and taking up attack positions without adequate reconnaissance by subordinate commanders—concluded that 3:00 P.M. was the earliest hour at which Longstreet could have begun his attack.[54] As a matter of fact, Longstreet's artillery opened fire about half an hour later. Without paying any attention to Colonel Sanger's study, Freeman, in his second account of the battle, accepted 9:00 A.M. as an hour at which Longstreet could have launched a strong attack. In an appendix, however, he states definitely that even at that time Cemetery Ridge was "adequately.defended" by the Federals and said, ". . . the traditional picture of an unoccupied ridge, waiting seizure while Longstreet loitered, is entirely false." [55]

Lee reached the vicinity of Seminary Ridge about 3:00 P.M. on July 1, and General Fuller has criticized him for not issuing a written order for the attack of the next day.[56] Although Lee had made up his mind to assume the offensive in plenty of time to write an order, the definite plan of attack was apparently not settled upon until the next morning. In the absence of a written order, he should have assembled his three corps commanders and have given a careful dictated verbal order, and should have seen that it was understood by everyone. This he did not do, although two of his corps commanders were new to that position. Suppose that Lee had issued a good order, and that the corps commanders on their part had issued good orders. Also suppose that Colonel Sanger was in error in his calculations, and that Longstreet could have delivered his attack at 1:00 P.M., and that the attack was made without more than the normal amount of confusion or misunderstanding on the part of various subordinates. What was the chance that Lee could have defeated the Federal army, which was then all present, except the Sixth Corps, which would have arrived before the contest was over? To get the answer, call the roll of the Federal corps and division commanders, and look at the casualty reports of organizations that were at any time involved in bitter fighting. In the attack that day Brigadier General A. R. Wright led his fine Georgia regiments to the crest of the ridge, drove back the Federal line, and momentarily seized some guns. But his eyes beheld and his brain comprehended the truth, and the next day he remarked with regard to reaching Cemetery Hill, "The trouble is to stay there after you get there, for the whole Yankee army is there in a bunch." [57] Though often quoted, the weighty significance of Wright's words has often been ignored.

Again on July 3 Lee issued no written order for the attack, and again he did not assemble his corps commanders to receive a careful verbal order. The attack that day cannot be viewed as anything more than a last hopeless venture. In spite of the small encouraging achievements of the day before, the bloody repulse of Johnson's attack against the Federal right on the morning of the 3rd was a warning of what was in store for the afternoon. It is true that the assaulting units in the afternoon were imperfectly coordinated and the Federal batteries took advantage of the fact to shift fire effectively.[58] But the unemployed reserve power on Cemetery Hill would have been more than sufficient to meet a better handled attack, or one in which a few more apparently available units might have been used.

Although the battle of Gettysburg was probably the worst that Lee fought, and one that he could not have won by better orders or better performance by subordinates, it did give him one of his greatest moments. When, just after the last charge, he met Wilcox, he extended his hand to the brigadier who was overcome with emotion on account of his shattered regiments, and he said calmly, "Never mind, General, all this has been my fault—it is I that have lost this fight, and you must help me out of it the best you can." [59] One can doubt if ever in history there was more lofty behavior on a battlefield. In his reports Lee carefully avoided placing blame upon his subordinates; and he never engaged in any of the written controversies about the battle after the war. While some remarks that he is reported to have made in later years are of doubtful authenticity, others appear to have been reliably recorded. His statement that he would have won if he had had Stonewall Jackson with him simply ignored Jackson's experiences at Port Republic and Cedar Mountain, as well as his conduct at Frayser Farm. There is no reason whatever to believe that Lee was ever accurately informed of the times of arrival of the different Federal corps on Cemetery Ridge, or that he realized that the Sixth Corps was practically unused in the battle, and that only four of Meade's seven infantry corps were heavily engaged. If Lee thought of Jackson, he might also have dwelt upon the fact that his last blow was aimed at a part of the line where Winfield Scott Hancock commanded, and fell most heavily on a corps commanded by John Gibbon—who at Groveton had shown himself fully a match for Stonewall. Were not Hancock and Gibbon and the others of the same racial stock as Jackson? Had they not had the same schooling? And had they not inherited the same traditions?

Fortune did not frown upon Lee at Gettysburg; Fortune smiled. General Alexander, who commanded the hundred guns that sought in vain to soften the Federal infantry for the last great assault, wrote that an attack by the Union Sixth Corps would have cut the Confederates in two, and he put the matter as strongly as he knew how when he said that Meade neglected an opportunity as great as McClellan allowed to pass at Antietam.[60] In both his ventures across the Potomac, Lee could have been destroyed on the field of battle. Meade would have had to prepare in time a great counterstroke and then wait with calm resolution as Lee had done at Second Bull Run. Since Lee merely accepted battle at Sharpsburg there has been no serious effort to show that he could have won that field. But because he was the attacker at Gettysburg and won local temporary successes, efforts to conjure up a possible decisive victory for him have persisted with great vigor. That they should have reposed so largely upon unjust charges against the able generals who led his corps in hopeless tasks, and who received such vague and imperfect orders, is an unhappy thought to contemplate.

It would seem that every possible excuse has been put forward to explain Lee's failure at Gettysburg. But the real explanation can be given in three words: the Union army.

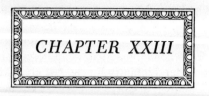

CHAPTER XXIII

A FEEBLE EFFORT AT PURSUIT

> We had them within our grasp. We had only to stretch forth
> our hands and they were ours. And nothing I could say or do
> could make the Army move. *Lincoln to Hay*

"THE army is in fine spirits." In such a manner General Meade reported within a few hours after a third of his guns and 10,000 of his infantry had smashed the enemy's last great assault—the forever epic but ill-advised charge of Pickett's heroic 15,000. The necessary basis for harvesting real "fruits of victory" thus was present. But what about the other equally important essential—the fortitude of the commander? Was Meade possessed of the determination, the will, the restless eagerness to exploit the situation fully? Or would he hesitate, magnify the difficulties that were certain to arise? And, dwelling upon uncertainties, would he grow cautious, and seek excuses for irresolution and delay? For the two days when he had been personally present on the field of battle, he had fought defensively, with very high cards in his hands. Could he change and become aggressive and, capitalizing upon the "fine spirits" of the army, wring from his men every effort of which they were capable? Could he tell them, "You have done well, but we have just begun—I must demand of you still greater things"?

A careful study of the dispatches that Meade had already sent to Washington prepares one for the next ten days, days that he was to use as ineffectively as McClellan had used the 14th, 15th, and the 16th of the preceding September. But this is to be said for Meade: in none of his dispatches to Halleck had he complained that he was greatly outnumbered by the enemy; in none had he issued dark threats as to what would happen if his demands were not met; in none had he said that if failure came the responsibility must rest upon someone other than himself. And his letters home also compare with those of McClellan to his own advantage in about the same ratio. Nevertheless, they are an important source of information for discovering the general's personality and military character, and they do no little damage to his record in the next fortnight. The home letters were not available to the early biographers, apologists, and extollers.

Some time during the night of the 3rd a message came in from Francis Barlow, who had been carried to a house in Gettysburg. Unfortunately, we have it only in the unsatisfactory form in which the chief of staff, who had been slightly wounded the day before, passed it on at 6:00 A.M. of the 4th to Newton and Howard: "General Barlow, in town, sends word that he believes the movement of the enemy to be a mere feint." [1] He added that Meade thought Barlow's opportunities for judging were good. Was the message meant to be a caution and a warning, or did the badly wounded Union general believe that Lee was trying to conceal a rather bad plight? Whether Newton and Howard understood the equivocal words cannot be said; but at least they were told specifically, "The general only desires to know where the enemy are, and not by any means to bring on an action." An hour later a dispatch was sent to Halleck,[2] who had it in twelve hours—which was as good time as one could wish. Enemy pickets had been withdrawn, and Meade's were following to discover what was really developing and to learn the extent of the enemy's movement. Information was still too scanty to reveal whether it was the beginning of a retreat or of some new maneuver. The message was no more than started on its way when a note arrived from Lee asking that arrangements be made for the exchange of prisoners at some point between the lines. That request should have revealed a good deal. Certainly, there was to be no fighting on Lee's part that day if he could avoid it; and eagerness to get rid of encumbrances could mean even more than that. Immediately Meade replied that he did not have the authority to make an exchange of captured men.[3] Rain fell in torrents during the afternoon, and any aggressive movement would have been difficult, even if Meade had felt so inclined; that he was not so disposed was proved by circulars to corps commanders.[4] Burying the dead, rectifying the lines, picking things up, and resting were the prescribed activities for the 56,139 effective fighting men that a field return for the day indicated as present.[5]

At noon Meade reported to Halleck that the situation had not changed much, though the enemy, abandoning many dead and wounded, had withdrawn his left, and the Federals occupied the town of Gettysburg. Ominous were the intimation that there would be a delay while supplies and ammunition were brought up, and the statement that it would be necessary to "rest the army, worn out by long marches and three days' hard fighting." Lincoln must have read the sentence with foreboding. Only two hours before, he had announced to the country that the latest word from the Army of the Potomac was such as to cover that army with the highest honor, and "to promise a great success to the cause of the Union." Though duly grateful to the army and its commander for the hard fighting of the last three days, the man who on June 30 had spoken of the best opportunity since the beginning of the war was wishing that within the next few days there could be garnered some great results of victory. Stanton, at work early in the morning, had wired General Dix at Fort Monroe at eight o'clock of the three-day battle, saying there were "prospects of a brilliant victory over Lee." [6]

At 4:15 P.M. Meade issued a congratulatory order stating: "An enemy, superior in numbers, and flushed with the pride of a successful invasion, attempted to overcome and destroy this army. Utterly baffled and defeated, he has now withdrawn from the contest." [7] Meade had no reason whatever to believe that Lee had more than the 80,000 men that he himself had accepted on June 28, that a Washington dispatch on June 30 stated were accepted there, and that Couch confirmed on July 4 in a dispatch to Meade which reached Washington at 10:00 A.M.[8] The real offense in the order, however, was not the false statement, but Meade's conception of the work that still lay ahead: "Our task is not yet accomplished, and the commanding general looks to the army for greater efforts to drive from our soil every vestige of the presence of the invader." Like the Pipe Creek order and the retreat order of the 2nd and the council of war, this sentence was to get Meade into very hot water. Ten days later John Hay wrote in his diary that the sentence caused Lincoln to remark: "This is a dreadful reminiscence of McClellan. The same spirit that moved McClellan to claim a great victory because Pennsylvania and Maryland were safe. The hearts of ten million people sunk within them when McClellan raised that shout last fall. Will our Generals never get that idea out of their heads? The whole country is our soil." [9]

Already Lee was making every effort to escape, without any driving whatever from the Federals; and this Meade certainly had good reason to know. His own chief signal officer wrote in his official report on September 18:

On July 4, at 5:40 A.M., the signal officer from a station on the college in Gettysburg reported to the general commanding "that the enemy had evacuated the position they held yesterday," and at 9:30 A.M, reported the new line occupied by them, and that they were retreating toward Hagerstown. This station was kept open all day, and information in regard to the movements of the enemy sent in by orderly. General Meade's headquarters were removed to the Baltimore pike, and this was made the terminus of all signal lines.[10]

No enemy troop columns could have been reported, but during the day and especially during the torrential rains of the afternoon the Confederate trains had assembled along the road to Chambersburg, and the head of the column started its movement from Cashtown at 4:00 P.M. Meade himself was inclined to believe that a retreat had started, for sometime during the day he expressed the opinion in a dispatch to General Smith, advancing from Carlisle, that Lee was retreating by way of Fairfield and Cashtown. At 7:40 the signal officers at Rock Signal Station (probably Little Round Top) reported that for the last twenty-five minutes there had been a steady stream of various types of vehicles on the Fairfield road. To some of his staff the case was certain, for Ingalls reported to Meigs at 8:10, "The enemy has been defeated and has retreated to the mountain passes, and will probably flee rapidly across the Potomac." [11] Though the statement was inaccurate, it is clear that Meade's quartermaster did not think it would take any driving to get Lee across the Potomac. But Meade, again uncertain, withheld from Halleck the fact that there was even any evidence that Lee had started a retreat, for at ten o'clock he sent a message to the General in Chief, that began, "No change of affairs since dispatch of 12 o'clock noon"—a statement that was not even truthful in view of the dispatch from the Rock Signal Station and of dispatches from Gettysburg College not in the records, but alluded to in them. He did not even communicate his opinion that Lee was retreating by way of Fairfield and Cashtown, but keeping everything very dark, he said: "I make a reconnaissance tomorrow, to ascertain what the intention of the enemy is." The last sentence was decidedly the best part of the dispatch: "My cavalry are now moving toward the South Mountain Pass, and, should the enemy retreat, I shall pursue him on his flanks." [12]

Apparently, however, information was reaching Washington that Meade did not send, and at 5:00 P.M. Stanton informed Dix that advices just in showed that Meade's victory was complete and Lee had started retreating toward Chambersburg at 3:00 A.M. Interesting indeed would be the basis for this statement, in view of the fact that Lee's verbal instructions for retreating were issued only at 1:00 A.M. No actual movements in its execution had been made, but as Lee was operating in a region loyal to the Federals it is perfectly possible that knowledge of his intention had been picked up and passed along. Whether there had been some cleverly obtained information, or whether the assertion had nothing substantial to support it, one cannot say. But the War Secretary believed it, and he said to Dix, "Whether [Lee] ever gets to Richmond may depend much upon your success in breaking his communication." [13]

No message directly from Gettysburg gave as much cause for optimism about the future as one Halleck received at 10:35 P.M. from General French at Frederick. A cavalry expedition that French had dispatched the evening before for Williamsport had returned after destroying Lee's pontoon bridge over the Potomac at that place, and had finished off the exploit by bringing back the lieutenant and thirteen of the men who had been guarding the structure.[14] With the bridge destroyed, the river swollen by the continued rains and sure to rise higher as a result of the deluge of the afternoon, circumstances seemed to be shaping for the destruction of the Confederate army. When Lincoln had stated on June 30 that he believed prospects were better than they had been at any time since the war had started, he did not have in mind such a happy event as the brilliant cavalry dash, or the discomfited guard, the ruined bridge, and a most acceptable storm thrown in by Providence. To those who read the message from Frederick, the rain had a pleasant sound and the rising Potomac was a cheering sight.

French's cavalry and the dripping skies were not the only agencies busily at work, for there was other planning and activity toward the completion of the work that had been begun in the three days of fighting. Haupt reported to Halleck at 11:00 P.M. from New Oxford (seven miles east of Gettysburg) about the opening of the railroad and the telegraph line into Gettysburg, about the forward movement of supplies, and the rearward flow of wounded. At 5:30 P.M. Meigs wrote to Ingalls: "To improve the victory, you will need, doubtless, many remounts. Stand on no ceremony, but, by purchases or impressment of all serviceable horses within range of your foraging parties, refit the artillery and cavalry in the best possible manner." To make the directive at the same time more urgent and clothe it with all needed authority he signed the dispatch, "By order of the Secretary of War." [15] Not just the vicinity of the battle was to be called upon to repair the waste in animals caused by the hard marches and the fighting, but the entire country; to quartermasters as far away as Indianapolis telegrams went ordering them to forward horses immediately to the Army of the Potomac, and Haupt telegraphed to the presidents of twelve railroads directing that "extraordinary efforts" should be made to get animals through without delay.[16] No one was trying harder to bring real victory out of Lee's severe reverse than the General in Chief. Before noon of July 4 he had sent an excellent dispatch to General Kelley at Cumberland, posting him on events and directing him to send forward all the force he could to the vicinity of Hancock, and there hold himself ready for a rapid movement to attack Lee's flank. "No time to be lost," urged Halleck.[17] With premonitions as to what might be the attitude of his old West Point classmate, Haupt had said in his near-midnight message to Halleck, "I fear that while Meade rests to refresh his men and collect supplies, Lee will be off so far that he cannot intercept him."

And so the nation's most momentous Fourth of July ended, with the people of the Northern states rejoicing over the victory, but with many afraid to write the letters that might come back, still having ahead of them days of anxious scanning of the great casualty lists.

On this Fourth of July one very great event had occurred of which the people and President could not learn at once. In the afternoon, a young captain had boarded a steamboat at Vicksburg with a dispatch to Halleck from Grant that began, "The enemy surrendered this morning." At last the great bastion on the Mississippi had fallen, and it yielded 30,000 prisoners, 50,000 small arms, many guns, and fifty-seven regimental colors.[18] A two months' operation had been completed in which soldiers have been able to find no false move made, no day wasted, no hour of irresolution, no moment of doubt in the face of difficulties or uncertainties; but a campaign to study carefully, as one outstanding in military art and generalship. And it was all announced very simply: "The enemy surrendered this morning." The great general, from whose lips no oath or blasphemous remark ever fell, did not give thanks to Heaven for what had been accomplished in the awful business of war. After his modest straightforward five words that would set the bells of victory ringing, there came three sentences about the paroling of prisoners, so that troops and transports would be ready for "immediate service"; then two sentences about the next moves on his agenda. As a communiqué, only the general who wrote it would ever write a better one. But everyone would have to wait to read this military masterpiece, for the nearest telegraph office was at Cairo, Illinois, 600 miles upriver.

Great efforts were quickly under way to care for the enormous number of wounded at Gettysburg, and they were in large part carried out by nongovernmental agencies. On the 4th the Adams Express Company in Baltimore began arranging a hospital corps; its superintendent asked Stanton for the necessary permission, and by 6:00 P.M. he had both the authority and the instructions.[19] The Sanitary Commission and the Christian Commission, which throughout the war did so much to lessen the suffering of the wounded and otherwise help the soldiers, were quickly mobilizing their resources and calling new volunteers to proceed to Gettysburg to aid the residents who had already begun to meet the great task that had fallen to them. Though their town was not much damaged, there were thousands of wounded of both armies to be cared for.[20] An enduring record of what took place has been left by Cornelia Hancock, a young Quaker living in New Jersey near Philadelphia, who had formed the resolve that she, like her brother and every male relative and friend she had, must go to war, and had commissioned her sister's husband, a philanthropic doctor in Philadelphia, to tell her when the moment had come:

The summons came on the morning of July fifth, 1863, when his horse and carriage was sent for me on a Fourth of July excursion boat that was returning to Salem by the Delaware River. It arrived in the early morning and was driven the five miles beyond the town to where I lived. When it was driven up in front of our house, my mother threw up both of her hands and exclaimed to father: "Oh, Tom, what has happened?" I had not risen, but hearing Mother's exclamation, and surmising, I said: "Oh, nothing, Mother. Doctor has sent for me to go to war!"

The young woman of twenty-three was no more prepared by experience for what she had suddenly to meet the next evening than were the men of Stannard's brigade who were thrown in to make a counterstroke against Pickett's battle-toughened veterans. But with equal fortitude she walked on the evening of the 6th into a church that was called a "hospital," where on boards placed on the backs of pews, and strewn with straw, the wounded lay as closely as they could be packed. She wrote:

> The townspeople of Gettysburg were in devoted attendance, and there were many from other villages and towns. The wounds of all had been dressed at least once, and some systematic care was already established. Too inexperienced to nurse, I went from one pallet to another with pencil, paper, and stamps in hand, and spent the rest of that night in writing letters from the soldiers to their families and friends. To many mothers, sisters, and wives, I penned the last message of those who were soon to become the "beloved dead."

After this introduction to the horrors of war she went early the next morning to the more than crude field hospital of the Second Corps, to begin more arduous activities in a sickening atmosphere; for burial of men and animals had not been swift enough for the hot days of July. Quickly the young woman learned; and order and some degree of adequacy, and then touches of comfort, replaced the stark want and need of the first days. By the 8th Cornelia, who "laid in the damp all night, and got up all right in the morning," was writing like an oldtimer. But the suffering, fortitude, patience, and courteous respect and appreciation of the soldiers had made her very bitter against the many persons in all parts of the North who were working against the war. At the end of two days, the young Quaker closed her letter home: "Kill the copperheads. Write everything, however trifling, it is all interest here." [21] That was doing well in brevity, but if Miss Hancock had had just a few more days of field service she might not have felt that propriety required that a full stop should interpose between her strongly contrasting thoughts. All in one sentence she might have said, "Kill the copperheads and write long letters." For terseness that would have vied with some of the orders of Stonewall Jackson.

It was not necessary for Meade to make the promised reconnaissance on the 5th in order to ascertain the intention of the enemy. When morning came Lee was gone. Almost as if he had never expected such a move, Meade wrote to Halleck at 8:30, "The enemy retired, under cover of the night and heavy rain, in the direction of Fairfield and Cashtown." The retreat was in agreement with what he had intimated to Smith, and before the month was over he found it necessary to defend himself in an unofficial letter to Halleck against the charge that Lee's movement had started during the day of the 4th. In defending himself he asserted that he had positive evidence that "not a man was withdrawn till after dark." So far as infantry and most of the artillery were concerned, this doubtless was true enough; but he was careful not to refer to the column of vehicles that his signal corps men had reported on the road to Fairfield in the late afternoon of the 4th. In reporting Lee's retreat he told Halleck that he would move at once on Lee's flank, by way of Middletown and South Mountain Pass, that his head-quarters would be that night at Creagerstown, that he had 55,000 effective men in the ranks, and that he wanted every available reen-forcement sent forward to Frederick without delay.[22] Within a few days, when prodded by Halleck for his slowness, Meade spoke as if many thousand of his men were barefooted. One of the things that should have been ascertained on the 4th was the exact number of men without shoes. There were thousands of dead and wounded that did not need their shoes, and Ingalls wrote in his report, "Ample supplies of forage, clothing, and subsistence were received and issued to fill every necessary want without in any instance retarding military move-ments." [23]

In the morning Haupt drove up to Meade's headquarters in a buggy, to announce that communication would be established that day with Washington by railroad and telegraph from Gettysburg, and to try to spur his old school friend on. However, he saw little disposition to move rapidly so as to intercept Lee; and, quite discouraged, he took an engine to Washington, where he reported the next day to Halleck on the gloomy prospects.[24] Meade, still at Gettysburg the following afternoon, sent a long dispatch to Halleck that arrived at 9:20 P.M., stating that he had "deemed it prudent to suspend the movement to Middletown" until he could be certain that the enemy was evacuating the Cumber-land Valley. "I find great difficulty," said Meade, "in getting reliable in-formation, but from all I can learn I have reason to believe the enemy is retreating, very much crippled, and hampered with his trains." [25] It looked as if he would not be convinced until the last Confederate sol-dier had crossed the river and had dutifully waved goodbye to Maryland. But Washington already had the melancholy news that the army had halted, and it added to the depression that President Lincoln felt over the congratulatory order. He was to spend that night at the Soldiers' Home, one of the retreats where he often sought escape from his burdens. At 7:00 P.M. he wrote to Halleck one of his most remarkable messages, one that showed his great discernment and his complete willingness to accept the judgments and actions of the General in Chief in the performance of his duty (that very week, Halleck had rebuffed Stanton for a minor intrusion affecting the protection of Washington):

I left the telegraph office a good deal dissatisfied. You know I did not like the phrase, in Orders, No. 68, I believe, "Drive the invaders from our soil." Since that, I see a dispatch from General French, saying the enemy is crossing wounded over the river in flats, without saying why he does not stop it, or even intimating a thought that it ought to be stopped. Still later, another dispatch from General Pleasonton, by direction of General Meade, to General French, stating that the main army is halted because it is believed the rebels are concentrating "on the road toward Hagerstown, beyond Fairfield," and is not to move until it is ascertained that the rebels intend to evacuate Cumberland Valley.

These things all appear to me to be connected with a purpose to cover Baltimore and Washington, and to get the enemy across the river again without a further collision, and they do not appear connected with a purpose to prevent his crossing and to destroy him. I do fear the former purpose is acted upon and the latter is rejected.

If you are satisfied the latter purpose is entertained and is judiciously pursued, I am content. If you are not so satisfied, please look to it.[26]

The President was not entirely fair to General French. Hearing the cannonading at Gettysburg on the 3rd, French had sent a detachment of his 900 cavalry to Falling Waters to destroy the pontoon bridge reported in that vicinity. Then on the 5th, after securing the South Mountain Passes, French sent an expedition to Harpers Ferry. Here it was found that the Confederates had floored the railroad bridge and had been crossing in small detachments.[27] (Just what troops these were is not clear.) Fortunately there were no Confederate engineers who were equipped to blow the bridge. Meade on the morning of the 3rd had specifically directed French to "re-occupy Harper's Ferry," so that the expedition sent should not have been just a raid like the dash for the bridge at Williamsport; but apparently it was so planned.[28] At least the officer in command of the little operation contented himself with

destroying the trestlework at the two ends of the great iron bridge over
the Potomac as well as the bridge over the canal, so as to deny their
use to the enemy. As a consequence Federal cavalry could no longer
reach the south bank of the river, and any interruption of the passage
of the "flats," about which Lincoln was so much annoyed, would have
had to be from the north side of the river. But there was no longer any
possibility of interrupting the ferrying operation from the north bank,
for Buford, who arrived near Williamsport about 5:00 P.M. of the
6th with his three hard-fighting brigades for the express purpose of destroying enemy trains, had to report failure: "The enemy was too
strong for me, but he was severely punished for his obstinacy." [29] Lee,
in possession of the shortest route to the crossing site, and protected by
the mountains, had been able to secure a firm hold upon the north bank
of the river near Williamsport.

Now the great folly of abandoning Maryland Heights and the shortsightedness of Hooker's idea and the soundness of Halleck's judgment
with regard to that position became only too clear. Whether or not a
misrepresentation by Butterfield caused Meade to give up his intention
to hold the place as a débouché can never be determined; but certain
it is that French's force of 11,000—infantry, cavalry, and artillery—
would have been in a position of great strategic value at Harpers
Ferry. The two brigades of cavalry which Stuart had left south of the
river had been hurriedly called northward by Lee, so that the south
bank of the river was unguarded, as Halleck had reported to Kelley.[30]
French could have thrown forward from Harpers Ferry a division of
5,000 that could not only have destroyed the bridge that his cavalry
had destroyed by a brilliant dash from Frederick, but could have *held*
the south bank of the river, preventing the two flats from taking Lee's
wounded across the river and bringing back the sorely needed artillery
ammunition and other supplies to the northern shore. Such a force
could have prevented the building of another bridge, and Lee's destruction should have followed. To the shortsightedness in abandoning
Harpers Ferry was added the pure folly of burning the trestle approaches to the railroad bridge, by which the Federals succeeded in
stalemating themselves, quite as if they were too chivalrous to take advantage of Lee's desperate plight: because Lee had no bridge, they
would partly destroy their own! More Federal cavalry was rapidly
becoming available for an operation across the river, and at noon on
the 6th Meigs informed Ingalls that 1,600 horses and over 2,000

cavalry, "just mounted or remounted," had already left Washington for Frederick.[31] In addition, the competent quartermaster general told the equally competent field quartermaster that several trains with from 100 to 275 horses were en route, and that telegrams had gone to divert the animals direct to Frederick. If stupidity on someone's part had led to the destruction of the trestles, could not the blunder have been rapidly repaired by the use of Meade's engineers and their abundant supply of pontoons? Could they not have thrown a bridge so that cavalry could cross and fall upon Lee's communications—a thing which Lee told Imboden that he expected would be done? This neglected opportunity will be left as the climax in Meade's futile pursuit of Lee.[32]

While Lincoln was writing his somewhat discouraged note from the Soldiers' Home, the steamboat with Grant's messenger was nearing Cairo. But the eager captain was to find himself anticipated by a few hours, for Admiral D. D. Porter, who had commanded the gunboats that had helped Grant so much, had made great haste to send word of the surrender of Vicksburg to the Secretary of the Navy. Quickly the news was flashed to the North, and a young woman of Marietta, Ohio, much interested in the commander of a regiment of the Iron Brigade, wrote on the 7th to her soldier, "There has been greater rejoicing over your victory in Pennsylvania than I have ever known, and within the last half hour dispatches have come saying that Vicksburg is ours, 'Great Babylon is fallen, is fallen.' I do not know how as a Nation we are going to bear our success, but I know as an individual I can't bear much more of anything." [33]

Lincoln, hearing the good news from Gideon Welles, did not waste time in rejoicing but, hoping that a spirit of emulation might be an additional spur to Meade, put the case bluntly to Halleck: "We have certain information that Vicksburg surrendered to General Grant on the 4th of July. Now, if General Meade can complete his work, so gloriously prosecuted thus far, by the literal or substantial destruction of Lee's army, the rebellion will be over." Halleck promptly passed the note on; thus the pressure was put heavily on Meade. Still the High Command was not inconsiderate; fairly and shrewdly it made a substantial pay-off for what he had done already, in an effort to urge him on by mixing rewards with prodding. At 3:00 P.M. Halleck telegraphed, "It gives me great pleasure to inform you that you have been appointed a brigadier-general in the Regular Army, to rank from July

3, the date of your brilliant victory at Gettysburg." [34] Thus, after the
war was over and hurrahs had died down there would be a substantial
reward for the general every month from the hands of the paymaster.
Nor could he have failed to conjecture that if he should just "complete
his work" there would come a permanent major generalship—the
highest rank the United States then had—with the paymaster dipping
a little deeper still into his money chest each month. Promptly to Grant
went that same permanent reward because he had finished his Vicksburg work.

Within two hours Halleck had a very gracious "Thank you" from
Meade, who had now reached Frederick; but Meade made no comment
on the statement that he had it in his power to end the rebellion. So
Halleck put on just a little more pressure, by telling his subordinate,
"Push forward, and fight Lee before he can cross the Potomac." If this
direction was intended as a dish for the general's supper the following,
written in response to Meade's request for Halleck's view as to what
his action should be if Lee got over the river first, may have been meant
for him to ponder during the night: "You have given the enemy a stunning blow at Gettysburg. Follow it up, and give him another before he
can reach the Potomac." If Lee escaped, circumstances would, Halleck
said, have to decide whether he should be pursued up the Shenandoah
Valley or east of the Blue Ridge. Of course Meade's inquiry, made with
full knowledge that Lee's bridge was gone and that the river was above
the fording stage and was still rising, completely confirmed the im-
pressions Haupt had gained on the 5th and the fears the President had
expressed on the evening of the 6th. Halleck's reply closed—as it began—with a call for vigor at the moment, so as to make unnecessary a
campaign south of the Potomac: "There is strong evidence that he
[Lee] is short of artillery ammunition, and, if vigorously pressed, he
must suffer." [35]

The next day Meade wrote a long letter to his wife, and it is important because it reveals much about his thoughts and attitude a few
hours after the President had told him plainly that it was within his
power to end the war, and after the General in Chief had thrown in two
prods for good measure. He wrote, "I arrived here yesterday; the army
is assembling at Middletown. I think we shall have another battle before
Lee can cross the river, though from all accounts he is making great
efforts to do so. For my part, as I have to follow and fight him, I would
rather do it at once and in Maryland than to follow into Virginia."

Excellent in a way; but there was no trace of determination, of urgency, in the letter that ended, "I am going to move as soon as I can get the army supplied with subsistence and ammunition." [36] Did Meade mean that five days after the battle his combat vehicles were not well supplied with ammunition, or that he was low on food? Ingalls's report stated that supplies had accumulated to such an extent at the Westminster railhead that they had to be shipped back to Washington after the base was changed to Frederick.[37] While Meade's statement about food and ammunition must be discounted, other comments in his letter are of much moment: "I see also that the papers are making a great deal too much fuss about me. I claim no extraordinary merit for this last battle, and would prefer waiting a little while to see what my career is to be before making any pretensions." Well, Lincoln had just told him he could end the war, which would have done about all for his career that he could have wished. Then Meade brought in something one would rather he had omitted, even in an intimate letter. Admitting he knew that "battles are often decided by accident, and that no man of sense will say in advance what their result will be"—a thesis which is true, but which he was prone to stress too much—he wrote, "I wish to be careful in not bragging before the right time." In speaking of Halleck's congratulatory dispatch, which he sent home for preservation because the General in Chief had used stronger words than he had deemed proper to use himself, he gave an appraisal of July 1–3 that cannot be improved upon: "I never claimed a Victory, though I stated that Lee was defeated in his efforts to destroy my army." Meade had not won; Lee had merely failed to win! What a contrast between his perfect description of Gettysburg and McClellan's prattle to his wife about Antietam being a masterpiece! Freely Meade confided the fact that for ten days he had been under a terrific strain, had not changed his clothes, had gone without a full night's rest and regular food, on many nights had not had a wink of sleep, and on several days had not even washed his face and hands. Though there can be no discounting the tremendous responsibility that rests upon a commanding general, who must be physically able to meet heavy exactions when necessary, Meade's report of his ten days is a melancholy tale, revealing what a tense and highly strung disposition he had. He should have known how essential it was to be in good condition; and since he was not blessed with the capacity to pick up sleep at odd moments—an ability that Napoleon valued highly and that Longstreet, Jackson, and

Lee also had—he should have removed himself from the vicinity of headquarters at night, undressed, and gone to bed.[38]

Though Lincoln lacked the revealing insight into Meade that reading his letter home would have given, he must have been much disturbed by a dispatch that arrived in midafternoon of the 8th. After telling of the heavy roads, the high spirit of the army, and the readiness of his men to make every needed exertion, Meade began to picture the difficulties ahead; though he spoke of his eagerness to have another trial with the enemy, he dwelt upon the uncertain fortunes of war, and predicted that he would find Lee in a strong position well covered with artillery. There was more than a hint of McClellan throughout the message, and Little Mac himself might have written, "I wish in advance to moderate the expectations of those who, in ignorance of the difficulties to be encountered, may expect too much." [39]

Lincoln not only forbore; he tried not to give up hope that something more could be wrung from Meade, and Halleck prodded again with the message: "There is reliable information that the enemy is crossing at Williamsport. The opportunity to attack his divided forces should not be lost. The President is urgent and anxious that your army should move against him by forced marches."

Immediately Meade started to argue. He not only argued; he contradicted himself. Though he had just written to his wife that "all accounts" concurred in saying that Lee was making frantic efforts to cross the river, he did not want the High Command to assert the same fact and use it as a prod. Consequently, he wired Halleck that his own information about the enemy crossing the river did not agree with what the General in Chief had just communicated; and he asserted that Lee had his whole force in position between Hagerstown and Williamsport. To make the situation appear more gloomy he added, "I have just received information that he has driven my cavalry force in front of Boonsborough." Then, apparently forgetting that he had just reported that morale was high and that the men were willing to undergo privations, he became very doleful about the state of his command: "My army is and has been making forced marches, short of rations and barefooted." The barefooted boys were getting over the ground pretty well—when required—for Meade reported that one corps had marched thirty miles the day before. The army as a whole had taken three days to cover thirty miles—parts of it, a still smaller distance. As if the spirit of McClellan was still present, Meade closed with a promise that must have seemed discouragingly familiar to the man in the White House: "I take occasion to repeat that I will use my utmost efforts to push forward this army." Halleck replied at once, disclaiming dissatisfaction, but nevertheless not retreating an inch from his previous position. He stated that troops arriving from New York and Fort Monroe would be sent directly to Harpers Ferry, and he ended with another prick: "You will have force to render your victory certain. My only fear now is that the enemy may escape by crossing the river." [40]

In sharp contrast to the timidity of the army commander was the boldness of his cavalry west of the mountains, where Buford and Kilpatrick, the latter reenforced by Huey's brigade of Gregg's division, were pushing the enemy energetically in spite of the fact that they were in the presence of greatly superior forces. Buford, undaunted because things had gone badly in the morning, had the situation under control in the afternoon, and reported that night:

> HEADQUARTERS FIRST DIVISION
> Boonsborough, July 8, 1863.
>
> I have had a very rough day of it. Early this morning the enemy advanced upon me in a pretty strong force (cavalry, infantry, and artillery). During the first part of the day they pressed me severely, and came near the town. Toward night, I turned the tables upon them, and drove them across the Antietam, toward Hagerstown and Williamsport. You never saw the division behave better. My loss is not heavy. The artillery fire was very hot. All of my fighting had to be on foot. The river is 5 feet higher than before, and rising. I have drawn in close to this place, to sleep. My train has been interfered with by the Eleventh Corps. I hope it may arrive in the night. There are no rebs this side of Antietam; none on the old battleground, and none at Sharpsburg. Plenty of them, however, can be found between Greencastle and Williamsport and between Hagerstown and Williamsport. Hurrah for Vicksburg.
>
> Very respectfully,
> Your obedient servant,
> *Jno. Buford,*
> Brigadier-General of Volunteers, Commanding.
>
> Colonel Alexander,
> Chief of Staff, Cavalry Corps.[41]

What a cavalryman! If the dispatches to Washington could have breathed the spirit of the tired but eager and dauntless Buford, all would have been well. Horsemen like Buford and Kilpatrick; infantry

corps that could do thirty miles in a day; the finest artillery that had
ever marched; a splendid signal corps; excellent supply service; a fine
staff; soldiers in high morale—all those things Meade had. But again
he was beginning to falter and grow afraid. Though he had repeatedly
asserted in letters that the outcome of a battle was largely a matter of
luck, he still would not fight unless he had a sure thing.

The next day, Thursday July 9, was a critical one, with General
Humphreys replacing Daniel Butterfield as chief of staff.[42] Well, indeed, was the gifted officer to fill this important position, but he always
regretted being taken away from field command, for he had a passion
to be where the battle was hot, and apparently took a peculiar pleasure
in the sound of whistling bullets. At 9:15 in the morning George Sykes
reported that his corps—with the two five-regiment brigades of fine
regulars—was going into camp beyond Boonsboro. The short march
he had made did not look as if he were being pressed very hard, and
he had nothing to say about tired, hungry, or shoeless soldiers, though
he passed on some information just received from Kilpatrick. At noon
Slocum reported that his corps had arrived at Rohrersville "in good
order." He could give no news of the enemy, but he passed the word
that he had found an excellent county map. Then, presently, Howard
sent in a report from a "deserter," who told a story that makes it seem
very probable that he had been sent out by Lee to frighten Meade into
believing that the Southern army was really in a fine condition and
not in any dangerous situation at all. Not eager to get away, but waiting to fight again; that was his story. In fact, he reported that Lee already had a bridge, which had been brought from Winchester, but was
not crossing since he wanted another battle. The Confederate soldiers
—who had not been told about Vicksburg—were in excellent spirits
and believed they could recover everything if only they could once get
the Yankees "agoing." [43]

Meade, whose headquarters had been advanced eight miles to Middletown on the afternoon before, had just finished a dispatch to Halleck
when the deserter forwarded by Howard was brought in. To the message already written was added a postscript repeating—for what it was
worth—the tale that the Confederate had told about the bridge which
Lee nonchalantly was disdaining to use except to bring supplies to his
army, as he awaited a chance to engage the Federals. It added a rather
ominous touch to the body of the message, in which Meade had stated

he was advancing in three columns, ending: "I think the decisive battle
of the war will be fought in a few days. In view of its momentous consequences, I desire to adopt such measures as in my judgment will tend
to insure success, even though these may be deemed tardy." Well indeed had the "deserter" done his work, for the General in Chief obviously also swallowed his story. At 3:00 P.M. he wired that it looked
as if Lee meant to fight north of the Potomac. He completely capitu-
lated to Meade in the words: "Do not be influenced by any dispatch
from here against your own judgment. Regard them as suggestions
only. Our information here is not always correct." He assured Meade
that he was trying to get every available man to him, but he had to
pass on the news that General Brooks's militia, which had marched so
bravely from Pittsburgh to join Kelley's force, had refused to cross the
state line—action very uncomplimentary to the Pennsylvanians, considering how many regiments had come from New York to defend Harrisburg. Having once broken, Halleck continued to deteriorate. An hour
and a half later, when he was informing Meade that three brigades,
plus two regiments and two complete batteries were on the way from
Washington, he himself suggested caution instead of boldness by
closing his dispatch, "I fully appreciate the importance of the coming
battle." [44] Caution was not paralyzing Buford, however. To the day he
gave only one sentence in his report; but it was characteristically a
good one: "July 9, attacked the enemy at 4:00 P.M. and drove him
handsomely about two miles." [45]

Behind the lines Herman Haupt, prototype of "trouble shooters,"
was also doing "handsome" things. On the 8th he untangled a snarl of
thirty-five trains between Frederick and Baltimore, and on the 9th he
wired Meigs from Hanover: "I am on my way to Gettysburg again.
Find things in great confusion. Road blocked; cars not unloaded;
stores ordered to Gettysburg, where they stand for a long time, completely preventing all movement there; ordered back without unloading; wounded lying for hours, without ability to carry them off; all
because the simple rule of promptly unloading and returning cars is
violated." The picture was dismal enough, but it did not take the magic
touch long to straighten matters out; for presently a dispatch from a
quartermaster at Gettysburg arrived and brought the word, "General
Haupt has just been in my office, and railroad matters to this point are
arranged so that there will be no confusion hereafter." Having now
straightened out two railroads, Haupt ordered some of his men to pro-

ceed in wagons from Gettysburg through Cashtown to Chambersburg, so as to repair the line to Hagerstown.[46] That would give another way to bring pressure on Lee if he did not get away—though Haupt thought he would.

Jubilantly enough Meade wrote the next day to his wife that the firm stand he had taken had broken Halleck down, and he had been told to use his own judgment.[47] In the early afternoon he reported to Washington somewhat in detail about the line the enemy had apparently taken up, upon which he was reported to be intrenching. He described his own advance and stated he would continue it "cautiously" the next day until he developed the Confederate position more fully.[48]

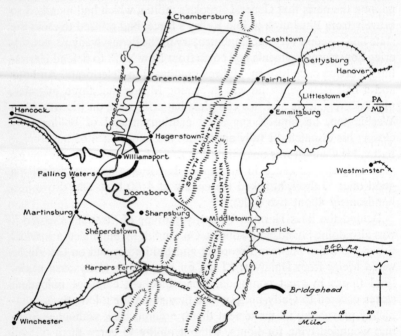

LEE'S ROUTES OF RETREAT AND BRIDGEHEAD

Lee's combat troops used the Fairfield Gap, his trains the Cashtown Gap. High waters kept him from crossing the river until the night of July 13.

Had he gone forward at this time personally and conducted a vigorous reconnaissance, there is no reason why he could not have uncovered with the aid of the cavalry and other advanced troops a considerable part of Lee's defensive position on the 10th. On this day when Meade was being so cautious, thinking—or pretending to think—that it was Lee's fixed purpose to wait north of the Potomac for the express purpose of having another battle, Lee seemed to Colonel Alexander more deeply anxious than he ever saw him.[49] The day before, he had had General Imboden, who was very familiar with the region, dictate information concerning crossings of the Potomac above Williamsport all the way to Cumberland; and he had left with Imboden the impression that he regarded his position as "precarious in the extreme." [50] All his wounded and the prisoners he had marched from Gettysburg had been ferried over the river; but still he had no bridge—in spite of the deserter's yarn. Dissatisfied at the speed with which pontoons were being built, Lee had put the work into the hands of another officer, who tore down warehouses to obtain suitable lumber. Supplies were meager, and though there had been no heavy rain since the night of the 7th, with the result that the waters were subsiding, the river was still too high for fording.[51] Such was Lee's true situation as Meade crept forward "cautiously," in seeming emulation of McClellan's advance over the same region the preceding September.

Finally on the 12th Meade had covered the eight miles that separated the line through Boonsboro—where much of his infantry had arrived before noon on the 9th—from the enemy position, which was behind Marsh Creek and two miles east of Williamsport. On this day there was reunited with the army a force under Brigadier General T. H. Neill that had followed Lee through the Fairfield Gap and had done no little damage to the Confederate rear guard.[52] It consisted of Neill's own brigade of Howe's division of the Sixth Corps, to which had been added Colonel John B. McIntosh's brigade of Gregg's cavalry division (with a section of two guns), and a battery of rifled pieces. Cut off from the rest of the army, Neill's force—augumented somewhat by militia units from Harrisburg under General W. F. Smith—was exposed to a stroke by Lee; and its conduct constitutes one of the bright spots in the pursuit. Neill, a West Point graduate, was more than generous in his report about the fine soldiership of McIntosh, a graduate of Annapolis, who seemed glad to change to horses after two years with ships; and he spoke about "the cool and professional manner" in which the converted seaman went about his land operations. Though recommended for promotion by Neill, the able colonel of the Third Pennsylvania Cavalry had to wait a year for the star appropriate to brigade command.

On the 12th Meade wired Halleck, "It is my intention to attack them tomorrow, unless something intervenes to prevent it, for the reason that delay will strengthen the enemy and will not increase my force." "Unless something intervenes"—Meade, the master of escape clauses, did not forget to insert that provision; and, as if to make doubly certain that something would intervene, he called a council of war. The next day at 5:00 P.M., after Washington had been waiting eagerly for news, the general reported that his corps commanders had been "five out of six" unqualifiedly against an attack; accordingly he was continuing his "reconnaissances with the expectation of finding some weak point, upon which, if I succeed, I shall hazard an attack." [53] How depressing the message was to Lincoln, we know; for John Hay had resumed his diary on the 11th, a day when the President had been buoyant and hopeful of a brilliant success, thinking that Meade in spite of his slowness "would yet show sufficient activity to inflict the *coup de grâce* upon the flying rebels." But after the very disappointing telegram came on the 13th the young secretary wrote: "Nothing can save them if Meade does his duty. I doubt him. He is an engineer." [54]

Although Meade did not have the chance to read the two short sentences in which Hay demolished him, he did read a message with a sharp reproof that Halleck, who was apparently seeking to reassert himself, sent at 9:30 P.M. on the 13th:

Yours of 5:00 P.M. is received. You are strong enough to attack and defeat the enemy before he can effect a crossing. Act upon your own judgment and make your generals execute your orders. Call no council of war. It is proverbial that councils of war never fight. Re-enforcements are pushed on as rapidly as possible. Do not let the enemy escape. [55]

But it was too late; already in a downpour of rain, by the bridge that had been completed at Falling Waters and the ford at Williamsport, the enemy was escaping. A difficult and very hazardous operation it was; but it was brilliantly executed, the wagon train, followed by the corps of Longstreet and Hill, using the bridge, while the sturdy men of Ewell's command breasted the high waters at the ford. At four o'clock the next morning, July 14, Captain Nahum Daniels, a Federal signal officer, discovered that the Confederates had evacuated their works, and tried unsuccessfully to get a message through by flags to the unsuspecting Meade. [56] An hour before that Kilpatrick, who was up bright and early in order to attack at seven, discovered that the enemy in his front had withdrawn, and at six o'clock Brigadier General George Custer drove Ewell's rearguard into the water at Williamsport. Moving with the rest of his command toward Falling Waters, Kilpatrick joined Buford. About two miles from the bridge the Confederate rear guard was encountered, and Federal troopers took a toll of two guns, three battle flags, and many prisoners, which Kilpatrick perhaps with exaggeration put at 1,500. Buford reached the river about noon, just as the enemy cut the bridge loose on the Maryland side, allowing it to swing in safety to the southern bank.[57] Lee, not content with a fine operation—remembering perhaps that he had not taken a single man from Burnside in the retirement at Fredericksburg —tarnished his record with a letter to Adjutant General Cooper claiming that the Federals had captured no men in battle, but only weary stragglers asleep by the roadside or in barns; but he did not explain how Kilpatrick's horsemen had come into possession of the colors of the Fortieth, Forty-seventh, and Fifty-fifth Virginia infantry regiments.[58] These units were a part of Heth's division, which with that of Pender formed the rear guard, the two under the command of Heth.[59] Longstreet, on the other hand, freely admitted the lost guns and colors and, without intimating that the number was a gross exaggeration, stated that Meade put the number of prisoners at 2,000.[60]

Major Eckert's telegraph instrument in the War Department clicked out the sad news at high noon of July 14; but the message—sent by Meade at eleven o'clock—put the best possible front on the situation. It stated merely that upon advancing to feel the enemy, and to attack "if the result of the examination should justify" an attack, he had discovered the enemy lines had been vacated. Immediately he had put his army in pursuit, the cavalry in advance. This version hardly agrees with the reports of Buford, Kilpatrick, and Daniels, the cavalrymen particularly being deprived of credit for acting independently. The message also revealed Meade's deficiency in humor, for he said to the General in Chief, "Your instructions as to further movements, in case the enemy are entirely across the river, are desired." [61] Halleck's photographs do not suggest that he smiled or swore easily; but Meade's request for instructions, after his critical and unyielding attitude toward all directions previously sent, should have done something to the scholarly countenance of the General in Chief. "Greatly grieved," was Hay's description of the reaction of his chief—his much revered "A. L." To the loyal assistant the President remarked: "We had them within our grasp. We had only to stretch forth our hands and they were ours. And nothing I could say or do could make the army move." [62]

Whatever private comments the news may have wrung from Halleck, it caused him to write a message much to the point though in the language of a model General in Chief. His dispatch, sent fifty minutes after receipt of Meade's, stated that the enemy must be pursued and cut up, but that detailed plans could not be given because of lack of information. His last sentence put the case just as it was without any effort at concealment: "I need hardly say to you that the escape of Lee's army without another battle has created great dissatisfaction in the mind of the President, and will require an active and energetic pursuit on your part to remove the impression that it has not been sufficiently active heretofore." That was too much for a general to whom the Fredericksburg ladies had recently been bringing wreaths and bouquets (the cautious Meade had been careful to tell his wife that they had come in a "delegation"). He promptly telegraphed that he considered the President's censure unjust and he wished to be relieved from command of the army. A half-hour later—at three o'clock—he reported the enemy entirely over the river, and told of the captures by his cavalry, with the incorrect statement that an entire brigade had been taken. Promising army commanders were certainly a scarce article, and Halleck replied that his telegram had not been intended as a censure "but as a stimulus to an active pursuit," and it was not deemed sufficient ground for Meade's request. [63]

Two days later Lincoln learned something of the fateful council of war through General Wadsworth at a White House tea. When asked by another officer as to why Lee had escaped, the hard-fighting general, whose infantry division had taken over from Buford on the first day at Gettysburg, replied gruffly, "Because nobody stopped him." In command of the First Corps during Newton's illness, he had been at the council on the night of the 12th; and his version of it differed somewhat from Meade's brief statement in the telegram to Halleck. French, commanding the Third Corps, Sedgwick, and Slocum strongly opposed an attack he said; but Meade, Warren, Pleasonton, and he himself were eager to assault, while Howard had little to say. The thought of the nonfighters seemed to be that Lee would attack the Federals if not himself attacked, giving them a great advantage; and neither they nor Meade had any idea that Lee was something more than eager to get away without a further combat. Wadsworth himself had stood out for a strong attack upon Lee's left flank, following the pattern of Stonewall Jackson at Chancellorsville, while Meade proposed three columns of attack.[64] (The fact that Meade himself later justified not attacking is merely another of his many contradictory statements.) Powerful indeed could have been the attack that the Federal commander was in a position to bring against Lee's maximum of 35,000 effective infantry and artillery; [65] for on the 10th he had shown 85,000 officers and men present for duty—which virtually meant available for combat—and to these must be added 10,000 received from Washington and brought by General Smith from Carlisle.[66] Kilpatrick reported that 500 militia—the Philadelphia Blues—had assisted him in repelling an enemy attack on the 13th—balancing the record of the Pittsburghers who would not set foot in Maryland.[67]

The contention that Lee's position was found to have been so strong that an attack would have been disastrous is not too convincing; for though Meade asserted it had been surveyed carefully he could not know the manner in which it was occupied.[68] Lee's eagerness to get away disproves the claim that he would have welcomed an attack. But was there not an alternative to an attack upon entrenched lines? General Haupt, who throughout his career was so resourceful in hard situations, stated that Meade could have held a strong defensive position with a part of his command, while he crossed sufficient force over the Potomac—keeping the two parts within supporting distance—to seize the south bank of the river and make bridging impossible for Lee.[69] Such a maneuver seems to turn on the location of Meade's pontoons. After the army had crossed into Maryland in June the bridges were dismantled and shipped to Washington for safe keeping. On July 5, foreseeing their use in the pursuit of Lee, Meade wisely telegraphed General Benham, "Put your bridge trains and troops in motion at once for Harper's Ferry." Four days later Benham, at his ordered destination after overcoming many difficulties, reported, "The two bridges are in the canal, and ready to be towed anywhere they may be needed up the river." [70] Thus Meade had the ability to move a part of his army over the river. What an aggressive commander could have accomplished by throwing part of his superior force to the other side of the Potomac can be imagined. Tardily on the 13th Meade thought of the unused bridges and grasped in a restricted way the opportunity they afforded. For two days Gregg's division of cavalry had been resting at Boonsboro after a short march from Middletown on the 11th. At 9:00

P.M., an order went to him to move the next day to Harpers Ferry, cross the river on the bridge the engineers would throw, and "annoy" Lee's trains and communications.[71] The move to Boonsboro had been perfectly futile, and Gregg, who had spent the 10th resting his division, could have crossed on the 11th instead of the 14th, to strike Falling Waters not later than the morning of the 13th.

"We had them within our grasp." Did Abraham Lincoln greatly exaggerate the possibilities in the situation? Herman Haupt, West Point classmate of George Meade, who saw in every problem the opportunities and not just the difficulties, certainly did not think so.

Though the people of the North were of course hopeful that some knockout blow might be dealt to Lee before he could cross to safety, news from the Army of the Potomac had competition for first place with the great riots that broke out in New York City on Monday July 13, riots which started as a protest against the draft, but soon turned into a general frenzy of destruction and assaults on Negroes. In haste, New York guard regiments were marched to Frederick to entrain for the city; and on the 15th Meade was directed to send a regiment of regular infantry and a battery.[72] On the 14th, the few troops that were available, the police, and volunteers began to get control over the great mob, which was almost entirely foreign-born. The militia regiments that began to arrive the next day were in a grim frame of mind; over a thousand rioters [73] fell before the rifles of the soldiers, but the reign of terror was at an end. Governor Seymour's address to the mob on the 14th, which began, "My Friends," did not set well with many who believed that his fierce opposition to the draft, like the inflammatory articles in bitterly anti-administration papers, was in part responsible for the outburst.

On the 17th, 18th, and 19th, the Army of the Potomac crossed back into Virginia at Harpers Ferry and six miles below at Berlin— present Brunswick—with its commander in an unhappy frame of mind, as shown by a sentence to his wife: "The proper policy for the Government would have been to be contented with driving Lee out of Maryland, and not to have advanced till this army was largely reinforced and reorganized, and put on such a footing that its advance was sure to be successful." [74] The general who had frequently announced that luck played a decisive role in military matters, was again wanting a sure thing. With a touch of McClellanism he added, "As, however, I am bound to obey explicit orders, the responsibility of the consequences must and should rest with those who give them." Two days before, when about to cross the river, he had stated to his wife that Lee's army was nearly equal to his own, and in reporting to Halleck on the evening of the 18th that most of Lee's army had crossed he showed some apprehension by remarking, "I see by the public journals it is intimated that a part of Bragg's army has been sent to Virginia. I presume if any reliable intelligence of this fact reaches you, I shall be fully advised." Apparently unannoyed by Meade's mild suggestion that he might fail in the duties of his office, the General in Chief replied at once: "You need have no fear of Bragg, Johnston, or Beauregard. Not a man will join Lee. His forces can only be re-inforced by a part of D. H. Hill's command, and even then they will be far inferior in numbers to your army." It is an important dispatch and shows conclusively that the High Command understood the situation. Two days later, Meade signed a strength return showing he had an aggregate present of 105,-623 men, with 92,847 present for duty, and no fewer than 86,291 present for duty equipped; his artillery numbered 330 guns.[75] As Lee's return for the same date showed an aggregate present of 50,178, exclusive of the cavalry,[76] Halleck's assertion was more than justified; almost two to one was the actual margin of strength that the Federal commander had.

Perhaps Halleck's blunt statement encouraged Meade to make a bold stroke in an attempt to take Lee in the flank as he moved in the direction of Culpeper.[77] With the Third Corps leading, he started through Manassas Gap on the evening of the 22nd; but the entire operation was bungled by General French, who acted with such slowness and caution that Lee's rear guard delayed him an entire day, allowing the escape of the whole Confederate army. French was new to field command, and Meade's failure to have one of his more experienced corps commanders in the lead throws upon him a large share of responsibility for the loss of an opportunity that Swinton described as very great.[78] Lee having successfully evaded a Federal attack, Meade went back through the mountains and followed more leisurely. August 1 has been officially taken as the end of the Gettysburg campaign, and that day found the armies in familiar territory, the Federals along the Rappahannock and the Confederates in the vicinity of Culpeper. But Lincoln's hopefulness had ended before that, for he had written in the remarkably frank letter that he set aside: "It would be unreasonable to expect, and I do not expect you can now effect much. Your golden opportunity is gone, and I am distressed immeasurably because of it." [79] But before the end of the month, in reply to a very irregular letter from General Howard, he had written in effect that he was letting bygones be bygones, and was "profoundly grateful for what was done, without criticism for what was not done." [80] In an exchange of long personal letters, Halleck and Meade removed any elements of seeming unfriendliness which had been engendered; but the General in Chief stood stanchly behind the President, and never intimated that Lincoln had looked for unreasonable accomplishments.[81]

The two armies watched each other, rested, and refitted through the hot days of August, with the people at home becoming more conscious of the grimness of war, because of the many casualties, the draft riots, and the picture of the execution of three men for deserting, a crime that Lee was combating in the same way, taking no fewer than ten lives by a firing squad on a single occasion.[82] Conscious of the blow that his defeat had been to the Confederacy, and fearing that he had lost the confidence of the people, if not also of his army, Lee on August 8 suggested to President Davis the desirability of selecting a new commander for the Army of Northern Virginia.[83] Three days later Davis in a warm letter expressed sentiments to many of which Lincoln also could have subscribed. Of the senseless clamor of the public he wrote:

". . . there has been nothing which I have found to require a greater effort of patience than to bear the criticisms of the ignorant, who pronounce everything a failure which does not equal their expectations or desires, and can see no good result which is not in the line of their own imaginings. . . . Expressions of discontent in the public journals furnish but little evidence of the sentiment of the army. . . . I say I wish I could feel that the public journals are not generally partisan nor venal.[84]

In the diary of Davis's chief of ordnance the situation of the Confederacy was recorded without effort to minimize or conceal its gravity. A few weeks before, Josiah Gorgas had evidently been indulging in much wishful thinking, for he had not seen the hopelessness of Vicksburg, and he looked upon Lee's venture on an invasion as full of promise. The trained soldier did not have the military judgment of Lincoln, who had appraised matters so correctly on June 30. After such rosy hopes, Gorgas had a severe and painful disillusionment, which he recorded on July 28. Naturally the loss of 45,000 fine rifles at Vicksburg and Port Hudson hurt him badly; and he thus unburdened himself: "It seems incredible that human power could effect such a change in so brief a space. Yesterday we rode on the pinnacle of success—today absolute ruin seems to be our portion. The Confederacy totters to its destruction." [85]

In the East, attention was turned southward to Charleston, where the first shots of the great war had been fired and the Union had been so greatly humiliated. Although the recent April attack by gunboats upon Fort Sumter had dismally and quickly failed, the determination by the Washington government to gain command of the harbor had not abated. Ground operations had been going forward in the approaches to the city, where low land was cut up by numerous and difficult streams, but with insufficient strength to do much more than immobilize a considerable number of Confederate troops, and to cause uncertainty and apprehension to the Richmond authorities. Finally in July, by the use of threats upon other points, the greater part of Morris Island—site of the battery that had fired upon the *Star of the West* in January, 1861—was seized, and some heavy ordnance was landed. On the narrow end of the island near the entrance to the harbor the Confederates had constructed a very strong earthwork—famed Fort Wagner. An assault on the morning of July 10 was easily repelled by the defenders, and a heavier attack on the 18th had also been broken with severe loss to the attacking Federals; among the killed in this action was Colonel Robert G. Shaw, leading the Fifty-fourth Massachusetts, the first colored regiment raised on "free soil." After that repulse Major General Quincy A. Gillmore, conducting the operations, set to work with progressive seige methods, advancing his parallels in the exhausting climate with the aid of naval guns.[86] Nor was Sumter forgotten as he worked his way toward Fort Wagner; on July 23 he reported to Halleck that the historic structure, where Anderson's little band of cannoneers had suffered, had been virtually demolished by the rain of heavy shells that he had poured into it. But it was not until September 7 that the defenders of Fort Wagner and of Fort Bragg—a small work nearer the island's tip—slipped away at night, abandoning their heavy guns to the attackers. Charleston itself had suffered a Federal bombardment; after the "Swamp Angel"—an 8-inch rifled Parrott gun with a resonant voice, emplaced in a marsh after tremendous labor—burst upon hurling its thirty-sixth 200-pound shell into the city, a battery was established nearer the target.[87] Then in real earnest shells began to fall among the wharves, the great warehouses, and the buildings from whose roofs in April, 1861, exulting Charlestonians had watched flames shoot up from Sumter and had applauded when the flag of the United States was shot down. No attempt to take Charleston itself was feasible, and even Sumter was stubbornly held by Confederate infantry, who made safe shelters in the mass of ruins, and against whom no assault was tried after an ill advised effort by the Navy on the night of September 7. But the lower portion of Charleston was largely abandoned, and, what was more important, blockade-runners no longer steadily took out cargoes of cotton under cover of night, or slipped into the harbor through the Federal fleet with their holds full of coveted munitions or eagerly desired luxuries of "graceful living." [88]

It was not only in Northern minds that there was the thought that Charleston's suffering had been brought upon itself and was deserved. Bitterly Gorgas wrote in his diary: "The sins of the people of Charleston may cause that city to fall; it is full of rottenness, every one being engaged in speculations. When the fate of Lee's army was, as we tho't trembling in the balance at Gettysburgh, the interest was less vivid in it than in a steamer which was expected in. . . . Her fall will be looked upon as a righteous doom." [89]

Throughout the summer there were alarming stories about the two new powerful raiders that were being built for the Confederates in Liverpool by the firm that had constructed the famous cruiser *Alabama,* currently causing so much havoc with United States commerce. As the toll of ships sunk by the guns of the "Anglo-rebel pirate"—as the *Alabama* was sometimes called in the Northern press—mounted, the anti-British feeling in the North increased. Early in September the Ambassador to Great Britain, Charles Francis Adams, learning that the new mystery ships were about to sail, protested once more to Earl Russell, Queen Victoria's Foreign Minister, ending his short note with the memorable sentence, "It would be superfluous in me to point out to your Lordship that this is war!" [90] The ships did not sail, and England bought them for her own navy. Thus at last the policy of Secretary of State Seward of badgering England and threatening war if she even recognized the Confederacy paid off—and paid off handsomely. The United States was in no position to have England—and possibly

France as well—arrayed against her as an actual shooting enemy, for she certainly had all the fighting she wanted at the time. But neither did the "Mother Country" want war, nor could she risk it. That fact Seward knew; and so he won his gigantic game of bluff. To her Majesty's minister there seemed to be more than just an outside chance that quiet Minister Adams—son of John Quincy Adams and grandson of John Adams of Revolutionary fame—might mean exactly what he said, "This is war." Never did a diplomat succeed better in finding precisely the right word; by the word "superfluous" the Yankee son of one President and grandson of another pushed Lord John into a tight corner.

As recently as June of this year a motion had been introduced in the House of Commons looking to the full recognition of the Confederacy, with perhaps the furnishing of aid.[91] The Northern successes of Gettysburg and Vicksburg, however, caused a quick shift of opinion, and only the more extreme Confederate sympathizers in England could after that have much belief in a Southern victory. Already they had noticed that, even when things were very black for the Federals, people in the North had shown their steady confidence by buying American securities that Europeans, doubtful about the future of the United States, wished to sell.[92] Then virtually on the same day the Federal armies won crucial victories at the end of the great, long battle line; one victory threw back an attempt to penetrate the North, the other victory secured the capture of an entire Southern army and caused the severance of the rebelling states into two sections. After Seward and Adams had won "The Battle of the Rams," danger of intervention in the war, or even of the recognition of the Confederacy, on the part of Britain virtually passed.

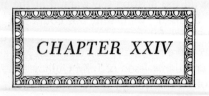

CHAPTER XXIV

MANEUVERS IN THE AUTUMN

> If you pursue and fight him, I think you will find out where
> he is. I know of no other way.   *Halleck to Meade*

Beyond the mountains, in the land of great rivers, events were also
going badly with the cause of Jefferson Davis. Mississippi was lost, as
well as much of Alabama, although Grant's proposed operation against
Mobile was not allowed, on account of concern over French activities
in Mexico, which the High Command believed might make it necessary
to conduct operations in Texas.[1] The Confederate attempt to cause
confusion in the North by sending Major General John H. Morgan on
a cavalry raid across the Ohio River into Indiana and Ohio on July 7
had ended with the capture of the enterprising and spectacular horseman—"bandit," the Northern press at times called him—near New
Lisbon, Ohio. Although Morgan did cause much alarm locally, he was
so closely pressed by pursuing cavalry that he scarcely had time to
enjoy the good meals that the fat land he traversed would have provided; and when the affair was all over, the results of the expedition
brought satisfaction to the North and not to the South.

With Morgan lodged in the penitentiary at Columbus, Ohio—but
so insecurely that he escaped—the attention of the people in the West
could be concentrated on affairs in east Tennessee. Rosecrans, who
had been compelled by shortage of supplies and inadequate cavalry to
be inactive at Murfreesboro, had found it possible to start an offensive
movement in the last days of June. Deceiving Bragg, whose force was
based on Chattanooga, he moved skillfully and crossed the Tennessee

River below Chattanooga, with the apparent intention of cutting Bragg's communications with Atlanta. Again Lee was hastily summoned for conferences in Richmond,[2] where he had not much more than arrived when a column under Burnside, operating against Buckner in east Tennessee, entered Knoxville on September 2. Soon thereafter it was decided that two brigades of Longstreet's corps would be sent to Charleston, while the rest of the corps went to help Bragg. The direct rail route to Chattanooga through east Tennessee having been cut by Burnside, it was necessary to route the troops through Richmond and Atlanta. The movement of 7,000 men with artillery and trains some 650 miles was more than a chore for the frail Southern railroads; it was a first-rate task apparently well handled.

Of course it was desirable that the Federals should not know what was up; it would be better still if they could be led to believe that it was Bragg who was reenforcing Lee, and not Lee sending help to Bragg. Lee apparently set about some counter intelligence work to induce such an idea, for on September 11 Halleck telegraphed Rosecrans that deserters reported that Bragg's army was sending troops to Lee, and he directed, "It is important that the truth of this should be ascertained as early as possible." Two days later, General Foster telegraphed to the General in Chief from Fort Monroe that "trains of cars had been heard running all the time, day and night, for the last thirty-six hours, on the Petersburg and Richmond road, evidently indicating a movement of troops in some direction." This might of course have been the movement of Bragg's men, but the next morning Foster reported that Longstreet's corps was reported to be going south through North Carolina. That was something very different indeed from the deserters' stories, and Meade was directed at once to ascertain, by giving battle if necessary, whether any of Lee's troops had left. On the same day, Meade replied that it was his view, based on a variety of meager and conflicting testimony, that Lee's army had been reduced by Longstreet's corps, and perhaps by some regiments of the commands of Ewell and Hill as well.[3]

Now it was a question of evaluating an important fact, and this Halleck did not do very happily. At 11:00 P.M. he telegraphed Foster that he thought Longstreet was going to North Carolina to suppress some of the very strong Union feeling there, and also to operate against Federal forces on the coast of that state, in the hope of causing detachments to be sent from Meade, when Longstreet would hasten back to

Lee for operations against the weakened Army of the Potomac.[4] It certainly was not an unreasonable speculation; and part of Longstreet's corps actually went to South Carolina, so that the Federal General in Chief was to a certain extent correct in not thinking of Chattanooga as the destination of the troop trains that had left Richmond. Halleck was directing a great war in an enormous theater, with a staff smaller than would now be used to send picture films or chocolate bars to the soldiers; and at 11:00 P.M., he was writing messages himself. Although Rosecrans seems not to have been directly informed of the departure of Longstreet, Halleck did direct Burnside on the 14th—after so advising Rosecrans the day before: "There are reasons why you should re-enforce General Rosecrans with all possible dispatch. It is believed that the enemy will concentrate to give him battle. You must be there to help." Actually Halleck may have thought that assistance would come to Bragg from General Joe Johnston's command in Alabama; but Rosecrans was of course gathering information for himself, and in his report he stated without reservation that he had strong indications that Bragg was expecting reenforcements from Virginia.[5] Thus Halleck's failure to be 100 per cent correct in interpreting Longstreet's departure from Lee's army was not as serious as it might have been.

Just as General Joe Johnston had joined Beauregard in time to defeat McDowell at First Bull Run and as A. P. Hill had arrived on the field of Antietam barely in time to turn the tide of battle on that hard field, so Longstreet came on the scene in northern Georgia not a moment too soon to play an important part in the battle of Chickamauga. Deceived into believing that Bragg was retreating upon Atlanta, Rosecrans had incautiously gone through the gaps in Mission Mountain into the valley of Chickamauga Creek, where in reality Bragg—who had evacuated Chattanooga—was laying a trap for him. McLaws's division arrived in time to be in the combat of September 19, but Longstreet in person and Hood's division did not participate until the next day. Hood himself, in the furious attack which he made, lost a leg; but his division was largely responsible for overpowering the Federal right and deciding the fortunes of the battle. Furious and bloody was the contest that raged in the wooded valley; one-fourth of Bragg's 66,000 men, and one-fifth of Rosecrans's 58,000 were killed or wounded. Though in hitting their adversaries the Federals were more efficient, the battle was a defeat for Rosecrans, who retreated to Chattanooga.[6]

Throughout the day Lincoln had the feeling that things were not going well; he had not been too encouraged by the brief dispatch he had received the night before from Rosecrans,[7] or the longer one that had come to Halleck. To Major Eckert there came at 7:45 P.M. a warning from the telegraph operator in Cincinnati: "You may expect bad news from Department of the Cumberland. General Rosecrans is in Chattanooga." [8] An hour later Halleck had the dispatch: "We have met with a serious disaster; extent not yet ascertained. Enemy over-whelmed us, drove our right, pierced our center, and scattered troops there." If Rosecrans could be so stirring in describing his own defeat, one wonders what he would have said if he had broken the enemy. The one encouraging part of the message was the statement that Thomas with seven divisions remained on the field at the last word. After stat-ing that troops from Charleston, Florida, Virginia, and all along the seaboard were among the prisoners taken, it concluded, "It seems that every available man was thrown against us." [9]

The situation looked desperate. The equinoctial night wore on, and was half gone when the man who, according to Ropes, was unfit to deal with military men telegraphed to his defeated general: "Be of good cheer. We have unabated confidence in you, and your soldiers and officers. In the main you must be the judge as to what is to be done. If I was to suggest, I would say save your army by taking strong posi-tions until Burnside joins you, when I hope you can turn the tide. . . . We shall do our utmost to assist you. Send us your present posting." Though communications with Burnside—who seemed to be delaying in the execution of previous orders—were far from satisfactory, the President at 2:00 A.M. of the 21st telegraphed him briefly, "Go to Rosecrans with your force without a moment's delay." [10]

In defeat Lincoln still saw victory, if Chattanooga could only be held. After Halleck had returned to his desk in the morning, the Presi-dent wrote to him that it was important that Rosecrans hold at or near the city; details were to be left to the field commander, but all possible assistance must be given. A characteristic last sentence drove home Lincoln's view of the situation: "If he [Rosencrans] can only maintain this position without gaining more, the rebellion can only eke out a short and feeble existence, as an animal sometimes may with a thorn in its vitals." [11] He was badly in error on the endurance of the Confederacy, but his appraisal of the seriousness of the loss of Chattanooga to the cause of Jefferson Davis was perfectly correct: Northern occupation of the city was indeed a thorn in the vitals of the South.

Succeeding telegrams from the defeated general brought more details but varied in regard to prospects until the night of the 23rd, when the message arrived: "We hold this point, and I cannot be dislodged except by very superior numbers and after a great battle." [12] The day before, encouraging news had come out of the enemy capital in a dispatch to Stanton from Brigadier General Charles K. Graham at Fort Monroe. He was the versatile and energetic officer who had led the successful raid across the lower Potomac on November 10, 1861—to McClellan's disapproval. At Gettysburg he had been wounded and captured in the fighting in the Peach Orchard; and he had made the long hard trip to Libby Prison, near Richmond. Because he was considered as an especially valuable officer, it was arranged to exchange him for Brigadier General James L. Kemper, who had commanded one of Pickett's brigades in the great assault and had fallen into Union hands severely wounded.[13] While in Libby, Graham had picked up much important information, and he telegraphed it promptly to Stanton when he arrived at Fort Monroe. Reporting that two divisions of Longstreet's corps with all their artillery had gone to Bragg, and that it was intimated that Lee himself might go to Tennessee, he added: "The news from Tennessee has produced no satisfaction. The rebel officers say that the accounts from the west are always favorable at first, but cannot bear the test of time." [14] To Stanton there was also coming a historic series of long dispatches from Charles A. Dana, who was his special representative with Rosecrans. The recent battle lost nothing as it was portrayed by the future editor of the *Sun:* "Thomas seemed to have filled every soldier with his own unconquerable firmness, and Granger, his hat torn by bullets, raged like a lion wherever the combat was hottest with the electrical courage of a Ney." The code clerks or the telegraphers did not know about the famous marshals of France, and they garbled the message; but Stanton would be denied nothing, and he obtained a repeat from Dana of the last words—perhaps uncoded.[15] Thus George H. Thomas and Gordon Granger had their records advanced in high quarters; but of Rosecrans himself Stanton formed an unfavorable opinion, believing that he had practically deserted the field.

Late at night of the 23rd there was a historic council of Halleck, Stanton, Seward, Chase, Watson, Colonels Hardie and McCallum, and Lincoln, whom John Hay summoned from his bed at the Soldiers' Home at Stanton's request.[16] It was decided to send the Eleventh and Twelfth Corps to Rosecrans, with Hooker in command [17]—a movement that was to be epoch-making in military annals, for nothing on a similar scale had ever been attempted. More than twice the number of men that had been sent to Bragg by the Richmond government would be sent to the Federal commander, and they would have to move twice the distance; the great Ohio River must be crossed twice, and there were no railroad bridges. At 2:30 A.M. of the 24th a dispatch to Meade told him to prepare the troops to move with five days' cooked rations, cars probably arriving on the morning of the 25th. A half-hour later a reply was back: the Twelfth Corps was on picket along the Rapidan, behind which Lee had been forced to retire from Culpeper; that would require from it some hard marching and fast preparation. To Rosecrans went a dispatch from the General in Chief informing him that 14,000 or 15,000 men from Washington would be in Nashville in about seven days.[18] It took courage to say that, considering that no plans whatever had been made, that rolling stock would have to be assembled, and that there would have to be four changes of cars: in Washington, from box and flat cars to passenger cars and box cars provided with seats; at the Ohio River near Wheeling; in Indianapolis, where there was no connecting track between two railroads that were a mile apart; and lastly at the Ohio River for the crossing to Louisville. Nor was it enough just to march men from one train to another; in addition, guns, wagons, and baggage had to be unloaded and reloaded, and men and animals had to be fed. Hooker was placed in command of the movement, and an order from Stanton authorized him to take military possession of all railroads, cars, locomotives, plants, and equipment that he deemed necessary.[19] Such action was superfluous, because the cooperation of the many railroads that were called upon was complete; and the fifty pages in the Official Records devoted to the move tell a thrilling story that can still be studied with profit by anyone interested in logistics.

At 11:00 A.M. of the 26th a dispatch from W. P. Smith, master of transportation for the Baltimore and Ohio, told Stanton that three trains had passed Martinsburg at half-hour intervals, and nine more trains were rolling close behind them. Everything was going perfectly, and responses from Ohio indicated the fullest condition of readiness at Bellaire for reentrainment, after the men, the vehicles, and the animals had crossed on the bridge of barges that had been constructed. A telegram of warm thanks was Stanton's reply. Colonel T. A. Scott had been called once more from the Pennsylvania Railroad and had been sent to Lousiville as a regulating officer. From him a telegram gave assurance that everything was in readiness for the transfer at Indianapolis, and that arrangements were complete for ferrying at Louisville; and a second dispatch reported that he would be ready to handle 5,000 men the next day, and a like number each succeeding day. On the 29th he informed Rosecrans that four trains had departed during the morning from Louisville for Bridgeport on the Tennessee River; the flow of trains would continue for the rest of the week. A similar report to the War Secretary brought the answer: "Your work is most brilliant. A thousand thanks. It is a great achievement." The next day Scott reported to Washington that the first four trains had reached Bridgeport, the railhead of the movement, a day ahead of the promised time. On October 2 Hooker telegraphed from Nashville to Stanton that the last of the Eleventh Corps had reached its destination the day before, and that the Twelfth Corps was passing through the city at the time. The message brought an expression of much satisfaction from Stanton and the words: "All success attend you and your operations." [20]

Trains of horses and baggage were still following the troops, but on the 6th a dispatch from Indianapolis stated that the last of these had departed.[21] Instead of 15,000 men, at least 18,000 were transported, and the number of horses was 50 per cent greater than the number for which transportation was first requisitioned; [22] but the increased load seemed to cause no trouble. Such was the Union's answer to the South's effort to capitalize upon its interior position and shorter lines of communication; in making it a new and brilliant chapter in military movements had been written. The American railroaders who achieved marvels of transport in World War II were the successors of great pioneers in railroading who in the war of the sixties left records that well could stir emulation.

Exhausted by hard work that seemed to lead to nothing, Buford at midnight on August 3 wrote to Pleasonton:

I am disgusted and worn out with the system that seems to prevail. There is so much apathy and so little disposition to fight and co-operation that I wish to be relieved from the Army of the Potomac. I do not wish to put myself and soldiers in front where I cannot get a support short of 12 miles. The ground I gain I would like to hold. The reconnaissance made on the 1st of August was a success, yet the First Corps gets the credit of saving me from disaster. I am willing to serve my country, but I do not wish to sacrifice the brave men under my command.[23]

It is impossible to believe that Meade's actions were not dictated by the attitude and views he had revealed to Mrs. Meade soon after recrossing the Potomac, and that he had an aggressive spirit. The bold cavalryman—who had repeatedly called the attention of his immediate commander to lack of support [24]—would have seen a complete explanation of everything if he could have read the letter that Meade had written home.

It was Lee that grew tired of doing nothing and broke the period of inaction, knowing of course that the Federal army had been reduced by the detachment of two corps, and that Meade's cautious spirit might have been increased. On October 7 Federal signal officers on Pony Mountain read Confederate signals that indicated a formidable movement by Lee. Federal General Martin McMahon wrote later: "For reasons never fully explained nor understood, the whole Army of the Potomac, which had marched all the way from Gettysburg for the purpose of engaging Lee, was ordered to retreat. It fell back in good order, certainly, but without apparent occasion." [25] After crossing the Rappahannock, Meade took heart, halted, and ordered Sedgwick back over the river to give battle in the direction of Brandy. But when it was discovered that Lee was also crossing the Rappahannock above him Meade had the retreat continued. On the 14th Warren, commanding the Second Corps in Hancock's absence, with a part of the Fifth Corps and assistance from the Third Cavalry Division, was attacked near Bristow, and won a smart victory. When he read the report of A. P. Hill, Jefferson Davis endorsed on it, "There was a lack of vigilance," while Lee, going over the battlefield the next morning with his subordinate remarked, "Well, well, General, bury these poor men and let us say no more about it." [26]

Not even battle success by a corps commander who was for the first time exercising field command stopped the rearward movement; Centerville was reached before Meade halted and took up a position to receive an attack. From that old familiar locality at noon of the 5th he sent a dispatch to Halleck that once more revealed his weak and halting generalship. After reporting the damage that Warren had done the day before to Heth—taking five guns and 450 prisoners—he stated that prisoners in Federal hands reported that Ewell and Hill together had 80,000 men, and that, starting with seven days' rations and good supply trains, Lee's purpose had been to secure Bull Run ahead of him. Evidently the Federal commander swallowed it all, and believed that Lee—in spite of the lessons of Gettysburg—would dare to come between himself and Washington. He was unable to decide whether Lee would tarry awhile to await opening of his communications with Gordonsville, or continue his advance. If Lee continued to turn his right, Meade's intention was to fall on him or continue to retire toward Washington, depending on whether he or Lee should first concentrate his command.[27]

Military literature can reveal few sadder messages than that—a complete surrender by Meade of all initiative, although he had much the larger army. His talk about "falling upon Lee" was of course idle chatter; for, no matter what information he might have, he would conclude that the enemy could concentrate more rapidly than he could. "I doubt him. He is an engineer," wrote keen John Hay, recalling probably that Little Mac was more of an engineer than a cavalryman —in spite of the saddle he had devised. Never did it occur to the hesitating and confused commander of the Army of the Potomac that, by being a little bold, he might call the tune and compel Lee to conform to his moves. He had not grasped one of the basic things in the catechism of an army commander: to try to make the other fellow do the guessing. Instead he always wanted to wait to see just what Lee would do; then—so he said—*he* would do something. But such a policy usually means never doing anything. Meade failed completely in the true evaluation of Lee's movement, as a maneuver to make the Union army fall back with the hope of striking a blow at part of it as it retired [28]—a program that would have been thrown completely out of gear by a little real aggressiveness on the part of Meade.

In a way, a letter to his wife was more devastating to Meade than the official one—bad as the latter was. He wrote from Centerville on the 17th, "Lee made a desperate effort to get in my rear, but I succeeded in out-manoeuvring him, and got into position at this place, Centreville, with my back to Washington, and ready for his attack if he had chosen to make it." [29] That statement made no pretense that he might "fall on Lee"; and it plainly intimated that he was in awe of Lee and believed he could do almost anything.

Lincoln saw the truth to which his general was blind. He was not worried about Washington with its 989 guns (433 south of the Potomac) and 21,000 officers and men present for duty. He knew that Lee had nothing like 80,000 men, and he grasped the fact that Lee's operation would give Meade an opportunity to do the Southern army great damage. On the 16th he wrote to Halleck that, although Lee had probably gathered in all "scraps" of troops he could find before he sallied forth, he could not have over 60,000 effective men, meaning probably aggregate present. The records prove that on September 30 Lee had 55,221 present, compared with Meade's 89,058. Lincoln, continuing, made this statement: "If Meade can now attack him on a field no more than equal for us, and will do so with all the skill and courage which he, his officers, and men possess, the honor will be his if he succeeds, and the blame may be mine if he fails." [30] Though he gave no positive order, Lincoln committed himself unequivocally; and publicity was given to the dispatch, so that there would be no doubt as to the President's willingness to assume full responsibility if the field commander could muster sufficient courage to act.[31] Certainly it was an unusual procedure. In forwarding a copy of Lincoln's letter, Halleck told Meade that 3,000 of Longstreet's men, who had gone to Charleston, might have returned to Lee; but that was the limit of reenforcements he conceded.[32]

Meade's actions were provoking Halleck, who telegraphed on the 18th after Meade had conjectured that Lee might be again going to the Valley, "If Lee has turned his back on you to cross the mountains, he certainly has seriously exposed himself to your blows, unless his army can move two miles to your one." An hour later the General in Chief passed on the information that Harpers Ferry had reported that the enemy had attacked near-by Charles Town—which gave some color to a move by Lee to the Valley—but in the evening he cleared up the matter by telegraphing that the attack on Charles Town had not been in great force and had been easily repelled. Then he went beyond the "two to one" thrust: "Lee is unquestionably bullying you. If you cannot ascertain his movements, I certainly cannot. If you pursue and fight him, I think you will find out where he is. I know of no other way." This angered Meade, and he replied, "If you have any orders to give me, I am prepared to receive and obey them, but I must insist on being spared the infliction of such truisms in the guise of opinions as you have recently honored me with, particularly as they were not asked for." That was going pretty far; but he saved himself by stating that he ought to be, and desired to be, relieved from command, if he was not giving satisfaction by acting upon his own judgment. Unfortunately there was no substitute and Halleck tried to pacify the ruffled Meade by telegraphing, "If I have repeated truisms it has not been to give offense, but to give to you the wishes of the Government. If, in conveying these wishes, I have used words which were unpleasing, I sincerely regret it." To this Meade replied, "Your explanation of your intentions is accepted, and I thank you for it," in which he again did violence to military proprieties, for an officer does not *accept* the explanations of his superior.[33]

Was George Meade sincere when he said so often, "If you don't like me, remove me—I don't care for the job, and never wanted it anyway"? or was it about the only bit of successful maneuvering he did, knowing full well the unavailability of a successor? Letters to his wife —including some later in the war—as well as his attitude afterward, when other officers received more recognition than he, make it not unreasonable to believe that when he spoke of his perfect willingness to be relieved, he had his fingers crossed just as tightly as when he talked about attacking the enemy.

Secretary Welles hit the nail squarely on the head when, after commenting in his diary on Lincoln's note of the 16th, he said about Meade, "If the President could tell him how and when to fight, his orders would be faithfully carried out, but the President is overtasking Meade's capabilities and powers."[34] There was the sad truth, clearly uttered.

After he had torn up the railroad to his satisfaction, Lee fell back toward the Rappahannock. Meade followed promptly on the 19th; and on November 7 he threw back over the river the part of Lee's army that had been left north of it, in a very successful action at Rappahannock Station and a smaller one at Kelly's Ford; but he did nothing to exploit his success. Again Lee took to the road, and on the 10th he was again over the Rapidan. After a month of hard marching and some small but sharp actions that went in the main favorably to the Federals, everything was about as it had been before. Though the Confederates were humiliated by the actions at Bristow on October 14 and the Rappahannock the next month, Lee had learned much about his new antagonist; he knew that there was little if any more boldness in Meade than there was in McClellan, and he might have entered in his book a judgment similar to Gideon Welles's. The knowledge he had gained was perhaps worth an army corps.

The public, sitting on the side, knew that Meade had missed several tricks in the recent maneuvering and was like a bridge player who ends a hand with three unused aces. He had to defend himself even against his wife. On October 21 he confessed to her that, after all, it had not been Lee's purpose to get in his rear, and that the Confederate general had had the best of it in the "deep game" that had been going on.[35] This was not far from admitting that Lee had been bullying him, as Halleck had plainly and vexatiously told him at the time. Not unnaturally, and probably very sympathetically, Mrs. Meade wrote to her husband of his own "retreat." That was *too* much; he could not allow such an awful error to stand, and he at once corrected the good woman. But he reproved her in a very nice way: unlike Halleck, she had not had the benefit of military study and experience. "You seem to be very much puzzled about my retreat, as you misname it. It was not a retreat, but a withdrawal of the army—manoeuvring to get into a proper position to offer battle, and made to prevent Lee from compelling me to fight at a disadvantage." "Offer battle." That was the most that Meade admittedly had had it in mind to do. He might get into a position from which he would not run; but he had had no intention of going out and aggressively seeking combat.

Near the end of November, Meade sought to redeem himself by assuming the offensive. On November 21 Kilpatrick sent to cavalry corps headquarters a detailed and carefully worked out intelligence report based on reports of deserters that put Lee's total strength at 39,000 men.[36] This was under the 45,614 effective total present that Lee actually showed on October 31, when Meade's return gave 84,321 as present for duty; [37] but Meade must have known that he had the two-to-one margin on his enemy that offensive operations might well require. On the evening of the 25th, a brief circular directed corps and independent commanders to be in readiness to march at 6:00 A.M., further instructions being promised before marching time.[38] It happened that Grant was again doing things in the west, this time at Chattanooga, to which he had gone a month before. Washington once more seized the chance to spur Meade on by kindling emulation, and on the 25th Assistant Secretary of War Watson telegraphed that a great and successful battle had been fought that day at Chattanooga, with some encouraging news also about Burnside, who had been shut up in Knoxville by Longstreet. To the dispatch Watson appended a telegram —signed briefly, "Grant"—that had come off the wires after he had finished his own message:

Although the battle lasted from early dawn until this evening, I believe

I am not premature in announcing a complete victory over Bragg. Lookout Mountain top, all the rifle-pits in Chattanooga Valley, and Missionary Ridge all entirely carried and now held by us. I have no idea of finding Bragg tomorrow.[39]

Meade responded beautifully and sent the message to Warren with instructions that it be read to his troops before they marched in the morning.[40] Well did the men of the Second Corps know that their old comrades of the Eleventh and Twelfth had had a part in the fight, but not until later would they learn of how Hooker's men had scaled rugged Lookout Mountain to fight the "Battle Above the Clouds."

Moving in unseasonably cold weather and on difficult roads, the

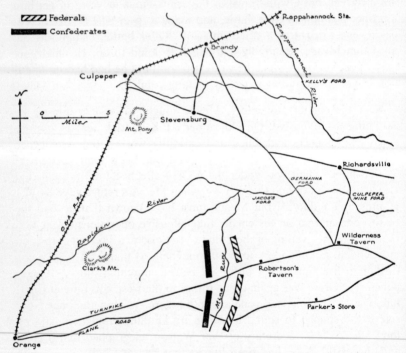

MEADE AND LEE, DECEMBER 1, 1863

army crossed the Rapidan on bridges thrown at Germanna and other fords, and, after reaching the Fredericksburg roads, turned west toward Lee's camps about Orange, developing on the 27th Lee's position along the western crest of the slope of Mine Run, one of the many tributaries of the Rapidan. On the 29th, reconnaissance by Sedgwick upon the right seemed to prove Lee's left unprotected by earthworks or slashings, and a plan of attack for the next day was drawn up. In the morning, Warren, who had the left of the line but had made a much more restricted flank movement than had been planned, found the Confederate position in his front too strong to warrant attack; and he so reported to Meade. On the right flank Sedgwick had opened his guns promptly at seven o'clock as directed, bringing quick replies from the wide-awake "rebels." In the woods there were two corps in column of brigades, animated by rivalry and eager to make the attack, when over the telegraph wires there suddenly came the message from Meade, "Suspend the attack until further orders," which he sent on learning that the situation with Warren was not just what was expected. The guns ceased their fire, and the troops that were to attack spent the day in waiting, while Meade went to the left to discover what had gone awry with Warren's part of the program. The Confederates took full advantage to straighten their position, and that evening when Meade inquired by telegram of Sedgwick as to the chances on his front the commander of the Sixth Corps had to report that the opportunity of the morning was gone. Meade accepted the judgment of his corps commander, and decided to put an end to his adventure and to return to his position in the vicinity of Brandy. Though the weather had been trying and the terrain hard for maneuvering, General McMahon recorded that the troops were in excellent spirits and in good physical condition, adding that "the heart was taken out of everybody when on the 1st of December the order came to retire across the Rapidan and resume the camps from which we had started out so gayly a week before." [41] Whatever Washington may have hoped for, Stanton's ten-word telegram on the evening of the 1st to General Benjamin Butler at Fort Monroe suggests that the retirement was no great surprise: "Meade is on the back track again without a fight." [42]

Thus ended the "Mine Run Fiasco," Meade's operation turning out to be nothing more than a practice march and a partial deployment, matters in which the Army of the Potomac was already accomplished. Operations for the year were over, and the command went into winter quarters, McMahon writing, "The troops burrowed in the earth and built little shelters, and the officers and men devoted themselves to unlimited festivity, balls, horse-races, cock-fights, greased pigs and poles, and other games such as only soldiers can devise."

From the cavalry that guarded the army as it rested in winter quarters, one important figure was missing: John Buford. He had—so far as the records show—sent his last report about enemy positions on November 15.[43] He became ill not long afterward and died in Washington on December 16. Before he died a commission as major general of volunteers had been placed in his hands, the commission appropriately dating from July 1, which had been his greatest day, though one cannot predict what distinction he might have achieved if he had lived, for obviously he had not reached his limit.

Though 1863 was an off year politically, the fall months brought some elections that were to prove that the administration had regained much of the prestige it had lost a year before, and was again well regarded. In the East, eyes were turned particularly on the Commonwealth of Pennsylvania, where a contest sharp and significant, like that at Gettysburg, was to be fought out. Governor Curtin, a strong supporter of the war, was opposed by Judge G. W. Woodward, whose loyalty was so questionable that he was reported to have said in 1861, "If the Union is to be divided, I want the line of separation run north of Pennsylvania." Strongly opposed to the draft law, he had joined with other Democratic judges on the state supreme court in pronouncing it to be unconstitutional. From his place as bench-warmer at Trenton, McClellan spoke up lustily in support of the man on the bench at Harrisburg, and wrote: "Having, some days ago, had a full conversation with Judge Woodward, I find that our views agree; and I regard his election as Governor of Pennsylvania called for by the interest of the nation." [44]

But too many Pennsylvanians had fallen on the field of Gettysburg, with thousands of comrades from New York, from Massachusetts, from Ohio, from Indiana, from far-off Minnesota, and from the other Northern states, for such talk to have much effect. The intrepid and stanch spirit of Pennsylvania-born John Reynolds, who had fallen so early in the battle, and the devotion of the men in the hospitals that had caused the young Quaker woman to write, "Kill the Copperheads," had touched deeply both the minds and the hearts of the people. They did not heed the advice of McClellan though he was a native of Philadelphia; they reelected Curtin by a good majority, and reestablished the Republicans in firm control of the government at Harrisburg.

Still more spectacular was the show and test that Ohio put on, for none other than arch Copperhead Vallandigham himself was a candidate for governor. The Buckeye state, in spite of great contributions to the war, had gone over to the opposition in the elections of 1862, having elected a Democratic secretary of state by a majority of 5,000. Now the banished Vallandigham conducted from Canada a furious campaign to win control of the state, and the many well attended meetings of Democrats seemed to indicate much enthusiasm for their eloquent leader. But when the votes were counted it was found that Ohio had given John Brough—a "war governor"—a majority of 60,000 over Vallandigham; and the figure was raised to 100,000 when the votes of the soldiers were counted.

Elsewhere throughout the country the local elections told the same general story, and Lincoln could feel that the Emancipation Proclamation, having "rounded the corner," was gaining support, while the troublesome questions of the habeas corpus and the draft had been surmounted. His direction on October 17 that 300,000 more men be drafted had apparently done him good rather than harm; and he could assume that his prompt rebuff on July 4 of Alexander H. Stephens, Vice President of the Confederacy, who had sought to come to Washington with a letter from Jefferson Davis,[45] had been widely approved in spite of the protests of the Copperheads and others who favored a negotiated peace. But, though Lincoln was too tough for many people, he was not harsh enough for the Radicals, a fact that promised difficulties in the future. He wanted no letter from the Richmond White House, even if it were written on Davis's best stationery and in his choicest hand. He wanted nothing short of the surrender of the Confederate armies in the field; but he harbored no vindictive thoughts, and he was laying no plans of vengeance or heavy punishment. Well did he know that on the problem of the reconstruction of the Southern states his views would differ greatly from those of many Republican leaders, and that he would have great difficulties to overcome if his policy were to prevail. But the problem lay in the future. The year 1863, with its great battles, its tense moments, its great decisions, and its accomplishments, was over.

Clearly there was a man of the year: U. S. Grant.

Discerning people had long seen that Grant was as resolute, as honest, as kind, and as selfless as Lincoln himself. Though he would never be able to write sentences such as the President had pronounced among the graves at Gettysburg on November 19, he had months before stirred the very discouraged people of the North with memorable sentences that have an imperishable place on the pages of our history. To a Confederate commander who had inquired about terms of capitulation Grant wrote one winter morning, after a night on a battlefield in freezing rain: "No terms except unconditional and immediate surrender can be accepted. I propose to move immediately upon your works." [46] In eight unstudied words the character of the man was revealed, and a touch of greatness haunts the sentence, "I propose to move immediately upon your works." Convincing the words also were to Grant's old friend, Brigadier General Simon Buckner, now his enemy; and presently Grant had Fort Donelson and was loading 15,000 prisoners on transports. The North had its first great victory, the South a stunning defeat in the loss of a place of much strategic value.

Lincoln had never seen Grant, but he had appraised him quickly. When the general was in public disfavor after the battle of Shiloh, and charges that he drank were being bandied about, Lincoln would pay no heed to those who clamored that he should be removed. He said simply: "I can't spare this man. He fights." [47]

After the great victory at Vicksburg on the nation's birthday, and the defeat of Bragg at Chattanooga in November, Grant's position as the outstanding Federal general was assured. In the winter of 1864, without any pressure from the President, Congress authorized the appointment of a lieutenant general, and in March Lincoln summoned Grant to Washington to elevate him to a position that none had held since Washington—for Scott was a lieutenant general only by brevet —and to make him General in Chief. Everything in the future was not to be simple and easy, for there were Lee and the Army of Northern Virginia, and Joe Johnston and his army; and there would be months of trial with heavy disappointment. But Lincoln would never again have the thought that the essential military commander was missing, after he had seen the cut of Grant's jaw, the quiet sureness of his eyes, the pervasive calmness of his manner, and the unpretentious uniform with the three-star shoulder straps.

The long search was over. Within a few weeks, Lincoln would remark, "Grant is the first General I have had."

LIEUTENANT GENERAL ULYSSES S. GRANT

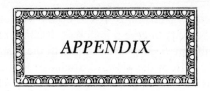

APPENDIX

I. ORGANIZATION OF THE FEDERAL FORCES

An order of the War Department dated May 4, 1861, prescribed the organization of the thirty-nine infantry regiments and the one cavalry regiment provided for by the call for three-year volunteers which was made on that date (*O.R., 122,* 151–154). The thoroughness of the document suggests that the call had been decided upon well before the day it was issued. The infantry regiments were to have minimum strength of 866 officers and men, and maximum strength of 1,046. Each regiment was to consist of ten similar companies; in addition it was to have a staff of six officers, three sergeants, a hospital steward, two principal musicians, and a band of twenty-four members. A company was to be composed of a captain, a first lieutenant, a second lieutenant, a first sergeant, four sergeants, eight corporals, two musicians, one wagoner, and sixty-four to eighty-three privates.

The regiments did not have a fixed battalion organization, and that term was used in a peculiar way, the regulations saying: "In all exercises and manoeuvres, every regiment, or part of a regiment, composed of two or more companies, will be designated as a battalion" (*U.S. Infantry Tactics,* authorized and adopted, May 1, 1861, art. 6). With one major on the regimental staff in addition to the lieutenant colonel, it was possible to handle the regiment as two battalions.

The cavalry regiment had a squadron organization, and was to consist of four to six such units, each squadron being composed of two companies. The strength of the regiment could vary from 660 to 1,168 men. No commander of field rank was assigned to a squadron, and the regiment had but one major. Horses were provided for in the simplest way—the men were to furnish them. For the "use and risk" of his animal a cavalryman was to receive fifty cents a day; if the horse became unserviceable, was killed, or died, the extra mounted pay stopped; if the trooper failed to replace an animal, he was to become a foot soldier.

Pay in volunteer organizations was to be the same as in the regular service, and the benefits in case a man was disabled or wounded were likewise to be uniform. Transportation pay to the place of muster was provided, as well as from the place of discharge to a man's home; the sum of $100 was also to be given at the time of discharge. Commissioned officers were to be appointed by the governors; but only two-thirds of those allowed to a regiment were to be appointed at the time its formation was begun. The remaining officers were to be designated when the regiment was completed, and they were to be chosen from the sergeants, upon the recommendation of the colonel, with the approval of the brigade commander.

The nine additional regiments of regular infantry (11th to 19th) that were ordered raised on May 4 were to be of a different type from the volunteer regiments. In conformity with the growing favor for a battalion organization, the regular regiments were to be composed of two or more battalions of eight companies each. Officers for the new regiments, as well as for the new regiment of regular cavalry and that of artillery, were assigned by an order of June 18 (revised Aug. 23). Most of the officers were regular officers, but a few were noted as volunteers. Each infantry regiment had the three majors proper for three battalions, but no regiment had more than eighteen captains. The roll of officers is an interesting one, for it contains names that were to become famous before the end of the war. William T. Sherman was to be colonel of the new Thirteenth Infantry, and Philip H. Sheridan was listed as one of his captains. Recruiting for the regiments was to be in the hands of the commanding officers, and a geographical region was assigned to each. Many of the regiments did not reach full strength, probably because men preferred to join volunteer organizations. At Gettysburg one of the ten regiments of Ayres's regular division had only three companies, and none had over eight (*O.R., 43,* 161). The assignments of some officers were changed quickly. Thus Sherman had a brigade at First Bull Run and Sheridan was soon colonel of a Michigan regiment. An interesting debate concerning the new regular regiments was held in the Senate the day after Bull Run (*Congressional Globe,* 37th Congress, 1st Session, pp. 220–221).

The service records of both volunteer and regular regiments are given in Dyer's monumental *Compendium.*

The order for the volunteer force specified that it would be organized into three divisions of from three to four brigades each, a brigade consisting of four regiments. A brigade staff had an adjutant, a surgeon, a quartermaster, and a commissary, in addition to an aide; but a division staff consisted only of an adjutant and two aides.

The absence of hospital facilities in the larger units is notable. Medical care seems to have been organized solely by regiments, each of which had a surgeon and a hospital steward, and was furnished three hospital tents—though this was not mentioned in the May 4 order. Delafield's Report (pp. 68–85) had emphasized the epoch-making work of Florence Nightingale for sick and wounded in the Crimean War, and had gone at length into the question of ambulances and medical treatment in European armies. An order of June 9 provided for women nurses. Those desiring appointment were to forward applications with credentials from two physicians and two clergymen of standing to Miss D. L. Dix, who was to issue accrediting certificates. The nurses would serve only in hospitals; they would not be in camps, "nor accompany regiments on the march." An order of Aug. 17 stated that "female nurses employed in permanent hospitals" would receive "forty cents per day and one ration in kind or by commutation, at the cost price."

Since volunteer regiments far in excess of the forty in the original call were being accepted, orders were issued on June 20 and 24 that all volunteer organizations should conform to the pattern laid down in the order of May 4. On Aug. 26, 1861, it was ordered that no minors be enlisted without the consent of their parents or guardians, but on Sept. 7 that no volunteers be discharged on account of minority. On Aug. 28 it was ordered that recruiting parties be sent from time to time to the home areas of their regiments for the purpose of keeping the organizations up to maximum strength. In his report for 1862 (*O.R., 123,* 904), Stanton wrote:

The advantage of filling up the old regiments is shown by many considerations. Various expedients have been adopted to accomplish that object. The official returns show that since the call for volunteers 49,990 recruits have been added to the old regiments. By the aid of some legislation it is hoped that this important object may be effectually attained.

The best possible legislation was the draft law, passed early the next year; and Phisterer writes, "Large numbers were sent as recruits to fill and strengthen old organizations already in the field" (*Statistical Record,* p. 12). Nevertheless, small regiments remained, for the error of organizing too many regiments had already been committed, and if they had all been brought to full strength more men would have been in service than was probably deemed necessary or practicable. (At Gettysburg there were no fewer than 228 regiments of infantry, not counting the twelve regular organizations.) The merging of regiments would have been logical, but after regiments had a combat record it would have been difficult, for men resist turning in their battle flags and losing an identity that they cherish.

The need of an adequate mounted arm led to the prompt abandonment of the requirement that a cavalryman furnish his own mount and horse equipment. An order of Aug. 3, 1861, provided for the equipping of volunteer cavalry on the same basis as the regular regiments; it also reduced the pay for the use and risk of a horse to forty cents a day. The procurement of animals was one of the vexing problems of the war, and on July 28, 1863, the Cavalry Bureau of the War Department was created, with "charge of the organization and equipment of the Cavalry forces of the Army, and of the provision for the mounts and remounts of the same."

Organization of the higher units varied greatly. At Gettysburg two corps had only two divisions; the other five had three divisions each. Some divisions had as few as two brigades; one had four; the number of regiments in a brigade varied from three to eight. (Attachment of reenforcing troops, such as Stannard's brigade from Washington, caused some of the unevenness.) The way in which the artillery was organized and assigned varied from time to time. At Fredericksburg divisions had from one to four batteries, and the Second Corps had two corps batteries; in addition there was extensive army artillery. At Gettysburg, however, there were no organic divisional batteries, five of the corps having artillery *brigades* of five batteries, while the Sixth Corps had a brigade of eight batteries, and the Twelfth Corps had only four. The cavalry corps had two brigades of horse artillery, one consisting of five and the other of four batteries. There was an army artillery reserve of the five brigades, four of which consisted of four batteries, while one had five. Because there were 362 guns (*O.R., 43,* 151) in sixty-seven batteries, there must have been forty-seven six-gun batteries and twenty batteries with four guns, unless there was some irregular distribution.

It was seen from the start that there would be army corps, and a War Department order of July 19, 1861, spoke of "Corps d'Armée," though nothing was said as to their composition. As noted in the text, Lincoln ordered the Army of the Potomac divided into corps in March, 1862. Pope's Army of Virginia was similarly divided into corps; but corps, like divisions within a corps and brigades within a division, had numbers relative to the army. It was not until July 17, 1862, that an act was passed legalizing army corps, and authorizing the President to form them at his discretion (Phisterer, *op. cit.,* p. 55). Five days later Lincoln announced the formation and composition of five corps, Fifth to Ninth; on Aug. 22, the First, Second, and Third Corps were designated. Other corps were subsequently created until there was a total of twenty-five infantry corps. Only one cavalry corps was formed, that of the Army of the Potomac, which came into existence April 15, 1863. The corps became the fixed large units, and only the President had power—except in an emergency—to appoint or remove their commanders. Special corps insignia were worn, resembling the division emblems of today.

II. STRENGTH RETURNS

A person accustomed to strength returns of today will be amazed at the great discrepancy in Civil War returns between the number of men reported as present and those given as present for duty. The difference would now be accounted for almost completely by the number of men sick and the number in arrest and confinement. The great discrepancy in the 1860's came largely from the fact that there were no service units such as all organizations, from a battalion up, now have. The ten wagoners of an infantry regiment were only a small fraction of the men needed for supply and administration, and other necessary men were detailed from regular combat units. Such men were carried on the morning reports of their units as on "special duty," and not as present for duty, because the duty was not with their own organization. Today the men would be in service or administrative units, and they would be accounted for as present for duty.

Although the present for duty figure as used in the Civil War eliminated most of the men engaged in supply and administration, a further effort was made to show the actual number of fighters who could be put into action, and the number present for duty equipped was given (Humphreys, *Virginia Campaign,* App. B, pp. 408–409). The returns of the Army of the Potomac for June 30, 1863, showed for the infantry corps and artillery reserve 86,703 officers and men as present for duty, and 84,158 as present for duty equipped (*O.R., 43,* 151). In general, it is impossible to divide the difference between the number present for duty and the aggregate present into its component parts, but Humphreys gave the breakdown for Apr. 30, 1864, as follows (the figures include both officers and men): on extra or daily duty, 19,095; in arrest or confinement, 931; sick, 4,576. Secretary of War Stanton conformed closely to modern practice, for in his reports, under the heading "aggregate available force for duty," he included all officers and men present, except those sick, not even excluding those in arrest or confinement.

Under the heading "effective total" the Confederates evolved a listing that would seem to be similar to what the Union army meant by "present for duty equipped," though they did it later, and the use that was made of the listing confounds one's expectation. In Aug., 1863, the return for the Army of Northern Virginia gave separately the number of men present for duty, and the effective total present (*O.R., 49,* 681). It is surprising to find that the two figures differ by only one man, and it would be interesting to know which soldier in Harry Heth's division had the unique distinction of being the one man in a total present of 71,954 (officers and men) who was regarded as available for duty, but was not considered as effective. Whatever may have been the reason, the man in question had been eliminated, or had recovered from his disability, or had regained his repute, by Oct. 31, for on that date Lee reported his effective total present, division by division, the same as the total present for duty of his enlisted men (*ibid.,* p. 811). Readers who may be surprised by that will be still more perplexed on the same page by the return of Maj. Gen. Arnold Elzey for his forces in the Department of Richmond. He gave 5,289 as the number of officers and men present for duty, while he put his effective total at the larger figure of 5,354! Perhaps he counted on 65 citizens of Richmond to show up rifle in hand on a day of trouble—like John Burns of Gettysburg fame—though they were not present to carry on the everyday chores of a soldier's life.

III. THE BREECH-LOADER QUESTION

Because of leakage of gas at the breech, the effective range of the Prussian needle gun was much less than that of good muzzle-loaders of the day; and the fact that it could be fired from the shoulder only for the early rounds was also a serious defect. It is often assumed that the needle gun was largely responsible for the prompt defeat of the Austrians by the Prussians in 1866. Foch in his well known *Principles of War* treated the opening battle at Nachod at length, and gave more stress to the German understanding of how to use superiority of fire than to better armament; he also pointed out that the Prussians won from the French in 1870 though their needle gun was inferior to the newly adopted French breech-loading chassepot (pp. 216–217). The conclusion to be drawn is obvious.

The Civil War occurred at a critical period in the evolution of both arms and cartridges, and there were many difficulties which had to be overcome. An instructive parallel is to be found in the development of the automatic rifle. Although such weapons had been produced before 1910, none had been issued as a military weapon by any power because of uncertainty of their action when, as under service conditions, grit and dirt got into the working parts (*Encyclopædia Britannica,* 11th ed., XXIII, 328). Twenty-five years elapsed before the Garand rifle was perfected and adopted by the United States Army. As to metallic cartridges, the *Encyclopædia Britannica* states that it was 1867 before solid-drawn cartridges were made from a single piece of metal (11th ed., article "Ammunition"). A document of 213 pages about the military display at the Paris Exposition of 1867, with the title *Report on the Munitions of War*, was written by Charles B. Norton and W. J. Valentine, the American commissioners. They stated that the "American" metallic cartridge was made from one piece of soft copper, and contrasted it with the British coiled Boxer cartridge; the requirements to be met by satisfactory cartridges were listed, but nothing was said as to whether the American cartridge was easy or difficult to make (pp. 1, 8–11, 13).

The question of ammunition expenditure was also causing debate at the time of the Civil War. The Delafield Report, after commenting upon the great expenditure of ammunition in the Crimean War, stated, "It is steadiness and aim at the object by the soldier that must be secured, a principle at variance with rapidity and celerity" (*Art. of War*, p. 8). A standard treatise of the day was John Gibbon's *Artillerist's Manual.* In the revised edition of 1863—after he had had distinguished service as a brigade and division commander—he wrote, "It is, then, only special corps to which this arm [breech-loader] should be supplied, and not to the main body of the army" (p. 113). Gibbon clearly was not thinking of a rifle with a good metallic cartridge, but the ammunition question also influenced him. Gen. Fuller states that the older generals in the Civil War preferred muzzle-loaders mainly on account of the ammunition problem (*Generalship of Grant*, p. 52). Gibbon, a brigadier general at thirty-five, could hardly be said to be old; Fuller's brief remark overlooks many facts in the status of military breech-loaders and metallic cartridges in the year 1861.

The cartridge boxes of the Union soldiers held only forty rounds, but it was common for commanders to require them to carry twenty additional rounds in their pockets. Ammunition was not packaged in convenient bandoleers as it is today, and the fear of undue waste was by no means mere conservatism. Bullets also were heavy, and the 100 rounds that Pope required troops to have upon going into battle, of which 60 were to be "upon their persons" (*O.R., 18,* 574), gave a load of seven pounds in metal alone.

The question of the initial armament of the Union forces depended upon weapons then on hand and those that could be bought abroad, and none of these were breech-loaders. In a report submitted on Nov. 21, 1862, the chief of ordnance, Brig. Gen. James A. Ripley, informed Stanton that up to that time 726,705 foreign muskets and rifles had been bought, while the National Armory had manufactured 109,810 rifles. From American manufacturers there had been bought 30,788 rifles, 31,210 carbines, and 86,607 pistols (probably revolvers). Before the war the combined capacity of the Springfield and Harpers Ferry armories had been only 22,000 weapons a year, but the output of the Springfield establishment alone had been raised to 200,000 rifles a year (*O.R., 128,* 852).

American ordnance men and the United States Army were not asleep; and in the year before the war George W. Morse, one of the best ordnance men in the service, had been set to work at the Harpers Ferry arsenal to change some muzzle-loaders to breech-loaders under a plan he had devised. Not only was all the machinery he had made for the work seized by the Confederates in Apr., 1861, but Morse himself "went over" to the South; and presently he built an arms plant at Greenville, S.C. (Hicks, *U. S. Ordnance*, I, 85–86; *Our Arms and Weapons*, pp. 74–75). Apparently Morse produced no breech-loaders for the South; but if he had remained with the North a feasible plan for converting might have been worked out earlier. Ripley's figures for Nov., 1862, show that only a small part of the Federal infantry could have been using breech-loaders by that time, even if a plan for converting had soon been agreed upon and if the ammunition problem could have been satisfactorily solved. For the conversion of 25,000 muzzle-loaders to breech-loaders in 1866, see Hicks, *op. cit.,* p. 91. The next year the British began to convert the Enfield rifle, selecting the plan of an American, Jacob Snyder, from 50 plans submitted. The breech-loaders adopted by Sweden, Russia, Italy, and France near the end of the sixties all used paper cartridges.

One must not draw unwarranted conclusions from the fact that the Federal cavalry had breech-loading carbines with which they often did effective work. Gen. Buford states that at Gettysburg men of one of his regiments "borrowed muskets" and fought with the infantry regiment that came to relieve it (*O.R., 43*, 927). Evidently the troopers did not scorn the muzzle-loader when it came to a hard fire fight against Lee's infantry.

It was not the breech-loader alone, but the breech-loader plus smokeless powder that completely altered infantry combat. With a breech-loader a man could load while lying down. That was a great gain, but the smoke from black powder quickly revealed his position. A rifleman today might in many circumstances prefer a good muzzle-loader firing smokeless powder to a breech-loader that gave out a revealing puff of smoke.

IV. THE CONVICTION AND EXONERATION OF PORTER

Gen. Pope did not himself prefer any charges against Gen. Porter, and although he felt deeply about Porter's action, as shown in letters to Halleck (*O.R., 18*, 816–827), his statements in his report of Sept. 3 were moderate. The actual formal charges against Porter were signed by Brig. Gen. B. S. Roberts, Pope's inspector general, and when under oath on the witness stand Pope said that he did not know, of his own knowledge, who had brought the charges (*ibid., 17*, 841). Though found not guilty of some of the specifications, Porter was found guilty of both charges against him, the most serious of which was his failure to obey the "4:30 P.M. order" that Pope had sent him (*ibid., 17,* 1051, and *16,* 511). The findings and the sentence of dismissal were approved by the President on Jan. 21, 1863 (*ibid.*, *17*, 1052).

At the time of the trial there was much doubt as to the actual enemy situation on the afternoon of Aug. 29, 1862. But when the case was reexamined in 1879—after a number of unsuccessful efforts to have it done before—the testimony of former Confederate officers left no doubt that Longstreet's divisions had arrived by noon or early afternoon and were in place generally in front of Porter. No one could have felt like punishing Porter for failure to execute an impossible order that might have led to disaster. But the board did more than recommend that the sentence be set aside, and that Porter be restored to the army. It stated that "Porter had understood and appreciated the military situation" (*ibid.*, *16*, 534). This both disregarded much clear evidence presented at the original trial, and by implication made a grave accusation against Porter. If Porter really understood the great enemy strength in his front, he should not have ordered an attack by two regiments supported by two more, but should have sent an officer of rank or gone himself to the army commander—who was not three miles away—to correct the grave misconception that his order revealed. Certainly any command and staff school would describe Porter's conduct as an example of very bad action. With regard to the note Porter sent back to Pope, which is not in the record—and an earlier note—the board stated, "But we are bound to presume that they reported the situation as Porter then knew it" (*ibid.*, p. 531). That is indeed very likely, and it may well have been the reason why Porter showed no interest whatever in the note at his trial. The fact that he did not present a copy of the note as part of his defense is full of significance, and likewise the fact that the board passed over the matter in silence. Nor did the board seek to explain why Porter said nothing whatever to Gen. Sykes about the order he had received. Is there anything more incredible than for a corps commander to spend the night in the presence of an especially able division commander and remain mute about an order which he has just received from army headquarters for the corps to attack?

With the full facts revealed about the enemy forces there is scant reason to doubt Fitz-John Porter merited exoneration of the charge of disobeying an order, as well as restoration to the army. But one may suggest that the board should have stopped short of finding the convicted general worthy of praise. Porter's counsel at the rehearing was

Joseph Choate, who went much further than the board itself. He even sought to explain away Porter's letters to Burnside, including that of Aug. 27 in which he expressed his wish to be away from Pope's army. Though Choate had never been in the army himself he did not hesitate to lecture three general officers on the criticisms that an officer may or may not make of his superiors. In a crafty manner he even asserted that Porter had stated he wanted to get away from Pope's command in order to attack Lee's communications! That apparently was too much for the generals, who made public their belief that the letter of the 27th was largely responsible for Porter's original conviction—which is very doubtful indeed—and criticized him for writing it. (The rehearing of the Porter case is given in full in Senate Executive Document No. 37, 1st Session, 46th Congress, 1879.)

The fact that the board praised Porter and asserted that he had a correct grasp of the enemy situation at the time he received Pope's order led Grant, who both as General and later as President had prevented a rehearing of the case, to change his mind. In Dec., 1882, he wrote an article "An Undeserved Stigma" in the *North American Review* (CXXXV, 536–546), to help reinstate Porter in popular esteem. It is questionable whether Grant ever carefully studied the records of the trial and was cognizant of the strong evidence against accepting the judgment of the reviewing board that Porter was well aware of the situation at the time he received Pope's ill-advised order to attack.

In forming a personal view of Porter's action on Aug. 29, 1862, it is permissible and desirable to recall his previous and subsequent record, although this was a matter of which the trial court could take no cognizance. As chief of staff for Gen. Patterson in his operations in the Shenandoah Valley in June and July, 1861, Porter must have been largely responsible for the rejection of the accurate reports given by Mr. (later Col.) Strother—who recorded the somewhat contemptuous or cavalier manner in which his reports were received by "the men of war." Patterson undoubtedly left much to Porter, in accordance with the exhortation he had received from Gen. Scott to make good use of his engineers "and other experienced staff officers" (*O.R., 1*, 670–671), and the Shenandoah operations might have been successful and Bull Run might have had a different outcome if Patterson had had a chief of staff who was more aggressive, less inclined to magnify enemy strength, and possessed of an otherwise different disposition.

At Antietam on Sept. 17 Porter had an opportunity not only to

dispel the cloud which hung over himself, but also to redeem completely the fallen estate of McClellan and make him a great hero, by
delivering a fatal blow to Lee's army. Porter commanded the reserve
by which the *coup de grâce* should have been delivered; in addition he
was held in high personal esteem by his commander and was accordingly in a position to make suggestions and give advice without hesitation. Two handsome generals stood close together that day with
tarnished reputations that could easily have been removed and replaced by great and lasting fame. All that was necessary was for one of
them to reveal the heart and courage of a bold field commander. Porter
certainly knew McClellan's plan of battle; perhaps he also knew of the
dispatch the latter had sent to the General in Chief at 1:20 P.M.
expressing his intention to attack in the center with his reserve. At
5:00 Porter wrote to Sykes, a few of whose men were engaged: "Burnside is driving the enemy. Please send word to the command you sent
to Pleasonton to support his batteries, and let him drive them" (*O.R.*,
28, 316). Pope's famous order to Porter may have been ill advised,
but at least it had meaning, while Porter wrote a sentence cluttered up
with pronouns whose antecedents are uncertain. Nouns are better for
battlefield messages, and the word "please" can usually be dispensed
with. Burnside was driving the enemy. McClellan knew it. Porter
knew it. But the best the latter could do was write a weak directive
cloaked with ambiguity. Perhaps it was about this time that McClellan
turned the inquiring glance to Porter, only to see a fateful shake of the
head. It takes a strong man to supplement himself with another who
makes up for his deficiencies; and, if the reporter wrote truly, McClellan got exactly what he wanted. He not only had his father-in-law as
chief of staff, but had as commander of his reserve a general not equal
to the great task of taking into a raging battle the last fresh troops,
with perfect confidence that the supreme moment had come and the
resolution to force the final and complete decision.

Porter's actions, both previously and subsequently, suggest that it
was habitual caution, not accurate knowledge of the enemy's strength,
that controlled his action at Second Bull Run and kept him from even
mentioning to George Sykes that he had received an order to attack.
Porter's successful fight at Hanover can be passed over, for he knew
he had an overwhelming force; McClellan would not otherwise have
ordered it. He did excellent fighting at Gaines's Mill and Malvern Hill;
but both those battles were defensive for the Federals. In the strange

letter of Aug. 31 to McClellan with the closing words "The bearer will tell you much," Porter wrote that his corps would fight "if cornered." That was exactly Porter's situation on June 27 and July 1. He was cornered: he had to fight.

V. TILLEY'S *LINCOLN TAKES COMMAND*

The book by John Shipley Tilley reveals much study of Volume I of the *Official Records* (as well as of the naval records), and is devoted entirely to the weeks and events that preceded the attack on Fort Sumter. It is very censorious of President Lincoln, Tilley evidently being one of those who—to use his own expression—view him through the large end of a telescope.

It would not have been possible to give in the introduction—entitled "The Background"—a full discussion of all the relevant events and incidents that preceded secession; but it is difficult to excuse failure even to allude to the Missouri Compromise. Tilley emphasizes the fact that the Senate in Jan., 1861, defeated the Crittenden proposal, which might have been accepted by a majority of the people. Inasmuch as he has not mentioned the Missouri Compromise—which was so hopefully regarded for a time but was repealed in 1854—it is not strange that Tilley does not raise the question whether the Crittenden proposal would really have settled anything.

Once secession had been voted by a state convention, Tilley seems to accept it wholeheartedly, if not indeed enthusiastically. After the vote of her convention, Florida was no longer one of the states in the Union (p. 11), and in his view the commanders of United States forts in Florida should have surrendered them without even waiting for instructions from Washington. Much is made of acts of such commanders that were "inflammatory" to the local citizens; but nothing is said about the effect upon people in the North of the way the authorities of the seceding states helped themselves to arms owned by the United States and stored in buildings that belonged to the United States. When, in describing the attitude in the North, Tilley (p. 32) speaks of Seward discovering a "higher law" in early 1861, he is not describing the situation accurately. Those words made the climax to Seward's first Senate speech more than ten years before (Hendrick, *Lincoln's War Cabinet,* p. 23). In a notable address in Feb., 1860, Seward completely reversed his former position; in Jan., 1861, to an audience of men and women that overflowed the Senate chamber into corridors and halls, he made a strong plea for conciliation and concession, and urged peace and union (*ibid.,* pp. 129, 130, 144). Accepting apparently in full the right of secession, Tilley makes no effort to explain any of Lincoln's acts by the fact that he considered the South as in rebellion.

Only the most casual reference was made in the text to Pensacola Harbor, where a situation resembling that at Charleston developed when Lieut. Adam J. Slemmer moved his handful of soldiers from a weak position in Fort Barrancas into strong Fort Pickens. The Florida forces were commanded by Col. William H. Chase, sixty-three years old, graduate of West Point and former officer of the United States Army. Tilley is lavish in his praise of Chase's behavior toward Slemmer, but is very critical of Slemmer. As a matter of fact, Chase was guilty of conduct reprehensible in a soldier when he tried to induce Slemmer to surrender his fort. It was not a case of military necessity, and Chase used political arguments when he wrote, "If a Southern Confederacy separates itself from the Union would it not be worse than folly to attempt the maintenance of Fort Pickens or any other fortified place within its limits?" (*O.R.,* *1*, 337–338). That question was not for Slemmer but for Washington to decide. Chase had probably often read the Article of War that specified death as a possible punishment for surrendering a fort; and it was scarcely honorable for him to attempt to lead into an error so severely punishable a young officer who wore the uniform that he had himself worn for many years. It would have been one thing for officials of Florida to trick Slemmer; it was quite another for a soldier to attempt it.

Because of the interposition of Senator Stephen R. Mallory—afterward Confederate Secretary of the Navy—an expedition with provisions and reenforcements for Fort Pickens was stopped outside the harbor by a special messenger dispatched from Washington on Jan. 29, 1861, and only the provisions were landed. The ships remained outside but Capt. Israel Vogdes was instructed to land his troops in case of an attack upon Fort Pickens. On Feb. 7 Vogdes wrote officially, "All the advantages of the present armistice are entirely on the side of the seceders" (*O.R.,* *1*, 358–359). For Slemmer he had nothing but high praise: "His resolution has probably been the means of preserving Fort Pickens from the seceders."

The armistice of which Vogdes spoke presents interesting and baffling questions, and Tilley tends to oversimplify its character (pp. 30–31). The understanding was verbal, and neither Vogdes nor any of the naval officers had been instructed to enter into an arrangement that would commit the United States for any period in the future.

The directive signed by both the Secretary of War and the Secretary of the Navy, which Tilley gives in part (p. 23), while instructing Vogdes specifically to land his troops in case of an attack or preparations for an attack upon Fort Pickens, definitely did not direct him to assure anyone that the United States government bound itself not to change his orders. One cannot believe that Vogdes did more than assure the Florida authorities that he would not land his troops unless he received orders to the contrary; nor can one believe that Chase thought that an army captain could commit his government unless he exhibited credentials of an extraordinary sort. Unquestionably the arrangement that was made grew out of the order from Washington, and just as unquestionably the Federal government appeared to give approval to it by not having it set aside at once; but Tilley argues almost as if a formal treaty, attested by seals and signatures of plenipotentiaries, set forth explicit commitments made by the United States of America.

It should also be noted that all drilling and training that the Florida troops did was a preparation for an attack on Fort Pickens. The unsuccessful effort to take the fort on Oct. 9, 1861, was by an assault; and storming columns can be and frequently are trained for their tasks at points remote from the scene of battle. Vogdes must have had this, and the deterioration of his own command from confinement on board a ship, in mind when he wrote that "all the advantages of the present armistice" lay with the "seceders."

A decision to reenforce Fort Pickens was made at the time that the final determination with regard to Sumter was arrived at, and on Apr. 1 Gen. Scott wrote an order for the land forces (*O.R., 1,* 365–366). On that very day Vogdes received an order written by Scott on Mar. 12 (*ibid.,* p. 360), directing him to land his men at the first favorable opportunity and hold Fort Pickens until further directed. (Tilley states that the reason for the order taking nineteen days to reach Pensacola was never "divulged"—as if something mysterious and sinister were involved.) When Vogdes asked Capt. Adams of the Navy to help carry out the order, the latter refused, on the ground that he had not received orders from his own superiors, and he wrote a long letter to the Secretary of the Navy asking for instructions (*Official Records of the Navy*, Ser. 1, Vol. IV, pp. 109–110; Tilley, pp. 49–50). Tilley plays the incident up with the heading, "A Captain Ignores a General's Order." That is very true—but it was a *naval* captain. Such officers habitually get orders from admirals, not from generals.

Adams wrote, "At present both sides are faithfully observing the agreement entered into by the U.S. Government with Mr. Mallory and Colonel Chase." This of course was a poor statement, for Adams had never seen anything that indicated that the "U.S. Government" had entered into any agreement whatever.

The castigation that Tilley gives Lincoln for violation of good faith is severe indeed, and he entitles a chapter "The Scrap-of-Paper Doctrine"—which is going a little far in view of the fact that there was no paper whatever with contracting signatures. But he ignores something even more significant. Not only had there been a change of administration of the United States; the Confederate government had taken over from Florida. Col. Chase was no longer the commanding officer, but Gen. Braxton Bragg, who had taken over military command at Pensacola as a representative of the Montgomery government. Here was something far different from a normal succession of administrations within a recognized state. Chase, an officer of a recognized government—the state of Florida—sought to pass on to an officer of an unrecognized government a verbal agreement which he had made; and it was natural that Lincoln did not feel himself bound by an agreement, at best rather peculiar, passed on to someone who in his mind had no credentials whatever.

More than two-thirds of *Lincoln Takes Command* deals with Fort Sumter. Lamon's visit is mentioned, and much is made of his conversation with Maj. Anderson and the ideas he left in that officer's mind; but no attention whatever is paid to the important statement made to Lamon by Governor Pickens, which Lamon reported to Lincoln. And there is not even a reference to the still more significant visit of Hurlbut, the native of Charleston, who returned to Washington and wrote the long report of his interview with James L. Petigru, the greatest jurist and most respected citizen of South Carolina. The reports of Lamon and Hurlbut must be kept in mind when considering Lincoln's decisions. Though such matters are ignored entirely, a six-page chapter "Lincoln Got What He Wanted" is devoted to the President's note of

May 1 to Capt. Fox. The effort to insinuate into the word "wanted" a particular one of its different shades of meaning, will hardly escape a reader.

It is impossible to condense into a single short sentence an adequate summary of the very complex Sumter incident, yet Tilley attempts it at the close of his introduction. After an unfavorable comment upon a paragraph from Edward Channing's history Tilley asserts (p. xxxvii) that the Confederates proceeded to bombard the fort upon the arrival of a relieving expedition off Charleston. Such a statement about Sumter can lead to ideas just as distorted or as incorrect—if not more so—than the sentences of Channing of which Tilley complained.

VI. R. M. JOHNSTON'S *BULL RUN*

A few discrete references were made in Chapter III to R. M. Johnston's *Bull Run: Its Strategy and Tactics*. It is one of the few books—if not the only one—on a campaign of the Civil War written by a professional historian who has made something of a specialty of military history. It has undoubted merits; but it contains errors and deficiencies that cause distrust.

With regard to the original call for 75,000 men, Johnston writes, "Some States refused their quotas and less than 45,000 were actually mustered in" (p. 4 n.). The only states that could be said to have refused their quotas were the four that afterward seceded, and the border states of Maryland and Kentucky. It is hardly just to say that Maine, New Hampshire, and Delaware refused to furnish the soldiers asked of them, when the men officially credited to them were respectively nine, one, and five below the numbers required. The western part of Virginia was also credited with furnishing 900 of the 2,330 asked for from the entire state (*O.R.*, *122*, 69 and n.). The number of men that the War Department gave as raised by the call, namely 91,816, is a little over twice the figure given by Johnston—he fails to mention whose count he accepted. Of the three-month men he is very critical, and one can doubt whether he understood that there was a legal reason for the short-term call. He does not note that the call for a little over 40,000 men that was made on May 3 was for three-year men. He states rather dogmatically that Lincoln's asking for 400,000 men in July "virtually admitted the uselessness of his previous measures" (p. 71). Had saving Washington and Baltimore, seizing Fort Monroe—which was never lost—and western Virginia, and recovering Harpers Ferry been useless? Actually of course Lincoln made *no* call for any men in July; and, as pointed out in the text, 208 regiments of three-year men were accepted before July 1 as a result of the call of May 3. Johnston must be considered as one of the historians unacquainted with Cameron's letter of July 1, 1861, to Lincoln, and also completely unaware of the difficulties of receiving, equipping, and caring for a large force, unless the most elaborate preparations have been previously made.

The raising of troops was not the only important incident of the first weeks of war about which Johnston has incorrect ideas. Consider his reference to the shooting in the last part of May of Col. Elmer E. Ellsworth. The twenty-four-year-old officer, known throughout the country as a master of spectacular drills, was in command of the New York Fire Zouaves, who were sent to occupy Alexandria when Federal forces crossed the Potomac on May 24. He was killed while descending the stairs in a small hotel, after he had gone to the roof to take down a Confederate flag. The man who shot him was the proprietor, who had represented himself as a roomer when Ellsworth entered. The assassin made an effort to empty the second barrel of his gun into the body of Corp. Francis E. Brownell, who was with his colonel; but the corporal was too quick, and the hotel propietor paid for his act with his life (Sandburg, *Lincoln*, I, 264). The killing of Ellsworth—which was witnessed by a reporter for the *New York Tribune*—helped inflame the North and was partly responsible for the enlistment of 208 regiments of volunteers by July 1 instead of the modest 40 called for. The young soldier's body lay in state in the White House, and this was not mere drama, for Ellsworth not only was popular in the North but was a close friend of Lincoln. Although an account of his death can be found in many places Johnston states that he was shot from a window (p. 19).

Johnston's failure to make proper distinction in military matters is shown by his reference to Samuel Cooper as adjutant general to Lee (p. 32). Cooper was adjutant and inspector general in the Confederate War Department, and was in fact the ranking four-star Confederate general. A strange error is made in the matter of cavalry organization when it is stated that there were two squadrons in a company of cavalry (p. 93 n.); the accurate figures in *O.R.*, *2*, 315 n., were accordingly incorrectly transformed. A more serious mistake occurs in the matter of armament. Johnston leaves the impression (p. 7) that all Federal troops were initially armed with the Springfield percussion rifle of caliber .58—an excellent weapon—when many of them had smoothbore muskets of caliber .69, and some had unserviceable Austrian arms. Then the error is further compounded by the assertion that the Springfield muzzle-loader was *soon* displaced by the breech-loader which the Prussian army was introducing at the time. Apparently it did not occur to Johnston that a gigantic manufacturing problem would have been involved—granted that there had been a satisfactory new weapon ready for adoption.

No book can be completely free of inconsistencies, and it is difficult for an author to avoid shifting his point of view a little. But Johnston achieves something like a record in his description of Gen. Scott's attitude toward McDowell and Patterson. He begins one paragraph with the sentence, "But however competent Scott might have been in his general views at the outset, he assumed far too readily that his subordinates were as fit to play the game of war as he was," and the next paragraph with "Scott probably felt little confidence in the abilities of his two army commanders" (pp. 68, 69).

Something of a bias against Lincoln is revealed by an incomplete quotation. Referring to Lincoln's message to Congress of July 4, 1861, Johnston writes: "The weightiest historian of the epoch has well characterized Lincoln's message when he says: 'No demagogue ever made a more crafty appeal' " (p. 71). The actual sentence that James F. Rhodes wrote was, "No demagogue ever made a more crafty appeal, and yet nothing could be further from the appeal of the demagogue." It was much to Johnston's credit that he gave the proper reference.

Referring to the way the Fourth Pennsylvania and the battery of the Eighth New York Militia marched back on July 21 from Centerville to Washington on account of the expiration of their terms of enlistment, and noting that Secretary Cameron was at McDowell's headquarters the evening before, Johnston states, "It is doubtful whether, even with a free hand, McDowell was the man to order a few deserters to be shot as an example; but with his superior present the blame cannot be laid at his door" (p. 148 n.). Indeed McDowell was not the man to give the order in question; he was too good a soldier and knew too well the Articles of War. The men in question were in no way deserters. Furthermore men are shot as deserters only after conviction and sentence of a court, followed by a careful review of the records of the trial. The return of the units to Washington while other soldiers were marching to battle is certainly not pleasant to contemplate. But throughout the war regiments left when their period of service ended, so that the occurrence of July 21, 1861, was not unique. The experience of the sixties furthermore merely repeated that of former wars. After capturing Vera Cruz and winning the battle of Cerro Gordo, Gen. Scott had to go into camp for several weeks while he waited for new regiments to replace seven he lost through expiration of term of service.

VII. THE WORK OF FRED A. SHANNON

It is difficult to write either briefly or with restraint about Shannon's very readable two-volume *Organization and Administration of the Union Army, 1851–1865*, which appeared in 1928, because it may have done much harm. Although it has probably not been read much by the general public, university and college teachers of American history, observing its extensive citations, may easily have been influenced by it, and may have formed false ideas about the competency of the administration and the army in the early stages of the Civil War.

The first section of the work is entitled "The State-Rights Principle Applied to the Army." Here at the outset is a certain distortion, for it was not a question of states' rights in raising an army, so much as the question of using existing machinery. The states all had military departments, and it was necessary to use their facilities even if it had been desired to do something else. In 1917 it would not have been possible to register men on June 5, in accordance with a draft law passed only on May 18, unless the entire operation of registration had been left to the states.

Shannon makes no reference to the very important letter from Cameron to Lincoln dated July 1, 1861, and leaves the impression that only the 42,000 men called on May 3, 1861, were raised. He quotes (I, 37) the Secretary of War as saying to a governor with regard to his quota of three-year regiments, "It is important to reduce rather than enlarge this number, and in no event to exceed it." By itself the sentence certainly seems to imply that the states were being restrained in their desire to furnish troops, and Shannon so interprets it. But it was spoken to Governor Andrew of Massachusetts (*O.R., 122*, 203), to whom six of the three-year regiments were allotted.

Massachusetts had had only 2 of the three-month regiments called in April, of which a total of 94 were raised, and a quota of 6 of the new organizations would indicate a total of something like 94 times 3, or 282, of the new long-term regiments. Actually this figure is not greatly in excess of the number of regiments Cameron evidently expected to be raised under the call of May 3, of which he stated he already had 208 on July 1. Shannon overlooks the important sentence in Lincoln's message to Congress on July 4, "One of the greatest perplexities of the Government is to avoid receiving troops faster than it can provide for them" (*O.R.*, *122*, 316). As observed before, Sir Frederick Maurice —who well understood the problems of receiving and caring for new troops—noted the significance of this statement in the important book that appeared two years before Shannon's.

Shannon states that there was no valid reason why Congress should not be called into session, speaks of unpardonable neglect in not calling an immediate session, and asserts that, if a special session had been called as quickly as the crisis demanded, authorization for 500,000 volunteers could have been secured in April instead of July; if this had been done, he says there would have been an army at Bull Run rather than an "armed mob" (I, 30, 31, 26). Reasons for not calling Congress at once have already been given; but no act of Congress could possibly have produced more troops than were in uniform by the time of Bull Run, or have had them better trained. The reference to an "armed mob" is an example of the nonsense of which Gen. Ballard—experienced in battles and military matters—complained. (Gen. Scott used the words when thoroughly exhausted, and before all the facts were in.)

A rather strong criticism of Nicolay and Hay ends with the charge (I, 50) that they did not mention the fact that New York alone wished to furnish 30,000 men for two years instead of a smaller number for three months, and that they make no reference to the hundreds of thousands of men who wished to volunteer but were refused. Actually according to *Harper's Weekly* for July 13, 1861, there were thirty-one New York regiments in and about Washington (V, 435); and all but a few of them served for at least two years (Dyer, *Compendium*, pp. 1405–1437). Thus New York certainly had her wish. As to the hundreds of thousands of volunteers that Shannon asserts were not accepted, it would be hard to give good evidence that as many as 10,000 men fit for service, who seriously desired to enlist, were denied the chance when it was possible to clothe and otherwise equip them, and take care of them properly in camps. That the period of restricted enlistment lasted only about two weeks after the call of May 3 is indicated by the fact that on May 19 Horace Greeley wrote to Lincoln expressing his great pleasure at hearing that all who were "efficient and ready" would in the future be accepted (Mearns, *Lincoln Papers*, II, 611).

A section of Shannon's work is devoted to "The Problem of Munitions." He asserts that the Prussian needle gun used a copper cartridge, and that its superiority had been well established by every known practical test (I, 118). One authority cited by him states, "The bullet was conical in shape and together with the powder was inclosed in strong paper" (*New International Encyclopædia*, 2nd ed., 1922, article "Small Arms"). The other source referred to was the article "Rifled Fire Arms," by a British writer, reprinted in *Eclectic Magazine of Foreign Literature, Science, and Art,* in Aug., 1861 (LIII, 556–561). Instead of asserting that the needle gun had passed tests convincingly, the article, after explaining both the merits and the defects of the gun, commended the British War Office for retaining the muzzle-loading Enfield rifle until "the perfection of the breech-loader." No reference whatever is made by Shannon to the statement in the important report of the Delafield Commission on the subject of breech-loaders.

Shannon gives the situation at the end of the war a bad twist by asserting that it was announced when the war was all over that a speedy plan had been devised for converting the million Springfield muskets and the half-million foreign and captured guns into breech-loaders (I, 142). The cited authority for the statement is a rather extensive report to Stanton, dated Oct. 20, 1865, from Brig. Gen. A. B. Dyer, chief of ordnance. But the report does not sustain Shannon's claim. Dyer wrote (*O.R.*, *126*, 143):

A plan for altering the muzzle-loading musket into efficient breech-loaders has been devised by the master armorer at Springfield Armory, which appears to be superior to any other that I have seen. I have taken measures to have 5,000 muskets altered according to it, and will have some of them issued to troops for trial as soon as the alterations can be made.

It was not even hinted by Dyer that the operation of conversion would be "speedy." As a matter of fact, the alteration of the muzzle-loaders to breech-loaders was very difficult, and in the following January sixty-six men were devoting all their time to preparations for altering, not 1,000,000 rifles, but only 5,000 (Laidley to Dyer, in Hicks, *Notes on U.S. Ordnance*, I, 90–91). As to the foreign arms, Dyer specifically recommended that they be sold "whenever suitable prices can be obtained for them."

The claim that the alteration of rifles that was ordered in 1865 could have been begun in 1861 has been referred to in the text. It was naïve, and comment is not necessary; but the master armorer at the Springfield arsenal and Gen. Dyer could have made some very interesting remarks.

Just as Shannon, in his criticism of troop raising in 1861, failed to set the actual and remarkable figures for that year side by side with those for 1917, and failed to warn his reader that a rifle highly satisfactory for a hunter or sportsman may be totally unsuitable for a military arm (as noted in the text, p. 119), so he did not say that Dyer specifically told Stanton that the first converted arms would receive service tests. The hard service received by a military rifle and the high degree of dependability that it must possess, are things that no responsible ordnance officer dare forget for one moment. If Shannon had had due regard for such things, some of his statements would have been omitted. Nor does it seem that he realized that before copper cartridges could be adopted for all the weapons in an army they must be capable of manufacture not only with accurate dimensions, but in quantity. (A distorted view about the needle gun was probably responsible for his statement on p. 131 of Vol. I that in Prussia the copper cartridge was already an old favorite.) Shannon's treatment soon conditions his reader for surprises, but hardly for the seeming belief that in the muzzle-loader powder and ball were rammed down the barrel at the same time (I, 113), and ignorance that the soldier had to bite the cartridge, tear it open, empty the powder into the barrel, and afterward insert the ball (*U.S. Infantry Tactics*, p. 32).

With obvious disapproval Shannon notes the War Department's scant enthusiasm for the first Gatling guns that were made in 1862, of which it bought a few (I, 147). The new weapon was mounted on wheels, had little if any offensive value, and made an inviting target for enemy artillery. Napoleon III became enthusiastic about a similar weapon, and to his regret substituted it for some traditional artillery. His new guns quickly revealed their positions by their smoke, and in the War of 1870 the Germans knocked them out with gunfire, and then advanced their infantry (Hicks, *Our Arms and Weapons*, p. 186). The Gatling gun became quite a different weapon after it was improved and smokeless powder was invented.

A long list could be made of topics properly belonging to army organization and administration that Shannon does not mention, although he includes such subjects as "The Slacker Problem," and the "Conscientious Objector." In fact, an appendix of six pages entitled "Army Organization" contains about all that there is that really comes under the title of the work. It is very incomplete and inadequate, failing to note, for instance, any changes or evolution that took place in the course of the war. Neither in the footnotes nor in the Bibliography is there so much as a reference to Army Regulations, to which, with a file of War Department General Orders for the period of the war, anyone with military experience would first turn if he wished to write about the organization and administration of the Union army. A good work with the title of Shannon's two volumes is a desideratum; but it could be written only by a person with much military knowledge and experience.

VIII. THE BOOK OF GENERAL GORDON

A very detailed and highly disparaging account of Pope's campaign, written by Maj. Gen. George H. Gordon, bears the title *A History of the Campaign of the Army of Virginia*. Gordon was a graduate of West Point, 1846, had extensive service in the Mexican War, resigned his commission in 1854, and entered the practice of law in Boston. He helped raise the Second Massachusetts, of which he became colonel, and commanded the Third Brigade of the First Division of Banks's corps at Cedar Mountain. Gordon's report of that action, in *O.R.*, *16*, 807–808, contains a gratuitous and ambiguous animadversion against McDowell, whom it incorrectly describes as commanding a division instead of a corps.

Even the first sentence of Gordon's book raises a debate, for he speaks of Jackson's turning "from his victorious battlefield of Cedar Mountain." Such a positive assertion about a battle whose outcome is hard to assess fairly, indicates the strong and uncompromising positions that he took, and his complete rejection of facts that contradicted his views. *The Dictionary of American Biography* states that the strong opinions and criticisms that hindered Gordon's promotion in the army are evident in his writings.

Gordon's work was an attack on Stanton and Halleck, and a defense—or glorification—of McClellan, as well as an indictment of Pope. Though it appeared before the *Official Records* were published, many reports had been printed, and he had access to War Department material. Accordingly it requires a little analysis, to show its general flavor and character.

The book asserts—without any evidence whatever—that Pope had no idea what order to issue on the morning of Aug. 27, 1862, and that McDowell suggested what should be done (p. 166). The whole charge is unimportant—and it is strange a soldier should make it. The sole question is: What order did Pope issue, and was it good?

Gordon makes much of the fact that Franklin reached Centerville at 5:00 P.M. on Aug. 30—as if he could have had some influence on the battle (pp. 419–420). Of McClellan's detaining him at Annandale, Gordon writes, "If Halleck considered that Franklin ought to move beyond Annandale, he should have so telegraphed McClellan, for he knew that McClellan believed that Franklin ought not to move beyond Annandale" (p. 439). It is true that Halleck's peremptory order of the evening of Aug. 28, that Franklin should go ready or unready, spoke only of moving "towards Manassas." But the General in Chief's purpose was perfectly clear—and also the first sentence of Army Regulations. What McClellan thought had no more to do with the question than what the man in the moon thought. He had received an order from his superior. Gordon's position is a strange one for a soldier.

Gordon defends Sumner at length against charges of marching slowly to Centerville (pp. 419–420). This is not the point at issue, and in 467 pages of text Gordon gives no space to Sumner's testimony before the Committee on the Conduct of the War that he could have marched two days earlier and have been in the battle, if he had not been held needlessly at Alexandria.

Gordon criticizes severely Pope's dispatch to Halleck from Centerville on Sept. 1, at 8:50 A.M. He sneers at even the first sentences, which are: "All was quiet yesterday and so far this morning. My men are resting; they need it much. Forage for our horses is being brought up." This dispatch, in which Pope first reported what he thought was disaffection in many officers of the Army of the Potomac, seems to the present writer to be highly creditable to him. But Gordon's indictment of it begins (p. 434): "This composition, so plainly acknowledging the incompetency of John Pope, and so plainly attempting to shift responsibility for that incompetency, was shown to the President of the United States. Abraham Lincoln feared that these accusations against Porter, and the baser insinuations against McClellan, as the fountain source of insubordination . . . might not be wholly false. . . . Pope's letter of accusation had been potent of evil. The President was prejudiced against Porter; and this prejudice was manifest in his approval of the findings and sentence of that court-martial before which General Porter was arraigned for those grave offenses which were set forth in Pope's letter. But the attempt to poison his mind against McClellan failed. Abraham Lincoln believed in General McClellan's patriotism and in his ability."

Is Gordon unaware of the grave charge he is making against Lincoln in asserting that it was Pope's letter and not the record of the trial and the summary by the judge advocate general that caused him to approve the findings and sentence of the court? John Hay's statement in his diary that Lincoln had remarked to him that McClellan wanted Pope to fail does not agree with Gordon's unsupported statement.

Although Gordon declares that Pope's letter influenced Lincoln against Porter, he maintains that Porter's letters to Burnside did not influence him: "The President expressed much gratification that through this source he could learn something" (p. 327). This amazing assertion is in no way supported. Although Gordon mentions some of Porter's criticisms of Pope—which he finds just—he does not quote Porter's statement that he wanted to be away from the approaching battle, or that much of the letter was private.

Gordon refers to "McClellan's impressive and moving appeal of the 30th, to be permitted to go with his troops into action," and criticizes Halleck for not alluding to it in the second of two telegrams (p. 428). But, though he writes with much detail, he fails to note that McClellan was essentially as much in the battle near Centerville as he had been in the battles of the Peninsular Campaign.

Gordon's attitude toward Stanton and Halleck is revealed by his reference to "the evil counsels and mischievous interference of his [Lincoln's] war secretary, Stanton, and his war secretary's abettor, Halleck" (p. 436). As already noted, Stanton gave no orders at all during the campaign, and Halleck was merely carrying out the duties of his office.

Though Gordon takes 467 pages to tell how very bad Pope was, he does not know who Pope's chief of staff was! He states that Gen. Roberts held that position (p. 99 n.). Throughout the campaign Col. George D. Ruggles was chief of staff; Roberts was at first chief of cavalry, and then inspector general.

It is hard to say how much influence Gordon's book has had. Ropes's very judicial *The Army Under Pope* acknowledges general indebtedness to it; but no influence is discernible, and the generous and warm appreciation of Pope with which Ropes concludes his study bears no resemblance to Gordon's climactic sentence (p. 462): "Whipped in detail should be Pope's epitaph." Freeman refers to Gordon without any word of caution and makes no mention of the more balanced book of Ropes; his general remarks appear to be built upon Gordon's work rather than upon a careful study and appraisal of Pope's dispatches to Halleck (see *Lee's Lieutenants*, II, 135–136, including n. 59).

Much hard work went into Gordon's book, and the battle detail may be accurate. But it is difficult to understand how a trained soldier —such Gordon was—could be so mercilessly and scornfully critical of Pope's tactical errors and mistakes of judgment, and accept McClellan's battle of Antietam (p. 436). Col. Strother recorded in his diary that on Sept. 15, 1862, Gordon rode up to him and spoke of the "glorious" accomplishment the day before at South Mountain. "Yes; a good beginning, but I am waiting for the end," Strother answered "coldly" (*Harper's Monthly*, XXXVI, 280—Feb., 1868). Inordinate personal attachment suggests itself and appears to be confirmed by the fact that Gordon speaks of "officers who adored General McClellan" (p. 419). Adoration is a strong attachment for soldiers to proclaim for each other, and it hardly indicates a calm, judicial, and objective attitude when the achievements of the "adored" are being compared with those of a disliked rival. Perhaps much can be explained by the simple fact that McClellan and Gordon were classmates at West Point.

IX. A MISCELLANY OF RECENT BOOKS

Attacks on Lincoln's War Secretary extend all the way from those that are mild to those that are virulent. An instance of recent relatively temperate criticism is that of George Fort Milton, who writes: "Stanton was not over-loyal to Lincoln. Again and again he would receive the most express direction of the President either to ignore it or to act exactly contrary to the course the Chief Executive had ordered him to take" (*Conflict,* p. 110). This assertion ignores completely the detailed analysis by Nicolay and Hay of the relations of the two men, both of whom they knew and observed constantly and closely. They state that for three years Stanton rendered Lincoln "steady personal service and devotion" (*Lincoln,* V, 138), and add: "His advice was always intelligent, consistent, and steady; his decisions were rapid and generally judicious and permanent. . . . As natural with two strong minds, they sometimes differed in their estimates of men or advisability of measures, but never in principle or object" (*ibid.,* p. 139). On the specific point that Milton raises, they write: "The anecdotes of his occasional blunt disregard of the President's expressed wishes are either untrue or are half-truths that lead to erroneous conclusions, and originated probably in a certain roughness of Stanton's manner under strong irritation" (*ibid.,* p. 142). The cross-purposes at which the President and Secretary of War found themselves were, according to the men who saw them most frequently, over "some minor and relatively unimportant matter" (*ibid.,* p. 142). Nicolay and Hay state, furthermore, the belief that the authentic cases of neglect by Stanton of a written direction were rare; and in the instance that they set forth at length, Stanton was right and Lincoln was wrong, as the latter admitted (*ibid.,* pp. 143, 145–147). Unfortunately Lincoln had made a hasty decision and an unwise commitment; but, because he believed that less harm would result from carrying it out than from breaking the engagement, he compelled Stanton to go through with it in spite of his clear statement that the order was an improper one that he could not issue. For the War Secretary's stern resistance in this case Lincoln showed no trace of ill feeling. One can indeed believe from his writing to Grant, "The Secretary of War is wholly free of any part in this blunder," that he admired Stanton for his fight. When men can deal with each other on such a plane it is unfortunate that there should be the distortion which is contained in Milton's sentence.

Implicit in what Milton writes about Stanton is a severe attack against Lincoln, who must have been a weak man if, with his knowledge, Stanton repeatedly acted contrary to his wishes, and an incompetent and undiscerning man if for three years Stanton "again and again" successfully practiced deception upon him. It would seem that Milton is unaware that he is in severe conflict with himself, for he asserts that

Lincoln was a man of force who usually asserted himself effectively (*ibid.*, p. 124); and he makes direct attacks upon Lincoln that are difficult, if not impossible, to reconcile with tributes on other pages. It is asserted that Lincoln "undertook to tie McClellan's hands by naming, without consultation, the four corps commanders for McClellan's army, three of them antagonistic to that General" (*ibid.*, p. 120). It would of course have been little short of treason for Lincoln to seek deliberately to hamper the commander of his principal field army in the broad way Milton has charged. But one need not go into the difficult question of motives, for one can keep to facts that Milton ignores. For months Lincoln had tried to get McClellan to appoint corps commanders; but he was as unsuccessful in this effort as he was in getting him to undertake military operations; thus he himself took the step that he knew was imperative (Nicolay and Hay, *Lincoln*, V, 169–170). After the battle of Williamsburg, McClellan asked to have the army divided into five corps instead of three (the First Corps was still at Fredericksburg) with Franklin and Porter as the new commanders. His request was immediately granted, though it is questionable whether the men McClellan chose were better than McDowell, Sumner, Heintzelman, and Keyes.

In asserting that Lincoln "probably had a hand" in the appointment of Pinkerton (*Conflict*, p. 114), Milton overlooks the fact that McClellan's official report took credit for the appointment (*O.R.*, 5, 51–52). That the general had spoken of having some new ideas on the subject of "intelligence" while he was in West Virginia has already been pointed out.

Milton's book is by no means an out-and-out McClellan defense. After listing Lee, Stanton, and Lincoln as obstacles, he writes: "But greater in importance than these three human and ponderable antagonists was an internal foe: McClellan's own inner infirmities were chiefly responsible for his failure" (*op. cit.*, p. 113). It would be difficult to write a more devastating bill of particulars against McClellan than Milton writes on p. 115. Yet in spite of that he states that if McClellan had had "a more cooperative President" he probably "could have brought the war to a close in the summer of 1862" (*ibid.*, p. 112). Still more positively he asserts that if Lincoln had "cordially and believingly sustained McClellan, probably the Civil War would have ended in 1862" (*ibid.*, p. 118). This pronouncement occurs only three pages after attention is called to McClellan's failure to throw in his reserves at Antietam as well as his falure to "attack the bleeding Lee that second day."

While the title *Conflict* is appropriate for a work wherein statements contend with one another in such a bewildering manner, it is not clear what authorities Milton used. In his Bibliography he refers to the *Official Records*, even commending them to the general reader. Yet it is hard to believe he used them accurately, for in one place (p. 309) he asserts that the set contains over 700 volumes and in another (p. 402) he puts down the number as 780. As a matter of fact, with deduction for the two books which were not published, but for which numbers were reserved, there are only 128 volumes in the set, including the index. Imposing though that number is, it is less than one-sixth of Milton's larger number. Among the works recommended for the reader the highly competent works of Michie and Generals Maurice, Ballard, and Fuller are absent—three of these especially significant because they come from distinguished participants in World War I. Freeman's *Lee* is commended; but it gives no support for Milton's assertion (p. 271) that at Gettysburg on July 1, 1863—presumably in the evening—Lee ordered Longstreet to attack the next morning at five o'clock. In fact, Freeman (III, 84, n. 53) carefully examines the question and gives the scanty basis for such a claim and the weighty testimony against it. In comparison with his position on the vital question of Lee's orders for the "Second Day," Milton's errors (pp. 266, 268, 269) in the date on which Meade relieved Hooker, the date on which Longstreet's scout Harrison reported to Lee, and the time of day when Reynolds was killed seem in some ways unimportant. Yet to put Meade in command of the army two days before the correct date, to have Lee receive news about the change of Federal commanders one day after he actually did, and to have Reynolds killed after the fighting of July 1 was over, instead of at the very beginning of the infantry action, may influence the views of the reader.

At the head of his Bibliography Milton speaks to the reader of books that "help the understanding of a war still half-hid in a fog of doubt and might-have-been." It is true that there are questions upon which uncertainty remains; but the war suffers mainly from distortions and inaccuracies where statements can be made that have high probability of precision, if indeed the facts are not beyond question.

In T. Harry Williams's *Lincoln and the Radicals* the name of Stanton occurs frequently. For the work of the radicals and of the

Committee on the Conduct of the War the present writer has no great sympathy. But it must be noted that the committee reports have much value. The testimony that officers gave may at times be open to question; but the reports contain many messages and orders which were written at the time and are beyond dispute; and they were an especially important public source for information before the publication of the Official Records.

Williams's point of view toward Stanton and his carelessness about facts are illustrated by his treatment of the trial of Gen. Porter (p. 224): "In mid-January the radical ax finally came down upon Fitz-John Porter. Pope's wild accusation after Manassas promoted [prompted?] Stanton to arrest Porter and bring him to trial before a court martial, which got under way in November. The secretary packed the court to make sure of a conviction."

It has already been noted that Pope filed no charges whatever against Porter. Furthermore, it was Halleck, not Stanton, who appointed the court and referred the charges for trial (*O.R., 17, 821*). Concerning all the officers except Maj. Gen. David Hunter, who was the president of the court, Williams makes a derogatory remark, sometimes rather irrelevant to the issue. The immaterial claim that Gen. B. M. Prentiss was captured at Shiloh because of surprise was denounced by Grant—who told what happened—as "without any foundation whatever" (*Memoirs,* I, 340). Williams also makes the error of naming N. B. Buford as Pope's chief of cavalry. As a matter of fact his cousin, John Buford, commanded a cavalry brigade under Pope. Napoleon Bonaparte Buford, a Western officer, happened to be in Washington convalescing; and he was put on the court because his service would not take him away from other duty. (Gen. Hunter also happened to be in Washington on leave.) Williams asserts that Ricketts was a personal enemy of Porter but fails to note that the accused general was asked if he objected to being tried by any member of the court; he replied that he did not (*O.R., 17, 824*). The Articles of War gave Porter the right to challenge any member of the court, a fact entirely overlooked by the author of *Lincoln and the Radicals,* who perhaps does not see the significance of the passage in the trial record, "The court was then duly sworn by the judge-advocate, and the judge-advocate was sworn by the president, in the presence of the accused." Porter saw the officers take their oaths, and the officers saw before them the man that they had to try.

Everyone who has felt the solemn responsibility of serving on a court-martial and is aware of the careful procedure, even in the matter of voting, has a right to resent the cavalier manner in which Williams impugns the integrity of the court that tried Porter, and his irresponsible charge that Stanton packed the court. He gives no indication that he has ever examined the 323-page record of the trial to see whether the sentence was sustained by the evidence; nor that he is aware of the fact that Porter's exoneration was based largely upon new evidence given by former Confederate officers which could not possibly have been presented in the original trial.

Otto Eisenschiml's *Why Was Lincoln Murdered?* is one of the most extreme of anti-Stanton books. Hendrick writes of its author, in *Lincoln's War Cabinet* (p. 237), that he "even suggests—without making the deliberate charge—that Stanton may have had a hand in the plot which ultimately culminated in Lincoln's assassination." With much restraint Hendrick describes the book as a "volume of grotesque depreciation." With the main contentions, inferences, and insinuations of Eisenschiml's book, the present work has no concern; but some comment is called for by a chapter that carries such a title as "Not Wanted—Victory in the East." (There is a chapter that makes the same strong claim with regard to the West.)

Eisenschiml states (p. 319), "The President apparently cared nothing about topographical obstacles, preferred frontal attacks where flank movements would answer the purpose and, in general, displayed a painful ignorance of all strategical principles." Reference is to Lincoln's preferring an operation toward Manassas to the Peninsula advance; and we have here a case of the common assumption by McClellan protagonists that it would not have been possible to turn the defenses of Manassas, and that nothing could have been done except attack the intrenchments. Though the intrenchments were extensive—lengthened somewhat by the use of wooden guns—there still was ample room for maneuver. And what should one say about the topography of the Peninsula, with its great swamps and its poor roads—where McClellan took his army? With the swampy Chickahominy interposing between the wings of his army, was he on favorable terrain, and did he execute any flank move or try to turn anything, and was he not preparing for siege operations? Although the very page from which the quotation above is taken contains a sentence from Ballard, Eisenschiml does not quote the judgment passed by that general—who knew something about military matters—upon the remarkable letter Lincoln wrote to McClellan on April 9, 1862, just after the methodical advance on Yorktown had commenced. Already quoted once, Ballard's remark is worthy of repetition, "The unexperienced lawyer summed up in three lines the situation which the professional soldier was constitutionally incapable of realizing" (*Military Genius of Lincoln*, p. 112).

Confident of Lincoln's "painful ignorance of all strategical principles," Eisenschiml calmly ignores the contrary judgment of some distinguished soldiers, including Generals Sherman, W. F. Smith, and James H. Wilson. Nicolay and Hay, after giving the views of the generals, add that Col. Robert N. Scott, the very able officer who brought out the first volumes of the *Official Records,* "frequently called Mr. Lincoln 'the ablest strategist of the war' " (*Lincoln,* X, 353–354).

Lincoln's actions actually receive a distorting twist from Einsenschiml: "He never was guilty of impressing his views on his generals in later years." What views had Lincoln *impressed* on McClellan? In the letter that he wrote to McClellan in Feb., 1862, asking specific questions with regard to the advantages of the general's proposal, he definitely stated that if the questions were satisfactorily answered he would consent to the scheme. A satisfactory answer Lincoln certainly did not receive; nevertheless he instructed McClellan to go ahead with his plan. Eisenschiml quotes Lincoln's well known statement to Grant in May, 1864, "The particulars of your plans I neither know nor seek to know." Though it would seem that language could not be plainer, the author of *Why Was Lincoln Murdered?* writes as if Lincoln had said that he did not care to know Grant's *plans*. The statement shows plainly that he was well informed of Grant's plans; and it was only McClellan's *plans* that he had ever wanted to know—not "particulars" about them.

Totally ignoring the judgment of the soldier Michie—who like Ballard was a competent critic—as to where responsibility lay for the indecisiveness of the battle of Antietam, Eisenschiml (p. 329) puts the blame on Burnside: "If Burnside had done what was expected of him on that fateful seventeenth of September, Lee's star would have set that night, and the cause for which he fought so valiantly would have received its *coup de grâce*." Nothing is said about the all-important question as to when orders to attack were sent to Burnside, or about McClellan's inexplicable failure to assist the attack on the left by advancing his reserve against Lee's center—in accordance with his own plan of battle. Eisenschiml indicts Burnside for not himself crossing the bridge during the battle, but does not note that Cox commanded the Ninth Corps in the attack, and Burnside was a supernumerary—because of McClellan's strange handling of command arrangements.

Eisenschiml may be unaware of the efforts that Stanton made on the night of September 17–18 to get ammunition through to McClellan, although his army was not in short supply. Having put responsibility for failure of complete victory on the 17th upon Burnside, Eisenschiml remains silent as to the 18th, for there is not the least chance to place responsibility for doing nothing on that day on anyone except McClellan. There is something actually ludicrous in the charge that Stanton did not want the war to end, on account of his radicalism. It was McClellan the *conservative* that had the chance to deal the fatal blow on September 17 and 18, before the appearance of the Proclamation of Emancipation. Because that act, not formally issued until the first of the following year, was specifically announced as a military measure, one can doubt if it would have appeared if McClellan had destroyed Lee in his position between Antietam Creek and the Potomac River.

As evidence that Lee's escape after Gettysburg was desired in Washington, Eisenschiml cites (p. 344) dispatches Halleck sent when he weakened on July 9 (*supra,* p. 747). Intrigues in the War Department while Lincoln slept at the Soldiers' Home—not Meade's telegrams—are tendered as the reason for Halleck's change in attitude. Why seek a strained and ugly explanation when there is at hand one as simple and adequate as that which Meade gave to his wife (Meade, *Letters,* II, 133), "The firm stand I took had the result to induce General Halleck to tell me to act accourding to my judgment."?

NOTES

NOTES TO CHAPTER XIV

1. Blackford, *War Years with Stuart,* p. 145.

2. It is sometimes stated that the cavalry was under the command of Col. B. F. Davis, 8th New York Cavalry; but Wool to Halleck, Sept 15, *O.R., 27,* 758–759, gives the report of the operation as made by Voss.

3. *Ibid., 28,* 305, 306. Curtin's dispatch acknowledged "your glorious message" about the battle of South Mountain and named Davis as the cavalry commander from Harpers Ferry, saying, "They cut their way through last night, and report that Colonel Miles would be obliged to surrender this morning, unless Jackson leaves to re-enforce Lee as against your army." He also forwarded to Stanton a message he had received from Greencastle about arrival of the cavalry.

4. Strother, "Personal Recollections," *Harper's Monthly,* XXXVI, 280 (Feb., 1868). The information about the destruction of Longstreet's wagons was also received.

5. *O.R., 27,* 549–799. The report stated that Col. Ford should never have been put in command on Maryland Heights, and that he had "shown throughout such a lack of military capacity as to disqualify him, in the estimation of this Commission, for a command in the service." Nevertheless Miles was severely blamed for not carrying out some of Ford's requests. The commission stated, "This leaving the key of the position to the keeping of Colonel Ford, with discretionary power, after the arrival of the capable and courageous officer [General White] who had waived his rank to serve wherever ordered, is one of the more striking facts illustrating the utter incapacity of Colonel Miles" (p. 799).

6. Freeman, *Lee,* II, 381. Authority is not given, but the number probably can be accepted.

7. Palfrey, *Antietam and Fredericksburg,* p. 56.

8. *O.R., 27,* 54.

9. *Ibid., 28,* 310.

10. Strother, *op. cit.,* p. 280. Palfrey, *loc. cit.,* wrote, "It was a day of idleness throughout, for a large part of the army."

11. *O.R., 27,* 55. A formal order for the organization of the army into "wings" and a "center" seems to be lacking, and the division of the army into two "wings" and a "center" used in the march from Washington had apparently been given up on the 15th. On Sept. 10 Burnside, in the role of a wing commander, gave an order to Hooker; Reno also signed himself as commanding the Ninth Corps, which had been Burnside's command. On the 14th a formal order put Burnside in command of the "right wing," but nothing was said about a left wing or a center (*ibid., 28,* 240, 290). On Sept. 15 the order was suspended, and Hooker was directed to report directly to army headquarters. In *O.R., 27,* 169–180, the organization of the Army of the Potomac for Sept. 14–17 is shown, but nothing is indicated of wings and a center. Palfrey, however, gave such a division and stated that it had been furnished to him by the adjutant general of the army (*op. cit.,* Appendix A).

Since McClellan's order of the 15th did not specifically state that Burnside would revert to the command of the Ninth Corps, there was some confusion. Gen. Cox wrote in "The Battle of Antietam," *B. and L.,* II, 631: "I urged Burnside to assume the immediate command of the corps and allow me to lead only my own division. He objected that as he had been announced as commander of the right wing of the army (his own and Hooker's), he was unwilling to waive his precedence or to assume that Hooker was detached for anything more than a temporary purpose." Cox's article is a good account of the battle.

12. Ruggles (aide-de-camp) to Sumner, *O.R., 107,* 839; Franklin's report, *ibid., 27,* 376; Ruggles to Franklin, *ibid., 107,* 839–840.

13. Henderson, *Stonewall Jackson,* p. 527.

14. Report of Gen. Williams, who succeeded to the command of the corps, *O.R., 27,* 474–478. This report is used in the account of the battle.

15. The 5th, 7th, and 66th Ohio, 3rd Maryland, 11th Pennsylvania, and 78th and 102nd New York.

16. Michie, *General McClellan,* p. 421.

17. Freeman, *Lee's Lieutenants,* II, 213; Alexander, *Military Memoirs,* p. 213.

18. Michie, *op. cit.,* p. 422.

19. Franklin's report, *O.R., 27,* 376–378.

20. Palfrey, *op. cit.,* p. 122.

21. *O.R., 27,* 63, 31.

22. *Ibid.,* p. 424. Cox's article in *B. and L.,* II, 630–660, gives a detailed account of the attack by the Ninth Corps.

23. *O.R., 27,* 424, 410, 63, 31. It is significant that McClellan could not give a copy of the order that showed the hour.

24. A good account of the defense is given by Freeman, *op. cit.* (chap. xiii, "Desperate Hours on the Antietam").

25. Cox, "The Battle of Antietam," *B. and L.,* II, 655.

26. Palfrey, *op. cit.,* p. 122.

27. *O.R., 28,* 315.

28. *N.Y. Tribune,* Sept. 20, 1862. The dispatch covers essentially the whole of p. 5.

29. Freeman examines some of the stories (*Lee,* II, 404 n.). His own version states that there was nothing theatrical in the meeting.

30. Strother stated also: "Some time between midnight and morning, being awakened by the going and coming of messengers to the General's tent, I heard McClellan's voice charging some officer with the following message: 'They are to hold the ground they occupy, but are not to attack without further orders' " (*op. cit.,* p. 285).

31. Livermore, *Numbers and Losses,* pp. 92–93. For breakdown of Union casualties see *O.R., 27,* 200.

32. *B. and L.,* II, 630. Mitchell was in a hospital eight months and died three years after discharge.

33. *O.R., 28,* 312.

34. *Ibid.* A duplicate, with the instructions by the chief of ordnance, is given *ibid., 107,* 842, and it carries the indorsement of the ordnance office, "Attended to at once, September 17—11 P.M."

35. *Ibid., 28,* 313–314, 327. For additional dispatches, see *ibid., 107,* 845–847.

36. Ripley (chief of ordnance) to McClellan, *ibid., 28,* 323.

37. *Ibid., 27,* 368–372, and *107,* 843–844.

38. *Ibid., 27,* 374.

39. *Ibid., 28,* 322.

40. Palfrey, *op. cit.,* p. 127.

41. Strother, *op. cit.,* p. 287.

42. Porter's report, *O.R., 27,* 340.

43. *Ibid.,* p. 68.

44. Henderson, *op. cit.,* p. 546; Freeman, *Lee,* II, 407.

45. There has been some tendency in Lee's biographers not to face the question squarely. Gen. Maurice is critical (Marshall, *An Aide-de-Camp to Lee,* p. 162 n., and *Lee,* p. 154).

46. Freeman, *Lee's Lieutenants,* II, 236–237, 154 n.

47. Letter of Oct. 10, *O.R., 18,* 820–821. "I am well aware of the hostility of some of the parties you mention as being my enemies as well as yours." Halleck went on to say that his official attitude would not be changed by such personal considerations. "If they want my place they will be perfectly welcome to it whenever the Government desires to make the change. I never wished the appointment, and have no desire to retain it."

48. *Ibid., 28,* 288, 289, 303.

49. Return of Sept. 20, *ibid.,* pp. 336, 337. The number included the Third and Eleventh Corps. Wool's Eighth Corps, divided into various garrisons, amounted to about 18,000 men.

50. *Ibid., 27,* 68.

51. *Ibid., 28,* 360.

52. McClellan, *Own Story,* p. 612; Michie, *op. cit.,* pp. 428–429.

53. McClellan, *op. cit.,* p. 613.

54. *O.R., 28,* 336, 376.

55. McClellan, *op. cit.,* p. 627.

56. *O.R.*, *27*, 13–14.

57. *N.Y. Tribune*, Sept. 29.

58. *O.R.*, *28*, 255, 272.

59. Stanton to Meigs, Oct. 25, *ibid.*, *27*, 21.

60. Oct. 26, *ibid.*, *28*, 491–493. Ingalls stated: "My orders for supplies have far exceeded any requisitions on me. . . . It has been my pride to know the fact that no army was ever more perfectly supplied than this has been, as a general rule." Much on the subject of clothing will be found in Halleck's report, *ibid.*, *27*, 4–24, and an abstract of shipments in *ibid.*, *28*, 487–88.

61. *Ibid.*, pp. 476–478.

62. *Ibid.*, pp. 492–493.

63. *Ibid.*, *28*, 451–452, and Ingalls's report, *ibid.*, *27*, 94–96. Ingalls said, "There was great delay in receiving our clothing. . . . For instance, clothing ordered to Hagerstown on the 7th of October for the corps of Franklin, Porter, and Reynolds, did not arrive there until about the 18th, and by that time, of course, there were increased wants and changes in position of troops." No figures were given—nothing, for instance, that shows how many men could not do duty on account of lack of shoes. There is no way to tell how many of McClellan's men could not have marched by, say, Oct. 5. He probably never had what could be called a reliable report of the actual condition and need of his troops made by careful inspectors.

64. Haupt, *Reminiscences*, pp. 139–143.

65. *O.R.*, *28*, 396, 403. McClellan began, "What arrangements are in progress in regard to supplying the army with hospital tents?" He did not tell how many such tents were in the army, or were stored with its excess baggage in Washington. Meigs's reply stated: "Each regiment, as raised, is supplied with its allowance of three hospital tents. Provision is made to keep up this supply, with a reasonable surplus." About 1,000 tents were in use in hospital camps in the District of Columbia.

McClellan's inquiry of Meigs was an irregular procedure. If he had a deficiency in the number allowed, Ingalls should have taken the matter up. If—as would seem to have been the case—he wanted something far beyond what was contemplated, he should have taken up the matter with Halleck.

66. *Ibid.*, *27*, 72, and *28*, 403.

67. *Ibid.*, *27*, 97, 15.

68. *Ibid.*, *28*, 416, 422–424.

69. McClellan to Halleck, Oct. 12, *ibid.*, *27*, 13. The figure 150 occurs in numerous communications on the subject.

70. *Ibid.*, *28*, 480. Probably it is impossible to straighten out the matter accurately, but see Meigs to Halleck, Oct. 21, *ibid.*, *27*, 17–20. McClellan's report went into the horse question at length, *ibid.*, pp. 77–81.

71. *Ibid.*, *123*, 584–585 (General Orders, No. 139, Sept. 24).

72. *Ibid.*, *28*, 621–623.

73. *Ibid.*, p. 627.

74. *Ibid.*, p. 55.

75. *Ibid.*, p. 54.

76. *Ibid.*, *27*, 81, and *28*, 464, 454.

77. *Ibid., 28,* 674.

78. *Ibid.,* p. 470.

79. *Ibid.,* pp. 494, 490. There is no reason to believe that McClellan would have understood how to use a larger body of horse, even if Virginia had been more suitable for cavalry action. He never spoke of the terrain when he referred to the ratio of cavalry to infantry recommended by European writers.

On October 24 or 25 Lincoln sent him the caustic telegram (*O.R., 28,* 485): "I have read your dispatch about sore-tongued and fatigued horses. Will you pardon me for asking what the horses of your army have done since the battle of Antietam that fatigues anything?" McClellan, replying, spoke of "two remarkable expeditions" that part of his cavalry had made, one of which was a 78-mile march in 24 hours after Stuart during the recent raid, and referred to reconnaissance and picketing. "If any instance can be found where overworked cavalry has performed more labor than mine since the battle of Antietam, I am not conscious of it." One can doubt whether all the work done was well planned or was needed, though the question is difficult. Earlier, when McClellan was at Harrison Landing, Lee withdrew the bulk of his cavalry for rest and recuperation, keeping a brigade at a time on duty. Sheridan, taking command of the cavalry of the Army of the Potomac in the spring of 1864, found the cavalry in poor condition due to excessive picket duty, much of which could be done by infantry. He changed the system, and was able to put the cavalry corps into good condition.

80. Lincoln's reply, referring to the message received from McClellan, *ibid.,* p. 496.

81. *Ibid.,* pp. 496, 497.

82. *Ibid.,* pp. 497–498.

83. *Ibid.,* p. 501.

84. Unfortunately terminology was not rigidly adhered to. Army Regulations indicated clearly that a musket was a smoothbore weapon; but a musket which had been subsequently rifled was called a rifled musket, perhaps for accounting reasons. On Oct. 9 one of McClellan's ordnance officers reported that the army had 80,000 Springfield and Enfield rifles, caliber .58; 20,000 rifles of caliber .54; 10,000 rifle muskets, caliber .69. Then he listed 5,000 rifles, smoothbore, caliber .69. Two days later, another ordnance officer made a return with the same figures, but all weapons were now muskets, except "10,000 muskets, caliber .69, rifled." The new report also listed "5,000 muskets, caliber .69, smooth" (*ibid.,* pp. 407, 412).

85. Apparently Cox's command entrained at Hancock (Stryker to Fisher, Oct. 10, *ibid.,* p. 34).

86. *Ibid.,* p. 504; *107,* 897–898.

87. *Ibid., 28,* 542.

88. *Ibid.,* p. 545.

89. *Ibid.,* p. 548. Haupt wrote in his *Reminiscences,* p. 156, "I had been confidentially advised of the change of commanders by Assistant Secretary Watson, and had brought out the bearer of the dispatches, General Wadsworth, I think, in a special train."

90. *O.R., 28,* 555. The telegram reads: "I have the honor to acknowledge the receipt of your letter of the 5th of November, covering General Orders, No. 182, upon the receipt of which I called upon General McClellan, who received from General Buckingham a copy of the order, and at once turned over the command of the Army of the Potomac to me. . . ."

91. *Ibid.,* p. 551.

92. Pickerill, *Third Indiana Cavalry,* p. 33. Pickerill states that McClellan "lost caste with the army," and that the authorities saw it would be safe to do what they had long felt should be done.

93. Halleck to Wright, Aug. 25, *O.R., 23,* 421; *N.Y. Tribune,* Nov. 10 (2 items).

94. Long, *Memoirs of Lee,* p. 233.

95. Capt. R. E. Lee, *Recollections and Letters,* pp. 414–419. Cazenove Lee quoted Gen. Lee as saying with regard to the battle of Gettysburg, "Jackson would have held the heights which Ewell took on the first day." Ewell took no heights; the controversy has been as to whether he should have tried to. For comments by Freeman, see *Lee,* III, 161 n.

Lee spoke as many as three times of the high temperature, saying, "I am unable to bear the heat now"; and he added that he had taken a severe cold and was "full of pains" and had been unable to sleep the preceding night. It was on the afternoon of that day (July 15) that he expected to go to the home of his cousin Cassius. In a letter written five days later, he again spoke of the weather as being "almost insupportable"; and though he reported improvement in his cold, he said he was "too painful" to make one of the visits he had planned. The second letter was written from "Ravensworth," a home of the Fitzhugh family ten miles west of Alexandria which he had left on July 19 (Freeman, *Lee,* IV, 477).

Eckenrode and Conrad (*McClellan,* pp. 281–282) accept the story recorded by Cazenove Lee so far as it regards McClellan but say nothing of the unjust indictment of Ewell that was closely associated with it. The other indorsement of McClellan upon which they rest their climax is contained in a letter from Colonel Theodore Lyman to his wife on June 2, 1864. The Lyman letters are an excellent source for events at the headquarters of the Army of the Potomac after Sept., 1863. Though he was an outstanding naturalist, Lyman was not a military student in any sense of the word; and he is accordingly a poor authority for things he did not see. As a matter of fact, he was in Europe during all of McClellan's military career, and did not return until June, 1863.

96. In illustration of efforts to deny the position here set forth, some quotations will be given from Thomas G. Frothingham's article on Antietam in *Proc. Mass. Hist. Soc.,* LVI, 173–208 (Dec., 1922). Of the fighting on the 17th he writes, "In fact the troops of both armies were fought to the point of exhaustion, with the exception of the 5th and 6th corps, and the cavalry of the Union Army, which were held in reserve against a possible disaster in any part of the battle." This makes military reserves resemble the reserve of a banker—something for a rainy day. Frothingham does not reveal that McClellan planned to strike the winning blow with his reserve, and that he so informed Washington at 1:30 P.M. It not only distorts the facts but does McClellan no service to give

the impression that he was unfamiliar with universally accepted military teachings and the explicit doctrine of Army Regulations on the use of reserves.

Frothingham concedes that after the divisions of Couch and Humphreys had joined McClellan on the morning of the 18th there was stronger reason for a new attack. He continues: "But was there any result to be gained that would be worth the inevitable losses, and worth the risk of some mischance? The main object of the campaign had been accomplished. Lee's army was crippled, and his invasion ended. It is more probable that there was greater risk of loss than possibility of additional gain for McClellan." Frothingham apparently wants his reader to believe that Lee could have so severely repulsed the greatly superior Union army with its excellent artillery and its fresh divisions that the entire North would have been open to his poorly clothed, badly fed, and battle-exhausted regiments to go where they pleased and do what they wished. Again he does the general no service by discounting the importance of Lee's lost order and failing to mention the fact that McClellan's dispatch to Lincoln immediately after finding it clearly revealed that he grasped the opportunity to do something far more than stop Lee's invasion. The competent criticisms of Michie are not mentioned, but the opinions of the Comte de Paris, who wrote several years before the publication of the records, are set before the reader. Myers in his book on McClellan accepts Frothingham's papers on Antietam and the Peninsula Campaign as authoritative.

97. It is possible that McClellan began to think of the Presidency soon after he went to Washington, as a natural result of the acclaim given him and of his belief in the incapacity of Lincoln and the administration. Something like a record in the case begins in the summer of 1862 when Fernando Wood and another Democratic politician visited him on the Peninsula. Wood was mayor of New York and was suspected of having distinctly secession sympathies. The two visitors urged McClellan to become an opposition candidate for President in 1864; he not only agreed to do this, but wrote a letter pledging himself to a conciliatory method of carrying on the war. He showed the letter to his good friend, Major General W. F. Smith, who said it looked like treason and who persuaded him either to withhold it or to destroy it. (The stories differ somewhat. See Myers, *McClellan*, pp. 310–311; Macartney, *Little Mac*, pp. 299–302). After the battle of Antietam, Wood reappeared, and so apparently did the letter.

The *Lincoln Papers*, edited by Mearns (II, 624–626), contain a letter McClellan wrote to the President on May 30, 1861, indicating that at that time he apparently had the strong desire to act entirely in conformity with Lincoln's views. The contrast with the Harrison Landing letter of July 7, 1862, in which he frankly gave political advice, is very marked.

Eckenrode and Conrad, in the Foreword to their book, announce the thesis that there are no military reasons for the "animadversions" cast on McClellan, and that the feeling toward him is thus entirely political, springing mainly from his candidacy against Lincoln in 1864. At the very end of the book they again charge historians with judging McClellan by the politics of the Civil War period.

NOTES TO CHAPTER XV

1. *O.R.*, *28*, 308, 314; Palfrey, *Antietam and Fredericksburg*, p. 17.

2. *O.R.*, *28*, 498.

3. It is commonly said that Burnside had twice previously declined the command of the Army of the Potomac.

4. Strother, "Personal Recollections," *Harper's Magazine*, XXXVI, 280 (Feb., 1868).

5. For example, the *N.Y. Tribune*, Nov. 10, 1862.

6. *O.R.*, *13*, 552–554, 546.

7. Burnside to Cullum, Nov. 9, 6:00 P.M., *ibid.*, p. 558.

8. *Ibid.*, p. 570.

9. Burnside's report, *ibid.*, *31*, 83.

10. *Ibid.*, *28*, 569, 570.

11. *Ibid.*, *31*, 83–84, 47. The President's letter is also given in Burnside's report, *ibid.*, pp. 97–99.

12. *O.R.*, *28*, 574, 579.

13. *Ibid.*, *31*, 47, 84.

14. *Ibid.*, *28*, 572.

15. *Ibid.*, pp. 583–584, 569, 572–573. The court to try Porter was appointed Nov. 25 (*ibid.*, *17*, 821).

16. Report of Gen. Ingalls, army quartermaster, to Gen. Burnside, *ibid.*, *31*, 146, showing that McClellan had greatly exaggerated the need of clothing for his army. He had marched under pressure from Washington before all the requisitioned clothing had been issued—leaving 50,000 uniforms at Harpers Ferry.

17. Freeman, *Lee*, II, 428; *O.R.*, *28*, 717–718.

18. For some comments, see Lee to Smith, Lee to Jackson, *O.R.*, *28*, 697, 715.

19. *Ibid.*, pp. 718, 716, 709. In a dispatch of Nov. 14 Lee stated to Randolph that the number of men in Longstreet's corps without shoes was 6,648—exclusive of Ransom's division, the reserve artillery, and the cavalry. The arrival of 3,000 pairs of shoes was expected. Some shoes and blankets sent recently to Staunton had gone to Jackson, who reported he still had men without shoes or blankets; but Lee did not know the exact number.

Lee's report of the number of men without shoes is in commendable contrast with the vague and general reports of shortages by McClellan, who never gave specific numbers. For instance, on Oct. 25 McClellan forwarded to Halleck a message from a subordinate which closed, "I will also remark that the men in my command are much in want of clothing" (*ibid.*, p. 485). A good commander would have had an inspection made to obtain definite figures on shortages, and would have checked to see whether the officer in question had made requisitions, and when, and whether his quartermaster had been following up the case. As a matter of fact, McClellan accepted rumors about shortages of equipment of his troops just as he accepted rumors about the enemy.

On Nov. 10, Lee wrote to Randolph, "Horses are now so scarce and dear that the dismounted men are unable to purchase them." Even if infantrymen might turn themselves into cavalrymen by purchasing horses, Lee had a problem in knowing what to do with his dismounted cavalrymen, for they could not be put into the infantry without their consent, and he did not believe they would consent.

20. *Ibid.*, p. 712.

21. Randolph to Lee, Lee to Randolph, Northrop to Randolph, *ibid.*, pp. 699–701, 716–717.

22. *Ibid.*, pp. 683–684, 713. Lee's letter of Oct. 26 to Randolph gave full details of reorganization of the army.

23. The documents are among those received too late for insertion in their proper places and are in the appendix to *O.R., 28*, 729–733. They contain some interesting statements by Lee and Hill upon the right of a superior to arrest a subordinate and release him without bringing charges. Jackson wrote emphatically that it was not sufficient for an officer to be able to explain afterward why he had not obeyed an order: "When an officer disobeys or disregards a known order, it is his duty to report it at once, with his explanation, without waiting to be called upon in each individual instance."

24. *Ibid.*, p. 722.

25. *Ibid.*, p. 552.

26. *Ibid.*, p. 574. The report seems accurate, except for the position of D. H. Hill. On Nov. 10 Lee wrote to Randolph that he was at the forks of the Shenandoah (*ibid.*, p. 711). Whether or not Halleck and Burnside knew at this time of the reorganization of Lee's army and of its order in battle, is hard to say. D. H. Hill's division, since its arrival after Second Bull Run, had been first under Jackson's command, then under Longstreet, and was now formally in the Second Corps.

27. In a long letter to Burnside dated Nov. 13, Sigel stated that it was probable that the intrenchments of Richmond had been strengthened by a second and more exterior line of defenses. He also gave a good deal of information about roads and streams, and urged a continuation of the campaign along the Culpeper-Gordonsville line (*ibid.*, pp. 574–576).

28. *Ibid.*, p. 573.

29. On Nov. 10 Lee wrote to Jackson (*ibid.*, p. 715) with regard to Burnside's movements: "If an advance toward Fredericksburg is discovered, it is plain that you cannot delay longer, and you must be prepared to move at any time. Make your arrangements accordingly, and be prepared to move at any moment." Stuart was watching Burnside closely, but there was "the difficulty of determining the first movements," and Lee said to Jackson, "You may learn more from the rear than we can in front."

30. In a telegram to Wright's adjutant on the 13th, Cox said of the reported movement of Jackson into West Virginia, "If this was true, it would be giving Burnside a chance to whip Lee, in Jackson's absence, and I, therefore, do not think it probable" (*ibid.*, p. 578). For Garrett's letters of the 14th and 15th, see *ibid.*, pp. 584, 586.

It was not strange that Garrett was apprehensive, for destroying his locomotives and tearing up his railroad had been a favorite exploit of Jackson ever since he had corralled a group of engines and wrecked them in Martinsburg in May, 1861.

31. Burnside's report states, "General Sumner's grand division started at daylight on the morning of the 15th, and the grand divisions of Generals Franklin and Hooker, together with the cavalry, started on the 16th." It is to be recalled that the report was written three years after the event. Actually, Hooker, who formed the rear guard, issued his march order on the 16th, and it stated that the center grand division would begin its movement at five o'clock the next morning (*ibid., 31,* 84, 762).

32. *Ibid., 28,* 549–551, 571–572.

33. Clarke to Parke, *ibid.,* p. 587.

34. *Ibid., 31,* 764.

35. Burnside to Cullom, *ibid.,* pp. 101–103. It is the basis of much that is said about the march and arrival. On Williams, see *ibid.,* p. 775.

36. *Ibid.,* p. 765. Blackford (*War Years with Stuart,* pp. 119–120) describes the capture on Aug. 28 in a farmhouse north of Groveton of a party of five Federal cavalrymen about to sit down to a meal of corncakes, butter, eggs, fried ham, and buttermilk. He was disdainful of their horses, and said they were given to Confederate infantry officers.

37. *O.R., 31,* 147 (Ingalls to Burnside), 775.

38. *Ibid.,* pp. 85–86.

39. *Ibid., 31,* 773.

40. *Ibid.,* pp. 773–774.

41. *Ibid.,* pp. 104–105.

42. *Ibid.,* pp. 777, 781–782.

43. *Ibid.,* pp. 783, 784–785.

44. Lee to Cooper, *ibid.,* p. 1026.

45. Various communications, *ibid.,* pp. 784–788. Sumner invited a committee of representatives from the town to meet in a conference. With them came two officers. Upon being informed that military personnel were not included in the invitation, the whole group returned to the town; then Sumner wrote to the mayor that he did not object to the presence of one or two officers. Apparently no written commitment was made by Lee.

46. *N.Y. Tribune,* Nov. 27.

47. *O.R., 31,* 103–104.

48. Lee to Jackson, to W. H. F. Lee, and to Ball, *ibid.,* pp. 1021–1022, 1013–1014.

49. There are three chief sources: the letter of explanation which Woodbury addressed to Parke on Nov. 24, just after his arrest, quoting from dispatches; Magruder's report of Nov. 25 to Woodbury; a memorandum for Burnside from Ingalls, *ibid.,* 793–795, 799–800, 148–149. Ingalls's very full and interesting memorandum, although undated, is attached to a report dated Mar. 19, 1864, and may well have been written soon after the pontoon incident; there would hardly have been occasion to deal so fully with the matter at the later date, and Ingalls could not have included all the details without at least consulting notes made at the time.

50. In his report after the war, dated Nov. 15, 1865, Burnside wrote that no

information that wagons would be needed with the pontoons that went down the Potomac had been given to Spaulding, and "neither to his knowledge had any information of that kind been given to General Woodbury." He continued, "Had this information been given to Colonel Spaulding, the necessary wagons could have been placed on the rafts and floated to Belle Plain, from which point the pontoons could have been hauled to Falmouth by teams from the army" (*ibid.,* p. 87). The engineers can hardly be excused for not sending the wagons—certainly Woodbury cannot be. Spaulding's attention was largely centered on the land train. It was obvious that the boats were to be used to bridge the Rappahannock, and not at Belle Plain or Aquia Creek. It is a military principle that loadings should be made complete, so that the loss of one vessel, for instance, will not render useless the loads of other ships. In the case of the Fredericksburg pontoons, the usefulness of both sets of boats was dependent upon the arrival of the land train.

51. Kelton, Halleck's assistant adjutant general, sent the following dispatch to Ingalls: "General Woodbury, in command of Engineer Brigade, with 48 pontoons, was reported at Aquia Creek on the 20th" (*ibid.,* p. 790). Whether Ingalls was at Aquia Creek or at Falmouth when the dispatch was received is not certain; but he was soon at Aquia Creek.

52. Ingalls to Burnside, *ibid.,* p. 790. The message stated that the land train had 20 pontoons "and wagons to carry 20 more, which are at Belle Plain." This raises another point—empty wagons had gone in the land train. Of course not only wagons are needed to haul pontoons, but horses. Woodbury should have known, however, that horses could have been obtained from Burnside's army, if it was impracticable to send horses with the river expedition; and there is nothing to indicate that there was a shortage of pontoon wagons in Washington when the 48 pontoons were dispatched down the river. Ingalls informed Burnside that about 26 wagons had been received by Magruder. "The quartermaster will furnish teams; common wagons cannot carry pontoons. I see no way of having enough at Fredericksburg before to-morrow evening." Magruder in his report to Woodbury spoke of "tardiness of the quartermaster's department" in furnishing the teams (*ibid.,* p. 800). Having used his boats to make a wharf for the quartermaster, Magruder may have been impatient, and believed the quartermaster had a big supply of extra four-horse teams concealed somewhere in the woods.

53. Burnside had evidently been trying to get in touch with the land train; and at 4:30 P.M. on the 22nd Gen. Franklin's assistant adjutant general forwarded from Stafford Court House a note written by Spaulding that morning that a sergeant had just brought in: "The roads are in such a shocking condition that I find I cannot make over 5 miles a day with my bridge train, and to do even this much I am obliged to haul many of my wagons for miles by hand, and work my men half the night." Spaulding had sent to Alexandria for a steamer to tow his rafts from the Occoquan down the Potomac; and he concluded: "My own horses, and part of the wagons, will proceed by land, but will not probably get through before the evening of the 25th instant" (*ibid.,* pp. 790–791).

54. Magruder reported, "Owing to an ill-made causeway, which, in the dark-

ness of the night, was impassable until I had repaired it, and the badly disciplined corps of teamsters furnished with the wagons, I could not force the train through until 9 a.m. of the 24th" (*ibid.*, p. 800).

55. *Ibid.*, pp. 792, 798, 793–795, 802. Not every officer would have taken the trouble to make the report at once.

56. *Ibid.*, pp. 171–172. Halleck wrote to Franklin May 29, 1863, of the "furor" which had been raised against him in the "public press" over the pontoons (*ibid.*, pp. 1008–1009). He rather implied that he could have disproved responsibility, but could certainly have done so only by throwing the blame on Woodbury, as he had come near doing in the telegram to Burnside. But when he appeared before the Committee on the Conduct of the War he tried to clear the engineer officer. Woodbury's letter also mentioned the criticism by the press.

57. *N.Y. Tribune*, Nov. 21, 1862.

58. *Ibid.*, Nov. 27.

59. Nicolay and Hay, *Lincoln*, VI, 199.

60. *N.Y. Tribune*, Nov. 22.

61. *Ibid.*, Nov. 21—a dispatch dated Nov. 18, stating, "Yesterday morning was lowering and rainy, but the threatened storm did not come."

62. Memorandum of Ingalls, *O.R., 31*, 150.

63. *Ibid.*, p. 86.

64. *Ibid.*, p. 800.

65. *Ibid.*, p. 798.

66. *Ibid.*, p. 797.

67. *N.Y. Tribune*, Nov. 28; *Nicolay and Hay, op. cit.*, p. 200. A second dispatch in the *Tribune*, on the same page as that referred to, did not mention Stanton.

NOTES TO CHAPTER XVI

1. *O.R., 31*, 1013–1015, 1018–1019.

2. Lee to Cooper, *ibid.*, pp. 1017–1018. In his letter of the 17th to Secretary Randolph, Lee had said that he did not know whether the move upon Fredericksburg was "a feint or a real advance upon Richmond." He added, "In the latter event, before it [the Federal force] can move from Fredericksburg, I think this whole army will be in position" (*ibid.*, p. 1016). With Jackson still in the Valley, Lee was greatly underestimating the difficulties he would have had if the pontoons had been on hand for Sumner and the other grand divisions which were close behind his column.

3. In his letter to Cooper of the 18th, Lee stated with reference to Stuart, "One of our scouts who joined him north of the Rappahannock, informed him that the enemy on Sunday [Nov. 16] moved from Bealeton back to Warrenton Junction; thence their main body marched toward Fredericksburg. At the date of his note he had ascertained nothing further."

4. *Ibid., 28*, 717–718, and *31*, 1021–1022.

5. Chilton to Pendleton, *ibid., 31*, 1019.

6. Lee to W. H. F. Lee, *ibid.*, p. 1013.

7. *Ibid.*, pp. 1020–1021.

8. The dispatch to Jackson in which Lee stated definitely that Stuart considered the information he had as conclusive that Burnside's whole army had marched for Fredericksburg carried the hour 9:00 A.M. The message to Davis stating that it was not certain that any force except Sumner's had moved, unfortunately shows no hour. Whether a communication was received from Stuart after the dispatch was sent to Davis is unimportant in view of other statements Lee made to Davis.

9. Freeman, *Lee*, II, 432.

10. *O.R., 31,* 823.

11. On Nov. 18 Lee wrote to Jackson: "But unless you think it is advantageous for you to continue longer in the valley, or can accomplish the retention and division of the enemy's force by so doing, I think it would be advisable to put some of your divisions in motion across the mountains, and advance them at least as far as Sperryville or Madison Court-House" (*ibid.*, pp. 1018–1019). Lee, with more information on the general situation than Jackson, should have issued an order, not merely said what he thought was advisable. He should have known that the Federals, with the upper Potomac well guarded, and a strong covering force for Washington at Centerville, had perfect freedom of movement, and that Jackson could not impede the main Union army.

The next morning he wrote: "As before stated, you can remain in the valley as long as you see that your presence there cripples and embarrasses the general movement of the enemy, and yet leaves you free to unite with Longstreet for a battle" (*ibid.*, pp. 1021–1022). What did he think Jackson could do that would embarrass the Federals, when Stuart's reports indicated the entire Army of the Potomac was either at Fredericksburg or in its vicinity? On the 23rd Lee wrote from "Camp Fredericksburg" that Burnside's whole army was apparently opposite the town. "Under this view of things, if correct, I do not see, at this distance," said Lee, "what military effect can be produced by the continuance of your corps in the valley" (*ibid.*, pp. 1027–1028). Still uncertainty and still no order, but only a *suggestion* that it would be well if Jackson moved to Culpeper. Two days later Lee tried to explain to Davis his long delay in calling up Jackson by stating: "I have waited to the last moment to draw Jackson's corps to me, as I have seen that his presence on their flank has embarrassed their plans and defeated their first purpose of advancing upon Gordonsville and Charlottesville" (*ibid.*, p. 1029). There would have been much validity in the explanation as late as the 18th; there was none after the reports from Stuart were in. Lee should have sent a warning order to Jackson on the 15th—the day of the first report about the Federal move—and ordered him to move on the first day he believed it best—which seems to have been the 17th.

12. *Ibid.*, pp. 1026–1027.

13. Lee to Davis and to Jackson, *ibid.*, pp. 1028–1029, 1027–1028.

14. Lee to Davis and to Jackson, *ibid.*, pp. 1034, 1035, 1029.

15. *Ibid.*, p. 814. See also Meigs to Burnside, pp. 817–818.

16. *Ibid.*, p. 777.

17. *Ibid.*, pp. 830, 832, 844–845, 840, 836, 837.

18. *Ibid.*, pp. 803, 1034.

19. *N.Y. Tribune*, Nov. 27; Kelley to Milroy, *O.R., 31*, 830.

20. Henderson, *Stonewall Jackson*, p. 574; Freeman, *Lee*, II, 441, 448–450.

21. *O.R., 31*, 841, 842.

22. *Ibid.*, pp. 61–63.

23. *Ibid.*, p. 64.

24. *Ibid.*, pp. 840–841.

25. Woodbury's and Comstock's reports, *ibid.*, pp. 169–171, 167–168.

26. *Ibid.*, pp. 174, 169.

27. *Ibid.*, pp. 175–176.

28. Hunt's report, *ibid.*, pp. 180–189.

29. Hunt's, Howard's, and Willcox's reports, *ibid.*, pp. 183, 262, 265, 310.

30. Franklin to Parke, with indorsement, *ibid.*, p. 844.

31. *Ibid.*, pp. 106–107, 448–449. The messages do not give the hours at which they were sent.

32. Franklin's report, *ibid.*, p. 449.

33. *Ibid.*, pp. 523, 846.

34. *Ibid.*, p. 89.

35. *Ibid.*, p. 523; *N.Y. Tribune*, Dec. 13.

36. *Ibid.*, p. 847. Strength return for Dec. 10, *O.R., 31*, 1121. The number of officers and men given as "present for duty" was set at 122,009, though it is not clear just what deductions had been made in addition to the sick. The number carried as "present for duty equipped" was put at 116,834, and this figure would certainly not include drivers of wagons and other vehicles on special detail from combat organizations. The aggregate present on the upper Potomac and Washington (mainly in the latter place) was put at 69,410 with 273 pieces of artillery. There were still many absentees, and the "present and absent" strength of Burnside's entire command was 328,834.

37. For a map of the battefield by a Confederate engineer, which gives the positions of troops without indicating subordinate commanders except Longstreet and Hill, see *ibid.*, p. 1128.

38. Return for Dec. 10, *ibid.*, p. 1057.

39. *Ibid.*, pp. 1050, 1053, 1054, 1061. On Dec. 8 Lee wrote to Davis: "I am reluctant to trouble Your Excellency with my wants; but unless the Richmond and Fredericksburg Railroad is more energetically operated, it will be impossible to supply this army with provisions, and oblige its retirement to Hanover Junction."

40. Freeman, *Lee,* II, 450–451.

41. A. P. Hill's division was only a few miles away, and it moved up early on the 12th and relieved Hood's division of Longstreet's corps, which had been holding the right of Lee's line. Hood stated, *O.R., 31*, 622, that he was relieved at 10:00 A.M.; but it is not clear whether or not he meant that the operation had actually been completed at that time.

42. *Ibid.*, pp. 1057, 663, 642.

43. Palfrey wrote (*Antietam and Fredericksburg*, p. 151): "It is a pitiful picture, but is probably a true one, that Burnside passed the evening of the 12th riding about, not quite at his wits' end, but very near it. As far as can be

made out, he finally came to the conclusion that he would attempt to do something, he did not quite know what, with his left, and if he succeeded, to do something with his right." Though not with the army at the time, Palfrey unquestionably talked to many officers who had been.

44. *O.R., 31,* 448–449, 91, 71. The hours given in Franklin's report do not agree with the fact that the first message Hardie sent to Burnside was marked 7:40.

45. Reynolds's and Meade's reports, *ibid.,* pp. 452–454, 510, 511.

46. The gap was between the brigades of Archer and Lane, and there has been much writing seeking to explain its occurrence. For the way in which Archer's and Lane's flanks were rolled up, see their reports, *ibid.,* pp. 657, 654–655.

47. *Ibid.,* p. 664. Early stated that the "cheering peculiar to the Confederate soldier" was "never to be mistaken for the studied hurrahs of the Yankees."

48. *Ibid.,* p. 634.

49. *Ibid.,* p. 523. One could feel differently toward Franklin if he had an established record of boldness and aggressiveness. For a critical discussion of his actions, see Palfrey, *op. cit.,* pp. 173–182. Palfrey was very severe on Burnside and in many ways quite indulgent with Franklin. Nevertheless he wrote: "But while it is easy to defend Franklin, and impossible not to sympathize with him, it is not easy to feel entirely satisfied with him." He found Franklin certainly wanting in audacity, and thought it strange that there was no evidence that he ever communicated with Burnside "in the way of suggestions, requests for instructions, or remonstrances." He made no allusion to Franklin's hesitancy in Pleasant Valley in September, or to the fact that a more energetic commander marching to the support of Pope on August 30 might have arrived in time to be of some use.

50. Statements by Capt. P. M. Lydig and Capt. R. H. I. Goddard, Burnside's report, *O.R., 31,* 127–128.

51. *Ibid.,* pp. 118–119.

52. Longstreet's report, *ibid.,* p. 570. Hood's division was partially engaged; that of D. H. Hill was shifted over to the Confederate right when Doubleday seemed to threaten to advance, and then was brought back because A. P. Hill's line had been broken (D. H. Hill's report, *ibid.,* p. 643).

53. For the detailed report of casualties, see *ibid.,* pp. 129–142.

54. Gen. Francis A. Walker wrote: "I well remember the 12th of December, 1862, carrying a message to Burnside from Couch, saying that so far as the latter could judge from the reports of citizens, contrabands, and deserters, a deep trench or canal ran around the town, between it and the hills, which would prove a serious obstacle to the passage of troops; and I never shall forget how indignantly and even angrily Burnside rejected the suggestion" (Bigelow, *Chancellorsville,* p. 388 n.). Couch said nothing of the matter in his report.

55. Carroll's and Whipple's reports, *O.R., 31,* 396–398, 392–394. Two officers and an orderly sent by Whipple at night to find Carroll's position so as to forward supplies never returned, having probably entered the enemy's lines.

56. Humphreys's report, *ibid.,* p. 432.

57. *Ibid.,* pp. 120, 117, 73, 65.

58. Butterfield to Hooker, *ibid.*, pp. 74–75. Burnside, in his testimony before the Committee on the Conduct of the War, said that Sumner had come to him and protested against making another attack, stating that higher commanders were unanimously against it, and that this led him to countermand his order (*C.C.W.*, 1863, 2: 653). See also Rush C. Hawkins, "Why Burnside Did Not Renew the Attack at Fredericksburg," *B. and L.*, III, 126–127.

59. *N.Y. Tribune*, Dec. 17.

60. Cutting to Burnside, *O.R., 31*, 126; Comstock's and Wonderly's reports, *ibid.*, pp. 168, 167.

61. Freeman, *Lee*, II, 472–473.

62. Hill's report, *O.R., 31*, 644.

63. Longstreet's report, *ibid.*, p. 570; *N.Y. Tribune*, Dec. 15.

64. *O.R., 31*, 122.

65. *Ibid.*, pp. 65–67, 95.

66. *Ibid.*, pp. 67–68.

67. *Ibid.*, pp. 180–190. There was something distinctly of the present day about the way in which the batteries on the heights on the left bank of the river carried on counter-battery fire and supported the infantry attack. Capt. Gustavus A. DeRussey, 4th United States Artillery, skillfully maneuvered four batteries up and down the river and did much to break up enemy demonstrations against the Federal left flank. Jackson spoke in his report about how well the batteries with Franklin were handled. The artillery with Sumner had a difficult time on account of congestion, and some of it returned to the other side of the river. The infantry divisions at first moved out to attack without their guns, but batteries were soon sent for. In order to help soften the enemy for the assault by Humphreys, two batteries were boldly advanced within 150 yards of the sunken road. The cannoneers stood calmly as the broken infantry retreated, and then by horse and hand removed their pieces. A volunteer group under Sgt. Anthony B. Norton returned and salvaged a limber of Battery B, First Rhode Island.

The Confederate artillery also was well handled; but the problem the gunners faced was much less difficult, because a large part of the targets consisted of closed-up infantry at close range and they had the chance to measure and record the ranges to different terrain features. For the exploit that increased the renown Maj. Pelham had already won, see Freeman, *Lee's Lieutenants*, II, 349–361.

Newman makes both an unsound and an unjust criticism of the artillery of the day in writing (*Tools of War*, p. 46), "In fact the field artillery was so useless that at Fredericksburg the Federal infantry attacked with no artillery support at all." Even today artillery may not be able to support the closing phase of an attack.

68. Butterfield to Hooker, *O.R., 31*, 76.

69. Burnside's final report, *ibid.*, pp. 95–96; Nicolay and Hay, *Lincoln*, VI, 213. Burnside wrote merely, "It is not worth while to give the details of this intended movement." William H. Mills writes that the crossing was to have been seven miles below Fredericksburg at Muddy Creek, in "From Burnside to Hooker," *Mag. Amer. Hist.*, XV, 44–56 (Jan., 1886).

70. *O.R., 31,* 886.

71. *Ibid.,* pp. 941–942.

72. A footnote in the *Official Records* reads: "This letter is printed from General Burnside's copy; it does not appear in Mr. Lincoln's papers." Nicolay and Hay state, "If the President ever received this letter he did not retain it" (*Lincoln,* VI, 216). Burnside's letter of the 5th to Lincoln seems to explain what happened: "In conversation with you on New Year's morning, I was led to express some opinions which I afterward felt it my duty to place on paper, and to express them verbally to the gentlemen of whom we were speaking, which I did in your presence after handing you the letter. You were not disposed then, as I saw, to retain the letter, and I took it back, but now return it to you for record, if you wish it." Although this paragraph was in Burnside's retained copy, it was not in the one received by the President, according to a note by the editors of the records. The "gentlemen" referred to must have been Stanton and Halleck.

73. *O.R., 31,* 940–941. The editors assumed that the letter had been withdrawn because no copy was found in the War Department file.

74. *Ibid.,* pp. 944–945.

75. *Ibid.,* pp. 917–918.

76. *Ibid.,* pp. 953–954.

77. *Ibid.,* p. 954.

78. Parke to Woodbury, *ibid.,* p. 994, and elsewhere.

79. General Orders, No. 12, *ibid.,* p. 985.

80. Mills, *op. cit.,* p. 21. Hebert (*Fighting Joe Hooker,* p. 163) quotes the statement.

81. Franklin to Halleck, June 1, 1863, *O.R., 31,* 1009–1010. In a brief report on Jan. 29, Lee wrote to Seddon, "The movements of the enemy on the 20th confirmed the belief that an effort would be made to turn our left flank, and that Franklin's and Hooker's corps were the troops selected for that purpose" (*ibid.,* p. 755).

82. For the huts, see *Harper's Weekly,* VII, 33, 34 (Jan. 17, 1863).

83. *O.R., 31,* 998–999. A footnote states that the order, not being approved by the President, was never issued, but appeared "in the public prints" as well as in Burnside's testimony before the Committee on the Conduct of the War.

On Apr. 23 Hooker wrote Stanton a long and very irregular letter, beginning, "I see that Burnside's stupid order, No. 8, has at last found its way into the newspapers" (*O.R., 40,* 855–856). Hooker went so far in denouncing Burnside as to refer to "his cowardice at the first Bull Run."

84. War Department G.O. 91, July 29, 1862, p. 20.

85. G.O. 144. See in general G.O. 1862, index, pp. 54–56. A colonel was "cashiered for repeated acts of cowardice in the face of the enemy," and another for "habitual drunkenness" (G.O. 115, 117). Eleven officers went out on one order for absence without leave "while the armies to which they belonged were fighting the enemy in the field" (G.O. 125); perhaps as a kindness to himself a captain was put out without the statement of the charge against him (G.O. 156). Col. Ford, after abandoning Maryland Heights in September, was dismissed in accordance with the recommendations of a commission

(G.O. 183). It is not apparent how charges were made, or who examined them. Injustices were unavoidable, and some effort must have been made to right them, for fourteen dismissals were revoked in 1862.

86. In 1863 only 17 officers were dismissed, and 8 had their dismissals revoked; on the other hand the number of officers reported in War Department orders as tried by courts-martial increased from 4 to 108 (G.O. 1863, index, pp. 168, 159–161). Everything considered, the record of the use of unlimited power seems to have been a good one.

87. *O.R., 31,* 993.

88. *Ibid.*

89. *Ibid.,* p. 1007.

90. *Ibid.,* pp. 1004–1005.

91. Burnside wrote in his final report, Nov. 13, 1865: "I am not disposed to complain of my lack of success in the exercise of the command; and in view of the glorious results which have since attended the movements of this gallant army, I am quite willing to believe that my removal was for the best" (*ibid.,* p. 96).

Sumner had previously requested to be relieved from field duty on account of age and health. He died before the end of March. For a high tribute, see Nicolay and Hay, *op. cit.,* p. 222.

Franklin felt aggrieved and promptly published a pamphlet about the battle of Fredericksburg—a very irregular procedure. Although not an official document, it was reprinted in one of the supplementary volumes of the records. His positive charge that Burnside had urged the removal of Stanton and Halleck after the battle of Fredericksburg caused the General in Chief to write to Burnside that he regarded the recommendation as a favor if a fact. In the extensive exchange of letters with Franklin the General in Chief pointed out some assertions that Franklin had made which must be taken as false. He terminated the correspondence on June 5 with a note in which he wrote, "What General Burnside may have said to the President or Secretary of War about me, in my absence, I, of course, do not know; but I have assurances that he never suggested my removal to either" (*O.R., 107,* 1019–1033, 1006, 1007–1012). It is to be recalled that Burnside's letter of Jan. 1 merely stated that officers and men lacked confidence in Stanton and Halleck—which was certainly not urging their removal.

In both 1863 and 1864 Franklin held subordinate command in operations in Louisiana and did nothing whatever to remove doubt about his fitness for the position of a grand division commander, or even a corps commander against a vigorous opponent. Greeley spoke of the "distinction" Franklin achieved at Sabine Pass in Sept., 1863, as "the first American General who managed to lose a fleet in a contest with land batteries alone" (*American Conflict,* II, 339).

NOTES TO CHAPTER XVII

1. For an account of Hooker's experiences in civil life, see Hebert's *Fighting Joe Hooker,* chap. ii.

2. Hebert (*ibid.,* p. 49 n.) gives as authority for his quotation: "Unidentified

clippings in the Hooker papers. Repeated in many newspapers and all articles concerning Hooker."

3. *O.R.*, *13*, 97, and *18*, 818. Bates, *Chancellorsville*, p. 17—a book decidedly pro-Hooker, but well written and valuable.

4. Bigelow, *Chancellorsville*, p. 6—a book without a peer in American military literature, as an exhaustive study of a single campaign.

5. "Ever since the battle of Antietam, Hooker has been looked upon as the inevitable General" (*N.Y. Tribune*, Jan. 27, 1863).

6. Nicolay and Hay, *Lincoln*, VI, 220.

7. *Harper's Weekly*, VII, 34 (Jan. 17, 1863).

8. *O.R., 31*, 998.

9. Sandburg, *Lincoln: The War Years*, II, 76.

10. Nicolay and Hay, *op. cit.*, 220, 264–272.

11. Welles, *Diary*, I, 229.

12. Nicolay and Hay, *op. cit.*, pp. 220–221.

13. *O.R., 31*, 1009, 1004.

14. Bigelow (*op. cit.*, p. 7) states: "His [Lincoln's] selection of Hooker to succeed Burnside was due not so much to his estimate of Hooker's military qualities as to the preference of his cabinet for Hooker as the only eligible general who was free of political aspirations, and therefore not a possible rival candidate for the Presidency."

Hebert (*op. cit.*, p. 166) speaks of Lincoln calling his advisers together, of a quick decision that Burnside must go, and of the elimination of McClellan as well as Rosecrans as possible successors. Contradicting Bigelow, he says that Lincoln favored Hooker, but that the issue was kept open by Stanton and Halleck. Quite as if he had the minutes of the whole procedure, Hebert writes that the question was narrowed down to a choice between Hooker and Meade, with Stanton and Halleck favoring Meade. Then Lincoln broke the deadlock by appointing Hooker. For this story there is no creditable authority. Hebert's only reference is to an article by Charles F. Benjamin, "Hooker's Appointment and Removal," in *B. and L.*, III, 239–241, written many years after the event and not documented. None of Benjamin's information could have been better than secondhand; furthermore, he does not speak of Lincoln calling together any advisers. In spite of the fact that Halleck wrote categorically three months after the event that he gave no advice whatever and was not consulted (*O.R., 31*, 1009, 1004), Hebert states, "Halleck, particularly, contended that there were reasons of an imperative character why he thought Hooker should be passed by"—which, if true, would make Halleck guilty of a monumental falsehood. Hebert makes no reference to the entry in Welles's diary, with its implication that there was no cabinet meeting. He also takes no notice of the view that Nicolay and Hay expressed. In short, he gives nothing to support his own account, and ignores all the evidence that contradicts it.

15. The frequent statement that Reynolds had been "sounded out" on the subject can probably be accepted.

16. Hooker ranked as major general of volunteers from May 5, 1862; Meade, from Nov. 29, 1862 (Phisterer, *Statistical Record*, pp. 252–253, entries 194, 228).

Rhodes's treatment of the case is very unsatisfactory (*History of the Civil War*, pp. 209–210). He states that both Reynolds and Meade were, in training and ability, qualified for command. The most that could be said is that they *looked* somewhat promising, because they had not had experience as army commanders, and Meade not even as a corps commander. Later, after he had commanded a corps, Meade was to write that his ability as an army commander had not been tested (Meade, *Life and Letters of Meade,* I, 388). It is amazing to find Rhodes citing Meade's letters to his wife and son as evidence of his fitness, and ignoring his subsequent record as commander of the army. The letters, though showing fine traits in the general, make a case against him, as will be seen in the sequel. Completely ignoring the question of relative rank, Rhodes writes, ". . . hence it must be concluded that Hooker's appointment was an instance of the popular voice overbearing expert opinion." What expert opinion?

Randall (*Lincoln the President,* II, 255, 254) notes that Hooker "had the experience and prestige of a corps commander," overlooking the fact that he was in command of *two* corps. His treatment of the change of commanders reverses events, for he presents a state of indecision existing with Burnside darting back "in a sensational night ride." It was Burnside's visit—of which the President had been informed—that precipitated the crisis, and the decision was too prompt for much in the way of "intrigue" after that. On the surprising order that Burnside showed Lincoln, Randall comments: "Having delivered the bolt, the general sped back to the army; obviously he was thinking more of disciplining certain generals, especially Hooker, than of accepting the alternative of resignation." Burnside probably was thinking of his *duty as a commanding general,* and of getting his army back to its camps from the "mud march."

17. *O.R., 40,* 4–5.

18. For example, *Harper's Weekly,* VII, 99 (Feb. 14, 1863), contained the appraisal: "There has been no question of his bravery, his energy, and his celerity in the field, qualities essential to an invading army. . . . He has issued no foolish addresses. In the hour of reverse he has neither thrown the blame upon the Government nor suffered others to do so."

19. *O.R., 40,* 3.

20. *Ibid.,* p. 4. Original in Collection of Alfred Whital Stern.

21. Hebert (*op. cit.,* p. 329, n. 33) states that the Hooker letter first appeared in the *Providence Journal,* May 6, 1879.

22. Nicolay and Hay, *op. cit.,* VII, 88; accepted by Bigelow, *op. cit.,* p. 10. Brooks (*Washington in Lincoln's Time,* pp. 52–55) describes in detail how in April Hooker read the letter to him and commented, "That is just such a letter as a father might write to his son." Hebert (*op. cit.,* p. 170) rejects much of this as being strictly "out of character" for Hooker to say. Of course, Brooks's memory may have played him tricks; but there is a chance that a very wide-awake man, intelligent enough to appeal to Lincoln, who lived through the times and talked with Hooker, understood Fighting Joe as well as his recent biographer.

23. *O.R., 28,* 569, and *31,* 987. The percentage of absentees to "aggregate present and absent" was 26.1 on Nov. 10, 1862, and 25.9 on Jan. 20, 1863.

Morell's troops on the upper Potomac have been dropped from the return for Nov. 10, because figures for them were not given in the later return. Both returns include the Washington command of Heintzelman.

24. Of a hard march De Forest wrote, "Perhaps it is worth while to mention that, after two or three days of repose, we were excessively proud of our thirty-four miles in a day, and were ready to march with any other brigade in the army for a wager" (*A Volunteer's Adventures,* p. 102).

25. Sterne, *Tristram Shandy,* bk. I, chap. xxv.

26. *N.Y. Tribune,* Dec. 24, 1862; Nicolay and Hay, *op. cit.,* VI, 218 n.

27. Bigelow, *op. cit.,* p. 36; *O.R., 31,* 96.

28. *Harper's Weekly,* VI, 67 (Jan. 31, 1863).

29. An apt description by De Forest, *op. cit.,* p. 46.

30. Nicolay and Hay, *op. cit.,* VII, 288, 289. A cannon ball that grazed Rosecrans killed his chief of staff, and three orderlies were shot by his side.

31. Livermore, *Numbers and Losses,* pp. 96–97.

32. Meade, *Life and Letters,* I, 383. Hebert states, "Public opinion was now up in arms against the military policy of the administration" (*op. cit.,* p. 164). The statement is so sweeping as to have almost no meaning.

33. *Harper's Weekly,* VII, 179, 226 (Mar. 21 and Apr. 11, 1863).

34. Nicolay and Hay, *op. cit.,* VI, 247.

35. *Harper's Weekly,* VII, 187 (Mar. 21).

36. Editorial, "The Wealth of Our Country," in *ibid.,* p. 194 (Mar. 28).

37. Phisterer, *op. cit.,* p. 62.

38. Nicolay and Hay, *op. cit.,* VII, 47. Fry had been adjutant general for McDowell at First Bull Run and afterward chief of staff for Gen. Buell. Nicolay and Hay state (p. 6) that he "was not only an accomplished soldier but an executive officer of extraordinary tact, ability, and industry."

39. *Harper's Weekly,* VII, 131 (Feb. 28, 1863).

40. *Ibid.,* p. 163 (Mar. 14).

41. *Ibid.,* pp. 194, 74, 86 (Mar. 28, Jan. 31, Feb. 7).

42. *Ibid.,* p. 162 (Mar. 14).

43. Nicolay and Hay, *op. cit.,* VI, chap. xx and p. 472.

44. Bill, *Beleaguered City,* pp. 100–101.

45. Gorgas, *Diary,* p. 31.

46. Lee to Seddon, Jan. 29, *O.R., 31,* 755.

47. *O.R., 40,* 12.

48. *Harper's Weekly,* VII, 109 (Feb. 14).

49. Halleck to Dix, Hooker to Halleck and reply, *O.R., 40,* 37, 44.

50. General Orders, No. 6, *ibid.,* p. 51.

51. Bigelow, *op. cit.,* pp. 39–40. *O.R., 40,* 61.

52. Sigel to Dickinson, and other communications, *O.R., 40,* 70–71.

53. General Orders, No. 26, *ibid.,* p. 42.

54. Bates, *op. cit.,* p. 26.

55. *O.R., 40,* 77–78, 73.

56. Circular, Mar. 21, *ibid.,* p. 152.

57. Lee to Davis, Feb. 26, *ibid.,* p. 643.

58. Bigelow, *op. cit.,* p. 46; *O.R., 40,* 180.

59. C. F. Adams, Jr., *Autobiography*, p. 161.

60. Bigelow, *op. cit.*, p. 44. Some of his criticisms are repeated in the text.

61. General Orders, No. 77, *O.R., 40*, 148–149.

62. Bigelow, *op. cit.*, p. 89.

63. *O.R., 40*, 148.

64. Brooks, *op. cit.*, pp. 50–52.

65. D. N. Couch, "The Chancellorsville Campaign," *B. and L.*, III, 155.

66. *O.R., 40*, 199–200. The dispatch explained the projected cavalry operation.

67. *Ibid.*, p. 158.

68. Hooker to Kelton, *ibid.*, pp. 99–100. Peck (at Suffolk) sent Hooker on Apr. 4 an accurate and full account of the situation in his front, describing the enemy forces as well as his own. He was well posted about Confederate activities (*ibid.*, pp. 190–191).

69. Freeman, *Lee*, II, 500.

70. Returns for Mar. 31, *O.R., 40*, 696, 180.

71. Bigelow, *op. cit.*, pp. 109–110, 142.

72. *Ibid.*, pp. 145, 151, 157, 168.

73. *O.R., 40*, 256–257.

74. On Feb. 1 Hooker had forwarded to Washington a letter of Jan. 30, addressed by Lee to Burnside, asking permission for two British subjects to pass through the Federal lines (*ibid.*, p. 37—reply on pp. 44–45).

Harper's Weekly, VII, 93 (Feb. 7, 1863), has a picture and a story of mounted pickets meeting in the middle of the Rappahannock.

75. Butterfield to Magaw, *O.R., 40*, 36–37.

76. *O.R., 31*, 989–990, 752–753.

77. *O.R., 40*, 255–256.

78. Butterfield to Commanding Officer, Fifth Corps, *ibid.*, pp. 262, 263.

79. *Ibid.*, p. 263.

80. *Ibid.*, pp. 266–267.

81. *Ibid.*, p. 268.

82. *Ibid.*, p. 264.

83. *Ibid.*, 18, 918–919.

84. *Ibid.*, 40, 263.

NOTES TO CHAPTER XVIII

1. Bigelow, *Chancellorsville*, p. 175.

2. *Ibid.*, p. 179.

3. *O.R., 40*, 273–274.

4. *Ibid.*, pp. 276–277.

5. Bigelow, *op. cit.*, p. 190.

6. *O.R., 40*, 277.

7. *Ibid.*, pp. 278–287.

8. Bigelow, *op. cit.*, p. 200.

9. *Ibid.*, p. 206.

10. *O.R., 40,* 288, 293.

11. Bigelow, *op. cit.*, p. 212.

12. *Ibid.*, pp. 213, 216.

13. *Ibid.*, p. 220.

14. *Ibid.*, pp. 218, 221.

15. *Ibid.*, pp. 215, 219.

16. For the high praise of a contemporary British soldier see Bates, *Chancellorsville,* pp. 55–56.

17. *O.R., 40,* 312, 313, 314, 305.

18. *Ibid.*, pp. 306–307, 310, 311–312.

19. *Ibid.*, pp. 301, 309, 315.

20. *Ibid.*, 39, 171.

21. Bigelow, *op. cit.*, p. 233.

22. *O.R., 40,* 322–324.

23. *Ibid.*, p. 324.

24. Bigelow, *op. cit.*, p. 235.

25. *O.R., 40,* 762.

26. Bigelow, *op. cit.*, pp. 132–133, 136, 245.

27. Doubleday, *Chancellorsville and Fredericksburg,* p. 11.

28. *Ibid.*, pp. 12, 13, 14.

29. *O.R., 40,* 342. Balloon "Eagle" was near Banks's Ford.

30. *Ibid.*, pp. 324, 326, 327. At 2:05 P.M. Butterfield informed Hooker that two deserters were just in from Early's division with the word that Hood's division had arrived the day before from Richmond. One of the men, originally from New York State, was described as "intelligent." Just the day before, Hooker was hoping the enemy would be reenforced from Richmond. Deserters were sent on to Washington without delay (Butterfield to Peck, May 2, 6:40 P.M., *ibid.*, p. 371).

31. Doubleday, *op. cit.*, pp. 13–14; Bigelow, *op. cit.*, pp. 250, 254.

32. *O.R., 40,* 328.

33. *Ibid.*, p. 338.

34. *Ibid.*, 342–343. Sedgwick's acknowledgment of the order countermanding the demonstration is in *O.R., 107,* 1034. A number of pages of interesting material on the Chancellorsville Campaign will be found in this supplementary volume.

35. *Ibid.*, pp. 346, 347. See also Schenk to Curtin, on pp. 347–348. There are numerous dispatches bearing on the alarm.

36. *Ibid.*, p. 325; Bigelow, *op. cit.*, p. 255; Young, *Gettysburg,* p. 129.

37. General Orders, No. 32, *O.R., 40,* 167.

38. *Ibid.*, p. 329.

39. *Ibid.*, pp. 332–333, 330.

40. *Ibid.*, 353.

41. Bigelow, *op. cit.*, p. 272.

42. *Ibid.*, pp. 276–277, with comments; *O.R., 40,* 360–361.

43. Probably the most accurate reconstruction of the night is in Freeman, *Lee,* II, 519–524 and Appendix V. Of a turning movement about Hooker,

Freeman writes on p. 515, "General Pope, somewhat similarly placed by Jackson's march on Manassas, had not hesitated to retire precipitately." The implication is not accurate. Pope struck to destroy Jackson; the fact that the movement caused him to move toward Washington was only incidental. One recalls that on Aug. 23, after Stuart's raid on Catlett, Pope had sought to destroy Jackson by a movement up the Rappahannock.

44. *O.R., 40,* 362.

45. Bigelow, *op. cit.,* pp. 279, 286.

46. Normally the leading unit in a march column is changed from day to day; but Slocum kept his own corps ahead both on the 29th and 30th. It was this march formation that resulted in Howards's being on the right of the line. An officer in permanent command of another unit in addition to his own is always—often unjustly—open to the charge that he favors his own command. In this case when "march conditions" ceased, Slocum had an interior position. There was of course opportunity for Hooker to change dispositions on May 1, though it was natural that he did not.

47. Sickles's and Birney's reports, *O.R., 39,* 386, 408.

48. Howard's report, *ibid.,* pp. 630, 628.

49. Bigelow, *op. cit.,* p. 288.

50. *Ibid.,* p. 289, citing the source. Not in *O.R.*

51. *O.R., 40,* 363.

52. The account of Jackson's attack is based on Bigelow, *op. cit.,* pp. 289, 291–328.

53. *Ibid.,* p. 319 n. As Jackson used a saddle without special trappings the horse was not suspected of belonging to an officer of high rank, and was turned over to the cavalry. It was recaptured by the Confederates in the summer and was recognized.

54. *Ibid.,* p. 338.

55. Numerous messages, *O.R., 40,* 353–356.

56. *Ibid.,* pp. 269–270, 300–301, 351.

57. Halleck had assigned Van Alen to duty with the Army of the Potomac on Apr. 24. What regard Hooker had for Van Alen is not apparent; but the editors of the *O.R.* describe him as acting chief of staff for Hooker at Chancellorsville before Butterfield reported. On May 7 he was removed from the staff and given charge of some defensive works. Perhaps Hooker meant to keep him busy with a shovel. He resigned July 14, 1863 (*ibid.,* pp. 249, 964; Phisterer, *Statistical Record,* p. 274, entry 964).

58. Van Alen to Butterfield, *O.R., 40,* 365. The order was repeated an hour later, after a dispatch from Sedgwick had been received.

59. Notably Hamlin. See Wood and Edmonds, *History of the Civil War,* p. 214. Knowing that troops to his left had been withdrawn, Howard should have looked more to his right. Hooker also, after ordering the movement of Sickles and its support by Slocum and Howard, should have seen that proper dispositions were made. Certainly no aggressive commander would have allowed an enemy force to march across his front as Jackson was doing, without taking some measures other than defensive. Though the absence of Sickles's divisions undoubtedly augmented the disaster on the night of May 2, his move

unquestionably put him in a position for a counterattack which could have been much more effective than passive resistance.

60. Bigelow, *op. cit.,* p. 345.

61. For high tribute to the fighting of both armies see Dodge, *Chancellorsville,* pp. 145–146, and Bigelow, op. cit., p. 377. There was no excuse for units to be out of ammunition, since plenty was over the river. Bigelow analyzes a statement by Doubleday on pp. 375–376.

62. Bigelow, *op. cit.,* pp. 350–351.

63. *Ibid.,* pp. 362, 380. Bigelow makes the strong statement, "It looks as if the medical director failed to do his full duty toward freeing the army of its disqualified and incompetent commander." Hooker probably would have protested. It would have been up to Couch to take the responsibility for action upon the official pronouncement of Letterman.

64. *Ibid.,* pp. 369, 366–367.

65. *Ibid.,* p. 397.

66. *Ibid.,* p. 396 n.

67. *Ibid.,* p. 400.

68. *O.R., 40,* 377–379.

69. *Ibid.,* p. 396.

70. *Ibid.,* pp. 769–770.

71. Bigelow, *op. cit.,* pp. 413, 416, 421, 411.

72. *Ibid.,* p. 422.

73. *Ibid.,* pp. 418–430; Barnes's report, *O.R., 39,* 514–516.

74. Bigelow, *op. cit.,* p. 429, mentioning Schurz and Dodge; Hebert, *Fighting Joe Hooker,* p. 220.

75. *O.R., 40,* 779–780.

76. *Ibid., 39,* 802.

77. Bigelow, *op. cit.,* p. 482.

78. *Ibid.,* pp. 440–459.

79. Freeman, *Lee's Lieutenants,* III, 41–42.

80. *O.R., 40,* 370, 413.

81. Babcock to Sharpe, *ibid.,* p. 421.

82. Bigelow, *op. cit.,* pp. 454–455.

83. Averell to Candler, with enclosure of Stoneman to Averell, *O.R., 40,* 352–353.

84. Bigelow, *op. cit.,* p. 458.

85. *Ibid.,* p. 478 n.

86. Dix, *Memoirs of John Dix,* II, 57.

NOTES TO CHAPTER XIX

1. Brooks, *Washington in Lincoln's Time,* pp. 56–68.

2. *O.R., 40,* 421–422.

3. *Ibid.,* pp. 433–434.

4. *Ibid.,* p. 413. Correspondence between Halleck and Hooker had, how-

ever, dropped off, after having been extensive for some time after Hooker assumed command. In his very brief report on the campaign Halleck stated: "General Hooker reported directly to the President, and received directions directly from him. I received no official information of his plans or of their execution" (*ibid.*, *39*, 156). Halleck forgot about his directive of Mar. 27 (*ibid.*, *40*, 158), and there is an error in the implication that Lincoln had given instructions.

5. *Ibid.*, p. 434. At 1:45 Lincoln wired Ingalls, "News has gone to General Hooker which may change his plans. Act in view of such contingency." The dispatch must refer to something about supply that is not explained in the *O.R.*

6. *Ibid.*, p. 435.

7. *Ibid.*, *39*, 171.

8. *Ibid.*, *40*, 435.

9. Brooks, *op. cit.*, p. 58.

10. *O.R.*, *40*, 434–435.

11. *Ibid.*, p. 438.

12. *Ibid.*, *40*, 437–438. Charles F. Benjamin, "Hooker's Appointment and Removal," *B. and L.*, III, 240–241, states that Lincoln returned to Washington on the night of the 6th, that he directed Halleck to remain till he knew "everything," and that Halleck, who was a skillful cross-examiner, got the full truth out of corps commanders and Hooker's staff about the battle, the implication being that he remained with the army several days. After Halleck brought back his findings, Benjamin asserts, a meeting was held by Lincoln, Stanton, and Halleck, at which it was decided that Hooker must not be allowed to fight another battle.

That Lincoln did not return to Washington on the night of the 6th is shown by his memorandum to Hooker, dated May 7; that Halleck was not left behind to conduct an investigation is proved in Stanton's telegram of the 7th to the governors and the generals by the first sentence: "The President and General in Chief have just returned from the Army of the Potomac." Benjamin gives a great deal of "inside" information, much of which certainly did not come to him first hand, and must have been in the nature of gossip or conjecture. Because he is incorrect and imaginative in simple factual matters, such as Halleck's being left behind to conduct an investigation, it would seem that not much confidence can be placed on what he said took place behind closed doors.

13. *O.R.*, *40*, 439.

14. *O.R.*, *39*, 192.

15. Freeman gives a detailed account of Jackson's death in *Lee's Lieutenants,* II, 675–682.

16. N. Malcolm, "Tactics," *Encyclopædia Britannica*, 12th ed., XXXII, 658–675, especially 673. This is a brilliant study by a one-time instructor in military history at the Staff College, Camberley, who commanded the British Army of Occupation in Germany after World War I.

17. The account of the Vallandigham incident is based largely on Nicolay and Hay, *Lincoln*, VII, 328–360.

18. Greeley, *American Conflict*, II, 493.

19. Bill, *Beleaguered City*, pp. 165–166.

20. *O.R.*, *44*, 305.

21. Bill, *op. cit.*, p. 175 and n. 5.

22. Dowdey, *Experiment in Rebellion*, p. 17. The York River road was of no value after the Peninsula campaign.

23. Annual report, Dec. 1, 1862, *O.R.*, *123*, 905–906; Hungerford, *B. & O. Railroad*, II, 42–43.

24. Freeman, *Lee*, III, 19.

25. Dowdey (*op. cit.*, pp. 283–286) describes a cabinet meeting of May 16 with all the vivid detail of one who had been present. He states that Lee was in attendance, and that the only person who opposed the invasion plan was Postmaster General John Reagan, who walked the floor that night "talking to his wife." Dowdey presents a rather dramatic scene the next morning—Sunday—with Reagan calling at the home of President Davis, apologizing for intruding but renewing his opposition to the cabinet decision and asking that it be reconsidered. The President listened, pale, thin, and frail, his hollow cheeks showing his own torment, but "said the decision was final." This story is not in agreement with Reagan's *Memoirs*, pp. 150–152, in which he stated that he remembered the crucial Saturday meeting with great clearness, and that Lee was *not present,* though he had attended earlier cabinet meetings. Reagan recorded that he was practically alone in opposing the invasion of the North; but he said nothing about walking the floor in his distress, nor did he mention Mrs. Reagan. Dowdey's account of the Sunday call on Davis with the sunlight streaming through the window of the little study, and Reagan's statement that he wrote a note to Davis without mentioning a visit to the President's house, are hard to reconcile.

26. Longstreet, *Manassas to Appomattox*, p. 331.

27. Freeman, *Lee's Lieutenants,* III, 21.

28. Swinton, *Army of the Potomac*, p. 340. Swinton adds in a footnote, "This, and subsequent revelations of the purposes and sentiments of Lee, I derive from General Longstreet, who, in a full and free conversation with the writer, after the close of the war, threw much light on the motives and conduct of Lee during this campaign."

29. *O.R.*, *45*, 868–869, 882.

30. *B. and L.*, III, 639 n.

31. *O.R.*, *69*, 896.

32. Longstreet, *op. cit.*, p. 232 n., wrote of D. H. Hill, "His record was as good as that of 'Stonewall' Jackson, but, not being a Virginian, he was not so well advertised."

33. *O.R.*, *40*, 846, 823, 821.

34. *Ibid.*, pp. 528, 527, 529, 542.

35. *Ibid.*, pp. 820–821, 834.

36. *Ibid.*, pp. 574, 504–506, 532.

37. *Ibid.*, p. 595.

38. *Ibid.*, *43*, 30.

39. Stanton to the President, inclosing a long report from Halleck, *ibid.*, *40*, 503–506.

40. *Ibid.*, *43*, 31–32.

41. *Ibid.*, *45*, 11, 7.

42. *Ibid.*, p. 18.

43. *Ibid.*, *40*, 525–527, and *45*, 886, 895.

44. *Ibid.*, *45*, 17, 12–13.

45. *Ibid.*, *43*, 34–35. This was the dispatch in which Lincoln told Hooker to fight Lee when opportunity offered, and to "fret him and fret him" if he remained where he was—a rather indefinite injunction, but one indicating Lincoln's desire for action.

46. Dowdey, *op. cit.*, pp. 16–17.

47. Freeman, *Lee's Lieutenants*, III, chap. i, "Much Pomp Ends in Humiliation," gives an excellent account of the review and the battle.

48. Hooker to Halleck, June 12, *O.R.*, *43*, 36.

49. Pleasonton to Butterfield, Butterfield to Pleasonton, *ibid.*, *45*, 49, 39. In several dispatches Pleasonton referred to infantry.

50. *Ibid.*, p. 58.

51. Pleasonton to Hooker, June 9, 7:40 A.M., *ibid.*, p. 38; Freeman *op. cit.*, p. 19.

52. *O.R.*, *45*, 48–49; Freeman, *op. cit.*, pp. 3–5.

53. *O.R.*, *45*, 47–48; Hooker to Halleck, June 12, and to Lincoln, June 14, *ibid.*, *43*, 36, 39. Hooker put Ewell and Longstreet's column at from 70,000 to 80,000 and Hill's corps at 30,000.

54. Supplemented by circular from Ingalls, *ibid.*, *45*, 67–68.

55. *Ibid.*, pp. 72–73.

56. *Ibid.*, *43*, 37, and *45*, 78–79.

57. *Ibid.*, *45*, 80; Freeman, *op. cit.*, p. 20.

58. *O.R.*, *45*, 81, 82.

59. *Ibid.*, *43*, 37.

60. *Ibid.*, *45*, 88–89.

61. Williams to Caldwell, June 13, *ibid.*, p. 95.

62. *Ibid.*, pp. 93–94.

63. Sandburg, *Lincoln*, II, 340.

64. *O.R.*, *45*, 36.

65. *O.R.*, *43*, 47–48, and *45*, 54.

66. *Ibid.*, *45*, 53, 44–45.

67. For Couch's order taking command and giving details about the Department Corps, see *ibid.*, pp. 68–69.

68. *Ibid.*, pp. 76–77, 79–80.

69. *Ibid.*, pp. 36–37, 44, 66.

70. *Ibid.*, pp. 50–51, 95.

71. *Ibid.*, *107*, 1055, and *43*, 39.

72. *Ibid.*, *43*, 40–41.

73. *Ibid.*, *45*, 124; *31*, 954.

74. *Ibid.*, *45*, 124.

75. *Ibid.*, pp. 126, 129.

76. Freeman, *op. cit.*, p. 27; Couch to Schenck, *O.R.*, *45*, 162. The number of wagons seems excessively large for Milroy's small command.

77. Couch to Stanton, *ibid.*, p. 264. Milroy's force gave some protection against Imboden's cavalry, which had turned westward toward Hancock.

78. Couch to Schenck, *ibid.*, p. 263.

79. Nicolay and Hay, *Lincoln*, VII, 208–209 n.; *O.R., 44*, 197. After discussing the connection of Halleck, Schenck, and Milroy with the holding and evacuation of Winchester, Lincoln concluded, "Serious blame is not necessarily due to any disaster, and I cannot say that in this case any of the officers are deserving of serious blame. No court-martial is deemed necessary or proper in the case." The original of Lincoln's letter to Milroy is owned by Foreman M. Lebold.

80. Freeman, *op. cit.*, p. 27.

81. *O.R., 45*, 136–138.

82. *Ibid.*, pp. 131, 140.

83. *Ibid.*, pp. 140, 241.

84. *O.R., 45*, 147.

85. *Ibid.*, pp. 150–151.

86. *Ibid., 43*, 45, 47.

87. Nicolay and Hay, *Lincoln*, VII, 212. It is to be noted that Lincoln said he believed Lee's return toward Harpers Ferry would give Hooker back the chance that McClellan had lost the previous fall. He closed by urging the "best cordial judgment" between Hooker and Halleck, offering to contribute his "mite" if the generals thought it "entitled to any consideration whatever."

88. *O.R., 43*, 45–47, and *45*, 151–152.

89. *Ibid., 45*, 171, and *43*, 48–50.

90. *Ibid.*, pp. 51, 52, 47–48.

91. *Ibid.*, pp. 52–53. Hooker inquired whether Halleck gave credit to the reported movements of the enemy as stated in the Chronicle of the 19th. Halleck replied: "I do not know to what particular statement in the Chronicle you refer. There are several which are contradictory." Then he gave the views described in the text.

92. *Ibid., 45*, 244.

93. *Ibid., 43*, 51, 55, 56, 57. Hooker complained that Gen. Slough, military governor of Alexandria, had not obeyed his orders, and asked that he be arrested, stating that he would prepare charges against him at once. Halleck explained that a certain brigade about which there was question did not belong to the division that had been put at Hooker's disposal, and he stated that no more troops could be withdrawn from Washington.

94. *Ibid., 107*, 1062. The dispatches described in the last note were sent on the 25th, and show that some sort of misunderstanding resulted from the Washington conference.

95. Butterfield to Hooker, Halleck to Hooker, June 24, *ibid., 45*, 286; *43*, 56.

96. *Ibid., 45*, 301–303.

97. *Ibid., 43*, 56.

98. *Ibid., 45*, 333.

99. *Ibid.*, pp. 240, 264.

100. *Ibid.*, pp. 225, 227, 271, 285–286.

101. Tyler to Halleck, *ibid.*, p. 294.

102. *Ibid.*, p. 295.

103. *Ibid.*, pp. 148–149.

104. *Ibid.*, p. 292.

105. A complete itinerary of the Army of the Potomac for the period June 5 to July 31, compiled in the office of the adjutant general of the Army, is given in *O.R., 43*, 140–150.

106. An excellent dispatch to Reynolds that would make him fully informed, *ibid., 45*, 314.

107. *Ibid., 43*, 57, and *45*, 369–370.

108. *Ibid., 43*, 920–921.

109. *Ibid., 45*, 323, 345–346.

110. It is sometimes stated that Jefferson Davis was responsible or remiss for failure to carry out Lee's wish in this matter. An intercepted dispatch from Cooper to Lee, dated June 29, gives a good deal of light on the question, and indicates that Davis knew nothing of the proposal until June 28 (*ibid., 43*, 75–76).

111. *Ibid., 45*, 347–348.

112. *Ibid.*, p. 328.

113. *Ibid.*, p. 348.

NOTES TO CHAPTER XX

1. *O.R., 43*, 58.

2. *Ibid.*, pp. 58, 59.

3. *Ibid., 45*, 336.

4. *Ibid.*, p. 312.

5. *Ibid.*, p. 349.

6. *O.R., 43*, 59.

7. *Ibid., 43*, 56, and *45*, 317.

8. *Ibid., 43*, 60. The hour at which this important dispatch was sent is not shown, but it was probably between 10:00 A.M. and noon.

9. *Ibid., 27*, 800.

10. *N.Y. Tribune*, July 1, 1863.

11. As previously observed, Johnston destroyed the bridge when he evacuated Harpers Ferry in June, 1861. It was not rebuilt until March, 1862, probably because the Federals did not control the lower Shenandoah Valley. The new bridge was washed away on April 22. Another was erected at once; but on June 7 it went before the flood that came from the storms that did so much to save Jackson from Frémont and McDowell. A new trestle bridge was built within a week, but it was replaced by an iron bridge during the summer.

12. *O.R., 28*, 520.

13. Hungerford, *B. & O.*, II, 24. Within two weeks the new bridge was tested by a high flood, and cars loaded with coal were placed on it to increase its resistance to the swollen river.

14. Randall, *Lincoln the President*, II, 272. Frothingham in his article on Antietam, *Proc. Mass. Hist. Soc.*, LVI, 173–208 (especialy 186), states that Harpers Ferry was without strategic value. It may be recalled that Jefferson Davis realized the strategic value of the position and Lee mentioned it to Johnston in a letter of June 7, 1861.

15. *O.R.*, *43*, 60.

16. Nicolay and Hay, *Lincoln*, VII, 226.

17. *O.R.*, *45*, 354, 355.

18. Young, *Gettysburg*, p. 144.

19. Meade, *Life and Letters*, I, 389.

20. *O.R.*, *43*, 60.

21. *Ibid.*, *45*, 369 (General Orders, No. 194), and *43*, 61.

22. Benjamin, "Hooker's Appointment and Removal," *B. and L.*, III, 239–243.

23. *O.R.*, *45*, 374; Meade, *op. cit.*, II, 1. Col. Hardie was the Gen. Hardie on Burnside's staff at the battle of Fredericksburg. Lacking confirmation by the Senate, his commission as brigadier general had expired on Jan. 22, 1863; he was promoted from colonel to brevet major general on Mar. 13, 1865 (Phisterer, *Statistical Record*, pp. 279, 248). At the time in question he must have been wearing the insignia of a colonel.

24. Randall, *op. cit.*, II, 273, seemingly uses Benjamin as authority.

25. Meade, *op. cit.*, II, 11, and I, 388.

26. *O.R.*, *45*, 373–374, 378.

27. Sawtelle to Ingalls, June 28, 7:00 P.M., *ibid.*, p. 380.

28. *Ibid.*, *43*, 61–62.

29. *Ibid.*, *45*, 374, 371, 372, and *43*, 144.

30. On the 28th Col. Lowell was at Poolesville with the 2nd Massachusetts Cavalry (Potter to Schenck, *ibid.*, *45*, 383).

31. Meade to Butterfield, Feb. 4, 1864, *ibid.*, *43*, 21.

32. *Ibid.*, pp. 62, 63.

33. *Ibid.*, *45*, 378, 382.

34. Meade to Butterfield, Feb. 4, Butterfield to Meade, Jan. 23, 1864, *ibid.*, *43*, 20–21; French's report, *ibid.*, pp. 488–489.

35. On the 27th Howard sent a dispatch to army headquarters that stated, "I have reports from different sources that Stuart's cavalry, or a part, crossed the river at Shepherdstown last night" (*ibid.*, *45*, 352).

36. *Ibid.*, *43*, 62–64.

37. Freeman, *Lee's Lieutenants*, II, 66.

38. Sawtelle to Ingalls, *O.R.*, *45*, 380.

39. Freeman, *op. cit.*, p. 67.

40. *O.R.*, *43*, 65.

41. Meade, *op. cit.*, II, 355.

42. *O.R.*, *45*, 930–931.

43. *Ibid.*, pp. 374–375.

44. Dawes, *Service with the Sixth Wisconsin*, p. 157.

45. *O.R.*, *45*, 924.

46. *Ibid.*, p. 913.

47. *Ibid.*, p. 914. A later dispatch described orders given Stuart.

48. *Ibid.*, p. 923.

49. Freeman's account (*op. cit.*, III, 60–68) of Stuart's experiences up to June 29 has been followed.

50. Longstreet, *Manassas to Appomattox*, p. 323; Freeman, *Lee*, III, 60–61. For an account of Mosby's challenge of the Harrison story and its refutation, see Young, *Gettysburg*, pp. 148–151.

51. Marshall, *Aide-de-Camp of Lee*, p. 250.

52. Henderson, *Stonewall Jackson*, p. 689.

53. In the order of June 23 (*O.R., 45,* 923), Lee had a very bad "if-but" sentence: "If General Hooker's army remains inactive, you can leave two brigades to watch him, and withdraw with the three others, but should he not appear to be moving northward, I think you had better withdraw this side of the mountain to-morrow night, cross at Shepherdstown next day, and move over to Fredericktown." When one comes to the word "but" he has been prepared for directions to be followed in case Hooker did not remain inactive. Instead directions that have already been given are repeated in an altered and amplified manner. Actually there were no instructions for the contingency of Hooker's moving northward, except by implication. Though Stuart was not told specifically to ride around Hooker in case the latter was moving north, he was forbidden to conduct such an operation if the Federal army did not move northward.

54. *O.R., 45,* 930–933, 942–943; Freeman, *Lee,* III, 53–55.

55. Bill, *Beleaguered City,* p. 170.

56. *O.R., 43,* 75–77.

57. *Ibid.,* pp. 17–19.

58. *Ibid., 45,* 947.

59. Davis to *Lee, ibid.,* 43, 75–77.

60. *Ibid.,* p. 936.

61. *Ibid.,* pp. 453–455.

62. Dix to Halleck, *ibid., 43,* 18–19, and *45,* 412.

63. Jones to Davis, *ibid., 45,* 957–959.

64. Lee to Davis, June 23, *ibid.,* pp. 924–925. Lee wrote: "The good effects of beginning to assemble an army at Culpeper Court-House would, I think, soon become apparent, and the movement might be increased in importance as the result might appear to justify. Should you agree with me, I need not say that it is desirable that the execution of the plan proposed should immediately begin. The enemy will hear of it soon enough, and a proper reticence on the part of our papers will cause them to attribute greater importance to it. I need not mention the benefit that the troops themselves would derive from being transferred to a more healthy climate." There is nothing in this to indicate that Lee believed that plans for such a concentration as he described were already under way. The letter arrived June 28, and Adj. Gen. Cooper replied on the 29th: "This is the first intimation that he [Davis] has had that such a plan was ever in contemplation, and, taking all things into consideration, he cannot see how it can by any possibility be carried into effect." Lee wanted the forces at Culpeper put under Gen. Beauregard.

65. Butterfield to Halleck, July 3, *ibid., 43,* 75.

66. *Ibid., 45,* 447–448.

67. Couch to Col. Frick, commanding at Columbia, *ibid.,* p. 385. The instructions said nothing about burning the bridge. They directed that its planking be taken up and stated that in no event should the bridge fall into the enemy's hands, which would certainly imply its destruction in case of necessity.

68. Schultz to Wilson, *ibid.,* p. 388. Instructions about firing the Harrisburg bridge "at a moment's notice" were specific.

69. Reno to Couch, 6:20 P.M., *ibid.*, pp. 387–388.
70. *Ibid.*, Atlas, II, Plate 116, 2.
71. *Ibid.*, 45, 390.
72. *Ibid.*, p. 385.
73. *Ibid.*, p. 390.
74. *Ibid.*, p. 391.

NOTES TO CHAPTER XXI

1. Dawes, *Service with Sixth Wisconsin*, p. 158.
2. "The people give and sell something to the men to eat, but I can't stand that way of subsisting, it causes dreadful straggling." Buford to Reynolds, *O.R.*, 43, 923–924.
3. Long, *Memoirs*, p. 274.
4. Meade, *General Meade*, II, 18.
5. *O.R.*, 43, 66–67.
6. *Ibid.*, p. 68.
7. *Ibid.*, 45, 414–417.
8. *Ibid.*, p. 416.
9. *Ibid.*, 43, 68–69; Blackford, *War Years with Jeb Stuart*, pp. 226–227.
10. *O.R.*, 45, 434, 436–437, 409. On the 29th Parker had wired Lincoln: "The people of New Jersey are apprehensive that the invasion of the enemy may extend to their soil. . . . The people of New Jersey want McClellan at the head of the Army of the Potomac. If that cannot be done, then we ask that he may be put at the head of the New Jersey, New York, and Pennsylvania troops now in Pennsylvania, defending these Middle States from invasion. If either appointment be made, the people would rise *en masse*." The New Jersey troops must have been keeping themselves in hiding until McClellan appeared, for Couch's return for June 30 listed no New Jersey units (*ibid.*, pp. 447–448). As to calling McClellan back Lincoln wrote with remarkable frankness, "I beg you to be assured that no one out of my position can know so well as if he were in it the difficulties and involvements of replacing General McClellan in command, and this aside from any imputations upon him."
11. Greeley, *American Conflict*, II, 376; Haupt, *Reminiscences*, p. 214.
12. With regard to Meade's failure to get proper rest and sleep see *infra*, p. 743: He had written on the 30th to Halleck, "I fear that I shall break down the troops by pushing on much faster, and may have to rest a day." Certainly there was no reason for him to be moving "much faster."
13. *Ibid.*, 45, 434. Meade's dispatch to Halleck of 7:00 A.M. July 1, began by acknowledging receipt of dispatches from Couch and Haupt (*ibid.*, 43, 70).
14. Stanton to Meade, *ibid.*, 43, 69; Hungerford, *B. & O. R.R.*, II, 39.
15. *O.R.*, 43, 70.
16. *Ibid.*, p. 71.
17. *Ibid.*, 45, 458–459.
18. *Ibid.*, 43, 70–71.

19. Meade to Halleck, *ibid.*, pp. 68–69.

20. *Ibid.*, p. 71.

21. *Ibid.*, p. 927.

22. *Ibid.*, *45*, 470.

23. *B. and L.*, III, 274–275 n. According to this account, pickets from Devin's brigade were covering the Chambersburg Road at the first contact, that brigade later moving to the right when Gamble came up.

24. *O.R.*, *43*, 924.

25. Doubleday, *Chancellorsville and Gettysburg*, pp. 126–127. Doubleday discusses the nature of the order sent to Howard—a matter of some dispute.

26. *Ibid.*, p. 132.

27. Wadsworth's report, *O.R.*, *43*, 265–267.

28. Buford's report, *ibid.*, p. 927; *B. and L.*, III, 276 n.

29. Doubleday, *op. cit.*, pp. 132 ff.

30. Howard's report, *O.R.*, *43*, 702.

31. *Ibid.*, pp. 924–925.

32. Doubleday's and Buford's reports, *ibid.*, pp. 250–252, 927.

33. Young, *Gettysburg*, p. 201; *O.R.*, *43*, 266.

34. *O.R.*, *43*, 187. Freeman put the number of "bewildered prisoners" taken at nearly 5,000 in *Lee*, III, 71, and close to 4,000 in *Lee's Lieutenants*, III, 97.

35. Young (*op. cit.*, p. 197) makes such an accusation.

36. *O.R.*, *43*, 366.

37. At 5:00 P.M. Howard wrote to Meade: "General Hancock arrived at 4 p.m., and communicated his intentions. I am still holding on at this time." At 5:25 P.M. Hancock reported quite as if he were in command (*ibid.*, pp. 696, 366). For a recollection of the conversation between Howard and Hancock at the time the latter arrived, as remembered by a staff officer, see *B. and L.*, III, 285.

38. *O.R.*, *43*, 704.

39. Dawes, *op. cit.*, p. 179.

40. Cutler's, Hunt's, and Schurz's reports, *O.R.*, *43*, 283, 231, 730; Freeman, *Lee's Lieutenants*, III, 93.

41. *O.R.*, *45*, 463–465.

42. *Ibid.*, *43*, 825, 366, 770, 777.

43. *Ibid.*, pp. 696, 704.

44. *Ibid.*, *45*, 468.

45. *B. and L.*, III, 284.

46. Freeman, *Lee's Lieutenants*, III, chap. vi, and especially p. 97. (His treatment in *Lee*, III, chap. vi, "The Spirit That Inhibits Victory," is equally severe.)

47. *O.R.*, *43*, 751.

48. Grover's report, *ibid.*, p. 284. Grover did not use the name Culp's Hill, but stated that the position was the extreme right of the Federal line, and that he held the same position until evening of the 3rd. Gen. Meade's son said that Wadsworth's division occupied the summit of Culp's Hill on the morning of July 2 (Meade, *op. cit.*, p. 65). Dawes stated specifically in his report that the Iron Brigade was sent to Culp's Hill (*O.R.*, *43*, 277).

49. Freeman, *op. cit.*, pp. 103, 92, 104 n. Douglas quotes Pendleton, of

Ewell's staff, and formerly of Jackson's, as remarking on account of Ewell's seeming indecision, "Oh, for the presence and inspiration of 'Old Jack' for just one hour" (*I Rode with Stonewall,* p. 247). Such a remark, even if made, has little to do with the question. If he made it, Pendleton forgot that, a year and a day before, his hero lost a whole afternoon in a way that has never been explained, and as a result McClellan's corps commanders extricated part of his army from its dangerous position at Frayser's Farm.

50. *O.R., 44,* 445, 319–320. Ewell noted that the Federals showed a formidable front on Cemetery Hill very quickly, and that he could not use artillery against the position; the hill could not be attacked from the town, and his troops were worn out with twelve hours of marching and fighting; in addition he had been told that Johnson's division would arrive soon. In 1870 Meade wrote a long letter in which he made much of a conversation with Ewell shortly after the war (*B. and L.,* III, 413–414). Ewell had told him that he had 20,000 men ready to attack Cemetery Hill at 4:00 P.M., but was held back by an order from Lee directing him to assume the defensive; he had sent an urgent request to Gen. Lee to be allowed to attack, "but the reply was a reiteration of the previous order." Just what Ewell said to Meade cannot of course be even guessed at; but it is hard to believe that he made a claim even approximating that with which he was credited. Doubtless he did refer to instructions from Lee that were of a cautioning nature.

Lee wrote, "General Ewell was, therefore, instructed to carry the hill occupied by the enemy, if he found it practicable, but to avoid a general engagement until the arrival of the other divisions of the army, which were ordered to hasten forward. He decided to await Johnson's division."

51. Freeman, *Lee's Lieutenants,* III, 172.

52. Lee's report, *O.R., 44,* 317–318.

53. Frédéric Culmann, quoted in *Infantry Journal,* XLIII, 45 (1936).

54. *O.R., 43,* 927. Buford added that Hancock "made superb disposition to resist any attack that might be made" on Cemetery Hill.

55. Freeman, *op. cit.,* p. 104. It is only after he refers to a dispatch that Sykes wrote to Slocum sometime after midnight July 1–2, that Freeman indicates that Ewell and Lee had reason to believe that Federal troops other than the First and Eleventh Corps were near at hand.

56. Meade, *op. cit.,* p. 62.

57. *O.R., 45,* 466.

58. *Ibid., 43,* 71–72.

59. *Ibid., 45,* 465, 467–468.

60. That Meade went forward without seeing Sedgwick is shown by a dispatch Butterfield sent to him at 2:40 A.M., July 2 (*ibid.,* p. 483).

61. Meade, *op. cit.,* p. 63.

62. *O.R., 43,* 927.

63. Birney stated that he marched from Emmitsburg over a road "rendered almost impassable by mud and the passage over it of the First and Eleventh Corps through the rain" (*ibid.,* p. 482).

64. Slocum, who had command over the Fifth Corps while it was on the Federal right, put the time of its arrival at 5:00 A.M.; Sykes put it at 8:00:

Barnes, at 7:00 (*ibid.*, pp. 759, 592, 600). The discrepancies may have been due to faulty memories or to the fact that one officer referred to the head of a column and another to its rear.

65. Frank A. Haskell, "The Battle of Gettysburg," *Harvard Classics,* XLIII, 357.

66. Writers disagree over the right third of the line. The deployment given is based on Meade, *op. cit.,* pp. 64–66, and the map in Young, *op. cit.,* p. 240.

67. Haskell, *op. cit.,* p. 360, says 8:00 A.M.

68. Col. Charles Candy, commanding the First Brigade of Geary's division, spoke of the brigade as occupying "a high range of hills," which indicates something more than Little Round Top (*O.R., 43,* 836).

69. Gen. Meade's testimony before the Committee on the Conduct of the War (Meade, *op. cit.,* p. 380).

70. *O.R., 43,* 483–484.

71. *Ibid., 45,* 486.

72. *Ibid.,* p. 487.

73. *B. and L.,* III, 411; Meade, *op. cit.,* p. 392.

74. *B. and L.,* III, 411.

75. Meade, *op. cit.,* p. 380.

76. *B. and L.,* III, 413.

77. *O.R., 43,* 482.

78. Sickles's own account written in 1886, see *B. and L.,* III, 414–419. For an account of Meade's son, written probably still later, see Meade, *op. cit.,* pp. 66 ff.

79. Hunt, "The Second Day at Gettysburg," *B. and L.,* III, 301–302.

80. Birney's report, *O.R., 43,* 482.

81. Storrick, *Gettysburg,* p. 32.

82. Haskell, *op. cit.,* p. 367.

83. *Ibid.,* p. 365.

84. *Ibid.,* p. 362.

85. Shown by an indorsement on the dispatch. *O.R., 45,* 474.

86. *Ibid.,* pp. 476–478.

87. Haupt to Ingalls, from Baltimore, July 1, Haupt, *Reminiscences,* pp. 214–216.

88. *O.R., 45,* 472.

89. Buford's report, *ibid., 43,* 928.

90. Haupt, *op. cit.,* p. 214.

91. *O.R., 43,* 72. The copy in Meade, II, 395, has "and" instead of "but" in the last sentence.

92. Capt. Frederick Bernays Wiener in "Decline of a Leader," *Infantry Journal,* XLV, 537 (1938), comments very sharply on the last sentence of Meade's dispatch.

93. For Sickles's account and criticism of Meade, see *B. and L.,* III, 416.

94. Meade, *op. cit.,* p. 72.

95. Young, *op. cit.,* pp. 264–265.

96. *Ibid.,* pp. 232–243 ("The Safeguarding of Little Round Top").

97. Hunt's account, *B. and L.,* III, 312.

98. Young, *op. cit.*, pp. 277–282, 270–276 ("Assaults on Culp's Hill," "The Attack on Cemetery Hill").

99. *O.R., 43,* 72.

100. Haskell, *op. cit.*, p. 383.

101. *O.R., 43,* 73–74.

102. Gen. Meade called attention to the newspaper articles, in a circular sent to corps commanders Mar. 10, 1864. See Meade, *op. cit.*, 413, with a discussion of the entire controversy in Appendices X and Y.

103. Slocum to Doubleday, Feb. 19, 1883, *ibid.*, p. 398.

104. *Ibid.*, p. 407.

NOTES TO CHAPTER XXII

1. Slocum's report, *O.R., 43,* 751.

2. For an account of Slocum's battle, see Meade, *Life and Letters,* II, 101–102.

3. Shaler's report, *O.R., 43,* 680–681.

4. *Ibid.*, p. 74.

5. Haskell, "The Battle of Gettysburg," pp. 386, 387.

6. Blackford, *Letters from Lee's Army,* p. 187. The Confederate captain, a brother of Lieut. Col. W. W. Blackford, the author of *War Years with Jeb Stuart,* was not too well impressed with the Cumberland Valley. On June 28 he wrote from Chambersburg, saying that the land was rich and highly cultivated, but the people were not; in the town itself there were some beautiful places that seemed to reveal some taste, and even culture and refinement, but in the country there was nothing but tasteless houses and immense barns, all alike. If there were any pretty women, they were not showing themselves (p. 184). Not unnaturally Blackford emphasized the discipline under which the Confederates were held and spoke of their generally good behavior. In this he probably did not exaggerate, for on June 30, the *N.Y. Tribune* reported that private property was being respected.

7. Hunt, "The Third Day at Gettysburg," *B. and L.,* III, 372.

8. Meade, *op. cit.*, 104. This very important statement occurs in that part of of the work in question that was not written by the son of Gen. Meade, who was in the battle, but by the grandson. Confirmation of such an understanding between the two generals is supplied by the message from Hancock to Meade on the evening of July 3, presently mentioned.

9. *O.R., 45,* 501–502.

10. *Ibid.*, pp. 506, 507.

11. *Ibid.*, p. 506.

12. *Ibid.*, p. 500.

13. Col. Long, of Lee's staff, had served before the war with Hunt's battery for the express purpose of receiving instruction in the use of artillery. At Appomattox the two officers reminisced, and Hunt criticized the Confederates for firing all over the field at Gettysburg. Amused at the comment, Long

replied, "I remembered my lessons at the time, and when the fire became so scattered, wondered what you would think of it" (Hunt, *op. cit.*, pp. 374–375).

In view of some statements Hunt made in his own report, his criticisms were not entirely fair. For although the Confederate fire was not landing well on the intended targets, it was sweeping an area behind the crest and was injuring animals and carriages (*O.R., 43,* 240).

14. *Ibid., 107,* 1069.

15. *Ibid., 43,* 240. Hunt said that the Confederate loss in matériel was equal to that of the Federals, and that marks on the trees showed that the Union fire had been more accurate.

16. Freeman, *Lee's Lieutenants,* III, 156.

17. Haskell, *op. cit.,* p. 402; Storrick, *Gettysburg,* p. 42.

18. Hunt, *op. cit.,* pp. 374–375.

19. The important position of commanding five batteries totaling twenty-eight guns was held by Capt. John G. Hazard. No subordinate officer could have observed the assault with much more concern than he, and he gave a dramatic account in his report. Of the ammunition situation in batteries of the Second Corps, he wrote: "The other batteries were in similar condition; still, they bided the attack. The rebel lines advanced slowly but surely; half the valley had been passed over by them before the guns dared expend a round of the precious ammunition remaining on hand. The enemy steadily approached, and, when within deadly range, canister was thrown with terrible effect into their ranks" (*O.R., 43,* 279–280).

20. Haskell, *op. cit.,* p. 404.

21. A distinguished observer of the Confederate operations was Col. Arthur J. Lyon Fremantle of the Coldstream Guards, who recorded his observations in a small book, *Three Months in the Confederacy.* He stated that the Confederates believed the "Rebel yell has a particular merit, and always produces a salutary effect upon their adversaries." On this account a unit was "sometimes spoken of as a good yelling regiment" (Storrick, *op. cit.,* p. 57).

22. Hall's report, *O.R., 43,* 436–441. Hall gave two diagrams to show how the Confederate attacking lines shifted to their left, and how his brigade and that of Webb operated. Extracts from his report and from that of Webb are given in *B. and L.* III, 390–391.

23. Storrick, *op. cit.,* p. 43.

24. *O.R., 43,* 366.

25. Storrick, *op. cit.,* p. 58.

26. Storrick, *op. cit.,* p. 49, puts the Federals at 5,000, the Confederates at 7,000.

27. Blackford, *War Years with Stuart,* p. 233.

28. Kilpatrick's and Merritt's reports, *O.R., 43,* 992, 943.

29. H. C. Parsons, "Farnsworth's Charge and Death," *B. and L.,* III, 393, 394.

30. *O.R.,* pp. 916, 993. Merritt spoke of his success (*ibid.,* p. 943).

31. *Ibid.,* pp. 74–75.

32. Merritt's report, *ibid.,* p. 943.

33. *Ibid.,* p. 187.

34. Shaler's report, *ibid.*, p. 682.

35. *O.R.*, *44*, 346. Freeman (*Lee's Lieutenants*, III, 190) notes that, if there is an error, the figure is too small.

36. Livermore, *Numbers and Losses*, pp. 102–103. The Federal strength return for June 30 gave 5,286 officers and 71,822 men as present for duty equipped in the seven infantry corps and the artillery reserve, the figure for the cavalry corps not being given. The aggregate present was 117,930 (*O.R.*, *43*, 151).

37. The "private letter" that Meade wrote in 1870 was published in *B. and L.*, III, 413–414. References in it to Sickles are unsatisfactory. Meade stated also that the Fifth Corps lost 50 per cent of its strength in supporting the Third Corps on July 2. The total casualties in the Fifth Corps were 2,187; but on June 30 it had 12,509 officers and men present for duty equipped (*O.R.*, *43*, 187, 151). Thus his statement looks like a great exaggeration.

For Sickles's reply to Meade, see *B. and L.*, III, 414–419. Just how much can be accepted in an article written so long after the event is uncertain. But in the controversy as to the exact orders given to Sickles on the morning of July 2, the case must go against Meade, for his failure to produce a written order. There is also reason to believe that Meade paid insufficient attention to Sickles's reports about his position.

38. Pinchon, *Dan Sickles,* chaps. xv, xvi.

39. Battine commented: "The only merit of the new position was that it acted like a breakwater upon which the fury of the attack spent itself, and by the delay enabled all the Federal troops to come into line" (*Crisis of the Confederacy,* p. 216).

Doubleday stated: "The movement, disastrous in some respects, was propitious as regards its general results, for the enemy had wasted all their strength and valor in gaining the Emmitsburg road, which after all was of no particular benefit to them. They were still outside our main line" (*Chancellorsville and Gettysburg,* p. 178).

40. Young, *Gettysburg,* p. 226. The letter is quoted by Helen D. Longstreet in *Lee and Longstreet at High Tide* (p. 9) and in part by Pinchon, *op. cit.,* (p. 267). Longstreet's statement cannot be entirely dismissed on account of the friendship that developed between himself and Sickles and Sickles's defense of his friend's actions on July 2.

41. Pinchon, *op. cit.,* p. 264.

42. Hunt, *op. cit.,* p. 375. For a discussion of the regulations about the authority of staff officers, see *ibid.,* 386–387. Hunt, after he had instructed suspension of fire on his own responsibility, learned that Meade was seeking him for the purpose of giving such an order (*ibid.,* p. 374).

43. *O.R.*, *39*, 249.

44. Hunt's report, *ibid.,* *43*, 239. Hunt said that a number of caissons and limbers had been exploded, and that it was very unsafe to bring up loads of ammunition.

44. *B. and L.*, III, 385–386.

45. *Ibid.*, pp. 386–387.

46. *O.R.*, *44*, 307, 606.

47. Freeman, *Lee*, III, 62. It is stated that Hill was under orders to march northward, as well as Longstreet. Lee's report does not say that any actual march orders for those commanders were "cancelled."

48. *O.R., 44,* 317.

49. *Ibid., 45,* 943–944.

50. Freeman, *op. cit.,* p. 62 n.

51. *O.R., 44,* 607.

52. Freeman, *op. cit.,* p. 65.

53. Longstreet, *Manassas to Appomattox,* p. 358.

54. Freeman, *op. cit.,* p. 84; D. B. Sanger, "Was Longstreet a Scapegoat?" *Infantry Journal,* XLIII, 39–45 (Jan.–Feb., 1936).

55. Freeman, *Lee's Lieutenants,* III, 760.

56. Fuller, *Decisive Battles,* p. 235.

57. Alexander, *Military Memoirs,* p. 422.

58. Hunt's report, *O.R., 43,* 240.

59. Freeman, *Lee,* III, 130, quoting Fremantle's eyewitness account.

60. Alexander, *op. cit.,* p. 432.

NOTES TO CHAPTER XXIII

1. *O.R., 45,* 513.

2. *Ibid., 43,* 78.

3. *Ibid., 45,* 514.

4. Haskell, "Battle of Gettysburg," p. 419; Imboden, "The Confederate Retreat from Gettysburg," *B and L.,* III, 423; *O.R., 45,* 519–520.

5. *O.R., 43,* 153. The figures for the 1st, 2nd, 5th, and 11th Corps were given as "present for duty"; for the 3rd Corps, as "effective strength"; for the 12th Corps, as "for duty equipped." That it was without doubt a "line of battle" figure is shown by Meade's dispatch at noon to Halleck, *ibid.,* p. 79.

6. *Ibid., 45,* 545, 529.

7. *Ibid.,* p. 519.

8. *N.Y. Tribune,* July 1, 1863; *O.R., 45,* 518.

9. Dennett, *Lincoln and the Civil War,* p. 67.

10. *O.R., 43,* 203.

11. *Ibid., 45,* 517, 516, 520.

12. *Ibid., 43,* 78.

13. *Ibid., 45,* 529; Imboden, *op. cit.,* p. 422.

14. *O.R., 45,* 524. The dispatch stated that the guard had consisted only of the one officer and thirteen men who were captured, but French may have misunderstood the report made by the commander of the expedition. John L. Collins, 8th Pennsylvania Cavalry, has given an account of the destruction of the bridge as related to him by some members of the raid, which had been carried out in a well planned manner ("A Prisoner's March from Gettysburg to Staunton," *B. and L.,* III, 430–433).

15. *Ibid.,* pp. 523, 524.

16. *Ibid.*, pp. 524, 568.

17. *Ibid.*, p. 528.

18. Grant, *Memoirs*, I, 567; *Harper's Weekly*, VII, 467 (July 25, 1863).

19. *O.R.*, *45*, 521.

20. Blackford describes some damage done by Confederates who fired from buildings, bringing retaliatory fire from Federals (*War Years with Stuart*, pp. 231–232).

21. Hancock, *South After Gettysburg*, pp. 2–4, 12.

22. *O.R.*, *43*, 79, 108–110.

23. *Ibid.*, p. 222.

24. Haupt, *Reminiscences*, pp. 223–224.

25. *O.R.*, *43*, 80–81.

26. *Ibid.*, *45*, 567.

27. French's report, *ibid.*, *43*, 489. It is to be recalled that Meade had directed French at 7:00 A.M. on July 3 to try to cut Lee's communications.

28. *Ibid.*, *45*, 501. French speaks of "an expedition to Harpers Ferry," but says nothing about failure to occupy the place. A remark added to Meade's direction shows it was passed on by French to Halleck, who received it at 6:45 P.M., July 3, so that there is no question about French's getting the order.

29. *Ibid.*, *43*, 928. The destruction of Lee's trains would have been nearly fatal. Imboden in his article, "The Confederate Retreat from Gettysburg," *B. and L.*, III, 426–427, written over twenty years after the event, gave a stirring account of his successful defense of the trains at Williamsport. It differs in important particulars from Buford's report. He states that his brigade and some wagoners were attacked by 7,000 men of Buford's and Kilpatrick's divisions and Huey's brigade. Buford makes it clear that Kilpatrick was at Hagerstown or in that direction, not arriving in the vicinity of Williamsport until near dark, when the fighting was over. The Federal cavalry was in a very hazardous position, because it was probable that Stuart's command would arrive soon (it did, according to Imboden). Buford's strike at Williamsport had to have protection on his right flank, and Kilpatrick appears to have given that essential. Buford spoke of having Merritt's and Gamble's brigades in the first line with Devin in support. He spoke of the Confederates as having a brigade—which was not the case, according to Imboden. There seems to be no doubt that Imboden handled the defense skillfully, though he may have been in serious error as to the Federal strength deployed against him.

30. For a note by Robertson, who was commanding his own as well as the brigade of Jones, see *B. and L.*, III, 253. Halleck of course did not know about the movement of the brigades of Robertson and Jones, but he stated, "Intercepted dispatches from Jeff. Davis show that the country between Lee's army and Richmond is entirely stripped of troops" (*O.R.*, *45*, 528).

31. *Ibid.*, p. 568.

32. Imboden, *op. cit.*, p. 428. Imboden guarded the prisoners on their march from the river, using only one regiment and not starting until the 9th.

33. Dawes, *Service with Sixth Wisconsin*, p. 163.

34. *O.R.*, *43*, 83, 82.

35. *Ibid.*, pp. 82, 83.

36. Meade, *op. cit.*, II, 132–133.

37. *O.R., 43*, 222.

38. With regard to July 3, Longstreet states that he rode to a woods "to lie down and study for some new thought that might aid the assaulting column" (*Manassas to Appomattox*, p. 39). At least one witness, Col. Fremantle, recorded that Longstreet went to sleep (quoted in Freeman, *Lee's Lieutenants*, III, 151–152). If Longstreet succeeded in getting a little sleep it was to his credit. Freeman records two naps that Jackson took, remarking with regard to the second incident, that nothing suggested he felt any concern over the task of getting his army out of the net that the enemy was spreading. He says also that few men have inherited stronger nervous systems than Lee, who could relax from strenuous efforts and go to sleep almost instantly (*Lee's Lieutenants*, I, 413, 415–416, and *Lee*, I, 451).

Foch took pains to record that, even during the critical days of the Battle of the Marne, he left his headquarters in the evening and went to a village six miles to the rear and went to bed (*Memoirs*, p. 87 n.).

39. *O.R., 43*, 84.

40. *Ibid.*, p. 85.

41. *Ibid.*, p. 925.

42. Butterfield was a good deal of a "Hooker man," and his continuance in his old position was quite out of the question.

43. *O.R., 45*, 615, 619.

44. *Ibid., 43*, 86–88.

45. *Ibid.*, p. 929.

46. *Ibid., 45*, 609, 619.

47. Meade, *op. cit.*, II, 133.

48. *O.R., 43*, 89.

49. Freeman, *Lee*, III, 140.

50. Imboden, *op. cit.*, p. 429.

51. *O.R., 43*, 214–215; Freeman, *Lee*, III, 141.

52. Neill's report, *O.R., 43*, 678–680. On July 5 a detachment of the 1st New York and 12th Pennsylvania cavalry captured about 645 men, 600 animals, 90 wagons, and 2 guns near Mercersburg, twelve miles southwest of Chambersburg (Beach, *First New York Cavalry*, pp. 263–266). The two regiments had been part of Milroy's command that had escaped from Winchester.

53. *O.R., 43*, 91–92.

54. Dennett, *op. cit.*, p. 66.

55. *O.R., 43*, 92.

56. *Ibid.*, pp. 210–211.

57. *Ibid.*, pp. 990, 929.

58. Meade sent a copy of Lee's letter to Halleck on Aug. 9. Lee was correct in stating that no large unit was captured. Meade incorrectly reported to Halleck on the afternoon of the 14th that his cavalry had captured a brigade of 1,500 (*ibid.*, pp. 989, 991, 93).

59. Heth's report, written Oct. 3, 1863, was bitter against Kilpatrick, who, he said "in order to glorify himself, has told a deliberate falsehood" (*ibid.*, p. 642). The alleged falsehood was that Kilpatrick "captured an entire brigade." Kil-

patrick wrote, in a special report about the action at Falling Waters dated Aug. 7: "We lost 29 killed, 36 wounded, and 40 missing. We found upon the field 125 dead rebels, and brought away upward of 50 wounded. A large number of the enemy's wounded was left upon the field, in charge of their own surgeons. We captured two guns, three battle-flags, and upward of 1,500 prisoners" (*ibid.*, p. 990). Kilpatrick's own casualties show that he did something more than gather up stragglers; and the absence of the word "brigade" from his report refutes Heth's accusation. There is of course no way to tell what verbal reports of the action at Falling Waters may have reached Meade, causing him to say in his telegram of July 14 that an entire brigade had been captured.

Buford in his report spoke of additional captures of 500 prisoners (*ibid.*, p. 929). Certainly the Federals were in a better position to know how many men they had captured than the Confederates, who seemed reluctant to concede over 500.

Among the Confederates killed at Falling Waters was Gen. Pettigrew, one of the few officers of rank who survived the charge of July 3.

60. Longstreet, *op. cit.*, p. 430.

61. *O.R., 43*, 92, 211. Daniels's report indicates that he had put the word of the Confederate evacuation through by telegraph to both Meade and Sedgwick by 6:00 A.M. at latest.

62. Dennett, *op. cit.*, p. 67.

63. *O.R., 43*, 92–94.

64. Dennett, *op. cit.*, pp. 67–68.

65. Lee's field return for July 20 gave 41,092 officers and men as present for duty, with an aggregate present of 50,178 which did not include Stuart's cavalry (*O.R., 44*, 292). The aggregate given as present in the last return—presumably on July 10—was 40,485, not including the cavalry, or the artillery of the Third Corps. It should be noted that Pickett's division—which on July 20 had 4,696 present—was absent on July 13, having been sent to Winchester by Lee on July 8 as a prisoner guard (*ibid., 45*, 983). Lee's concern about his own position was indicated by his telling Pickett he must be ready to come to the assistance of the army.

66. *Ibid., 43*, 152. A field return for July 14 gave an aggregate of 98,932, including 10,567 in detachments at Harpers Ferry, Frederick, Maryland Heights, and South Mountain in McReynolds's cavalry (*ibid.*, p. 154). It is hard to determine the time when all these reenforcements arrived, or their quality. On July 11 Meade informed Halleck that he had placed Brig. Gen. B. F. Spinola's 1,700 men (sent by Dix) in the rear, on Spinola's statement that their nine months' enlistment period was about over and they were not too reliable. Halleck replied that the men had told him they would serve throughout the crisis under anyone but Spinola, whom they regarded as worthless, and he authorized Meade to relieve the latter and send him away. Meade evidently took no action, for the brigade was given as at South Mountain on July 14 (*ibid.*, pp. 90, 91, 154).

On July 11, Dix reported that he had forwarded 10,000 men from Fort Monroe since the previous morning, that he would send 4,000 to 5,000 men, making with Spinola's brigade about 17,000 (*ibid., 45, 655*). Whether these additional men could have been called up earlier, and could have been forwarded over the heavily worked railroad, and whether Meade would have merely left them at some place in the rear, is a matter for pure conjecture. On the 10th Halleck had told him, "Bring up and hurl upon the enemy all your forces, good and bad" (*ibid., 43, 89*). Meade disregarded the injunction, at least in part, and it is idle to claim that Halleck was slow in sending reenforcements when Meade had 3,300 men at Harpers Ferry—in addition to 1,700 on Maryland Heights—and 1,700 on South Mountain. See, however, S. R. Pennypacker, *General Meade*, p. 209.

67. *O.R., 43,* 996.

68. For Meade's statement before the Committee on the Conduct of the War, see Pennypacker, *op. cit.,* p. 212.

69. Haupt, *op. cit.,* p. 229.

70. *O.R., 45,* 547, 618.

71. *Ibid., 43,* 928, and *45, 676.*

72. *O.R., 44,* 915, 918. Greeley, *American Conflict,* II, 501–508; Nicolay and Hay, *Abraham Lincoln,* VII, chap. i, "The Enrollment and the Draft." Shannon, *Union Army,* devotes one section of his second volume to "The Slacker Problem" and draft troubles in various parts of the country. Stating that the War Department did not give due notice to state and local authorities about the draft, he states (p. 209) that the draft was begun with absolutely no precaution, and without the police commissioners being notified. His supporting reference is completely irrelevant. Nicolay and Hay write: "Even on Saturday morning, the 11th of July, when the draft was begun at the corner of 43rd Street and Third Avenue, there was no symptom of disturbance. The day passed pleasantly away, the draft was carried on regularly and good-humoredly, and at night the Superintendent of Police as he left the office, said the Rubicon was passed and all would go well." On July 6, Gen. Fry notified Governor Seymour that a draft had been ordered in some seven districts, including the Ninth, where the riot broke out and where 2,521 were to be called. No date was set; but he invited the Governor's attention to a communication sent on July 1, and requested him to carry out the suggestions (*O.R., 124,* 471).

Undoubtedly there were grave faults in the draft law of 1863, and mistakes in judgment and other errors in carrying it out, but it would take a well informed person with experience in such matters to pass sound criticism on the New York situation. Much was learned from experience.

73. Governor Seymour's estimate, given in Nicolay and Hay, *op. cit.,* p. 25.

74. Meade, *op. cit.,* II, 136.

75. *O.R., 43,* 96, 152.

76. *Ibid., 44,* 291–292.

77. H. H. Humphreys, *Andrew A. Humphreys,* p. 204. In a letter of July 25, Gen. Humphreys wrote of the maneuver as exceedingly bold.

78. Swinton, *Army of the Potomac,* p. 374. Gen. Humphreys stated that if the operation had been six hours earlier it would have been the most brilliant ever accomplished in the country. He was inclined to understatement, and his words have great weight.

79. Nicolay and Hay, *op. cit.,* pp. 280–281. Lincoln knew that Meade was aware of his dissatisfaction, and so he felt impelled to say clearly just how he had felt. There had been a chance to win the war, he wrote. "As it is, the war will be prolonged indefinitely." Second thought probably suggested that nothing could be gained by sending the letter, and that Meade would have insisted on being relieved.

80. Meade, *op. cit.,* II, 137, 138. Lincoln did not deny his disappointment, saying that he was "deeply mortified by the escape of Lee across the Potomac." But he added, "General Meade has my confidence as a brave and skillful officer and a true man." Meade, in forwarding the letter to his wife, wrote that Howard had "thought it proper to write to Mr. Lincoln, deprecating his dissatisfaction with me, and informing him I had the full confidence of the army." Howard wrote on July 10, before Lee had crossed the Potomac; Lincoln replied on July 21.

81. Halleck to Meade, July 28, *O.R., 43,* 104–105. The letter closed, "I need not assure you, general, that I have lost none of the confidence which I felt in you when I recommended you for the command." Of the failure to attack Lee at Williamsport, Meade wrote in his reply of July 31: "Now, as I said before, in this, perhaps I erred in judgment, for I take this occasion to say to you, and through you to the President, that I have no pretensions to any superior capacity for the post he has assigned me to" (*ibid.,* pp. 108–110).

On July 29 Lincoln wrote to Halleck that he feared Meade thought the government wished him to bring on a general engagement with Lee as soon as possible. He believed the opportunity for a successful action was over, but stated clearly that he deferred to the judgment of the General in Chief. Halleck at once telegraphed the message to Meade, who replied the next day, stating that he had been under the impression that an attack upon Lee was still urgently desired (*ibid.,* pp. 105–107).

82. *Harper's Weekly,* VII, 509, 616–617 (Aug. 8 and Sept. 19, 1863), showed the shooting of three men at Leesburg on June 19 and of five more men later. In stating that the June execution was the first for deserting, the editor forgot the picture he had published on Dec. 28, 1861. See also Freeman, *Lee's Lieutenants,* III, 219.

83. *O.R., 108,* 752–753; quoted at length by Freeman, *Lee,* III, 156–157. Lee wrote, "I hope Your Excellency will attribute my request to the true reason, the desire to serve my country, and to do all in my power to insure the success of her righteous cause."

84. *O.R., 49,* 639–640.

85. Gorgas, *Civil War Diary,* p. 55.

86. Gillmore, "The Army Before Charleston in 1863," *B. and L.,* IV, 71.

87. W. S. Stryker, "The 'Swamp Angel,'" *B. and L.,* IV, 72–74.

88. Gillmore states that blockade running was "constantly and most successfully carried on at Charleston throughout the years 1863–64" (*ibid.,* p. 68). But Ammen, quoting an official naval report, states that after July 19, 1863, two or three blockade runners within the harbor managed to escape, "and one or two may have gotten in, but that ended the business of blockade-running at Charleston" (*The Atlantic Coast,* p. 146). Greeley writes that the practice was

terminated (*op. cit.*, II, 482). Freeman writes that in the fall of 1863 the fast British merchantmen found Wilmington the only "ready port" for munitions (*Lee,* III, 164–165).

89. Gorgas, *op. cit.*, p. 51.

90. Adams, *Education of Henry Adams*, p. 172. Hendrick states that Russell had given orders to prevent the sailing of the ships five days before he received Adams's "threat" (*Lincoln's War Cabinet*, p. 215).

91. *Harper's Weekly*, VII, 467 (July 25, 1863).

92. Between Jan. 1, 1861, and Jan. 1, 1863, more than $200,000,000 of American securities held abroad were sent to New York for sale, and all found ready purchasers (*ibid.*, p. 194 (Mar. 28, 1863)).

NOTES TO CHAPTER XXIV

1. Under date of Aug. 9, John Hay wrote in his diary with regard to Lincoln's views: "He is very anxious that Texas should be occupied and firmly held in view of French possibilities. He thinks it just now more important than Mobile. He would prefer that Grant should not throw his army into the Mobile business before the Texas matter is safe. He wrote in that sense, I believe, to Grant today" (Dennett, *Lincoln and the Civil War*, p. 77). Grant in his *Memoirs* (I, 578–589) put chief responsibility for the decision against his Mobile proposal upon Halleck, though he referred to Lincoln's view. He of course never saw Hay's statement, and it is hard to say how much Halleck was influenced by Lincoln.

2. Freeman, *Lee,* III, 163.

3. Halleck's report, *O.R., 50,* 34, 35.

4. *Ibid.*, p. 36.

5. *Ibid.*, p. 54.

6. Livermore, *Numbers and Losses*, pp. 105–106. Livermore states that 1,000 Union soldiers hit 292 of their enemy, while the comparable figure for the Confederates was 172.

7. Dennett, *op. cit.*, p. 82; *O.R., 50,* 136: "Have captured ten pieces of artillery. Took prisoners from thirty different regiments, and with the blessing of God will do more to-morrow."

8. *Ibid., 52,* 750. The message is signed "Stevens."

9. *Ibid., 50,* 142.

10. *Ibid.*, p. 146.

11. *Ibid.*, p. 148.

12. *Ibid.*, p. 168. In midafternoon of the 22nd, Halleck had received a message stating that the mass of the army was intact and in good spirits, and that the disaster was not as bad as had been first feared. But at 10:00 P.M. Lincoln had a more doleful telegram: "We are now in Chattanooga in line of battle, the enemy threatening our whole front; have pushed to our picket line. Whether they will attack today uncertain. General Burnside will be too late to help us. We are about 30,000 brave and determined men, but our fate is in the hands of God, in whom I hope" (*ibid.*, pp. 160, 161).

13. *Ibid.*, *119*, 280, 284–286. Further interesting details about this somewhat exceptional exchange can be found through the index of the volume cited.

14. *Ibid.*, *49*, 223. Graham also reported that storehouses in Richmond were filled with provisions.

15. *Ibid.*, *50*, 194–195, 199.

16. Dennett, *op. cit.*, p. 93.

17. Secretary Chase wrote in his diary that Lincoln and Halleck were disinclined to weaken Meade, but that he and Seward had supported Stanton in urging it (Sandburg, *Lincoln*, II, 427). Hay made no such statement, and Chase's statements cannot always be accepted without question.

18. *O.R.*, *48*, 147, 150.

19. *Ibid.*, p. 151.

20. *Ibid.*, pp. 161–163, 177, 178, 180, 184.

21. *Ibid.*, p. 198.

22. Smith to Stanton, *ibid.*, p. 173.

23. *Ibid.*, *45*, 835. With regard to his action on the 1st, Buford wrote (*ibid.*, *43*, 932): "I then ordered everybody to fall back, and was followed and pressed by at least 5,000 infantry and three batteries as far as Brandy Station. The fighting was very handsomely executed; there were several charges and sabers were used with success."

24. On Aug. 4 Pleasonton passed on to headquarters two of Buford's dispatches, and commented, "General Buford has, I fear, grounds for complaint in not being properly supported." On Aug. 1 Buford complained directly to Meade that the engineers would not help him cross a stream: "If I am to advance, I would like to see some disposition shown to aid me. Everything seems to be awaiting orders" (*ibid.*, *45*, 839, and *43*, 931).

25. Martin T. McMahon, "From Gettysburg to the Coming of Grant," *B. and L.*, IV, 83. The article is the chief source for the account of the Bristow Campaign.

26. Freeman, *Lee*, III, 183; Long, *Memoirs of Lee*, p. 311.

27. *O.R.*, *49*, 326.

28. Freeman, *op. cit.*, pp. 71, 174.

29. Meade, *Life and Letters*, II, 153–154.

30. *O.R.*, *49*, 239, 186, 764, 332.

31. Sandburg, *op. cit.*, II, 438–439. Lincoln's letter was often misinterpreted as an order.

32. *O.R.*, *49*, 332.

33. *Ibid.*, pp. 345, 346, 354.

34. Welles, *Diary*, I, 47.

35. Meade (*op. cit.*, p. 154): "His [Lee's] object is to prevent my advance. and in the meantime send more troops to Bragg. This was a deep game, and I am free to admit that in the playing of it he has got the advantage of me."

36. *O.R.*, *49*, 476.

37. *Ibid.*, pp. 811, 405. Lee's return: aggregate present, 95,251; present and absent, 97,192. Meade's: aggregate present, 95,455; present and absent, 151,855.

38. *Ibid.*, p. 488. It had been planned to have the movement take place on

Nov. 24, and a detailed order was issued on the 23rd; but rain delayed the operation (*ibid.*, pp. 480–481).

39. *Ibid.*, p. 489.

40. *Ibid.*, p. 488.

41. McMahon, *op. cit.*, pp. 88, 91. McMahon's article is the basis of the brief account of the Mine Run operation given in the text.

42. *O.R.*, *49*, 537.

43. *Ibid.*, p. 461.

44. Greeley, *American Conflict,* II, 508.

45. *Harper's Weekly*, VII, 467 (July 25, 1863).

46. *O.R.*, *7*, 161.

47. Church, *Grant*, p. 231.

BIBLIOGRAPHY

Only books quoted or cited as authority are given. In the case of periodicals or other works for which an author's name is not the key word, the work is given alphabetically with its full title, and also under the abbreviation used for it, to avoid any confusion.

Adams, Charles Francis, Jr., *Autobiography*. Boston, Houghton, 1916.

Adams, Henry, *The Education of Henry Adams: An Autobiography*. Boston, Houghton, 1918.

Alexander, E. P., *Military Memoirs of a Confederate: A Critical Narrative*. New York, Scribner, 1907.

Allan, William, *Stonewall Jackson's Campaign in the Shenandoah Valley of Virginia from November 4, 1861, to June 17, 1862*. London, Rees, 1912.

Ammen, Daniel, *The Atlantic Coast*. New York, Scribner, 1883.

Anderson, Frank M., *The Mystery of "A Public Man": A Historical Detective Story*. Minneapolis, Univ. of Minnesota Press, 1948.

Aston, Sir George, *The Biography of the Late Marshal Foch*. New York, Macmillan, 1929.

B. and L. See Battles.

Ballard, Colin R., *The Military Genius of Abraham Lincoln*. London, Oxford Univ. Press, 1926.

Barnard, J. G., *The Peninsular Campaign and Its Antecedents, as Developed by the Report of Major-General George B. McClellan and Other Published Documents*. New York, Van Nostrand, 1864.

Bassett, John Spencer, *A Short History of the United States, 1492–1938* (3rd ed.). New York, Macmillan, 1939.

Bates, David Homer, *Lincoln in the Telegraph Office*. New York, Century, 1907.

Bates, Samuel P., *The Battle of Chancellorsville*. Meadville, Pa., E. T. Bates, 1882.

Battine, Cecil W., *The Crisis of the Confederacy*. New York, Longmans, 1905.

Battles and Leaders of the Civil War (4 vols.). New York, Century, 1884–1888.

Beach, William H., *The First New York (Lincoln) Cavalry*. New York, Lincoln Cavalry Assn., 1902.

Beatty, John, *Memoirs of a Volunteer, 1861–1863*. New York, Norton, 1946.

Beyer, William Gilmore, *On Hazardous Service: Scouts and Spies of the North and South*. New York, Harper, 1912.

Bigelow, John, Jr., *The Campaign of Chancellorsville: A Strategic and Tactical Study*. New Haven, Yale, 1910.

Bill, Alfred Hoyt, *The Beleaguered City: Richmond, 1861–1865*. New York, Knopf, 1946.

Blackford, Susan Leigh, *Letters from Lee's Army*. New York, Scribner, 1947.

Blackford, W. W., *War Years with Jeb Stuart*. New York, Scribner, 1945.

Brooks, Noah, *Washington in Lincoln's Time*. New York, Century, 1895.

C.C.W. Reports of the Committee on the Conduct of the War, Senate Documents, 37th Congress, 3rd Session, Washington, 1863, and 38th Congress, 2nd Session, 1865. In each case there are four volumes and only part of volume 1 is devoted to reports of the committee.

Channing, Edward, *A History of the United States,* Vol. VI (The War for Southern Independence). New York, Macmillan, 1930.

Church, William Conant, *Ulysses S. Grant and the Period of National Preservation and Reconstruction*. New York, Putnam, 1897.

Congressional Globe.

Crawford, Samuel W., *The History of the Fall of Fort Sumter: The Genesis of the Civil War*. New York, S. F. McLean & Co., 1898.

Dabney, R. L., *Life and Campaigns of Lieutenant-General Thomas J. Jackson*. New York, Blelock & Co., 1866.

Dana, Charles A., *Recollections of the Civil War*. New York, Appleton, 1899.

Davis, Jefferson C., *The Rise and Fall of the Confederate Government* (2 vols.). New York, Appleton, 1881.

Dawes, Rufus R., *Service with the Sixth Wisconsin Volunteers*. Marietta, Alderman, 1890.

De Forest, John William, *A Volunteer's Adventures: A Union Captain's Record of the Civil War*. New Haven, Yale, 1946.

Delafield, Richard, *Report on the Art of War in Europe, in 1854, 1855, and 1856* (Executive Document No. 59, 36th Congress, 1st Session, Senate). Washington, George W. Bowman, 1860.

Dennett, Tyler, *Lincoln and the Civil War in the Diaries and Letters of John Hay*. New York, Dodd, 1939.

Diary of a Public Man (anonymous—prefatory notes by F. Lauriston Bullard). Chicago, Abraham Lincoln Book Shop, 1945.

(D.A.B.) Dictionary of American Biography. New York, Scribner, 1928–1936, 1943.

Dix, Morgan, *Memoirs of Adams John Dix* (2 vols.). New York, Harper, 1883.

Dodge, Theodore A., *The Campaign of Chancellorsville* (2nd ed.). Boston, Ticknor, 1881.

Doubleday, Abner, *Chancellorsville and Fredericksburg.* New York, Scribner, 1882.

Douglas, Henry Kyd, *I Rode with Stonewall.* Chapel Hill, Univ. of North Carolina Press, 1940.

Dowdey, Clifford, *Experiment in Rebellion.* Garden City, Doubleday, 1946.

Dyer, Frederick H., *A Compendium of the War of the Rebellion.* Des Moines, Dyer, 1908.

Eckenrode, H. J., and Conrad, Bryan, *George B. McClellan: The Man Who Saved the Union.* Chapel Hill, Univ. of North Carolina Press, 1941.

Edmonds, J. E. See Wood.

Eisenschiml, Otto, *Why Was Lincoln Murdered?* Boston, Little, 1937.

Field Service Regulations, Operations. Washington, War Department, 1944.

Flower, Frank A., *Edwin McMasters Stanton.* Akron, Saalfield, 1905.

Foch, Ferdinand, *The Memoirs of Marshal Foch,* trans. T. Bentley Mott. Garden City, Doubleday, 1931.

——, *The Principles of War,* transl. J. de Morinni. New York, Fly, 1918.

Fox, Gustavus Vas, *Confidential Correspondence of Gustavus Vas Fox,* ed. Robert Means Thompson and Richard Wainright. New York, De Vinne Press, 1918–1919.

Freeman, Douglas Southall, *R. E. Lee: A Biography* (4 vols.). New York, Scribner, 1935.

——, *Lee's Lieutenants: A Study in Command* (3 vols.). New York, Scribner, 1945.

Fuller, J. F. C., *Decisive Battles of the U.S.A.* New York, Harper, 1942.

——, *The Generalship of Ulysses S. Grant.* New York, Dodd, 1929.

Gibbon, John, *The Artillerist's Manual,* 2nd ed. New York, Van Nostrand, 1863.

Gordon, George H., *History of the Campaign of the Army of Virginia.* Boston, Houghton, 1880.

Gorgas, Josiah, *The Civil War Diary,* ed. Frank A. Vandiver. University, Univ. of Alabama Press, 1947.

Gorham, George C., *Edwin M. Stanton* (2 vols.). Boston, Houghton, 1899.

Grant, Ulysses S., *Personal Memoirs of U. S. Grant* (2 vols.). New York, Webster, 1885.

Greeley, Horace, *The American Conflict: A History.* Hartford, Case, 1864–1866.

Hancock, Cornelia, *South After Gettysburg: Letters of Cornelia Hancock from the Army of the Potomac, 1863–65.* Philadelphia, Univ. of Pennsylvania Press, 1937.

Harper's Weekly.

Haskell, Frank A., "The Battle of Gettysburg," *Harvard Classics,* ed. C. W. Eliot, Vol. XLIII. New York, Collier, 1910.

Haupt, Herman, *Reminiscences of General Herman Haupt.* Milwaukee, Wright & Joys, 1901.

Hebert, Walter H., *Fighting Joe Hooker.* Indianapolis, Bobbs-Merrill, 1944.

Henderson, G. F. R., *Stonewall Jackson and the American Civil War.* New York, Grosset, 1936.

Hendrick, Burton J., *Lincoln's War Cabinet.* Boston, Little, 1946.

Herndon, W. H., and Jesse W. Weik, *Herndon's Life of Lincoln,* ed. Paul W. Angle. Cleveland, World, 1942.

Hicks, James E., *Notes on United States Ordnance* (2 vols.). Mount Vernon, N. Y., James E. Hicks, 1946.

——, *What the Citizen Should Know About Our Arms and Weapons.* New York, Norton, 1941.

Hosmer, James Kendall, *The Appeal to Arms:* Vol. XX of *The American Nation: A History,* ed. Albert Bushnell Hart. New York, Harper, 1907.

Hudson, Frederick, *Journalism in the United States from 1690 to 1872.* New York, Harper, 1873.

Humphreys, Andrew A., *The Virginia Campaign of '64 and '65: The Army of the Potomac and the Army of the James.* New York, Scribner, 1883.

Humphreys, Henry H., *Andrew Atkinson Humphreys.* Philadelphia, Winston, 1924.

Hungerford, Edward, *The Story of the Baltimore and Ohio Railroad, 1827–1927* (2 vols.). New York, Putnam, 1928.

Instructions for Field Artillery. Philadelphia, Lippincott, 1861.

Johnston, Joseph E., *Narrative of Military Operations.* New York, Appleton, 1874.

Johnston, R. M., *Bull Run: Its Strategy and Tactics.* Boston, Houghton, 1913.

Journal of Southern History.

Lamon, Ward Hill, *Recollections of Abraham Lincoln, 1847–1865,* ed. Dorothy Lamon. Chicago, McClurg, 1895.

Lee, Robert E., *Recollections and Letters of General Robert E. Lee.* Garden City, Doubleday, 1904.

Leech, Margaret, *Reveille in Washington, 1860–1865.* New York, Harper, 1941.

Lincoln Papers. MS. collection in Library of Congress.

Livermore, Thomas L., *Numbers and Losses in the Civil War in America, 1861–65*. Boston, Houghton, 1901.

Long, A. L., *Memoirs of Robert E. Lee*. New York, Stoddard, 1886.

Longstreet, Helen D., *Lee and Longstreet at High Tide*. Gainesville, Ga., Author, 1904.

Longstreet, James, *From Manassas to Appomattox: Memoirs of the Civil War in America*. Philadelphia, Lippincott, 1896.

Macartney, Clarence Edward, *Little Mac: The Life of General George B. McClellan*. Philadelphia, Dorrance, 1940.

McClellan, George B., *McClellan's Own Story: The War for the Union*. New York, Webster, 1887.

McClellan Papers. MS. collection in Library of Congress.

Magazine of American History.

Marshall, C., *An Aide-de-Camp of Lee: Papers of Colonel Charles Marshall*, ed. Sir Frederick B. Maurice. Boston, Little, 1927.

Massachusetts Historical Society, *Proceedings*.

Maurice, Sir Frederick B., *Robert E. Lee, the Soldier*. Boston, Houghton, 1925.

——, *Statesmen and Soldiers of the Civil War: A Study in Conduct of War*. Boston, Little, 1926.

——, ed. See Marshall.

Meade, George Gordon, *The Life and Letters of George Gordon Meade*, ed. G. G. Meade the Younger (2 vols.). New York, Scribner, 1913.

Mearns, David C., ed., *The Lincoln Papers* (2 vols.). Garden City, Doubleday, 1948.

Michie, Peter S., *General McClellan*. New York, Appleton, 1901.

Milton, George Fort, *Conflict: The American Civil War*. New York, Coward-McCann, 1941.

Moore, Albert B., *Conscription and Conflict in the Confederacy*. New York, Macmillan, 1924.

Moore, Frank, *Rebellion Record: A Diary of American Events with Documents, Narratives, Illustrative Incidents, Poetry, etc.*, ed. Frank Moore. New York, Putnam, 1861–1863: Van Nostrand, 1864–1868.

Morley, John Viscount, *Recollections* (2 vols.). New York, Macmillan, 1917.

Myers, William Starr, *General George Brinton McClellan*. New York, Appleton-Century, 1934.

Newman, James R., *The Tools of War*. Garden City, Doubleday, 1942.

Nicolay, John G., *The Outbreak of Rebellion*. New York, Scribner, 1882.

——, and John Hay, *Abraham Lincoln: A History* (10 vols.). New York, Century, 1890.

Norton, Charles B., and W. J. Valentine, *Report on the Munitions of War*

(Paris Universal Exposition, 1867). Washington, Government Printing Office, 1868.

O.R. See *War of the Rebellion.*

Palfrey, Francis Winthrop, *The Antietam and Fredericksburg.* New York, Scribner, 1882.

Patterson, Robert, *A Narrative of the Campaign in the Valley of the Shenandoah in 1861.* Philadelphia, J. Campbell, 1865.

Phisterer, Frederick, *Statistical Record of the Armies of the United States.* New York, Scribner, 1883.

Pickerill, W. N., *History of the Third Indiana Cavalry.* Indianapolis, Aetna, 1906.

Pinchon, Edgcumb, *Dan Sickles: Hero of Gettysburg and "Yankee King of Spain."* Garden City, Doubleday, 1945.

Porter, Horace, *Campaigning with Grant.* New York, Century, 1907.

Randall, James Garfield, *The Civil War and Reconstruction.* Boston, Heath, 1937.

——, *Lincoln the President: Springfield to Gettysburg* (2 vols.). New York, Dodd, 1945.

Reagan, John H., *Memoirs, with Special Reference to Secession and the Civil War.* New York, Neale, 1906.

Rhodes, James Ford, *History of the Civil War, 1861–1865.* New York, Macmillan, 1917.

——, *History of the United States from the Compromise of 1850* (3 vols.). New York, Harper, 1895.

Ropes, John Codman, *The Army Under Pope.* New York, Scribner, 1881.

Sandburg, Carl, *Abraham Lincoln: The War Years* (4 vols.). New York, Harcourt, 1939.

Schaff, Morris, *The Battle of the Wilderness.* Boston, Houghton, 1910.

Shannon, Fred Albert, *The Organization and Administration of the Union Army, 1861–1865* (2 vols.). Cleveland, Clark, 1928.

Sherwood, Robert E., *Roosevelt and Hopkins: An Intimate History.* New York, Harper, 1948.

Storrick, W. C., *The Battle of Gettysburg.* Harrisburg, McFarland, 1946.

Strother, D. H., "Personal Recollections of the War," serial in *Harper's Magazine,* Vols. XXXIII–XXXVI, 1866–1868.

Swinton, William, *Campaigns of the Army of the Potomac.* New York, Richardson, 1866.

U.S. Infantry Tactics. Philadelphia, Lippincott, 1861.

Upton, Emory, *Military Policy of the United States.* Washington, Government Printing Office, 1912.

Vandiver, Frank A., ed. See Gorgas.

War of the Rebellion: Official Records of the Union and Confederate Armies. Washington, Government Printing Office, 1882–1900.

The publication (consistently referred to in footnotes as *O.R.*) is in four series, each series being divided into volumes, and the volumes into parts. After the earlier volumes of Series I were in print a continuous sequence of Serial numbers in Arabic was added for the later issues, taking account of the issues already published, on which it was impossible to place the corresponding numbers. References in the present work to the *O.R.* use Serial number (in italic) and page number alone. Thus *18,* 48 means Serial 18, page 48. The following key demonstrates the application of the missing Serial numbers to the earlier issues:

Serial	1 = Series I, Vol.	I		
	2 =	II		
	5 =	V		
	12 =	XI,	Part	i
	13 =	XI,	"	ii
	14 =	XI,	"	iii
	15 =	XII,	"	i
	16 =	XII,	"	ii
	17 =	XII,	"	ii, supplement
	18 =	XII,	"	iii
	27 =	XIX,	"	i
	28 =	XIX,	"	ii
	31 =	XXI		

Webb, Alexander S., *The Peninsula, McClellan's Campaign of 1862.* New York, Scribner, 1881.

Welles, Gideon, *Diary of Gideon Welles.* Boston, Houghton, 1911.

Whitman, Walt, *Complete Prose Works.* Philadelphia, McKay, 1892.

Whitton, F. E., *The American War of Independence.* New York, Dodd, 1931.

Williams, T. Harry, *Lincoln and the Radicals.* Madison, Univ. of Wisconsin Press, 1941.

Wilson, James Harrison, *The Life of John Rawlins.* New York, Neale, 1916.

Wood, W. Birkbeck, and J. E. Edmonds, *A History of the Civil War in the United States, 1861–5.* New York, Putnam, 1905.

Young, Jesse Bowman, *The Battle of Gettysburg.* New York, Harper, 1913.

INDEX

Ranks shown are the highest held in connection with mention in these two volumes. The abbreviation C.S. denotes civil as well as military officers of the Confederate States. A hyphen is used between nonconsecutive page numbers to indicate scattered references to a subject as well as a continuous treatment.

[1] The forces that were in the general vicinity of the Potomac River until March, 1862.

[2] The force had no official name, but was composed of troops in the Department of Northeastern Virginia, which McDowell commanded.

[3] The force had no official name, but was composed of troops in the Department of Pennsylvania, which Patterson commanded.

[4] The army was organized soon after McClellan took command of the Division of the Potomac, on July 27, 1861, and its history through 1863 is the main subject of these volumes.

Cobb, Howell, Sec. of Treas. in Buchanan's cabinet, resigns, 18; Sec. of Treas., C.S., 380

Codori house (Gettysburg), 693, 699

Collins, John L., cited, 850

Collis, Capt. Charles H. T., remarkable march by, 209

Columbia, Pa., 669

Columbus, Ohio, 760

Committee on Conduct of the War, 504, 538, 676–697

Communications, failure of, at Sumter, 53

Comstock, Capt. Cyrus B., in Fredericksburg campaign, 502, 521, 570; in Chancellorsville campaign, 572, 576, 600

Confederate States, formation of, 16–17; take over from separate states, 34; question of foreign recognition of, 150, 557; receive British loan, 555; bill to recognize in House of Commons, 759

Conrad, Bryan, see Eckenrode and Conrad

Conscription, see Armies, Confederate

Cooke, Brig. Gen. Philip St. George, in Peninsular campaign, 217

Cooper, Col. Solomon, adjutant general, resigns to join Confederacy, 54, 390; Gen., C.S., 346, 509, 511, 751

Copperheads, 611

Corinth, Miss., 243; evacuated by Confederates, 191, 194; battle of, 472

Corps, Confederate

For First Corps, see Longstreet, Fredericksburg campaign and afterward; for Second Corps, see Jackson, Fredericksburg and Chancellorsville campaigns, Ewell, Gettysburg campaign and afterward; for Third Corps, see A. P. Hill, Gettysburg campaign and afterward

Corps, Federal [1]

I, in Peninsular campaign, 145; in Antietam campaign, 450, 451; in Fredericksburg campaign, 487, 526; in Chancellorsville campaign, 561, 569, 572, 577, 589, 591, 594, 595; in Gettysburg campaign, 635, 637, 641, 645, 672, 676, 677, 680, 683, 686–688, 690, 691, 693, 694, 700, 706, 710, 720, 752; in autumn 1863 operations, 766. See also McDowell, pp. 145–204, passim; Hooker (Antietam campaign); Reynolds (Fredericksburg, Chancellorsville, and Gettysburg campaigns); Doubleday and Newton (Gettysburg campaign)

II, in Peninsular campaign, 145, 169, 235, 236; in Antietam campaign, 379, 451; in Fredericksburg campaign, 487, 526, 532; in Chancellorsville campaign, 561, 569, 574; in Gettysburg campaign, 621, 635, 637, 672, 682, 692, 695, 699, 720, 721; in autumn 1863 operations, 767, 772. See also Sumner (Peninsular, Second Bull Run, and Antietam campaigns); Hancock (Gettysburg campaign)

III, in Peninsular campaign, 145, 169, 183, 235, 236; in Fredericksburg campaign, 486; in Chancellorsville campaign, 561, 569, 572, 580, 584; in Gettysburg campaign, 635, 637, 641, 672, 676, 677, 687, 692, 693, 695, 698, 699, 703, 710, 720, 721, 752, 755. See also Heintzelman (Peninsular and Second Bull Run campaigns); Stoneman (Fredericksburg campaign); Sickles (Chancellorsville and Gettysburg campaigns)

IV, in Peninsular campaign, 145, 169, 183. See also Keyes

[1] Corps I–VI as designated by the President in accordance with the act of Congress of July 17, 1862, were essentially the same as the corps with the same numbers previously formed in the Army of the Potomac. See Phisterer, Statistical Record, pp. 55–56.

Fort Johnston, S.C., 20
Fort Macon, N.C., C.S., 481
Fort Marcy (Washington), Va., 305
Fort Monroe, Va., important Federal base, 12, 66, 539, 561, 667, 668, 732, 761, 764
Fort Moultrie, S.C., 17, 19
Fort Pickens, Fla., 790–792
Fort Runyon (Washington), Va., 125
Fort Sumter, S.C., 6, 17, 19, 33; Anderson occupies, 20; armament of, 33, 49; conflicting reports about, 36; demand for surrender and capture of, 45–52; cabinet discussion about, 387–388; question of signals at, 389–390; reduction of, by Federals, 757
Fort Wagner, S.C., C.S., attack on and capture, 757
Foster, Maj. Gen. John G., at Fort Sumter, 33, 49, 50, 58, 386; in coastal operations, 565, 630, 668, 761
Fox, Gustavus V., Asst. Sec. of Navy, proposal and efforts with regard to Sumter, 38–39, 43, 53–54, 56; with regard to the Monitor, 152, 156
France, Mexican operations, 557, 760
Franklin, W.Va., 199
Franklin, Maj. Gen. William B., 137; in Peninsular campaign, 164, 165, 169, 229, 235, 237; in Second Bull Run campaign, 282, 289, 322, 338, 340, 353, 361, 376; in Antietam campaign, 380, 381, 445; in Fredericksburg campaign, 487, 495, 496, 503, 523, 525, 526, 528, 529, 531, 532, 544; relieved of command because of charges by Burnside.
Frayser's farm, battle of, 237–238
Frederick, Md., 72; in Antietam campaign, 362, 366, 368; in Gettysburg campaign, 631, 639, 641, 644, 645, 656, 711, 734, 738, 741, 747, 754
Fredericksburg, Va., 2, 9, 170, 251, 258; in Second Bull Run campaign, 275, 281, 282; in Fredericksburg campaign, 482, 488, 495, 500; battle of, 528–534; in

Chancellorsville campaign, 567, 575, 583, 591, 592, 595, 599
Freeborn, tugboat for Fort Sumter expedition, 53
Freeman, Douglas Southall, cited, 155, 203, 205, 212–213, 232, 238, 302, 318, 337, 381, 425, 452, 454, 514, 520, 614–615, 689, 690, 691, 725–727, 852, 856
Fremantle, Lieut. Col. A. J. L., cited, 718, 848
Frémont, Maj. Gen. John G., 118, 176, 642; in Valley campaign, 172, 187, 188, 190, 193, 197, 198, 202, 204; declines to serve under Pope, 259
French, Maj. Gen. William H., 452, 580; in Gettysburg campaign, 646, 656, 658, 709, 711, 734, 739, 752, 755
Front Royal, Va., 172, 540
Frothingham, Thomas G., cited, 405, 417–418, 816–817
Fry, Brig. Gen. James B. provost marshal general, 557, 831, 854
Fuller, Maj. Gen. J. F. C., cited, 357, 727, 784
Fulton, C. C., correspondent, 246
Furloughs, evils from, etc., 418–419

Gaines's Cross Roads, Va., 292
Gaines's Mill, battle of, 226–229
Gainesville, Va., 310, 311; battle of, see Second Bull Run
Gamble, Col. William, in Gettysburg campaign, 674, 682–684, 702
Garnett, Brig. Gen. R. S., C.S., in West Virginia operations, 106, 111 (killed)
Garrett, John W., President B. & O. R.R., 285, 459, 495, 648
Gatling guns, 800–801
Geary, Brig. Gen. John W., in Valley campaign, 174, 181; in Gettysburg campaign, 673, 688, 694, 695, 708, 709
General in Chief, Scott retires and McClellan appointed, 131; McClellan relieved, 157; no successor appointed, 158; Halleck appointed, 251; Grant appointed, 776

Henry, A. C., 606
Henry, Joseph, 117
Henry House Hill, *see* battles of Bull
    Run
Herndon, Va., 637
Herron, Brig. Gen. F. J., 554
Heth, Maj. Gen. Harry, C.S., 607,
    767, 782; in Gettysburg cam-
    paign, 617, 684, 690, 724, 751
Hicks, Maj. James E., cited, 784, 785,
    800
Hill, Lieut. Gen. Ambrose P., C.S.,
    6; in Peninsular campaign, 225,
    227, 237, 238; in Second Bull
    Run campaign, 314, 327; in An-
    tietam campaign, 374, 454, 455,
    461; in Fredericksburg campaign,
    494, 518; in Chancellorsville
    campaign, 591, 607; in Gettys-
    burg campaign, 617, 622, 625,
    628, 631, 645, 665, 677, 681, 685,
    686, 691, 700, 705, 709, 713, 715,
    724, 725; in autumn 1863 opera-
    tions, 761, 762, 767
Hill, Maj. Gen. D. H., C.S., 183, 227;
    in Antietam campaign, 373–375,
    381, 452, 457; in Fredericksburg
    campaign, 492, 494, 518, 528;
    his postwar remark on Gettys-
    burg campaign, 616–617; at
    Petersburg, 667
Hitchcock, Maj. Gen. Ethan Allen,
    adviser to Lincoln, 158, 159, 168
Holmes, Capt. Oliver W., at Antietam
    (wounded), 458
Holmes, Brig. Gen. T. H., C.S., 237
Holt, Joseph, Sec. of War under
    Buchanan, commends Anderson,
    23, 31; refuses Hayne's demands,
    32; his report to Stanton, 245
Hood, Maj. Gen. John B., C.S., 227,
    324, 457, 492, 532, 565, 603; in
    Gettysburg campaign, 617, 619,
    625, 705; in battle of Chicka-
    mauga, 762
Hooker, Maj. Gen. Joseph, on lower
    Potomac, 142–143; in battle of
    Williamsburg, 168; in Second
    Bull Run campaign, 295, 312,
    317, 327, 334, 354; in Antietam
    campaign (wounded), 382, 447,
    448, 450; in Fredericksburg cam-

paign, 487, 495, 496, 498, 499,
    526, 533, 544; given command
    of Army of Potomac, 546, 549–
    550; earlier life, 547; reorganiza-
    tion of army, etc., 560, 561, 562;
    secretively plans operation, 565,
    566, 568, 569; his skillful flank
    march, 572–575; halts and is at-
    tacked by Lee at Chancellors-
    ville, 576, 578, 591, 592; injured,
    594, 595; fails to relinquish com-
    mand, 595; sends dispatch to
    Lincoln, 597; holds council of
    war and retires, 600–602; blames
    others for failure, 604; order to
    his army, 607; actions in first
    part of Gettysburg campaign,
    618–620, 622, 627, 631, 634,
    635, 636, 638, 639; crosses Po-
    tomac, 641; makes issue over
    abandonment of Maryland
    Heights and asks to be relieved,
    650, 651; farewell order, 656;
    takes Eleventh and Twelfth
    Corps West, 764–766; in battle
    of Chattanooga, 772
Hopewell Gap, Va., 324
Howard, Maj. Gen. Oliver O., in
    Chancellorsville campaign, 569,
    572, 579, 584, 587–589, 600,
    604; in Gettysburg campaign, 64,
    658, 673, 677, 685, 686, 688,
    690, 691, 698, 713, 721, 731,
    746, 752; writes Lincoln, 756
Howe, Brig. Gen. Albion P., in battle
    of Chancellorsville, 595, 596
Huey, Col. Pennock, in Chancellors-
    ville campaign, 574, 590; in
    Gettysburg campaign, 695, 745
Huger, Maj. Gen. Benjamin, C.S., in
    Peninsular campaign, 184, 237
Humphreys, Maj. Gen. Andres A., 9,
    13; in Antietam campaign, 460;
    in battle of Fredericksburg, 533;
    in Chancellorsville campaign,
    580; in Gettysburg campaign,
    673, 695, 698, 705, 720, 721;
    made chief of staff, Army of
    the Potomac, 746; cited, 781–
    782
Hunt, Brig. Gen. Henry J., chief of
    artillery, 524, 537, 567, 629, 690,

situation, 113; comment on him
by Beauregard, 124; fails to appraise weakness of Munson's
Hill, 124; minimizes McDowell's
work in fortifying Washington,
125; quarrels with Scott, 125;
believes Washington in danger,
126; writes to Scott about, 126;
wants control of all officers in
Washington, 127; Margaret
Leech's appraisal of, 127; continues to overestimate enemy,
127, 129; his analysis of his own
force, 129; speaks of "the great
battle before us," 130; appointed
General in Chief, 131; takes over
War Department orders, 132;
predictions about his fall campaign, 133; illness of, 136; objects to Lincoln's Special War
Order No. 1, 138; long and
rambling letter to Lincoln, 140;
allowed to proceed with Peninsular campaign, 141; disapproves
Hooker's suggestion about clearing enemy batteries from Potomac, 142–143; his canal-boat
difficulty, 144; popularity with
army, 145; Michie on, 145;
efforts to explain his inactivity,
146; his training problem compared with World Wars I and II,
147; his political friends generally enemies of the President,
148; marches to Centerville, 153;
adheres to Pinkerton's strength
reports, 154; vanity of, 155;
holds council of war at Fairfax,
156; his Urbanna proposal disapproved by subordinates, 156;
given freedom of movement and
receives assurance about Merrimac, 156; unjustly says administration refused Urbanna move,
156; relieved as General in Chief,
157; reports troops left at Washington, 159; requests some of
Wool's regiments, 161; notified
of detention of McDowell, 163–
164; reveals lack of resolution,
164–165; mystery about his
strength, 165; appraised by John

ston, 166; follows Johnston, 168;
reaches field at Williamsburg,
168; in front of Richmond, 169;
given permission to reorganize
army, 169; puts base at White
House, 170; speaks of superior
enemy force, 182; inability to
estimate enemy strength, 185;
reprimanded by Stanton, 215; informed of reenforcements, 215;
given command of Department
of Virginia, 216; reports that
Beauregard has arrived in Richmond, 218; informed that Mc
Dowell will be sent, 219; moves
headquarters to Dr. Trent's, 219;
asks for James guns, 220; reports
deserter's story about Jackson,
220; becomes boastful, 224; vacillates between elation and
gloom, 224–225; urges action on
Burnside, 225; awaits attack on
June 27th, 226; decides to retreat
to James River, 229; famous
message to Stanton, 229; his retreat unnecessary, 231; undeserved praise of, 232; fails to
have reconnaissance made, 232;
uses only Quaker Road, 233; his
wagons exaggerated, 233; not
present at Frayser's farm, 237;
gives command to Porter at Malvern Hill, 239; requests more
gunboats, 241; last dispatch from
Chickahominy, 242; misrepresents his retreat as a change of
base, 248; requests more men,
249; lack of balance increases,
249; gives Lincoln political advice, 250; letter to Hill Carter,
250; replies to Pope, 252; letter
to Adjutant General, 252; inaccurate statements about own and
enemy strengths, 255; has many
absentees, 255; protests his recall, 258; procrastinates, 263;
seizes but relinquishes Malvern
Hill, 273; leaves Harrison's Landing, 274, 278; reports to Halleck,
275, 276; message to Porter, 281;
arrives at Aquia, 289; thinks
Haupt's plan risky, 304; suggests

751; Hooker's crossing in Gettysburg campaign, 641; Meade's recrossing, 754

Powhatan, vessel in Fort Sumter expedition, 53-55

Prairie Grove, Ark., battle of, 554

Prentiss, Maj. Gen. Benjamin M., 809

Press, The, 128, 673

Price, Maj. Gen. Sterling, C.S., 465

Prime, W. C., his accusation against Stanton, 230

Quaker Road, Va., used in McClellan's retreat, 233–234, 237

Raccoon Ford, Va., 227, 603

Railroads, temporarily taken over by government, 207; commanded by Stanton, 614; in movement of troops West, 765

Ramsdell, Charles W., cited, 390

Randall, James G., cited, 399, 830

Randolph, George W., Sec. of War, C.S., 168, 488, 509, 510, 511

Ransom, Maj. Gen. Robert C., C.S., 492, 565, 638

Rapidan River, Va., 1, 156; in Cedar Mountain operation, 265; in Second Bull Run campaign, 274, 277, 278; in Fredericksburg campaign, 487; in Chancellorsville campaign, 568, 572, 603; in autumn 1863 operations, 765, 770, 772

Rappahannock River, Va., 2, 137, 155, 156; in Second Bull Run campaign, 275, 278, 280, 282–284, 288, 357; in Fredericksburg campaign, 486, 494, 506, 512, 513, 526; in Chancellorsville campaign, 566, 568, 572; in autumn 1863 operations, 767, 770

Rappahannock Station, 279, 284

Rawlins, Brig. Gen. John A., 11

Reagan, John, Sec. of War, C.S., cited on cabinet meeting, 837

Rectortown, Va., 174, 194, 475

Regiments, Confederate
Alabama: 2nd, 683; 5th, 587; 22nd, 683; Georgia: 18th, 639; Louisiana: 1st, 93; Maryland: 1st, 181; South Carolina: 4th, 93;

Texas: 1st, 228; 4th, 228; Virginia: 33rd, 95; 40th, 751; 44th, 112; 47th, 751; 55th, 751

Regiments, Federal
Connecticut: 5th, 265; Illinois: 8th Cav., 4, 235, 641, 682, 719; 12th Cav., 446, 682, 852; Indiana: 7th, 687, 690; 11th, 71; 19th, 683; 27th, 451; 3rd Cav., 4, 641, 682, 684; Maine: 4th, 522; 10th, 265, 451; 19th, 699; Maryland: 1st, 181; 3rd, 812; Massachusetts: 1st, 699; 2nd, 451, 457; 6th, 63; 7th, 595; 8th, 63; 18th, 601; 19th, 524, 600; 20th, 183, 524; 54th, 757; 2nd Cav., 841; Michigan: 2nd, 96, 97; 7th, 524; 24th, 683; 1st Cav., 277; Minnesota: 1st, 699; New Jersey: 3rd, 123, 134; 11th, 553, 720; New York: 5th, 351; 7th, 63; 28th, 265, 451; 74th, 143; 78th, 812; 89th, 524; 102nd, 812; 122nd, 720; 1st Cav., 134, 852; 8th Cav., 4, 446, 682; 15th Engrs., 522, 523; 50th Engrs., 502, 522, 523; Ohio: 3rd, 109; 5th, 812; 7th, 812; 8th, 717; 11th, 303; 12th, 303; 23rd, 308, 382, 474; 66th, 812; 1st Cav., 300; Pennsylvania: 11th, 812; 46th, 265, 451; 118th, 601; 3rd Cav., 749; 8th Cav., 235, 274, 574, 590, 600; 8th Cav., 852; Rhode Island: 2nd, 93; United States: 14th, 73; Vermont: 1st Cav., 4; West Virginia: 1st Cav., 262; Wisconsin: 2nd, 683; 3rd, 451; 6th, 595, 683; 7th, 683

Remagen, 506

Reno, Maj. Gen., Jesse L., in Second Bull Run campaign, 274, 279–281, 283, 288, 311, 324, 327, 354; in Antietam campaign (killed), 361, 376, 381, 383

Reynolds, Maj. Gen. John F., 774; in Second Bull Run campaign, 281, 284, 310, 327; in Chancellorsville campaign, 526, 529, 550, 561, 589, 600; in Gettysburg campaign, 626, 627, 641, 645, 656, 673, 676, 682; reaches

OHIO

PENN

N

Marietta

Ohio River

Parkersburg

Little Kanawha River

392

W

E

S

T

OHIO

Mt. Jackson

Harrisonburg

VIRG

Staunton

VI

Charleston

Summersville

Gauley Bridge

Big Kanawha River

382

R

I

R

James

Lynchburg

Appomattox

TENNESSEE

RR

AND

VIRGINIA

Christiansburg

372

0 5 10   20   30   40   50 Miles

Danville

NORTH

C

8 |°

80°

79°